T0192238

Communications
in Computer and Information Science   1956

Editorial Board Members

Rationale

The CCIS series is devoted to the publication of proceedings of computer science conferences. Its aim is to efficiently disseminate original research results in informatics in printed and electronic form. While the focus is on publication of peer-reviewed full papers presenting mature work, inclusion of reviewed short papers reporting on work in progress is welcome, too. Besides globally relevant meetings with internationally representative program committees guaranteeing a strict peer-reviewing and paper selection process, conferences run by societies or of high regional or national relevance are also considered for publication.

Topics

The topical scope of CCIS spans the entire spectrum of informatics ranging from foundational topics in the theory of computing to information and communications science and technology and a broad variety of interdisciplinary application fields.

Information for Volume Editors and Authors

Publication in CCIS is free of charge. No royalties are paid, however, we offer registered conference participants temporary free access to the online version of the conference proceedings on SpringerLink (http://link.springer.com) by means of an http referrer from the conference website and/or a number of complimentary printed copies, as specified in the official acceptance email of the event.

CCIS proceedings can be published in time for distribution at conferences or as postproceedings, and delivered in the form of printed books and/or electronically as USBs and/or e-content licenses for accessing proceedings at SpringerLink. Furthermore, CCIS proceedings are included in the CCIS electronic book series hosted in the SpringerLink digital library at http://link.springer.com/bookseries/7899. Conferences publishing in CCIS are allowed to use Online Conference Service (OCS) for managing the whole proceedings lifecycle (from submission and reviewing to preparing for publication) free of charge.

Publication process

The language of publication is exclusively English. Authors publishing in CCIS have to sign the Springer CCIS copyright transfer form, however, they are free to use their material published in CCIS for substantially changed, more elaborate subsequent publications elsewhere. For the preparation of the camera-ready papers/files, authors have to strictly adhere to the Springer CCIS Authors' Instructions and are strongly encouraged to use the CCIS LaTeX style files or templates.

Abstracting/Indexing

CCIS is abstracted/indexed in DBLP, Google Scholar, EI-Compendex, Mathematical Reviews, SCImago, Scopus. CCIS volumes are also submitted for the inclusion in ISI Proceedings.

How to start

To start the evaluation of your proposal for inclusion in the CCIS series, please send an e-mail to ccis@springer.com.

Kousik Dasgupta · Somnath Mukhopadhyay ·
Jyotsna K. Mandal · Paramartha Dutta
Editors

Computational Intelligence in Communications and Business Analytics

5th International Conference, CICBA 2023
Kalyani, India, January 27–28, 2023
Revised Selected Papers, Part II

 Springer

Editors
Kousik Dasgupta 🆔
Kalyani Government Engineering College
Kalyani, India

Somnath Mukhopadhyay 🆔
Assam University
Silchar, India

Jyotsna K. Mandal 🆔
University of Kalyani
Kalyani, West Bengal, India

Paramartha Dutta 🆔
Visvabharati University
Santiniketan, West Bengal, India

ISSN 1865-0929   ISSN 1865-0937 (electronic)
Communications in Computer and Information Science
ISBN 978-3-031-48878-8   ISBN 978-3-031-48879-5 (eBook)
https://doi.org/10.1007/978-3-031-48879-5

This Springer imprint is published by the registered company Springer Nature Switzerland AG
The registered company address is: Gewerbestrasse 11, 6330 Cham, Switzerland

Paper in this product is recyclable.

Preface

It is with immense pleasure that we present the proceedings of the Fifth International Conference on Computational Intelligence in Communications and Business Analytics (CICBA 2023), organized by the Department of Computer Science & Engineering at Kalyani Government Engineering College, Kalyani, during January 27–28, 2023. CICBA has evolved into a flagship event at the intersection of computational intelligence, communications, and business analytics, fostering international collaboration and the dissemination of cutting-edge research.

CICBA 2023 welcomed distinguished keynote speakers, each a luminary in their field. We were honoured to have with us Bhabatosh Chanda from the Indian Statistical Institute, Kolkata, Amit Konar from Jadavpur University, Kalyanmoy Deb from Michigan State University, Hisao Ishibuchi from the Southern University of Science and Technology, China, Jayant Haritsa from IISc Bangalore, Narayan C. Debnath from Eastern International University, Vietnam, Celia Shahnaz from Bangladesh University of Engineering and Technology, Hiroyuki Sato from The University of Electro-Communications, Japan, Debashis De from Maulana Abul Kalam Azad University of Technology, West Bengal, India, and Mohd Helmy Bin Abd Wahab from University Tun Hussein Onn Malaysia, Malaysia.

In technical collaboration with IEEE CIS Kolkata, IEEE Kolkata Section, and IETE Kolkata, CICBA 2023 garnered substantial interest from the global research community. Springer CCIS Series was our esteemed publication partner, ensuring the high quality and widespread dissemination of the conference proceedings.

We are pleased to present the submission statistics for CICBA 2023. We received 187 initial submissions, which is evidence of our conference's growing significance. 52 papers were approved and registered, representing an impressive acceptance rate of 27%.

The conference proceedings are organized into two volumes, each featuring distinct tracks. In Volume 1, you will find 26 insightful papers in the "Computational Intelligence" track. Volume 2 is divided into two tracks: "Theories and Applications to Data Communications" with 17 papers, and "Theories and Applications to Data Analytics" with 9 papers. These contributions represent the cutting edge of research in computational intelligence and business analytics and cover a wide range of topics.

As we reflect on the history of CICBA since its inception in 2017, we are pleased with its growth and impact. This conference series has consistently attracted high-quality research from around the world. We are grateful for the contributions of our esteemed keynote speakers, organizing committees, and evaluators, who have made CICBA a remarkable venue for the exchange of knowledge.

We sincerely thank all the authors who submitted their work, the reviewers who diligently evaluated the submissions, and the participants who contributed to vibrant discussions during the conference. Your collective efforts have enriched the academic discourse in computational intelligence, communications, and business analytics.

We hope you find these proceedings enlightening and inspiring, and that they serve as a valuable resource for researchers and practitioners in the field. We look forward to future editions of CICBA, which we are committed to making even more intellectually stimulating and professionally rewarding.

Sincerely,

Kousik Dasgupta
Somnath Mukhopadhyay
Jyotsna K. Mandal
Paramartha Dutta

Organization

Chief Patron

Anindita Ganguly   D.T.E, Govt. of West Bengal, India

Patron

Sourabh Kumar Das   Kalyani Government Engineering College, India

General Chair

Nikhil R. Pal   Indian Statistical Institute Kolkata, India

Organizing Chairs

Swapan Kumar Mondal   Kalyani Government Engineering College, India
Sourav Banerjee   Kalyani Government Engineering College, India

Program Committee Chairs

Kousik Dasgupta   Kalyani Government Engineering College, India
Somnath Mukhopadhyay   Assam University, India
Jyotsna K. Mandal   University of Kalyani, India
Paramartha Dutta   Visva Bharati University, India

International Advisory Board

A. Damodaram   JNTU, India
Amit Konar   Jadavpur University, India
Atal Chowdhury   Jadavpur University, India
Aynur Unal   Stanford University, USA
Banshidhar Majhi   VSSUT, India
Carlos. A. Coello Coello   CINVESTAV-IPN, Mexico

Edward Tsang	University of Essex, UK
Hisao Ishibuchi	SUSTech, China
Kalyanmoy Deb	MSU, USA
L. M. Patnaik	IISc Bangalore, India
P. N. Suganthan	Qatar University, Qatar
Pabitra Mitra	IIT Kharagpur, India
S. N. Srirama	University of Tartu, Estonia
Subir Sarkar	Jadavpur University, India
Sushmita Mitra	ISI Kolkata, India
Umapada Pal	ISI Kolkata, India

Organizing Committee

Angsuman Sarkar	Kalyani Government Engineering College, India
Malay Kumar Pakhira	Kalyani Government Engineering College, India
Manju Biswas	Kalyani Government Engineering College, India
Anup Kumar Biswas	Kalyani Government Engineering College, India
Sandip Nandi	Kalyani Government Engineering College, India
Anup Mallick	Kalyani Government Engineering College, India
Surya Sarathi Das	Kalyani Government Engineering College, India
P. S. Banerjee	Kalyani Government Engineering College, India
Tapan Kumar Santra	Kalyani Government Engineering College, India
Kuntal Bhowmick	Kalyani Government Engineering College, India
D. K. Jha	Kalyani Government Engineering College, India

Technical Program Committee

Alok Chakraborty	National Institute of Technology Meghalaya, India
Anamitra Roy Chaudhury	IBM Research, India
Angsuman Sarkar	Kalyani Government Engineering College, India
Animesh Biswas	Kalyani University, India
Anirban Chakraborty	IISc Bangalore, India
Anirban Mukhopadhyay	University of Kalyani, India
Arindam Sarkar	Belur Vidyamandir, India
Arnab Majhi	NEHU, India
Arundhati Bagchi Misra	Saginaw Valley State University, USA
Asif Ekbal	Indian Institute of Technology Patna, India
B. B. Pal	University of Kalyani, India
B. K. Panigrahi	Indian Institute of Technology Delhi, India
Basabi Chakraborty	Iwate Prefectural University, Japan

Biswapati Jana	Vidyasagar University, India
Chandreyee Chowdhury	Jadavpur University, India
Debaprasad Das	Assam University, India
Debarka Mukhopadhyay	Christ University, India
Debashis De	Maulana Abul Kalam Azad University of Technology, India
Debasish Chakraborty	ISRO Kolkata, India
Debotosh Bhattacharjee	ISRO Kolkata, India
Deepsubhra Guha Roy	University of Tartu, Estonia
Dhananjay Bhattacharyya	Saha Institute of Nuclear Physics, India
Dilip Kumar Pratihar	Indian Institute of Technology Kharagpur, India
Farukh Hashmi	National Institute of Technology Warangal, India
Gopa Mandal	Jalpaiguri Govt. Engg. College, India
Girijasankar Mallik	University of Western Sydney, Australia
Hasanujjaman	Govt. College of Engg. & Textile Tech, India
Himadri Dutta	Kalyani Govt. Engg College, India
Hrishav Bakul Barua	TCS Innovations Kolkata, India
Indrajit Saha	National Inst. of Tech. Teachers' Training & Research Kolkata, India
Indranil Ghosh	Institute of Management Technology Hyderabad, India
J. K. Singh	Jadavpur University, India
Jabar H. Yousif	Sohar University, Saudi Arabia
Jaydeb Bhaumik	Jadavpur University, India
Jayeeta Mondal	TCS Innovations Kolkata, India
Jeet Dutta	TCS Innovations Kolkata, India
Joshua Thomas	Penang University, Malaysia
Jyoti Prakash Singh	National Institute of Technology Patna, India
Kakali Dutta	Visva Bharati University, India
Kamal Sarkar	Jadavpur University, India
Kartick Chandra Mondal	Jadavpur University, India
Kaushik Dassharma	Calcutta University, India
Khalid Yahya	Istanbul Gelisim University, Turkey
Kouichi Sakurai	Kyushu University, Japan
Koushik Majumder	Maulana Abul Kalam Azad University of Technology, India
Koushik Mondal	Indian Institute of Technology (ISM) Dhanbad, India
Kousik Roy	WB State University, India
Krishnendu Chakraborty	Govt. College of Engg. and Ceramic Technology, India
M. S. Sutaone	College of Engineering Pune, India

Manju Biswas	Kalyani Govt. Engg. College, India
Megha Quamara	IRIT, France
Mili Ghosh	North Bengal University, India
Mita Nasipuri	Jadavpur University, India
Mohammed Hasanuzzaman	Munster Technological University, Ireland
Mohsin Kamal	National University of Computer and Emerging Sciences, Pakistan
Moirangthem Marjit Singh	NERIST, India
Moumita Ghosh	Narula Institute of Technology, India
Mrinal Kanti Bhowmik	Tripura University, India
Muhammad Naveed Aman	National University of Singapore, Singapore
Nabendu Chaki	University of Calcutta, India
Nguyen Ha Huy Cuong	University of Danang, Vietnam
Nibaran Das	Jadavpur University, India
Nilanjana Dutta Roy	Institute of Engineering and Management, India
Partha Pakray	National Institute of Technology, Silchar, India
Partha Pratim Sahu	Tezpur University, India
Parthajit Roy	University of Burdwan, India
Pawan K. Singh	Jadavpur University, India
Prasanta K. Jana	Indian School of Mines Dhanbad, India
Prashant R. Nair	Amrita Vishwa Vidyapeetham, India
Prodipto Das	Assam University Silchar, India
Rajdeep Chakraborty	Netaji Subhas Institute of Technology, India
Ram Sarkar	Jadavpur University, India
Ranjita Das	National Institute of Technology Mizoram, India
Ravi Subban	Pondicherry University, India
S. B. Goyal	City University of Malaysia, Malaysia
Samarjit Kar	National Institute of Technology Durgapur, India
Samir Roy	NITTTR, Kolkata, India
Samiran Chattopadhyay	Jadavpur University, India
Sandeep Kautish	Lord Buddha Education Foundation, Nepal
Sankhayan Choudhury	University of Calcutta, India
Santi P. Maity	Indian Institute of Engg, Science and Technology Shibpur, India
Sharmistha Neogy	Jadavpur University, India
Shashank Mouli Satapathy	VIT University, India
Shrish Verma	National Institute of Technology Raipur India
Sk. Obaidullah	Aliah University, India
Somenath Chakraborty	West Virginia University Institute of Technology, USA
Soumya Pandit	Sheffield Hallam University, UK
Soumya Shankar Basu	Sheffield Hallam University, UK

Sriparna Saha	Indian Institute of Technology Patna, India
Subarna Shakya	Tribhuvan University, Nepal
Subhadip Basu	Jadavpur University, India
Subrata Banerjee	National Institute of Technology Durgapur, India
Sudarsun Santhiappan	BUDDI AI, India
Sudhakar Sahoo	Institute of Mathematics & Applications, India
Sudhakar Tripathi	National Institute of Technology Patna, India
Sudipta Roy	Assam University Silchar, India
Sujoy Chatterjee	UPES Dehradun, India
Sukumar Nandi	Indian Institute of Technology Guwahati, India
Suman Lata Tripathi	Lovely Professional University, India
Sunil Mane	College of Engineering Pune, India
Sunita Sarkar	Assam University Silchar, India
Tamal Datta Chaudhury	Calcutta Business School, India
Tandra Pal	National Institute of Technology Durgapur, India
Tanmoy Chakraborty	IIIT Delhi, India
Tanushyam Chattopadyay	TCS Innovations Kolkata, India
Tapodhir Acharjee	Assam University Silchar, India
Tien Anh Tran	Vietnam Maritime University, Vietnam
Utpal Sarkar	Assam University Silchar, India
Varun Kumar Ojha	University of Reading, UK

Contents – Part II

Theories and Applications to Data Analytics

Contents – Part I

Theories and Applications to Data Communications

A Novel Approach of Fragile Watermarking for Authentication and Tamper Detection Exploiting Local Binary Pattern (LBP)

Manasi Jana[1], Biswapati Jana[2(✉)], and Subhankar Joardar[3]

[1] Department of Computer Applications, Haldia Institute of Technology, Haldia, West Bengal, India

[2] Department of Computer Science, Vidyasagar University, West Midnapore, West Bengal, India
biswapatijana@gmail.com

[3] Department of Computer Science and Engineering, Haldia Institute of Technology, Haldia, West Bengal, India

Abstract. Data communication and transmission through internet has been rapidly increased now a days specially during and after COVID-19 pandemic situation. So, it is essential to preserve multimedia data from outlawed access. Here, a novel approach of fragile watermarking for authentication and tamper detection has been suggested. Firstly, an input image is split up into non-overlapping blocks of sized 3×3. A reference block has been chosen randomly to get the watermark which is hidden at the LSBs (Least Significant Bits) of the non-reference blocks of input image. The proposed scheme takes the advantage of Local Binary Pattern (LBP) feature of the image which is used to generate the watermark. The proposed scheme maintains high quality watermarked images with 51.68 dB average PSNR and 0.9955 average SSIM. The proposed scheme has been analysed against different attacks like cropping and copy-move forgery which shows 100% Tamper Detection Rate (TDR) for cropping attack and 99.39% for copy-move forgery attack. The presented scheme also exceeds other methods with respect to PSNR and SSIM value as depicted in comparative analysis.

Keywords: Fragile watermarking · Tamper detection · Authentication · LBP (Local Binary Pattern)

1 Introduction

Now a days, it is extremely convenient to capture, transmit and storage of multimedia data through internet. However, it is a big concern to guard these data from outlawed alteration. Watermarking [1] and Steganography [2] are two potential solutions to keep the integrity of digital data. Many researchers have

K. Dasgupta et al. (Eds.): CICBA 2023, CCIS 1956, pp. 3–16, 2024.
https://doi.org/10.1007/978-3-031-48879-5_1

paid their attentions to solve this issue by devising watermarking techniques on spatial [3] and frequency domain [4]. In spatial domain watermarking schemes, the watermark is directly placed into the pixels of cover image. In frequency domain, the watermark is embedded into the coefficient values after applying different transform functions such as DCT (Discrete Cosine Transform), DWT (Discrete Wavelet Transform), DFT (Discrete Fourier Transform) etc. on cover image. Recently, more attention has been paid on tamper detection, authentication and recovery [5] at an efficient manner. The watermarking technique is classified into three techniques such as fragile, semi-fragile and robust. Fragile and semi-fragile techniques are used to detect unauthorised manipulation even at very low modification. Robust watermarking technique is designed for copyright protection and ownership verification. In the proposed method, a fragile watermarking method exploiting LBP is designed for authentication and tamper detection. The objective and motivation of this paper is to design a fragile watermarking technique for document authentication at high tampering rate.

The following is a summary of our suggested scheme's main contributions.

(i) Only LSB of each pixel has been modified to embed watermark which results in watermarked image with high imperceptibility.
(ii) The random reference block and shared secret key have been used to enhance reliability of the presented scheme.
(iii) The time complexity of the suggested method is very less due to LSB substitution of watermark embedding of presented scheme.
(iv) It produces a high authentication checking due to its very high TDR (Tamper Detection Rate).

The remaining part of the paper is collocated as follows. Section 2 narrates the related studies of the presented scheme. Section 3 introduces the presented scheme with example. Experimental results have been introduced at Sect. 4. Lastly, the paper is culminated at Sect. 5.

2   Related Studies

In the past, different watermarking techniques are proposed on spatial domain [6] and frequency domain [7]. In 1995, Walton [8] has instigated watermarking scheme to accomplish authentication. However, it can not recognize the exact

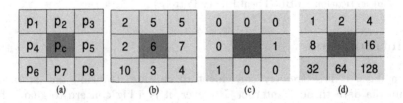

Fig. 1. Numerical example of LBP value generation

tamper pixels. Zhang and Frank [9] have proposed a LBP based semi-fragile watermarking method but it suffers from low imperceptibility of the water-marked image. The Local Binary Pattern (LBP) feature of an image has sug-gested by Ojala et al. [10,11]. LBP is used in the field of texture classification [12], image classification, face detection and pattern recognition. A numerical exam-ple of LBP value generation of a 3×3 block is shown in Fig. 1. Here, p_c (Fig. 1(a)) is the central pixel and p_i, $i = 1$ to 8 represent eight neighbouring pixels of a 3×3 block. The LBP (β) value of this block (Fig. 1(b)) is computed using Eq. (1) and Eq. (2).

$$\beta = \sum_{i=1}^{8} F(p_i - p_c) \times 2^{i-1} \tag{1}$$

$$F(z) = \begin{cases} 1 & \text{if } z \geq 0 \\ 0 & \text{Otherwise} \end{cases} \tag{2}$$

where $F(z)$ is a sign function.

The LBP value (β) of this 3×3 block $= (16 + 32)_{10} = (48)_{10}$. Based on LBP feature we have suggested a novel fragile watermarking for authentication and tamper detection which produces pixel wise tamper localization.

3 The Proposed Scheme

Here, a LBP based fragile watermarking is presented for authentication and tamper detection. The proposed scheme can be divided into two phases (a) Creation of watermark and embedding procedure (b) Authentication and tamper detection procedure.

3.1 Creation of Watermark and Embedding Procedure

A schematic diagram of proposed scheme has been illustrated in Fig. 2. The creation of watermark and embedding procedure can be done as follows.

Step 1: Divide $M \times N$ sized input image (I) into 3×3 non-overlapping blocks B_j, where $j = 1$ to $\lfloor \frac{M}{3} \rfloor \times \lfloor \frac{N}{3} \rfloor$ in raster scan order.

Step 2: Select one 3×3 block as reference block (B_r) from B_j, $j = 1$ to $\lfloor \frac{M}{3} \rfloor \times \lfloor \frac{N}{3} \rfloor$ and treat all other ($\lfloor \frac{M}{3} \rfloor \times \lfloor \frac{N}{3} \rfloor$ -1) blocks as non-reference blocks.

Step 3: Find LBP value (β) of the reference block B_r using Eq. (1) and Eq. (2). Let, each bit of (β) is denoted by $\beta_8, \beta_7, .., \beta_1$ and calculated using Eq. (3).

$$\beta_i = \lfloor \frac{\beta}{2^{i-1}} \rfloor \mod 2 , \quad i = 1 \text{ to } 8 \tag{3}$$

Step 4: Take a secret key key_1 and convert into binary equivalent as $k_8, k_7, k_6, .., k_1$ using Eq. (4) and Eq. (5).

$$k = \mod (key_1, 255) \tag{4}$$

$$k_i = \left\lfloor \frac{k}{2^{i-1}} \right\rfloor \ mod \ \ 2, \qquad i = 1 \ to \ 8 \tag{5}$$

Step 5: Find watermark bits (ψ_i) using Eq. (6).

$$\psi_i = \beta_i \ \ XOR \ \ k_i \ , \quad i = 1 \ \ to \ \ 8 \tag{6}$$

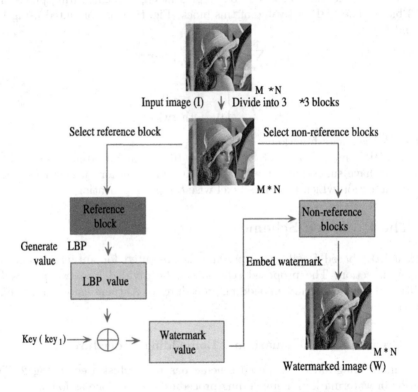

Fig. 2. Schematic diagram of watermark embedding

Step 6: Embed watermark bits (ψ_i) at LSBs of eight pixels of a non-reference block using Eq. (7).

$$p_i = \left\lfloor \frac{p_i}{2} \right\rfloor \times 2 + \psi_{9-i} \ , \quad i = 1 \ to \ 8 \tag{7}$$

Step 7: Repetition is applied on Step 6 until the watermark is embedded into all non-reference blocks of the input image (I) which results in a watermarked image (W).

3.2 Authentication and Tamper Detection Procedure

A schematic diagram of authentication and tamper detection has been illustrated in Fig. 3. The steps for authentication and tamper detection are as follows.

Step 1: A watermarked image (W) is split up into 3×3 non-overlapping blocks B_j, where $j = 1$ to $\lfloor \frac{M}{3} \rfloor \times \lfloor \frac{N}{3} \rfloor$ in raster scan order.

Step 2: Select the reference block (B_r) from $\lfloor \frac{M}{3} \rfloor \times \lfloor \frac{N}{3} \rfloor$ blocks which has been selected during watermark embedding and rest $\lfloor \frac{M}{3} \rfloor \times \lfloor \frac{N}{3} \rfloor$ - 1 blocks are treated as non-reference blocks.

Step 3: Find LBP value (β) of reference block (B_r) using Eq. (1) and Eq. (2).

Step 4: Take the secret key key_1 and convert into binary equivalent using Eq. (4) and Eq. (5).

Step 5: Find out calculated watermark (ψ^c) using Eq. (6).

Step 6: Extract retrieved watermark (ψ^e) from a non-reference block (B_j), $j \neq r$ using Eq. (8) and Eq. (9).

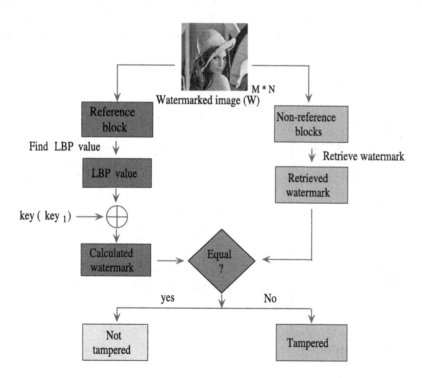

Fig. 3. Schematic diagram of authentication and tamper detection

$$\psi'_{9-i} \leftarrow p_i - 2 \times \lfloor \frac{p_i}{2} \rfloor \quad , \quad i = 1 \ to \ 8 \tag{8}$$

$$\psi^e = \sum_{i=1}^{8} \psi'_i \times 2^{i-1} \tag{9}$$

Step 7: Compare calculated watermark (ψ^c) and retrieved watermark (ψ^e). The non-reference block (B_j), $j \neq r$ is treated as tampered block if any mismatch is found between calculated watermark (ψ^c) and retrieved watermark (ψ^e), otherwise it is treated as non-tampered block. If any non-reference block is identified as tampered then the watermarked image (W) has been recognized as an un-authenticated and tampered watermarked image (T). It is a fragile watermarking method because the content integrity can be identified due to single bit modification.

3.3 Illustrative Example

An illustrative example of watermark embedding of the suggested method has been illustrated in Fig. 4. A 6×6 sized input image (I) has been taken and split up into 3×3 sized non-overlapping four blocks B_j, $j = 1$ to 4. One

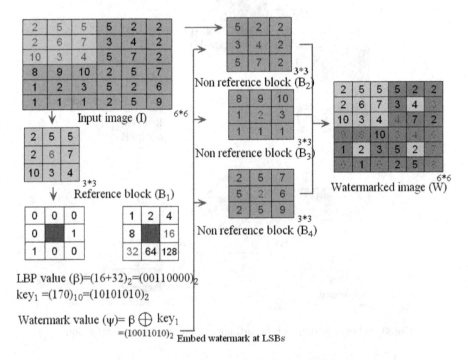

Fig. 4. An example of watermark embedding

block (say, B_1) has been selected as reference block and rest three blocks $(B_2, B_3$ and $B_4)$ are treated as non-reference blocks. The LBP value (β) of reference block (B_1) is $(16 + 32)_{10} = (48)_{10} = (00110000)_2$. Let, the secret key $(key_1) = (170)_{10} = (10101010)_2$. So, the watermark $(\psi) = \beta \ XOR \ key_1 = (10011010)_2$. A schematic diagram of watermark generation of proposed method has been illustrated in Fig. 5. After embedding watermark at LSBs of pixels of B_2, B_3 and B_4 using Eq. (7), a watermarked image (W) has been generated. An example of authentication and tamper detection of suggested method has been illustrated in Fig. 6. A tampered watermarked image (T) (6×6) has been taken and split up into four non-overlapping 3×3 sized blocks B_j, $j = 1$ to 4. Let, the pixel value 9 of block B_3 of watermarked image (W) has been changed to 10. Here B_1 is the reference block and B_2, B_3 and B_4 are non-reference blocks. For authentication checking, first the LBP value (β) of B_1 has been generated using Eq. (1) and Eq. (2) that is $(00110000)_2$. The calculated watermark $(\psi^c) = \beta \ XOR \ key_1 = (10011010)_2$. The extracted watermark (ψ^e) retrieved from LSBs of pixels of B_2 is $(10011010)_2$ which is same as calculated watermark (ψ^c) that means B_2 has not been tampered. The extracted watermark (ψ^e) retrieved from B_3 is $(00011010)_2$ which is not same as calculated watermark (ψ^c). So block B_3 has been tampered that means T is not an authenticated image.

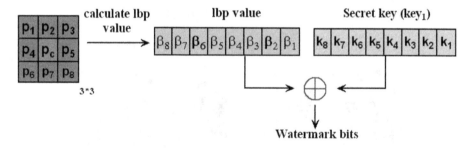

Fig. 5. Schematic diagram of watermark generation

4   Experimental Results

The experiment of suggested scheme is carried out using Matlab (R2016a) software. Eight gray scale input images (512×512) and four color images (512×512) have been taken for experiment as shown in Fig. 7. The proposed scheme has been also tested using different types of gray scale images and color images which produce same results. Watermarked images are generated after embedding watermark at LSBs of pixels of non-reference blocks of input image as shown in Fig. 8. Two parameters like PSNR and SSIM are taken to analyse the grade of the watermarked images. The PSNR and SSIM are calculated using Eq. (10), Eq. (11) and Eq. (12) respectively.

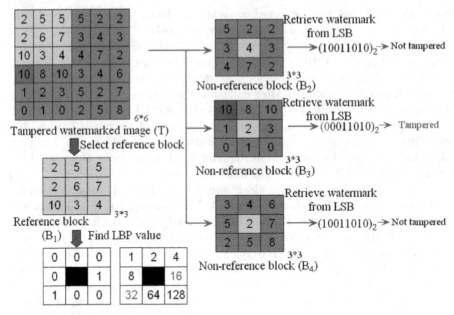

LBP value $(\beta)=(16+32)_{10}=(00110000)_2$

Let, $key_1 = (170)_{10}=(10101010)_2$

Calculated watermark value $(\psi^c) = \beta \oplus key_1=(10011010)_2$

Fig. 6. An example of authentication and tamper detection

(a) Lena   (b) Airplane   (c) Cameraman   (d) Tiffany

(e) Woman   (f) Crowd   (g) Lake   (h) Pepper

(i) Baboon   (j) House   (k) Parrot   (l) Tower

Fig. 7. Input images (512×512) used in proposed scheme

(a) Lena   (b) Airplane   (c) Cameraman   (d) Tiffany

(e) Woman   (f) Crowd   (g) Lake   (h) Pepper

(i) Baboon   (j) House   (k) Parrot   (l) Tower

Fig. 8. Watermarked images (512 × 512) produced in proposed scheme

Table 1. Tamper detection analysis

Attacks	Images (512 × 512)	Tampered blocks	Tamper detected blocks	TR (%)	TDR (%)
Cropping	Lena	1445	1445	5	100
		2890	2890	10	100
		7225	7225	25	100
		14450	14450	50	100
Copy-move forgery	Lake	1445	1439	5	99.58
		2890	2864	10	99.10
		7225	7179	25	99.36
		14450	14384	50	99.54

$$PSNR = 10 Log_{10} \frac{255^2}{MSE} \tag{10}$$

$$MSE = \frac{1}{M*N} \sum_{x=1}^{M} \sum_{y=1}^{N} \left(I(x,y) - W(x,y) \right)^2 \tag{11}$$

where MSE is Mean Square Error between the watermarked and input image.

$$SSIM \quad (I,W) = \frac{(2\mu_I\mu_W + C_1)(2\sigma_{IW} + C_2)}{(\mu_I^2 + \mu_W^2 + C_1)(\sigma_I^2 + \sigma_W^2 + C_2)} \tag{12}$$

where μ_I and μ_W are local means of I and W, σ_I and σ_W are standard deviations of I and W images respectively. C_1 and C_2 are constants.

The efficiency of the proposed plan is measured in terms of PSNR (Peak Signal-to-Noise Ratio), NCC (Normalized Cross Correlation), Q-index (Quality

Table 2. PSNR (dB), NCC, Q-index, BER, SSIM of proposed scheme

Images (512 × 512)	PSNR (dB)	NCC	Q-index	BER	SSIM
Lena	51.69	0.9998	0.98	0.05	0.9971
Airplane	51.67	0.9997	0.99	0.05	0.9972
Cameraman	51.69	0.9997	0.99	0.05	0.9966
Tiffany	51.67	0.9998	0.97	0.05	0.9970
Woman	51.71	0.9996	0.96	0.05	0.9966
Crowd	51.68	0.9998	0.99	0.05	0.9969
Lake	51.69	0.9997	0.98	0.05	0.9971
Pepper	51.68	0.9998	0.99	0.05	0.9860
Baboon	51.72	0.9996	0.97	0.06	0.9858
House	51.68	0.9998	0.98	0.05	0.9964
Parrot	51.67	0.9997	0.98	0.05	0.9972
Tower	51.66	0.9996	0.96	0.05	0.9965
Average	51.68	0.9997	0.98	0.05	0.9969

Table 3. Comparison of proposed plan with other methods

Images (512 × 512)	[13]	[14]	[15]	[16]	[17]	Proposed
Avg. PSNR (dB)	51.13	51.12	51.06	34.41	51.14	51.68
Avg. SSIM	0.9969	0.9966	0.9968	0.9058	0.9969	0.9969

Index), SSIM (Structural Similarity Index Measure) and BER (Bit Error Rate) as shown in Table 2. The average PSNR value of the proposed plan is 51.68 dB which is very high due to the modification of only one LSB (Least Significant Bit) of each pixel. The values of NCC, SSIM and Q-index are nearer to 1 resulting in high imperceptibility of the proposed method. The efficiency of the proposed plan has been tested by using two parameters TR (Tampering Rate) and TDR (Tamper Detection Rate). If we choose the reference block from the first row or column or last row or column, then we get excellent TDR against any attacks. TR and TDR are measured using Eq. (13) and Eq. (14) respectively.

$$Tampering \quad Rate \quad (TR) = \frac{N^{tamper} \times 100}{N^{total}}\% \qquad (13)$$

where, N^{total} is the total number of blocks, N^{tamper} is the number of tampered blocks of tampered watermarked images.

$$Tamper \quad Detection \quad Rate \quad (TDR) = \frac{N^{detect} \times 100}{N^{tamper}}\% \qquad (14)$$

where, N^{detect} is the number of detected tampered blocks and N^{tamper} is the number of tampered blocks of tampered watermarked images.

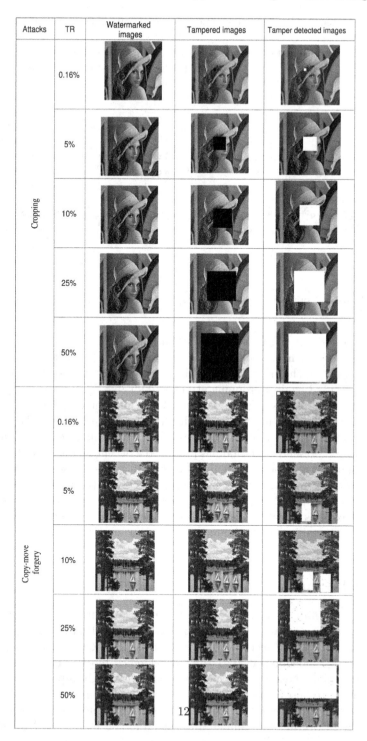

Fig. 9. Tampered images and tamper detected images on different attacks at different tampering rate

Table 4. Comparison of time complexity with other methods

Embedding time (Sec)	[18]	[19]	Proposed
	179.96	13.10	12.03

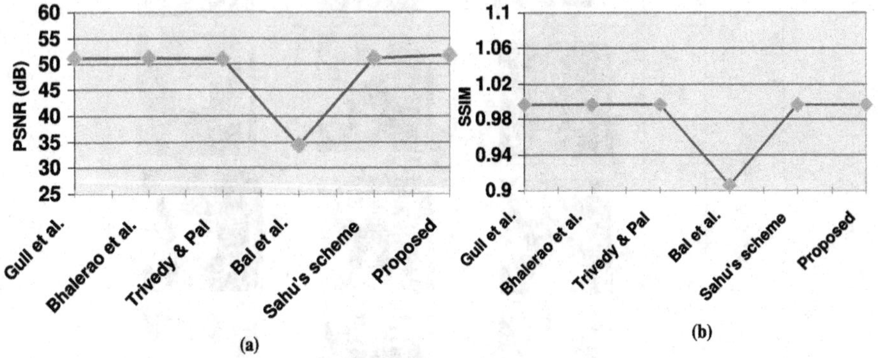

(a)   (b)

Fig. 10. Comparison of PSNR (dB) and SSIM with other methods

The effectiveness of the suggested scheme has been measured by applying different attacks such as cropping and copy-move forgery attack at different tampering rate as shown in Fig. 9. Table 1 shows that the suggested scheme having 100% TDR against cropping attack and 99.39% TDR against copy-move forgery attack. Table 3 shows the comparison of presented method with other methods like Gull et al. method [13], Bhalerao et al. method [14], Trivedy and Pal's method [15], Bal et al. method [16] and Sahu's method [17]. The table reveals that the presented method has produced a decent quality of watermarked image than other methods. As depicted in Fig. 10, the suggested scheme shows its superiority than other schemes in terms of PSNR (dB) and SSIM values. We have also compared the proposed scheme with other methods in term of time complexity as shown in Table 4. The experiment is applied on Lena image (512×512). The table depicts the superiority of the suggested scheme than other schemes.

5   Conclusions

This scheme introduces a novel fragile watermarking method with high level tamper detection and authentication exploiting Local Binary Pattern (LBP). The LBP feature and a secret key have been used to generate a secure watermark which is embedded at LSBs of non-reference blocks. The experimental results reveal that the suggested method results in a high imperceptible watermarked image. It also shows 100% TDR against cropping attack and 99.39% TDR against copy-move forgery attack. In future, the proposed scheme can be extended by recovering the tampered regions and can be analyzed by different image manipulation attacks.

References

1. Sharma, S., Zou, J.J., Fang, G.: A novel multipurpose watermarking scheme capable of protecting and authenticating images with tamper detection and localisation abilities. IEEE Access **10**, 85677–85700 (2022)
2. Jana, M., Jana, B.: An improved data hiding scheme through image interpolation. In: Das, A.K., Nayak, J., Naik, B., Pati, S.K., Pelusi, D. (eds.) Computational Intelligence in Pattern Recognition. AISC, vol. 999, pp. 157–169. Springer, Singapore (2020). https://doi.org/10.1007/978-981-13-9042-5_14
3. Qingtang, S., Zhang, X., Wang, H.: A blind color image watermarking algorithm combined spatial domain and SVD. Int. J. Intell. Syst. **37**(8), 4747–4771 (2022)
4. Singh, R., Izhar, L.I., Elamvazuthi, I., Ashok, A., Aole, S., Sharma, N.: Efficient watermarking method based on maximum entropy blocks selection in frequency domain for color images. IEEE Access **10**, 52712–52723 (2022)
5. Jana, M., Jana, B., Joardar, S.: Local feature based self-embedding fragile watermarking scheme for tampered detection and recovery utilizing ambtc with fuzzy logic. J. King Saud Univ.-Comput. Inf. Sci. **34**(10), 9822–9835 (2022)
6. Pal, P., Jana, B., Bhaumik, J.: An image authentication and tampered detection scheme exploiting local binary pattern along with hamming error correcting code. Wireless Pers. Commun. **121**(1), 939–961 (2021)
7. Jana, M., Jana, B.: A new DCT based robust image watermarking scheme using cellular automata. Inf. Secur. J. Glob. Perspect. **31**, 1–17 (2021)
8. Walton, S.: Image authentication for a slippery new age. Dr. Dobb's J. **20**(4), 18–26 (1995)
9. Wenyin, Z., Shih, F.Y.: Semi-fragile spatial watermarking based on local binary pattern operators. Opt. Commun. **284**(16–17), 3904–3912 (2011)
10. Ojala, T., Pietikainen, M., Harwood, D.: Performance evaluation of texture measures with classification based on kullback discrimination of distributions. In: Proceedings of 12th International Conference on Pattern Recognition, vol. 1, pp. 582–585. IEEE (1994)
11. Ojala, T., Pietikäinen, M., Harwood, D.: A comparative study of texture measures with classification based on featured distributions. Pattern Recogn. **29**(1), 51–59 (1996)
12. He, D.-C., Wang, L.: Texture unit, texture spectrum, and texture analysis. IEEE Trans. Geosci. Remote Sens. **28**(4), 509–512 (1990)
13. Gull, S., Loan, N.A., Parah, S.A., Sheikh, J.A., Bhat, G.M.: An efficient watermarking technique for tamper detection and localization of medical images. J. Ambient Intell. Humaniz. Comput. **11**(5), 1799–1808 (2020)
14. Bhalerao, S., Ansari, I.A., Kumar, A.: A secure image watermarking for tamper detection and localization. J. Ambient Intell. Humaniz. Comput. **12**, 1057–1068 (2021)
15. Trivedy, S., Pal, A.K.: A logistic map-based fragile watermarking scheme of digital images with tamper detection. Iran. J. Sci. Technol. Trans. Electr. Eng. **41**(2), 103–113 (2017)
16. Bal, S.N., Nayak, M.R., Sarkar, S.K.: On the implementation of a secured watermarking mechanism based on cryptography and bit pairs matching. J. King Saud Univ.-Comput. Inf. Sci. **33**(5), 552–561 (2021)
17. Sahu, A.K.: A logistic map based blind and fragile watermarking for tamper detection and localization in images. J. Ambient Intell. Humaniz. Comput. **13**, 1–13 (2021)

18. Singh, D., Singh, S.K.: DCT based efficient fragile watermarking scheme for image authentication and restoration. Multimedia Tools Appl. **76**(1), 953–977 (2017)
19. Gul, E., Ozturk, S.: A novel triple recovery information embedding approach for self-embedded digital image watermarking. Multimedia Tools Appl. **79**(41), 31239–31264 (2020)

A Machine Learning Based Video Summarization Framework for Yoga-Posture Video

Sana Afreen[ID], Tanmoy Ghosh[ID], Soumya Bhattacharyya(✉)[ID],
Anirban Bhar[ID], and Sourav Saha[ID]

Narula Institute of Technology, Kolkata, West Bengal, India
{soumya.bhattacharyya,anirban.bhar,sourav.saha}@nit.ac.in

Abstract. Video summarization techniques aim to generate a concise but complete synopsis of a video by choosing the most informative frames of the video content without loss of interpretability. Given the abundance of video content and its complex nature, there has always been a huge demand for an effective video summarization technique to analyze various dynamic posture centric videos. Yoga session video summarization is one of the interesting application areas of dynamic posture centric video analysis that is lately drawing the attention of computer vision researchers. The majority of available general video summarizing methods fail to detect key yoga poses in a yoga session video effectively, as they do not consider posture-centric information while extracting key frames. In this paper, we propose a machine learning based video summarization framework, which is capable of extracting a series of key postures in a yoga session video by tracking a few key-posture points corresponding to vital parts of the human body. Compared to the widely used FFMPEG tool, the proposed method appears to have a higher proportion of matched keyframes but a lower proportion of missing key-frames and redundant non key-frames with respect to the ground truth set, demonstrating its potential as an effective yoga posture video summarizer.

1   Introduction

In today's cyber technology driven world, video has become the most popular data format in our daily lives. The proliferation of video-based applications has led to an exponential explosion of video data. Almost 90% of current Internet traffic is video data, and it continues to grow significantly [5]. In addition, video analysis is widely employed in artificial intelligence jobs such as automatic driving, intelligent monitoring, and interactive robotics [14]. Under these conditions, automatic video analysis techniques are in high demand.

1.1   Motivation

Given the massive abundance of video content and its complex nature, there has been huge demand for effective video summarization which facilitates video

K. Dasgupta et al. (Eds.): CICBA 2023, CCIS 1956, pp. 17–29, 2024.
https://doi.org/10.1007/978-3-031-48879-5_2

analysis tasks for various complicated computer vision applications. Video summarization techniques make many video-processing tasks simpler while dealing with long and complex video streams [1]. A video summary highlights the key content of the video and eliminates redundancy by picking only a subset of keyframes for producing a condensed version of the original video without losing the interpretability. It is also used in many challenging video-based computer vision applications, such as video captioning, action recognition, and anomaly detection [1]. Some of the direct applications of video summarization are presented below.

1. Personal video summarization: Automatic video summarization of personal videos is very efficient for quickly generating a set of interesting moments from a lengthy video.
2. Sport-highlights: Video summarization can detect interesting moments in a sport-video.
3. Movie trailer generation: Video summarization can also be used to make movie trailers.
4. Theme-based Video Search Engine: Video Summarization can be used in search engines as the theme of the target video for retrieval of relevant videos.

Video Summarization can also be used to extract key posture frames from a video for action recognition. Nowadays, automated human activity analysis in a video is a highly promising field. The computational ability of an automated system to recognize and comprehend bodily motion offers numerous advantages for effective analysis of various forms of physical activities or exercises [17].

1.2   Contributory Scope of the Proposed Work

Yoga, which originates from India, is a popular form of healthy exercise that encourages harmony between the body (physical) and mind (mental). It is one of the world's oldest sciences that has been proven useful for maintaining and preserving physical and mental health. Medical professionals also nowadays acknowledge the therapeutic effects of yoga [8]. However, incorrect yoga postures may lead to sprains and muscle soreness. To prevent such injuries, it would be advantageous to have an automated computer vision tool capable of analyzing yoga posture videos. The main challenge in such a posture analysis task is to identify the key postures of an individual within a stipulated time frame. Figure 1 shows a sequence of desirable key postures for a Yoga Posture Video (Surya Namaskar). Most of the existing general video summarization approaches fail to identify such key postures from a yoga posture video as they do not explore posture-specific features while producing key-frames of a video.

In view of the above mentioned unexplored scope of research efforts on utilization of the power of artificial intelligence for yoga-posture video summarization, the primary objective of our proposed work is to leverage the capacity of machine learning techniques to develop an effective yoga-posture video summarization framework. The proposed framework is capable of extracting a sequence of key postures of an individual in a yoga posture video by tracking a few key-posture points corresponding to a few vital parts of the human body.

Fig. 1. 13 Keyframe Sequence of a Yoga Posture Video (Surya Namaskar)

In the subsequent section of this paper, we present a survey of related works. Section 3 details the proposed methodology along with the descriptions of key modules such as the key posture-point detection module, the posture vector generation strategy for ANN-based classification module, and the foundational principle of the key-posture frame identification module. Section 4 reports the performance evaluation results of the framework in comparison with the popular FFMPEG algorithm [13] and ground truth set. Finally, we conclude the paper in Sect. 5 by presenting a summary of the proposed work and its future scope.

2 Related Work

Numerous approaches are reported in the literature for video summarization. The video summarization approaches may be categorized based on sequential frame comparison, global frame comparison, minimum correlation between frames, minimum reconstruction error in frames, temporal variance between frames, maximum video frame coverage, reference key frame, curve simplification, key frame extraction using clustering, object- and event-based key frame extraction, and panoramic key frames. Hannane et al. [6] uses each frame of a video series for comparing with the previously retrieved key frame. This frame is regarded as the new key frame if the difference between the extracted key frame and the current key frame is large. The colour histogram is used to compute similarity between two frames of a video. The key benefit of this strategy is that it is straightforward but produces many redundant key frames. Liu T et al. uses the concept of lowering the summation of the relationship between frames to generate meaningful key frames from a shot. The crucial frames that were retrieved are inextricably linked. In this concept a graph-based technique is implemented to extract important frames and their associations. The shot is represented as a weighted graph, and the shortest path is determined using the A* method. The frames in the shot that have the least amount of connection and correlation are called key frames. Key frames can be retrieved by decreasing the variance between the preview frame and the collection of frames in a shot. The interpolation method creates the prevision frame. In [4], Chao et al. proposed a method for selecting a pre-defined group of key frames reducing frame reformation error. Sze K. W. et al. [16] combined the prevision frame-based technique with a pre-defined set of key frame selection approach exploring the motion-based characteristics. Luo J et al. proposed a video summarization methodology based on the maximum number of frames in a shot that a candidate key frame could represent [9]. This approach may help to estimate the total number of key frames but it is computationally demanding.

In [10,11], clustering techniques are applied on the sequence of video frames to form clusters of similar frames. In this approach, each cluster center or a frame with highest entropy in its cluster may be considered as a key-frame of the video stream. Cluster of similar frames can be generated using popular clustering techniques such as K-means or fuzzy C-means. Clusters are usually generated using the color feature as similarity metric. Cluster-based techniques have the benefit of covering the global properties of the frame. The downside of this approach is that cluster construction and feature extraction from a frame have a significant computational cost.

In [2], Basavarajaiah et al. provided a classification of various summarization approaches based on deep-learning techniques. Most deep-learning based video summarization techniques represent the visual content of the video frames as deep feature vectors and cast video summarization as a structured prediction problem to estimate the probability of a frame being a key frame by modelling temporal dependency. Nonetheless, an assessment of existing video summary methodologies revealed a dearth of research into the development of video summarization frameworks for dynamic posture-specific videos, such as yoga sessions. The vacuum of research efforts for extracting key frames from dynamic posture-centric videos drives us to work on developing video summarization frameworks for yoga posture centric videos.

3   Proposed Methodology

In this section, we describe the proposed methods of extracting key frames from yoga-posture videos. The primary purpose of key-frame extraction for yoga posture video summarization is to eliminate redundant frames to reduce computational load. In our proposed model, we have deployed a deep learning model to identify ten key-posture points corresponding to ten vital body parts of a single person in an image frame. Subsequently, a feature vector is constructed based on these key-posture points for ANN-based classification of postures. The

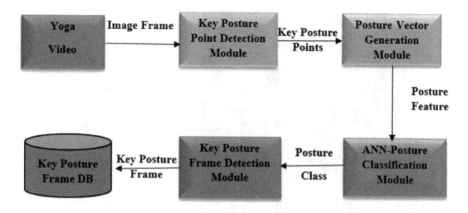

Fig. 2. Overview of the architecture of the proposed framework

class-outcomes of the ANN classifier are further analyzed to identify keyframes in the video. The overall architecture of the proposed framework is outlined in Fig. 2.

Key-Posture point detection from human posture image or video plays a central role in posture analysis. However, it is a challenging task due to the wide variety of articulated poses, numerous degrees of freedom of body-parts around junction points, and occlusions. Recent work [15] in computer vision-based human action analysis has shown significant progress on pose estimation using deep learning techniques. Newell et al. [12] have shown that the stacked hourglass architecture may provide a significant boost in predicting the junction points of the human body in a video. Bazarevsky et al. presented a very lightweight convolutional neural network architecture, namely BlazePose, for human pose estimation [3]. They used an encoder-decoder network architecture to predict heatmaps for all joints, followed by another encoder that regresses directly to the coordinates of all joints. During inference, the network produces 33 body key-points for a single person. We have deployed a similar model in this work to identify 10 key-posture points corresponding to 10 vital body-parts of a single person in an image frame, as shown in Fig. 3. Our solution requires a typical initial pose alignment as a baseline posture to extract all the key-points (Fig. 3) in the initial frame sequence. Subsequently, a tracking module attempts to predict the relative displacement of each key-point in a given frame around their respective neighbourhood based on their locations in the previous frame sequence. The prediction of the tracking module uses the convolutional neural network architecture presented by Bazarevsky et al. in [3]. Once all the key-points are localized in a frame, a feature vector is formed based on their relative locations to represent the posture so that we can deploy a classifier to identify its posture class. In the next section, the feature vector generation scheme is described in detail.

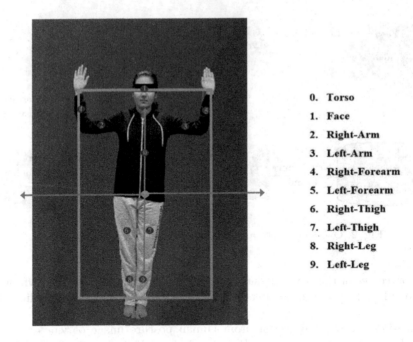

0. **Torso**

1. **Face**

2. **Right-Arm**

3. **Left-Arm**

4. **Right-Forearm**

5. **Left-Forearm**

6. **Right-Thigh**

7. **Left-Thigh**

8. **Right-Leg**

9. **Left-Leg**

Fig. 3. 10 posture key points of a Human Body (Proposed Framework)

3.1 Posture Feature Vector Generation

The feature vector is primarily formed based on the relative locations of the isolated key-points of the body. In order to determine the relative locations of the key-points, a minimal rectangle bounding all the key-points is obtained so that its center can represent the origin of our referential coordinate system. The normalized vertical and horizontal displacements of every key-point with respect to the origin of our referential coordinate system are considered as feature points while generating the feature vector. In order to make the entire feature vector for a posture, the aspect ratio of the bounding rectangle is also added. Below, the process of the Posture Feature Vector is outlined for an identified set of key posture points in an image frame.

Step 1: Determine the Minimal Enclosing Rectangle, which will include all the ten key posture points of the body.

Step 2: Determine the center (X_0, Y_0) of the Minimal Enclosing Rectangle to represent the origin of referential coordinate system.

Step 3: Normalize the vertical and horizontal displacements of every key-point from the origin of the referential coordinate system (i.e., $X_k - X_0, Y_k - Y_0$ for k-th key point). The sequence of these displacement values for all the ten posture key points, along with the aspect ratio of the Minimal Enclosing Rectangle, forms the feature vector.

Table 1. Posture feature vectors of a few Yoga postures

Posture Video Frame	Posture Feature Vector
 Posture Frame - 01	<-0.06 , -0.19, -0.03 , -0.5, -0.02 , -0.32, -0.05 , -0.32, 0.04 , -0.3, 0.02 , -0.31, 0.01 , 0.16, 0.01 , 0.15, 0.04 , 0.5, 0.06 , 0.47, 0.12>
 Posture Frame - 02	<0.07 , -0.2, -0.01 , -0.5, 0.05 , -0.3, 0.0 , -0.32, -0.03 , -0.27, -0.08 , -0.3, 0.06 , 0.14, 0.06 , 0.16, 0.07 , 0.46, 0.08 , 0.49, 0.16>
 Posture Frame - 03	<0.19 , -0.01, 0.35 , -0.35, 0.33 , -0.05, 0.28 , -0.09, 0.36 , 0.2, 0.32 , 0.13, -0.06 , 0.27, 0.26 , 0.11, -0.36 , 0.35, 0.33 , 0.22, 1.04>
 Posture Frame - 04	<0.12 , -0.04, 0.39 , -0.31, 0.32 , -0.02, 0.25 , -0.06, 0.38 , 0.24, 0.33 , 0.18, 0.02 , 0.13, -0.15 , 0.18, -0.06 , 0.19, -0.39 , 0.31, 1.27>

The size of the feature vector is twenty-two as both vertical and horizontal displacements of every key-point is considered. Table 1 shows the feature vectors for four posture frames as examples. It is worth noting that the variance among feature vectors of similar postures is smaller than the variance among feature vectors of dissimilar postures.

3.2 Key Frame Identification Based on Machine Learning

In this section, our proposed algorithm for generating key frames from a yoga-posture video is detailed. The proposed algorithm works on a frame of the video if the key posture-point detection model succeeds in returning the locations of specified key-posture points in the frame. The key-frame generation module decides whether a frame is a key-frame based on the posture prediction model and its posture-match-score in comparison with a few model postures corresponding to the predicted posture-class.

The principal idea behind the proposed algorithm stems from some basic intuitive assumptions such as (a) a yoga-exercise can be considered as a typical sequence of a few specific intermediate key-postures which constitute the key-frame sequence of the yoga-exercise video; (b) each intermediate key yoga posture is rendered through a sequence of progressive postures, the majority of which are close to the key posture under construction in terms of relative locations of the key-posture-points in a frame (c) The best match in the sequence of progressive

---

Algorithm 1: Algorithm for Key-Posture Frame Extraction

Input: $videoFile$: A Yoga Posture Video File

Output: $keyFrameList$: A list of Key Frames

1 **Function** $GetKeyFrameList (videoFile)$
2   **while** $((curFrame \leftarrow videoFile) \neq NULL)$ **do**
3        $keyPosturePtList \leftarrow genKeyPosturePt(curFrame)$;
4   **if** $keyPosturePtList == NULL)$ **then**
5 | **break**
6   **end**
7        $featureVector \leftarrow genFeature(keyPosturePtList)$;
8        $curPostureClass \leftarrow predictPostureClass(featureVector)$;
9   **if** $curPostureClass == prevPostureClass)$ **then**
10          $postureMatchScore \leftarrow$
               $getMatchScore(featureVector, curPostureClass)$;
11   **if** $postureMatchScore \geq curBestMatchScore$ **then**
12             $curBestMatchScore \leftarrow postureMatchScore$;
13             $bestMatchFrame \leftarrow curFrame$;
14   **end**
15   **end**
16   **else**
            /* Posture Transition   */
17          $transitionFrameCnt[curPostureClass] + +$
               $maxTransitionFrameCnt \leftarrow getMaxVal(transitionFrameCnt)$;
18          $maxTransitionClass \leftarrow getMaxValIndex(transitionFrameCnt)$;
19   **if** $maxTransitionFrameCnt > Threshold)$ **then**
               /* record the best matched frame as key frame   */
20             $keyFrame[keyFrameCnt] \leftarrow bestMatchFrame$;
21             $keyFrameCnt \leftarrow keyFrameCnt + 1$;
22             $prevPostureClasss \leftarrow maxTransitionClass$;
23             $bestMatchFrame \leftarrow curFrame$;
24             $curBestMatchScore \leftarrow postureMatchScore$;
25   **reset** $transitionFrameCntArray$;
26   **end**
27   **end**
28   **end**

---

postures while rendering an intermediate key yoga posture may be conceived as one of the keyframes of the yoga-exercise video.

The algorithm based on the above intuitive assumptions is presented as Algorithm 1 in this article. For a video with n frames, the algorithm's computational time complexity is $O(n)$. In order to ensure a transition between two intermediate key-postures in the video, only the initial frames of a posture-sequence towards rendering a new intermediate key-posture are checked against a threshold value. One of the benefits of this strategy is that it lets the module pull out keyframes while the video is still being recorded.

4   Experimentation, Results and Discussions

The performance of the proposed algorithm is evaluated by studying six different yoga postures, namely Suryanamaskar, Bhujangasan, Brikshasan, Dhanurasan, Trikonasan, and Ustrasan, and we have considered four videos as a sample set for each yoga posture. The results are compared to a ground truth set of manually extracted key frames as well as the widely used key frame extraction module of FFMPEG [7,13]. Here, we have presented comparative results in respect of the ground truth set for both qualitative and quantitative analysis of the proposed method. Table 2 lists keyframes of a video sample corresponding to the Suryana-maskar Yoga Posture. Three sets of keyframes obtained by the Ground Truth Strategy, the FFMPEG Strategy, and the Proposed Method are shown for qualitative analysis. It is evident from Table 2 that the set of keyframes extracted by our method is more similar to the ground truth set as compared to FFMPEG's algorithm.

In order to analyze the efficacy of our algorithm quantitatively, the following evaluation metrics are considered as an intuitive basis of comparison with respect to ground truth. Table 3 summarizes the quantitative results in terms of average percentages of matched keyframes, missing keyframes and redundant non-keyframes in comparison with FFMEPG.

1. Number of Matched Keyframes: Similar keyframes may be found in both the ground truth set and a set obtained through a video summarization algorithm. A larger value for the number of similar keyframes signifies better efficacy. This means that better summarization expects a bigger overlap between the keyframe set from the ground truth and the keyframe set from an algorithm.
2. Number of Missing Keyframes: Some of the keyframes of a ground truth set may not be found in a set obtained through a video summarization algorithm. A smaller value of the number of such missing keyframes denotes better efficacy of an algorithm.
3. Number of Non-Keyframes: Sometimes, a video summarization algorithm may extract irrelevant frames (termed "non-keyframe") from a video. For example, the third frame extracted by the FFMPEG algorithm may be considered a non-keyframe with respect to the ground truth set. The number of these non-keyframes should be very low for a video summarization algorithm to work well.

Table 2. Sequence of Keyframes Extracted by Ground Truth Strategy, FFMPEG Algorithm, and Proposed Algorithm for Qualitative Analysis

Table 3. Overall Comparative Results of the Proposed Algorithm and FFMPEG Algorithm

Algorithm Used	Matched Key-Frame (%)	Missing Key-Frame(%)	Non-Key-Frame(%)
FFMPEG	56	19	25
Proposed Algorithm	74	13	13

Table 4 reports the results of twenty-four yoga posture video samples based on the above-mentioned evaluation metrics. It can be observed that the proposed method demonstrates better performance in comparison with the FFMPEG algorithm.

Table 4. Comparative Results of the Proposed Algorithm and FFMPEG Algorithm with respect to Ground Truth Strategy for Quantitative Analysis

Yoga Posture Video		Number of Key-frames in Ground-Truth	Number of Matched Key-frames		Number of Missing Key-frames		Number of Non Key-frames	
Yoga Posture	Sample-ID		FF-MPEG	Proposed Method	FFMPEG	Proposed Method	FFMPEG	Proposed Method
Suryanamaskar	1	16	12	14	4	2	4	2
	2	16	11	13	5	3	5	3
	3	16	13	13	3	3	4	2
	4	16	12	14	4	2	3	3
Bhujangasan	5	9	7	8	2	1	2	1
	6	9	8	8	1	1	1	1
	7	9	7	7	2	2	2	2
	8	9	7	7	2	2	1	2
Brikshasan	9	12	8	10	4	2	3	1
	10	12	8	10	4	2	4	1
	11	12	9	10	3	2	3	1
	12	12	9	11	3	1	5	2
Dhanurasan	13	10	7	8	3	2	5	1
	14	10	7	8	3	2	4	1
	15	10	7	7	3	3	5	1
	16	10	8	8	2	2	5	1
Trikonasan	17	8	6	7	2	1	3	2
	18	8	5	7	3	1	4	2
	19	8	5	7	2	1	4	1
	20	8	6	7	2	1	3	2
Ustrasan	21	8	7	7	1	1	4	2
	22	8	7	7	1	1	4	2
	23	8	6	7	2	1	5	1
	24	8	5	7	3	1	4	2
Total		252	187	212	64	40	87	39

5   Conclusion

In this paper, a novel key-frame extraction method for yoga posture video summarization is presented. The primary purpose of key-frame extraction for yoga posture video summarization is to eliminate redundant frames to reduce computational cost while analyzing the yoga postures. In our proposed model, we have deployed a deep learning model to identify 10 key-posture points corresponding to 10 vital body parts of a single person in an image frame. Subsequently, a feature vector is constructed based on these key-posture points for ANN-based classification of postures. The outcomes of the ANN classifier are further analyzed to identify keyframes in the video. In the future, we may aim to trace the key posture points in the extracted key-frames for dynamic yoga posture analysis. The majority of the existing video summarization algorithms determine the key-frames in a video stream based on generic image feature-level differences between consecutive frames but do not explore the posture-specific features like the proposed algorithm. We have provided comparative results in respect of the ground truth set for both qualitative and quantitative analysis of the proposed method. The proposed framework appears to be capable of extracting a meaningful collection of key-frames from yoga posture videos that is reasonably comparable to the ground truth set, implying its suitability as an effective yoga posture video summarizer.

References

1. Ajmal, M., Ashraf, M.H., Shakir, M., Abbas, Y., Shah, F.A.: Video summarization: techniques and classification. In: Bolc, L., Tadeusiewicz, R., Chmielewski, L.J., Wojciechowski, K. (eds.) ICCVG 2012. LNCS, vol. 7594, pp. 1–13. Springer, Heidelberg (2012). https://doi.org/10.1007/978-3-642-33564-8_1
2. Basavarajaiah, M., Sharma, P.: Survey of compressed domain video summarization techniques. ACM Comput. Surv. **52**(6), 1–29 (2019)
3. Bazarevsky, V., Grishchenko, I., Raveendran, K., Zhu, T., Zhang, F., Grundmann, M.: Blazepose: on-device real-time body pose tracking. arXiv preprint arXiv:2006.10204 (2020)
4. Chao, G.C., Tsai, Y.P., Jeng, S.K.: Augmented 3-d keyframe extraction for surveillance videos. IEEE Trans. Circuits Syst. Video Technol. **20**(11), 1395–1408 (2010)
5. Gygli, M., Grabner, H., Riemenschneider, H., Van Gool, L.: Creating summaries from user videos. In: Fleet, D., Pajdla, T., Schiele, B., Tuytelaars, T. (eds.) ECCV 2014. LNCS, vol. 8695, pp. 505–520. Springer, Cham (2014). https://doi.org/10.1007/978-3-319-10584-0_33
6. Hannane, R., Elboushaki, A., Afdel, K., Naghabhushan, P., Javed, M.: An efficient method for video shot boundary detection and keyframe extraction using sift-point distribution histogram. Int. J. Multim. Inf. Retriev. **5**(2), 89–104 (2016)
7. Liu, G., Zhao, J.: Key frame extraction from mpeg video stream. In: 2010 Third International Symposium on Information Processing, pp. 423–427. IEEE (2010)
8. Long, C., Jo, E., Nam, Y.: Development of a yoga posture coaching system using an interactive display based on transfer learning. J. Supercomput. **78**(4), 5269–5284 (2022)

9. Luo, J., Papin, C., Costello, K.: Towards extracting semantically meaningful key frames from personal video clips: from humans to computers. IEEE Trans. Circuits Syst. Video Technol. **19**(2), 289–301 (2008)
10. Moir, G.L., Graham, B.W., Davis, S.E., Guers, J.J., Witmer, C.A.: An efficient method of key-frame extraction based on a cluster algorithm. J. Hum. Kinet. **39**(1), 15–23 (2013)
11. Nasreen, A., Roy, K., Roy, K., Shobha, G.: Key frame extraction and foreground modelling using k-means clustering. In: 2015 7th International Conference on Computational Intelligence, Communication Systems and Networks, pp. 141–145. IEEE (2015)
12. Newell, A., Yang, K., Deng, J.: Stacked hourglass networks for human pose estimation. In: Leibe, B., Matas, J., Sebe, N., Welling, M. (eds.) ECCV 2016. LNCS, vol. 9912, pp. 483–499. Springer, Cham (2016). https://doi.org/10.1007/978-3-319-46484-8_29
13. Niedermayer, M., Sabatini, S., Giovara, V.: Ffmpeg documentation (2012). http://ffmpeg.org/ffmpeg-all.html#Video-Encoders
14. Peng, B., Lei, J., Fu, H., Jia, Y., Zhang, Z., Li, Y.: Deep video action clustering via spatio-temporal feature learning. Neurocomputing **456**, 519–527 (2021)
15. Sigal, L.: Human pose estimation. In: Computer Vision: A Reference Guide, pp. 573–592. Springer (2021)
16. Sze, K.W., Lam, K.M., Qiu, G.: A new key frame representation for video segment retrieval. IEEE Trans. Circuits Syst. Video Technol. **15**(9), 1148–1155 (2005)
17. Yan, C., Li, X., Li, G.: A new action recognition framework for video highlights summarization in sporting events. In: 2021 16th International Conference on Computer Science and Education (ICCSE), pp. 653–666. IEEE (2021)

Real-Time Human Fall Detection Using a Lightweight Pose Estimation Technique

Ekram Alam[1,3]($\boxtimes$), Abu Sufian[2], Paramartha Dutta[3], and Marco Leo[4]

[1] Department of Computer Science, Gour Mahavidyalaya, Mangalbari, West Bengal, India

[2] Department of Computer Science, University of Gour Banga, Malda, India

[3] Department of Computer and System Sciences, Visva-Bharati University, Bolpur, India
ealam4u@gmail.com

[4] National Research Council of Italy, Institute of Applied Sciences and Intelligent Systems, 73100 Lecce, Italy

Abstract. The elderly population is increasing rapidly around the world. There are no enough caretakers for them. Use of AI-based in-home medical care systems is gaining momentum due to this. Human fall detection is one of the most important tasks of medical care system for the aged people. Human fall is a common problem among elderly people. Detection of a fall and providing medical help as early as possible is very important to reduce any further complexity. The chances of death and other medical complications can be reduced by detecting and providing medical help as early as possible after the fall. There are many state-of-the-art fall detection techniques available these days, but the majority of them need very high computing power. In this paper, we proposed a lightweight and fast human fall detection system using pose estimation. We used 'Movenet' for human joins key-points extraction. Our proposed method can work in real-time on any low-computing device with any basic camera. All computation can be processed locally, so there is no problem of privacy of the subject. We used two datasets 'GMDCSA' and 'URFD' for the experiment. We got the sensitivity value of 0.9375 and 0.9167 for the dataset 'GMDCSA' and 'URFD' respectively. The source code and the dataset GMDCSA of our work are available online to access.

Keywords: Fall Detection · Pose Estimation · GMDCSA · Movenet · Lightweight Fall Detection · Real-time Fall Detection

1 Introduction

Human fall is one of the major reasons for hospitalization in elder people around the world [1]. Detection of human falls is very vital so that medical help can be provided as early as possible. Human fall detection can be done using wearable, ambient, or vision sensors [2]. Vision-based fall detection system is more suitable, especially for elder people [3]. There is no need to attach the vision sensor to

K. Dasgupta et al. (Eds.): CICBA 2023, CCIS 1956, pp. 30–40, 2024.
https://doi.org/10.1007/978-3-031-48879-5_3

the body like wearable sensors. Wearable sensors need to be charged frequently whereas vision sensors can work on a direct home power supply. Human fall detection is one of the useful application of computer vision [4,5]. In this paper, we have proposed a lightweight human fall detection system using pose estimation [6,7]. We have used a lightweight and fast pose estimation model 'Movenet Thunder' [8] for our work. The main contributions of this work are as given below.

Real Time 'Movenet' processes the video with 30+ FPS [9] (real-time) in the majority of current low computing devices like mobile phones, laptops, and desktops. So the proposed system can work in real-time on these devices. We tested our work on an average computing laptop with inbuilt webcam.

Lightweight The proposed system does not required very high computing power and can work on any normal laptop/desktop or mobile device.

Local Computation All computation can be processed locally. There is no personal data (images/frames) transfer from edge [10] to the cloud and vice versa. Only the output (fall) is sent to the caretaker center for necessary medical help. In this way, our system also preserves the privacy of the subject.

GMDCSA Dataset A new fall detection dataset named GMDCSA was introduced.

The rest of the paper is structured as follows. Section 3 describes related work briefly. Section 2 gives an overview of the pose estimation using 'Movenet'. Section 4 discusses the methodology of our work. Section 5 describes the datasets which were used in this work. Section 6 provides the results of this work in the form of different metrics. Finally, Sect. 7 concludes the proposed work with possible future scopes.

2   Background Study

We have used a lightweight pose estimation model named 'Movenet Thunder' [8]. This model accepts an RGB frame or image of the size 256×256 and extracts the normalized coordinate and confidence values of the 17 key-points of the human body joints. The 17 key-points are shown in Fig. 1. The indices (from 0 to 16), Keypoints, Y values, X values, and confidences value of a sample image are shown in Table. 1.

The values of y,x, and confidence are normalized from 0 to 1. The top left position is the origin(0,0) and the bottom right position has the value (1,1). When the keypoints are clearly visible then confidence tends to 1 (100%) otherwise it tends to 0 (0%).

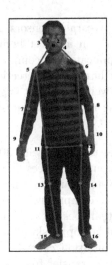

Fig. 1. 17 Keypoints of the Movenet pose estimation model

Table 1. Index, Keypoint, Y value, X value and confidence of an sample image

Index	Keypoint	Y Value	X Value	Confidence
0	Nose	0.22416662	0.579579	0.7201656
1	Left Eye	0.20926172	0.5974146	0.8043867
2	Right Eye	0.20485064	0.5642889	0.5905826
3	Left Ear	0.22323	0.6126661	0.7964257
4	Right Ear	0.21771489	0.5370738	0.7529471
5	Left Shoulder	0.3235461	0.6375601	0.8950565
6	Right Shoulder	0.2964768	0.48282918	0.65825576
7	Left Elbow	0.43468294	0.63684213	0.7667525
8	Right Elbow	0.42770475	0.4406372	0.8829603
9	Left Wrist	0.54110587	0.6462866	0.6282949
10	Right Wrist	0.5392799	0.42464092	0.8215329
11	Left Hip	0.54277164	0.57565194	0.85804665
12	Right Hip	0.53679305	0.48321638	0.88962007
13	Left Knee	0.69595444	0.609515	0.8796475
14	Right Knee	0.7019378	0.46842176	0.6786141
15	Left Ankle	0.85588527	0.56420994	0.7951814
16	Right Ankle	0.8588409	0.47616798	0.82729894

3   Related Work

This section briefly describes some recent related works. Asif et al. [11] introduced a single-shot fall detection technique using 3D poseNet. Chen et al. [12]

proposed a 3D posed estimator which was used as input for the fall detection network. Apicella and Snidaro [13] proposed a fall detection method based on CNN, RNN and PoseNet pose estimation. Leite et al. [14] introduced a multi (three) channel CNN-based fall detection system. Optical flow, pose estimation, and visual rhythm were used as inputs for three different streams of the CNN. Open-Pose [15] was used for pose estimation. Chen et al. [16] proposed a fall detection system using the Yolov5 network [17]. Liu et al. [18] proposed a fall detection system based on BlazePose-LSTM. This system was introduced especially for seafarers. Beddiar et al. [19] introduced a work based on the angle formed by the line from the centroid of the human face to the centroid of the hip to the line formed from the centroid of the hip to the horizontal axis. Amsaprabhaa et al. [20] proposed a multimodal gate feature-based fall detection system.

4   Methodology

The methodology of the proposed work is shown in Fig. 2. The input can be an image, frames of a video, or the live video stream. The input images/frames were resized to 256×256 as preprocessing before feeding it to the Movenet. After preprocessing, pose estimation was done using the Movenet. The Movenet extracts the key-point co-ordinates with their confidence score as shown in Table 1. Confidence score can vary from 0 (0%) to 1 (100%) for each keypoints. If all key-points with very low confidence are also used for fall detection then it might select the wrong keypoints and this will reduce the performance of the system. If the high confidence value threshold are used it may ignore some good keypoints which might be useful for the detection of the fall. After experimenting with different threshold values of the confidence score, we finally selected 0.5 as threshold value because it gave good results. We have selected only those key-points whose confidence scores are greater than 0.5. The fall activity and sleeping activity are

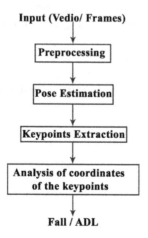

Fig. 2. Proposed work methodology

very similar and there are high chances of detecting a sleeping activity as fall. If there is a sleeping like activity on the floor then the system should detect it as fall activity, but if there is a sleeping like activity on the bed then the system should detect it as ADL (not fall) activity. To filter out this we compared the approximate y value of the top of the bed with the y value of the nose, eyes, ears, shoulders, elbows and wrists (upper body part). If the y value of these key-points (upper body part) are greater than the approximate y value of the top of the bed, then the activities of these frames are not fall and filtered out for the fall detection. After that the coordinates (x, y values) of the keypoints of the upper body parts were compared with the coordinates of key-points of the lower body parts(hips, knees, ankles). If the differences of the y value of the upper body keypoints (UBK) with lower body keypoints (LBK) is less than or equal to 0.05 (threshold-y) and the absolute differences of the x value is greater than 0.5 (threshold-x) then there is a chance of a Fall and the fall counter is increased by one. The selection of the values for the threshold-y and threshold-x were done after doing many experiments with different values. These values gave the best results. If in the next frame this is false then counter reset to 0. If this happens continuously for 2 or more frames (minimum counter value 2), then the system detects it as a fall, and a fall alert is sent. Detail of the analysis is shown in Fig. 3. The source code of the proposed work is available here https://github. com/ekramalam/RTHFD.

5   Dataset

We used two datasets for the proposed experiment, the URFD [21] dataset and a dataset (GMDCSA) created by us. The URFD dataset contains 40 ADL (not fall) activities and 30 fall activities. The GMDCSA dataset contains 16 ADL (not fall) activities and 16 Fall activities. The GMDCSA dataset has been created by performing the fall and the ADL activities by a single subject wearing different set of clothes. The web camera of a laptop (HP 348 G5 Laptop : Core i5 8th Gen/8 GB/512 GB SSD/Windows 10) was used to capture the activities. The description of the ADL and Fall video sequences of the GMDCSA dataset are shown in Tables 2 and 3 respectively. The link to access this dataset is as follows https://drive.google.com/drive/folders/ 1ohDEXki8Wz12cJ1XzyKIK4T6y1_hAf3p?usp=sharing.

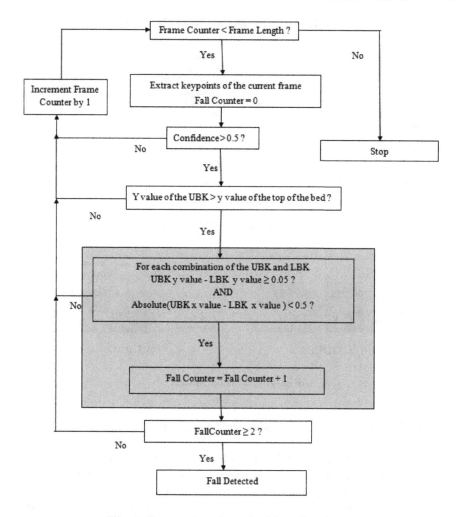

Fig. 3. Proposed work methodology flowchart

6   Result

The performance of a model can be measured using different evaluation metrics
[1] like sensitivity, specificity, precision, etc. The values of True Positive (TP),
True Negative (TN), False Positive (FP), and False Negative (FN) are needed
to calculate the values of these metrics. The value of TP, TN, FP, and FN can
easily be found from the confusion matrix as shown in Fig. 4. The value of TP,
TN, FP, and FN for the two dataset GMDCSA and URFD are shown in Table 4.
Table 5 shows the values of sensitivity, specificity, precision, false positive rate,
false negative rate, accuracy, and F1 Score.

These values can be calculated using the values of TP, TN, FP, and FN
as shown in Table 4. Table 5 also shows the expressions of the corresponding

Table 2. GMDCSA Dataset: ADL Activities

File Name	Length	Description
01.mp4	08 sec	Sitting on the bed to sleeping right side on the bed. Face towards camera
02.mp4	06 sec	Sitting on the bed to sleeping left side on the bed. Face towards camera
03.mp4	06 sec	Sitting on the bed to sleeping left side on the bed. Face towards ceiling
04.mp4	05 sec	From sleeping left side on the bed (Face towards ceiling) to sitting on the bed
05.mp4	10 sec	Coming to the bed and reading book in sitting position. Front view of the subject. One leg folded
06.mp4	12 sec	Sitting on the bed (front view) to reading the book while supporting towards the wall. Side view, Leg straight
07.mp4	07 sec	Reading book while sitting on the chair. Front view
08.mp4	06 sec	Walking in the room
09.mp4	04 sec	Reading book while walking in the room
10.mp4	03 sec	Reading book while walking in the room
11.mp4	09 sec	Walking to sitting on the chair and then reading book
12.mp4	07 sec	Reading book while sitting on the chair to stand up and keeping the book on the chair and going out of the room
13.mp4	06 sec	Walking to sitting on the chair (side view)
14.mp4	05 sec	Sitting on the chair (side view) to walking
15.mp4	07 sec	Walking to picking a mobile phone from the ground and then sitting on the chair
16.mp4	03 sec	Picking the mobile phone from the ground while sitting on the chair

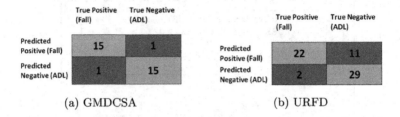

(a) GMDCSA   (b) URFD

Fig. 4. Confusion Matrix

metrics. The Sensitivity is more important than other metrics for any medical classification problem like human fall detection. The values of sensitivity are 0.9375, and 0.9167 for GMDCSA and URFD respectively. These values are good enough for a lightweight system. The specificity for GMDCSA is 0.9375 whereas for URFD it is 0.7250. The performance of our model is better using the GMD-CSA dataset than the URFD dataset. This may be because the ADL activities of URFD contained many complex falls-like activities. Some of these activities were classified wrongly as falls by our system.

Some of the sample outputs of this experiment using the GMDCSA and URFD datasets are shown in Figs. 5 and 6 respectively. The captions of the subfigure tell whether the frames are from the ADL sequence or the fall sequence. The number in the brackets of the caption is the file name of the video of the corresponding dataset. Figure 5 shows three sample ADL frames and three fall frames from the GMDCSA dataset video sequences. Similarly, Fig. 6 shows three sample ADL frames and three fall frames from the GMDCSA dataset video sequences.

Table 3. GMDCSA Dataset: Fall Activities

File Name	Length	Description
01.mp4	06 sec	Falling from sitting on the chair to the ground. Left side Fall. Full body not visible
02.mp4	06 sec	Falling from sitting on the chair to the ground. Left side Fall. Full body not visible
03.mp4	05 sec	Falling from sitting on the chair to the ground. Left side fall
04.mp4	04 sec	Falling from sitting on the chair to the ground. Right side fall
05.mp4	05 sec	Walking to falling. Right side fall
06.mp4	05 sec	Walking to falling. Right side fall
07.mp4	05 sec	Walking to falling. Right side fall
08.mp4	04 sec	Walking to falling. Left side fall
09.mp4	04 sec	Standing position to falling. Forward Fall. Full body (head) not visible
10.mp4	04 sec	Standing position to falling. Forward Fall. Full body (right eye) not visible
11.mp4	06 sec	Standing position to falling. Backward Fall
12.mp4	06 sec	Standing position to falling. Backward Fall
13.mp4	04 sec	Standing position to falling. Backward fall. Full body (head) is not visible
14.mp4	05 sec	Standing position to falling. Backward fall. Full body (both ankles) is not visible
15.mp4	06 sec	Sitting on the chair (side view) to right side fall
16.mp4	06 sec	Sitting on the chair (side view) to left side fall.

Table 4. The value of TP, TN, FP, and FN for the dataset GMDCSA and URFD

Dataset	TP	TN	FP	FN
GMDCSA	15	15	1	1
URFD	22	29	11	2

Table 5. Results of the experiment

Metric	Expression	Dataset	
		GMDCSA	URFD
Sensitivity	TP/(TP + FN)	0.9375	0.9167
Specificity	TN/(FP + TN)	0.9375	0.7250
Precision	TP/(TP + FP)	0.9375	0.6667
False Positive Rate	FP/(FP + TN)	0.0625	0.2750
False Negative Rate	FN/(FN + TP)	0.0625	0.0833
Accuracy	(TP + TN)/(P + N)	0.9375	0.7969
F1 Score	2TP/(2TP + FP + FN)	0.9375	0.6216

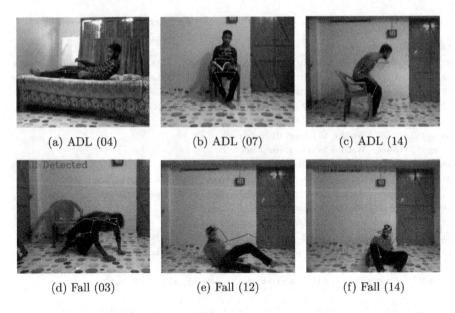

(a) ADL (04)   (b) ADL (07)   (c) ADL (14)

(d) Fall (03)   (e) Fall (12)   (f) Fall (14)

Fig. 5. Sample outputs using the GMDCSA dataset

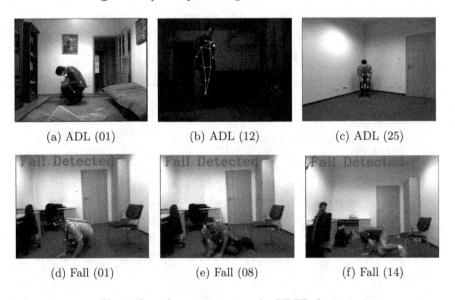

(a) ADL (01)   (b) ADL (12)   (c) ADL (25)

(d) Fall (01)   (e) Fall (08)   (f) Fall (14)

Fig. 6. Sample outputs using the URFD dataset

7   Conclusion and Future Scope

In this paper, we proposed a lightweight and fast human fall detection system using 'Movenet Thunder' pose estimation. Our proposed system is very fast and requires very low computing power. It can run easily in real-time on any low-computing device like mobile, laptop, desktop, etc. All computation is done locally, so it also preserves the privacy of the subject. The metrics are also good enough considering the low computing requirement of the system. The proposed technique gave good results using the GMDCSA dataset. The sensitivity values are good for both datasets. The Movenet pose estimation model is a fast and lightweight model, but its accuracy is moderate. Also, our system can not work for more than one subject at the same time. In the future, we are thinking to improve our system so that it can work in multi-person [22] environments with high accuracy while maintaining the low computing requirement.

References

1. Alam, E., Sufian, A., Dutta, P., Leo, M.: Vision-based human fall detection systems using deep learning: a review. Comput. Biol. Med. **146**, 105626 (2022)
2. Wang, Z., Ramamoorthy, V., Gal, U., Guez, A.: Possible life saver: a review on human fall detection technology. Robotics **9**(3), 55 (2020)
3. Gutiérrez, J., Rodríguez, V., Martin, S.: Comprehensive review of vision-based fall detection systems. Sensors **21**(3), 947 (2021)
4. Alam, E., Sufian, A., Das, A.K., Bhattacharya, A., Ali, M.F., Rahman, M.H.: Leveraging deep learning for computer vision: a review. In: 2021 22nd International Arab Conference on Information Technology (ACIT), pp. 1–8. IEEE (2021)
5. Wang, X., Ellul, J., Azzopardi, G.: Elderly fall detection systems: a literature survey. Front. Robot. AI **7**, 71 (2020)
6. Munea, T.L., Jembre, Y.Z., Weldegebriel, H.T., Chen, L., Huang, C., Yang, C.: The progress of human pose estimation: a survey and taxonomy of models applied in 2d human pose estimation. IEEE Access **8**, 133330–133348 (2020)
7. Chen, Y., Tian, Y., He, M.: Monocular human pose estimation: a survey of deep learning-based methods. Comput. Vis. Image Underst. **192**, 102897 (2020)
8. Bajpai, R., Joshi, D.: Movenet: a deep neural network for joint profile prediction across variable walking speeds and slopes. IEEE Trans. Instrum. Meas. **70**, 1–11 (2021)
9. MoveNet: Ultra fast and accurate pose detection model. — TensorFlow Hub — tensorflow.org. https://www.tensorflow.org/hub/tutorials/movenet. Accessed 21 Oct 2022
10. Sufian, A., Alam, E., Ghosh, A., Sultana, F., De, D., Dong, M.: Deep learning in computer vision through mobile edge computing for IoT. In: Mukherjee, A., De, D., Ghosh, S.K., Buyya, R. (eds.) Mobile Edge Computing, pp. 443–471. Springer, Cham (2021). https://doi.org/10.1007/978-3-030-69893-5_18
11. Asif, U., Von Cavallar, S., Tang, J., Harrer, S.: SSHFD: single shot human fall detection with occluded joints resilience. arXiv preprint arXiv:2004.00797
12. Chen, Z., Wang, Y., Yang, W.: Video based fall detection using human poses. In: Liao, X., Zhao, W., Chen, E., Xiao, N., Wang, L., Gao, Y., Shi, Y., Wang, C., Huang, D. (eds.) BigData 2022. CCIS, vol. 1496, pp. 283–296. Springer, Singapore (2022). https://doi.org/10.1007/978-981-16-9709-8_19
13. Apicella, A., Snidaro, L.: Deep neural networks for real-time remote fall detection. In: Del Bimbo, A., Cucchiara, R., Sclaroff, S., Farinella, G.M., Mei, T., Bertini, M., Escalante, H.J., Vezzani, R. (eds.) ICPR 2021. LNCS, vol. 12662, pp. 188–201. Springer, Cham (2021). https://doi.org/10.1007/978-3-030-68790-8_16

14. Leite, G.V., da Silva, G.P., Pedrini, H.: Three-stream convolutional neural network for human fall detection. In: Wani, M.A., Khoshgoftaar, T.M., Palade, V. (eds.) Deep Learning Applications, Volume 2. AISC, vol. 1232, pp. 49–80. Springer, Singapore (2021). https://doi.org/10.1007/978-981-15-6759-9_3
15. Cao, Z., Simon, T., Wei, S.-E., Sheikh, Y.: Realtime multi-person 2d pose estimation using part affinity fields. In: Proceedings of the IEEE Conference on Computer Vision and Pattern Recognition, pp. 7291–7299 (2017)
16. Chen, T., Ding, Z., Li, B.: Elderly fall detection based on improved YOLOV5s network. IEEE Access 10, 91273–91282 (2022)
17. Ultralytics, Yolov5, https://github.com/ultralytics/yolov5. Accessed 14 Jan 2023
18. Liu, W., et al.: Fall detection for shipboard seafarers based on optimized Blazepose and LSTM. Sensors 22(14), 5449 (2022)
19. Beddiar, D.R., Oussalah, M., Nini, B.: Fall detection using body geometry and human pose estimation in video sequences. J. Vis. Commun. Image Represent. 82, 103407 (2022)
20. Amsaprabhaa, M., et al.: Multimodal spatiotemporal skeletal kinematic gait feature fusion for vision-based fall detection. Expert Syst. Appl. 212, 118681 (2023)
21. Kwolek, B., Kepski, M.: Human fall detection on embedded platform using depth maps and wireless accelerometer. Comput. Methods Programs Biomed. 117(3), 489–501 (2014)
22. Kocabas, M., Karagoz, S., Akbas, E.: MultiPoseNet: fast multi-person pose estimation using pose residual network. In: Ferrari, V., Hebert, M., Sminchisescu, C., Weiss, Y. (eds.) ECCV 2018. LNCS, vol. 11215, pp. 437–453. Springer, Cham (2018). https://doi.org/10.1007/978-3-030-01252-6_26

Design of a Vehicle Overspeed Management System Using Blockchain-Assisted IoV

Manju Biswas[1]([✉]) [ID], Subhajit Mallick[1] [ID], Shounak Bose[1] [ID], Ghanashyam Nandi[1],
Sourav Banerjee[1] [ID], and Utpal Biswas[2] [ID]

[1] Kalyani Government Engineering College, Kalyani, India
`falsecse.manju@gmail.com`, `mr.sourav.banerjee@ieee.com`
[2] University of Kalyani, Kalyani, India

Abstract. The Internet of Vehicles (IoV) is a network of vehicles integrated with sensors, software, and intermediary technologies to connect and exchange data over the Internet according to predetermined standards. Traditional vehicular ad-hoc networks (VANET) have evolved into the Internet of Vehicles as a result of recent significant breakthroughs in the new but promising paradigm of the Internet of Things (IoT) and its fusion with cutting-edge wireless communication technology. Recent data shows traffic accidents are a big cause of concern. In recent years, speeding has been a factor in 60% of road accidents. Road transport must eventually transition to the Internet of Vehicles to solve this problem and many others related to road safety. With the help of the internet of vehicles, driving will significantly change. Blockchain secures the entire process of sharing information among IoVs and adds features like traceability, thus people can be confident that the system is secure and reliable. This paper highlights the problem that road transport in India is very unsafe, and put forward a proposed model of blockchain-assisted IoVs as a solution to tackle this issue.

Keywords: Internet of Vehicles · Internet of Things · VANET · Blockchain · Vehicle Overspeeding · Traffic Management

1 Introduction

The Internet of Automobiles (IoV), which originated from Vehicular Ad-Hoc Networks (VANET), is anticipated to develop into an "Internet of Autonomous Vehicles" in the future. The IoV ecosystem depends on contemporary infrastructure and architectures that share the computational load among numerous processing units in a network for these to work together harmoniously. Many of these architectures rely on open-source software & systems to work [1].

Vehicle-to-vehicle (V2V) [2, 3], vehicle-to-human or personal device (V2H or V2P), vehicle-to-infrastructure (V2I), vehicle-to-roadside unit or other similar Infrastructure (V2I or V2R), and vehicle-to-sensors are the five primary types of connections needed inside the IoV infrastructure (V2S). Connected vehicles use IEEE Wireless Access in Vehicular Environments for V2V and V2I communication (WAVE). Wi-Fi and 4G/5G

K. Dasgupta et al. (Eds.): CICBA 2023, CCIS 1956, pp. 41–50, 2024.
https://doi.org/10.1007/978-3-031-48879-5_4

[4] are mostly used by V2I pairs, MOST/Wi-Fi is used by V2S pairs, Bluetooth, NFC, CarPlay, and CarPlay or Android Auto are used by V2H pairings. The basic architecture of IoV is shown the Fig. 1.

The Internet of Vehicles is set to fundamentally transform the driving experience. Implementing smart city infrastructure [5] and communicating with our vehicles through the IoV will make it safer than ever. Here are some of the applications that make it very important to the automotive industry [6].

- Accident Avoidance
- Traffic control
- Theft avoidance
- Improved Road Safety
- Faster Travel and Convenience
- Emergency response
- Environmental Benefits

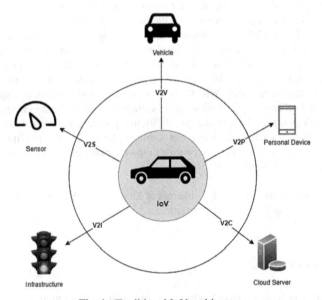

Fig. 1. Traditional IoV architecture

The traditional architecture of IoV is illustrated in Fig.-1. Typical communication patterns in a traditional IoV architecture include V2V (vehicle to vehicle), V2I (vehicle to infrastructure), V2P (vehicle to pedestrian), V2P (vehicle to platform), and V2C (vehicle to cloud). These communication channels are used to transfer data that has been gathered from sensors on the vehicle and will be processed and stored on a platform. In order to give drivers and passengers access to information and services, applications are lastly developed.

A blockchain is a machine for storing statistics in a manner that makes ma-chine changes, hacking, and dishonesty hard or impossible. A community of computer structures referred to as a blockchain simply copies and disseminates a virtual log of transactions throughout the complete community [7]. The application of blockchain technology in the Internet of Vehicles (IoV) is being examined to determine its effectiveness as a security solution for Vehicular Ad Hoc Networks (VANETs). Specifically, the proposal suggests utilizing blockchain to verify vehicle identity and authenticate data. [8]. The management of facilities, including work order tracking, preventative maintenance, and life cycle assessments, can be changed by blockchain [9].

Due to the decrease or removal of those unpleasant manual tasks blockchain will expedite processes and reduce expenses. Almost any process, such as space management, work orders, environmental health and safety planning, and preventive maintenance, might be modified using this [10]. A lot of road accidents happen in India daily. According to the data from 2021 published by NCRB, overspeeding is responsible for 58.7% of all accidents [11], while reckless or careless driving and overtaking accounted for 25.7%. The most significant traffic rule violation linked to fatalities (69.3%) and injuries (73.4%) resulting from accidents was exceeding the speed limit. From all this data, it is clear that overspeeding is a real problem and a major cause for concern. Simply put, an overspeeding vehicle gives other forthcoming vehicles very less time to react, and it becomes extremely difficult to avoid a collision. It is how accidents happen due to overspeeding.

Making nearby vehicles aware of overspeeding and reckless vehicles will be a huge step forward in terms of avoiding these accidents. Other vehicles can take precautionary actions and make the difference between life and death. It is especially true for long expressways and sharp turns. At sharp turns and on long highways in foggy weather, it becomes impossible to know when an overspeeding vehicle may be coming close. In such situations alerting nearby vehicles of a possible danger can be immensely beneficial. If the nearby infrastructures or checkpoints can be made aware of such vehicles, catching the rogue driver and stopping the vehicle at such checkpoints will be easier. And only then can further action be taken, and a possible accident could be prevented.

The remaining portion of this section is structured as follows. Similar previous studies are reviewed in Sect. 2. The system model and operational procedures for the proposed model are explained in Sect. 3. Finally, Sect. 4 provides a summary of the findings and outlines potential areas for future research.

2 Literature Review

Fadhil et al. [12] discussed IoT has enabled greater connectivity between devices, including vehicles, resulting in improved safety, convenience, and intelligence in our daily lives. The development of IoT-enabled vehicles has given rise to the Internet of Vehicles (IoV), which represents an advanced version of Vehicular Ad Hoc Networks (VANETs) designed primarily to enhance road safety. However, despite the increasing number of IoT-connected vehicles, there remain various unknown challenges and untapped potential in the IoV. This paper provides an overview of IoV technology, as well as its limitations.

Labrador et al. [8] discussed, however, one aspect of this that will guarantee its implementation is vehicular communication. However, the ongoing concerns about security and privacy should not exclude vehicular communication. According to the findings, the Internet of Vehicles can leverage blockchain as a security mechanism for data verification and vehicle identification.

Ramaguru et al. [7] discussed vehicle ownership has been rising exponentially as a result of cities' burgeoning populations and ongoing urbanization. As a result, traffic management has grown to be a major issue in modern society. This paper offers a 10 V-based traffic management strategy to address the issue that plagues us regularly.

Mendiboure et al. [13] discussed one of the primary security vulnerabilities identified in the distributed SD-IoV control layer is the absence of authentication and authorization protocols for applications, whether they are from the network, third-party sources, or users. This means that there are no limitations on the impact these applications can have on SDN controllers and network performance.

Wang et al. [14] discussed In order to tackle centralized problems and improve the architecture of the Internet of Vehicles (IoV), blockchain technology is employed to establish a secure and decentralized vehicular environment. The purpose of this research is to provide a comprehensive analysis of the various ways in which blockchain can be utilized in the IoV. The paper begins by introducing both blockchain and IoV.

Kumar et al. [15] discussed the internet of vehicles is projected to play a crucial role in the development of the next generation of intelligent transportation systems. By 2020, the expansion of the internet of vehicles will generate revenues of about 2.94 billion USD.

Ghazal et al. [16] discussed a proposed autonomous healthcare system for medical equipment that utilizes Internet of Vehicles-based artificial neural networks (IoV-ANN) to enhance efficiency. The IoV-ANN system provides a secure network for monitoring and tracking the location of vehicles via GPS. This article highlights how the IoV-ANN system aids in reducing traffic congestion to facilitate the smooth operation of emergency vehicles.

Khoukhi et al. [17] discussed innovative technologies and solutions incorporated into "smart cities" to manage municipal resources like transportation, electricity, and other crucial infrastructure.

Hossain et al. [18] discussed current research on green Internet of Vehicles (IoV) systems tends to focus only on certain energy-related issues, neglecting discussions on the influence of modern energy-efficient techniques and the emergence of 6G networks. This paper seeks to address this gap by outlining essential considerations for managing energy harvesting, communication, computation, traffic, and electric vehicles (EVs) across five distinct scenarios.

Wang et al. [19] discussed an overview of the Internet of Vehicles (IoV), outlining its core concepts, application scenarios, and unique characteristics. However, given the complexity of IoV technology, further research is necessary to fully understand its capabilities.

3 Proposed Work

Suppose that a car is travelling too fast or irresponsibly. This paper aims to notify and alert other vehicles nearby about the presence of a rogue vehicle so that they can be more aware of the situation and avoid any possible accident or actively take necessary steps to be on the safer side such as making sure that they have seat belts tied on, or slowing down their vehicle, or stopping the vehicle completely. To make sure that the overspeeding vehicle is caught as soon as possible, this paper aims to notify nearby checkpoints or toll naka [20] where the vehicle can be caught and further legal and precautionary actions can be taken.

In our system model (Fig. 2), we address overspeeding vehicles using Blockchain assisted IoV. The model comprises three primary sections: the detection section, the Blockchain section constituting ledger entry into blockchain, and the alert mechanism.

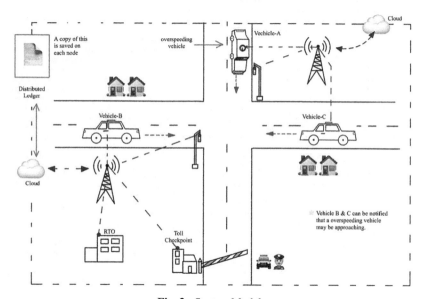

Fig. 2. System Model

3.1 Detection Technique

The process of this alert and stopping of overspeeding starts with actually detecting an overspeeding vehicle. For this, the speedometer sensor reading of the vehicle can be used or the GPS of the vehicle could also be utilized to detect movement speed or a combination of both for increased reliability. If the speed is found to be above a particular threshold of safe speed, then the system will flag this vehicle as overspeeding.The flowchart of this complete process from the detection of an overspeeding vehicle to the alert system and eventually catching the overspeeding vehicle is represented in the form of a flowchart given in Fig. 3.

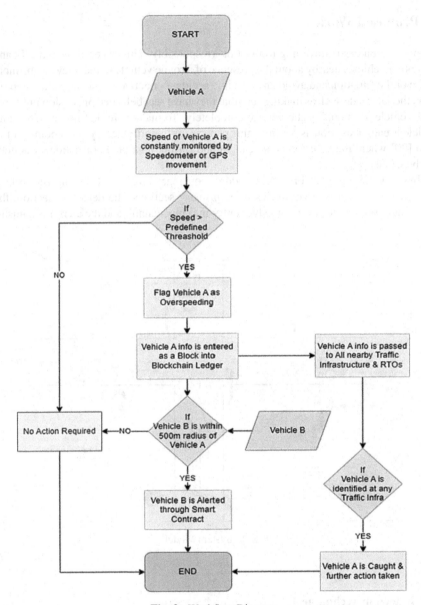

Fig. 3. Workflow Diagram

3.2 Public Ledger Entry

Now, after the detection of a particular overspeeding vehicle (here Vehicle-A), this information will be further processed for the alert mechanism to work. This complete transaction of essential information about the over-speeding vehicle will happen through blockchain [21].

The information about the overspeeding vehicle will be uploaded in the form of a block. This information may contain identification info about the vehicle such as the registration number, and also the latitude & longitudinal information to locate the vehicle. This block of data uploaded works like a distributed public ledger, where any node can access/view the information and can verify the authenticity of the data.

The workflow diagram for our proposed IoV overspeed management system using blockchain is illustrated in Fig. 3. The sequential stages involved in the detection, blockchain entry, and alert mechanism are outlined in this diagram.

3.3 Alert Mechanism

The alert mechanism is done automatically through the smart contract. This works based on the logic that if a new block of data is added to the blockchain, nodes that are essentially IoVs, that are within a particular radius (let's take that to be 500 m) get the alert that an overspeeding vehicle may be approaching. So, in the above diagram, vehicle-B and vehicle-C would be alerted about the existence of the overspeeding vehicle, vehicle-A in the nearby vicinity. This alert location & zone can be calculated by the latitude and longitudinal value of the overspeeding vehicle. This model also aims to inform the traffic infrastructure or administrative infrastructure such as the nearest checkpoints (or toll nakas), in the same way about the overspeeding vehicle so that they can be caught and stopped and further actions can be taken.

3.4 Suggested Blockchain-Enabled Network Model

The nodes participate in the blockchain network and thus validate the data transactions that happen on the network. This is what makes the blockchain network decentralized and secure. The node network for our proposed model is shown in Fig. 4.

The Fig. 4 outlines a blockchain-enabled IoV network model that connects vehicles, traffic infrastructure, RTO offices to Central Information Centre, in the form of a distributed ledger to facilitate secure and transparent communication between all entities.

Our proposed model deals with a very specific aspect of this whole IoV ecosystem which is over-speeding which is a major hurdle in the way of better road transport. This paper suggests using blockchain for the information exchange for its security [22] and traceability. It is believed that shortly the world will see advancements in terms of automation in vehicles and thus the day is not far when the Internet of Vehicles will be a reality and a common vehicle feature. Also, since the inception of blockchain, the whole Web ecosystem is slowly shifting towards a more decentralized approach. Thus, this paper is proposing blockchain as the underline technology that will support this IoV ecosystem. This combination of blockchain with IoV has hardly been researched before, especially to deal with the over-speeding vehicle. This paper hopes to gain some valuable insights from all the research for model building for the cause we are trying to develop.

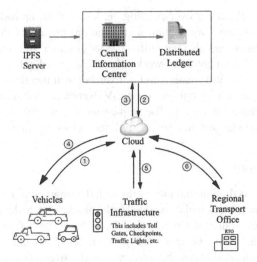

Fig. 4. Blockchain-enabled IoV network Model

4   Conclusion and Future Scope

The IoV is expected to make road transport a lot better. It will be safer than ever owing to the development of smart city infrastructure and its connectivity with our vehicles through the IoV. Even in this generation of vehicles, we have cruise control, automatic gear switch, and many features that automate the driving experience. These imply that we are eventually moving towards a driverless, autonomous future where vehicles will be self-driven. However, we are not there yet, and we need several breakthroughs to achieve such limits, especially in the context of Indian roads. Thus, what we believe is that the near future is leaning more towards a mixed form of driving, like AI will assist drivers in every aspect of driving to make road transport robust and one of the safest transports. Thus our model aims to only alert the nearby vehicles because of our assumption that AI will not be given administrative and hardware level control of a vehicle. This is because AI needs to be more failsafe and tamperproof to be given autonomy at that level. In the future scope, we hope to include more authentication services such as Pollution Under Control Certificate (PUCC) verification and other IoV-related communications through blockchain.

References

1. Gerla, M., Lee, E.–K., Pau, G., Lee, U.: Internet of vehicles: from intelligent grid to autonomous cars and vehicular clouds. In: IEEE World Forum on Internet of Things (WF-IoT), Seoul, Korea (South), pp. 241–246 (2014). https://doi.org/10.1109/WF-IoT.2014.680 3166
2. Das, D., Banerjee, S., Chatterjee, P., Ghosh, U., Biswas, U.: A secure blockchain enabled V2V communication system using smart contracts. IEEE Trans. Intell. Transp. Syst. **24**, 1–10 (2022). https://doi.org/10.1109/TITS.2022.3226626

3. Das, D., Banerjee, S., Chatterjee, P., Ghosh, U., Mansoor, W., Biswas, U.: Design of a blockchain enabled secure vehicle-to-vehicle communication system. In: 4th International Conference on Signal Processing and Information Security (ICSPIS), Dubai, United Arab Emirates, pp. 29–32 (2021). https://doi.org/10.1109/ICSPIS53734.2021.9652424
4. Das, D., Banerjee, S., Chatterjee, P., Ghosh, U., Biswas, U., Dasgupta, K.: Blockchain enabled SDN framework for security management in 5G applications. In: Proceedings of the 24th International Conference on Distributed Computing and Networking (ICDCN '23). Association for Computing Machinery, New York, pp. 414–419 (2023). https://doi.org/10.1145/3571306.3571445
5. Das, D., Banerjee, S., Mansoor, W., Biswas, U., Chatterjee, P., Ghosh, U.: Design of a secure blockchain-based smart IoV architecture. In: 3rd International Conference on Signal Processing and Information Security (ICSPIS), DUBAI, United Arab Emirates, pp. 1–4(2020). https://doi.org/10.1109/ICSPIS51252.2020.9340142
6. Dandala, T.T., Krishnamurthy, V., Alwan, R.: Internet of vehicles (IoV) for traffic management. In: IEEE International Conference on Computer, Communication and Signal Processing (lCCCSP-2017), pp. 1–4 (2017). https://doi.org/10.1109/ICCCSP.2017.7944096
7. Ramaguru, R., Sindhu, M., Sethumadhavan, M.: Blockchain for the internet of vehicles. In: Singh, M., Gupta, P.K., Tyagi, V., Flusser, J., Ören, T., Kashyap, R. (eds.) Advances in Computing and Data Sciences. Communications in Computer and Information Science, vol. 1045, pp. 412–423. Springer, Singapore (2019). https://doi.org/10.1007/978-981-13-9939-8_37
8. Labrador, M., Hou, W.: Implementing blockchain technology in the internet of vehicle (IoV). In: International Conference on Intelligent Computing and its Emerging Applications (ICEA), pp. 5–10 (2019). https://doi.org/10.1109/ICEA.2019.8858311
9. Naushad, R.: Blockchain in facility management. https://medium.datadriveninvestor.com/blockchain-in-facility-management-d8c9b7186c4c. Accessed 17 Jan 2023
10. Intellis, what are the benefits of blockchain for facilities managers in 2020. https://www.intellis.io/blog/what-are-the-benefits-of-blockchain-for-facilities-managers-in-2020#:~:text=An%20advantage%20of%20Blockchain%20is,safety%20planning%2C%20and%20space%20management. Accessed 16 Jan 2023
11. Accidental Deaths & Suicides in India 2021. https://ncrb.gov.in/sites/default/files/ADSI-2021/ADSI_2021_FULL_REPORT.pdf. Accessed 26 Dec 2022
12. Fadhil, A.A., Sarhan, Q.I.: Internet of vehicles (IoV): a survey of challenges and solutions. In: 21st International Arab Conference on Information Technology (ACIT), pp. 1–10(2020). https://doi.org/10.1109/ACIT50332.2020.9300095
13. Mendiboure, L., Chalouf, M.A., Krief, F.: Towards a blockchain-based SD-IoV for applications authentication and trust management. In: Skulimowski, A.M.J., Sheng, Z., Khemiri-Kallel, S., Cérin, C., Hsu, C.-H. (eds.) Internet of Vehicles. Technologies and Services Towards Smart City. Lecture Notes in Computer Science, vol. 11253, pp. 265–277. Springer, Cham (2018). https://doi.org/10.1007/978-3-030-05081-8_19
14. Wang, C., Cheng, X., Li, J., He, Y., Xiao, K.: A survey: applications of blockchain in the internet of vehicles. EURASIP J. Wirel. Commun. Netw. **2021**(1), 1–16 (2021)
15. Yadav, L., Kumar, S., KumarSagar, A., Sahana, S.: Architechture, applications and security for IOV: a survey. In: 2018 International Conference on Advances in Computing, Communication Control and Networking (ICACCCN), pp. 383–390. IEEE (2018)
16. Ghazal, T.M., Said, R.A., Taleb, N.: Internet of vehicles and autonomous systems with AI for medical things. Soft Comput., 1–13 (2021)
17. Khoukhi, L., Xiong, H., Kumari, S., Puech, N.: The internet of vehicles and smart cities (2021). https://doi.org/10.1007/s12243-021-00891-7

18. Wang, J., Zhu, K., Hossain, E.: Green internet of vehicles (IoV) in the 6G era: toward sustainable vehicular communications and networking. IEEE Trans. Green Commun. Networking **6**(1), 391–423 (2021)
19. Wang, M., Wang, S.: Communication technology and application in internet of vehicles. In: 2021 IEEE 4th International Conference on Information Systems and Computer Aided Education (ICISCAE), pp. 234–237. IEEE (2021)
20. Das, D., Banerjee, S., Biswas, U.: Design of a secure blockchain-based toll-tax collection system. In: Sharma, D.K., Peng, S.-L., Sharma, R., Zaitsev, D.A. (eds.) Micro-electronics and telecommunication engineering. Lecture Notes in Networks and Systems, vol. 373, pp. 183–191. Springer, Singapore (2022). https://doi.org/10.1007/978-981-16-8721-1_18
21. Roy, R., Haldar, P., Das, D., Banerjee, S., Biswas, U.: A blockchain enabled trusted public distribution management system using smart contract. In: Ortiz-Rodríguez, F., Tiwari, S., Sicilia, M.A., Nikiforova, A. (eds.) Electronic Governance with Emerging Technologies. Communications in Computer and Information Science, vol. 1666, pp. 25–35. Springer, Cham. https://doi.org/10.1007/978-3-031-22950-3_3
22. Banerjee, S., Das, D., Biswas, M., Biswas, U.: Study and survey on blockchain privacy and security issues. In: Cross-industry use of Blockchain Technology and Opportunities for the Future, pp. 80–102. IGI Global (2020)

A Study on Algorithms for Detection of Communities in Dynamic Social Networks: A Review

Subrata Paul[1(✉)], Chandan Koner[2], Anirban Mitra[3], and Shivnath Ghosh[1]

[1] Department of CSE, School of Engineering, Brainware University, Barasat,
West Bengal 700125, India
subratapaulcse@gmail.com
[2] Department of CSE, Dr. B C Roy Engineering College, Durgapur, West Bengal 713206, India
[3] Department of CSE, ASET, Amity University, Kolkata, West Bengal 700135, India

Abstract. Community within the social networks is demarcated as collection of nodes which are thickly associated among them whereas sparingly associated to nodes exterior to the community. The problem of community detection is a key topic of research and has gained enough attention over last two decades. Considering the case of Dynamic Social Networks those changes with time community detection is an important issue. The existence of overlapping communities has complicated the task of community detection. In this review work, the authors have illustrated a few community detection algorithms that discover communities within dynamic social networks. An analysis of the discussed algorithms with a focus on the further research work has been done and a real life examples have been cited in the paper.

Keywords: Community social networks · Dynamic Social Networks · Community Detection · Overlapping Communities · community detection algorithms

1 Introduction

Communities within a social network are described as a collection of nodes which are highly associated with each other beyond the remaining nodes within the network. Detection of the emergent community has been a significant characteristic that is generally used for the extraction of meaningful information from networks. However, an extreme challenge that is faced during the community detection is that there does not exist any universal definition for the community structure [1]. Detection of communities although is possible in small scale networks, but it becomes computationally intractable if the size of the network is large. Although various algorithms have been projected for optimal uncovering of communities within a short span of time, but majority of these approaches are grounded on the optimization of objective functions [2].

Evolution of communities in social networks is a natural phenomenon and is generally characterized on the basis of how densely a node is connected within its graphical

K. Dasgupta et al. (Eds.): CICBA 2023, CCIS 1956, pp. 51–64, 2024.
https://doi.org/10.1007/978-3-031-48879-5_5

representation. Considering the case of Dynamic Social Networks, many communities are seen to evolve and subsequently some of them dilutes with time [21]. Therefore, this problem of detection for the evolution of communities within real world social networks has gained quite significance of the past few years. On the basis of requirements of the kind of identified communities alongside the features of the assessed graphs, several accepted notions have been put forward regarding communities. Some of these notions are dependent on various properties of graph like nodes are member of a single or multiple community, links are associated with weights or not, whether a hierarchy can be extracted from the community or not etc. Actually, the design of an algorithm is to be made concerning the way the extraction of communities is to be done from large graphs [3]. Communities that exist among major real-life networks are having the feature of overlapping where a node is a member of several communities at the same instant. Considering the case of social networks, every person is a member of several communities like the community of his colleagues, family, college friends, hobbies, etc [4].

In majority of the real-world networks, it is viewed that a greater extent of the nodes simultaneously is a member of numerous communities. In these cases, Traditional community detection approaches fail in the identification of overlapping communities. Clique percolation has been the widely accepted approach which is used in the identification of overlapping communities within the networks. The basis of this algorithm is that cliques are more likely to be generated from internal edges that are connected densely than the external edges that are sparingly connected [2]. Such overlapping communities to which each of us belong ranges from those which are in relation with research activities or private life. Additionally, members of these communities also belong to individual communities, those results in an enormously complex web of communities within them. There is a need for the systematic study [5] of communities for such large networks [6].

Let us now discuss some of the examples of Dynamic Network Datasets for dynamic communities that are viewed in present circumstances.

1.1 Facebook Buy and Sell Group

Facebook, an online commonly used social networking platform has come up with a feature of marketplace, where any user can buy or sell any of his commodities through the pages. The commodities posted are made available to the user as per their likings in that page. Dynamic communities are formed within a particular page when a set of users post similar kind of items for sale within a same day. Hybrid communities also tend to develop if a particular user sells two or more different commodities within the same page for a day.

1.2 WhatsApp Group for an International Conference

Considering the case of the occurrence of an international conference where a whatsapp group has been created for the authors whose paper are going to be published for the conference. Community creation is twofold in this case. The first community is formed by the set of authors who are going to present their paper on the same track. Second set of community is formed by the authors who have their same type of query on a particular topic. This second type communities may emerge from time to time if any important issue arises during the functioning of the event and even after its occurrence.

2 Literature Review

Various works related to the detection of communities have been done over the past years. Baudin et al. [4] in their work had designed a technique for the detection of community that overlaps and entitled the same as clique percolation method (CPM). Formally this technique denotes community as leading union of k-cliques which is reachable from every node by a sequence of neighboring k-cliques. If the cliques overlap on k-1 nodes, they are said to be contiguous. The scalability of this technique is questionable for the large graphs with medium k values. A community detection algorithm for Fluid Communities has been done by Pares et al. [7] where the notion of fluids was proposed to interact with the environment. Their expansion and contraction occur reluctantly as an outcome of this interaction. Propagation methodology sets up the fluid Communities that signify the state-of-the-art in terms of its scalable nature alongside its computational cost.

In their work, Palla et al. [6] has introduced a methodology for the analysis of the basic statistical characteristics of interwoven sets within the communities which shows overlapping nature. Upon defining the novel set of characteristic magnitudes concerning statistics of communities, an effective practice was needed for exploration of overlapping communities for a large scale. It was visualized that overlapping nodes were important where the distributions have shown the common features of networks. Aston and Hu [8] have proposed DSCAN (Dynamic SCAN) for improvement of SCAN that would allow for an update in local structure for a lesser time than the runtime of SCAN on the entire network. The test of DSCAN was made on real world dynamic networks and was seen to perform sooner much better than SCAN within one a single timestamp to another in relation to the size of alteration. A methodology was also deduced with genetic algorithms that would detect the existence of communities within dynamic social networks that works faster and perform segment-wise.

The task of Community detection has aimed in the discovery of different properties for complex networks with the search of consistent groups. Label Propagation Algorithm (LPA) simulates epidemic poison with the spread of labels proving itself a widespread algorithm for this task. The variation of this algorithm aims at its improvements so as to enhance its features for making them adaptable to the altering environment with the preservation of the benefits it has over the traditional approaches. Garza and Schaeffer [9] has classified and summarized the advancements made in the LPA algorithm over the combination of various LPA units have been carried out on two kinds of kinds of minor synthetic networks. Label propagation algorithm (LPA) being a conventional and operational technique, is instable and displays the random behavior. Li et al. [10] in their work has proposed an enhanced label propagation algorithm namely LPA-MNI where they made a combination of modularity function along with node importance to the existing algorithm. This algorithm has recognized communities at initial level in accordance with the value of modularity. Newman within his work [11] has reviewed various algorithms that deals with the search of communities within networks groups of vertices wherever connections are denser whereas scarcer among connections. The review discusses few traditional approaches that include spectral bisection, Kernighan-Lin algorithm with the hierarchical clustering approaches. It was also shown that these approaches don't display better outcomes with the real-world data and thus a focus was made on the applicability of algorithms that works efficiently with these data. Khan and Niazi [2] has presented a survey on the significant literature with the usage of CiteSpace. Identification of the evolving inclinations with the use of network approaches for identification of evolving nature is being seen. Significant, centrally located and active nodes were identified with the use of scientometric analyses.

3 Existing Community Detection Algorithms

In the present section a detailed review has been made on the approaches used by selected algorithms for the detection of communities in dynamic social networks.

3.1 DSCAN: Improvements to SCAN

SCAN [12] put on enhancements to the density-grounded detection. With these adjustments SCAN is allowed in creating communities short of user-defined threshold that consists of epsilon. It also has the capability in updating dynamic network timeslots. An updated algorithm DSCAN (Dynamic SCAN), has the ability in handling dynamic networks.

The threshold of SCAN i.e ε which lies within the range (0, 1), describes the least resemblance among two adjacent nodes which necessarily happens for two nodes for being ε neighbors. This ε-neighborhood serves as an example of how a community is organised.

If dependence is done on user stipulations for ε, it has the possibility to reduce performance if improper ε is used while executing the algorithm with several values of ε can be expensive. This algorithm is tested for numerous networks, and found that probable good epsilons concerning some network to lie within the series of (0.4, 0.8). Lower value of ε shall result into some larger community, whereas higher value of ε shall lead to numerous smaller communities. In order to generate ε-neighborhood for any node, it is checked that whether the value of ε belongs to the range (0.4, 0.8) and further an average for the outcomes are generated. Since the results produces are analogous, therefore the ease of computing with multiple values of ε is done.

Algorithm: DSCAN
Input: Graph timestamps (0 ... T), ε, μ
run SCAN for G_0
for t in 1 till T:
    ΔE = edge changes between G_{t-1} and G_t
    $G_t = G_{t-1}$
    for e in ΔE:
    if e is an addition:
    add e to G_t
    else:
    remove e from G_t
    updateNetwork (G_t, e, ε, μ)

1st Method: updateNetwork
Input: Graph G, edge altered e, ε, μ
u, v = nodes of e
for x $\in$ (u, v):
    if x = = u:
    x' = v
    else:
    x' = u
    if x is a core:
    propagateId(x, generateNewId(), ε, μ)
    if e was a removal:
    if x' is not density connected from x and id(x') = = id(x):
    if x' is a core:
    propagateId(x', generateNewId(), ε, μ)
    else:
    makeHubOrOutlier(x')
    else:
    if x was a core:
    for nei in neighborhood of x:
    if id(nei) == id(x) and nei has not been changed:
    propagateId(x', generateNewId(), ε, μ)
if x has not been altered:
    makeHubOrOutlier(x)
    for nei in neighborhood of x:
    if nei is not a core and does not neighbor a core:
    makeHubOrOutlier(nei)

2nd Method: propagateId
Input: Vertex v, id, ε, μ
if v is a core:
    push v onto the queue
while |queue| > 0:
u = pop from top of queue
    if u was not checked already:
    id(u) = id
    if u is a core:
    push all ε-neighbors of u to the queue

3rd Method: making of HubOrOutlier
Input: Vertex v
Id's = id's of neighbors of v
if $\|$ids$\|$ > 1:
    make v a hub
else:
    make v an outlier

With this Algorithm, the network is dynamically updated. The SCAN algorithm is applied to the first timestamp in a series of timestamps for a network. Further for every successive timestamp, acquire the alteration in edges among two timestamps. Within Method 1, an update in the network is carried out on from nodes of every edge of the network which has been demonstrated within the 1st Method. Update in network is made in such a manner that the node becomes central, if it was previously not or gets removed from the central position. After an update in the existing cluster id or generation or generation of a fresh cluster id, dissemination occurs by every operationally associated nodes so as to obtain a fresh community. 2nd Method describes transmission of id over communities that has been recently generated. This method also updates the network when it loses the ability in forming the cluster. 3rd Method displays the way of handling the nodes for making them hub or an outlier [8].

3.2   The Label Propagation Algorithm

The label propagation algorithm (LPA) follows a local or bottom-up segmental procedure which is motivated with its widespread spread. Initially, the input graph may be pre-processed by eliminating zero-degree singleton nodes or by iteratively eliminating one-degree nodes. Subsequent to initialization phase every node viewed within lines 2-4 of the algorithm is assigned a (universally unique) label. In the next step, an iterative broadcast of labels commences within every iteration as viewed in lines 8–16 of the algorithm where the label of every node is rationalized. All calculations necessitated during the iteration are sequential.

For familiarizing with alternative types of input networks, various types of community detection arrangements have been discussed that deals with overlapping community detection with LPA [9].

Community Overlap Propagation Algorithm (COPRA) [13] permits usage of multiple labels per node with the assignment of belonging coefficient to each of these. Synchronous adoption of nodes, neighbors are labeled and belonging coefficient is calculated for every iteration t

$$b_t(c, v) = \frac{1}{|\Gamma(v)|} \sum_{u \in \Gamma(v)} b_{t-1}(c, u) \qquad (1)$$

For those Labels having coefficient beyond 1/k (k refers to a pre-defined parameter) are reserved, except none of the labels meet the terms alongside the earlier, where the labels having highest coefficient is preferred (ties are determined arbitrarily).

In Speaker-Listener Label Propagation Algorithm (SLPA) [14], very node is well-appointed with memory for the storage of numerous labels. Whenever a label is updated, node performs as listener while its neighbors act as speaker. There is an exchange of label between speakers to listener. Acceptance of label by listener follows listening rule while transmission of label by speaker occurs through speaking rule.

For Overlapping-node detection, recognition of overlapping nodes comprises of application of metric that can be local or global above nodes with evaluation of whether the resultant value surpasses a specified threshold. Considering optimistic cases, overlapping of node occurs. Metrics which has been illustrated for this purpose consists of neighbor purity [15] that includes numerous alternative communities where node participates and variation in weights [16]. For calculation of neighbor transparency, co-occurrence within communities might be accessed through multiple LPA rounds [17] that would enhance the runtime of the algorithm.

3.3 LPA-MNI Algorithm

For solving the instability problem of LPA, LPA-MNI, is designed on the basis of node importance and modularity. Initial community estimation is done by this algorithm. Additionally, all nodes that belong to the identical rough communities are assigned similar labels. Lastly, label propagation is implemented for community detection.

Update of labels occurs by application of three random strategies that hints to unpredictability of its outcome. LPA-MNI employs a node significance valuation technique to prevent instability. Update of node occurs through descending order in accordance with the significance of every node throughout the iteration. Upon reaching the maximum value for a number of more than one label this algorithm shall compute the significance of every label besides selection of label having major significance for apprise within the node label. Randomness problem is thus solved by these stages making the consequence of LPA-MNI as deterministic and precise [10].

Framework of LPA-MNI Algorithm

Input: The Graph, which consist of set of nodes and edges.

Output: The outcome of community detection

1: Initialization of communities for every nodes of the network.

2: Calculate the node significance for every node in accordance with $DC(i) = \frac{k_i}{n-1}$.

3: D ← Assemble of nodes according to their significance.

4: For every node i ∈ D, removal of i from its individual community besides positioning it inside the community of neighbor j, j. Next, calculate of increase in modularity through the procedure. Node I should be positioned in such a way so that its gain is maximized. In this procedure, each node is analyzed successively in order D till this gain remains unaffected and the preliminary rough community are attained.

5: In step 4, assignment of identical label to nodes within the similar preliminary community.

6: t is set to 1.

7: For every i ∈ D, updating of label is done in accordance with the function, $C_x(t) = f(Cx_{i1}(t),..., Cx_{im}(t), C_{xi(m+1)}(t-1),..., C_{xik}(t-1))$, whenever the quantity of supplementary label grasps maximum, significance of neighboring nodes are computed according to $DC(i) = \frac{k_i}{n-1}$, and most significant node's label are allocated to present node.

8: If the labels within the network turn out to be stable, the algorithm is stopped. Otherwise, t is set as $t+1$ and a return back is made to step 7 [10].

3.4 Kernighan-Lin Algorithm

This algorithm follows a greedy optimization approach which allocates benefit function Q for the partitions within the network and further efforts in optimizing the advantages over probable separations. This benefit function consists of sum of edges which falls within these groups devoid of the numbers which falls among them. Further the algorithm has two phases.

Initially every probable pairs of vertices are considered out of which, one vertex is selected from every group, and alteration ΔQ within the benefit function is computed that would be produced on swapping. In the next stage, pair which maximizes this alteration is chosen and swapping is done. There occurs a subsequent repetition of this procedure, where a vertex already swapped is restricted to swap again. After every vertex within a single group has been swapped at least once, this phase concludes. During the second phase of this algorithm, categorization of swaps was invaded to search for the pint that has highest Q value. At this point, the graph is bisected.

Preparing a two-phase procedure for the functioning of the algorithm allows for the likelihood that there is no monotonic increase in value of Q. Even though there is a decrease in the value of Q, higher values which might appear during future swaps will exist within the algorithm [11].

3.5 The Algorithm of Girvan and Newman

General community detection algorithms necessitate in finding natural divisions within the vertices without involvement of the user in specifying the quantity of communities, their dimensions or the way they are formed. This algorithm [18] successfully fulfills these criteria with the addition of three absolute features that includes: (1) This algorithm follows a divisive approach, where edges are gradually eliminated from a network, after its comparison with agglomerative hierarchical clustering method; (2) selection of edges for removal is done with the computation of the betweenness scores; (3) these betweenness scores are computed at each step after removal of an edge.

Edge betweenness can be illustrated as quantity of geodesic (i.e., shortest) paths among vertex pairs which are being tracked throughout the considered edge, added over entire vertex pairs. Calculation of this magnitude is done for every edge in time and is given as O (mn) for graphs consisting of m edges and n vertices [19, 20].

3.6 Clique Percolation Method (CPM) Algorithm

Union-Find structure

CPM algorithm depends on the Union-Find structure or disjoint-set data structure. Its structure resembles forest, where trees resemble as disjoint subsets whereas nodes resemble as essentials.

There are several actions on nodes which include Find (p), Union $(r_1;\ldots; r_i)$ and MakeSet (). The find function yields root node of tree that contains Union-Find node p. The union function accomplishes tree union signified with their roots through the creation of one root as a parent of the remaining ones. The final function Makeset generates a fresh tree containing a single node p that corresponds to fresh empty set.

A CPM community is signified by means of a collection of every (k - 1) cliques contained within them. Characterization of such communities are done through Union-Find structure where nodes consist of (k - 1)-cliques. Iteration is carried by this algorithm over every k-cliques for testing whether the present k-clique is appropriate for a community, with the test of whether (k - 1)-clique is contained within them.

The CPM algorithm takes the entire k-cliques into consideration in sequence. For each of the k-clique, iteration is carried over its (k - 1)-cliques $c_{k-1}^1, c_{k-1}^2, ..., c_{k-1}^k$, that recognizes set p_i to which this algorithm be appropriate within the Union-Find. Further this algorithm accomplishes union operation on its entire set p_i [4].

3.7 CPMZ Algorithm

An agglomerative k-clique community (CPMZ community) is being thought as an amalgamation of either a single or several CPM community. The central idea behind the CPMZ algorithm is the identification of every (k - 1)-clique for the set that comprises of z-cliques. For every k-clique, consideration is made for every (k -1)-cliques. Since a (k - 1)-clique is signified as a collection of the aforementioned z-cliques, where communities of (k - 1)-clique shall denote individual which comprises of every z-cliques.

On having a closer look at the CPMZ Algorithm, it is being viewed that the iteration in for loop existing on the 3rd Line takes place for every k-clique c_k for graph G. Communities for (k -1)-clique consists of its entire z-cliques. This has been the reason for computation of its intersection within set P, as illustrated within 12th Line. P set is computed for each of (k - 1)-cliques and its computation of its union is done on set S form 4th till the 13th line. Thereafter, merging of the entire S sets are done in 18th Line. Possibility of S being empty subsequent to loop at the 5th Line shall illustrate the situation in which no (k - 1)-cliques within c_k has been detected earlier. If (k - 1)-clique for c_{k-1} has not been perceived, then its z-cliques will not have a possibility to associate with a mutual Union-Find set, and subsequently calculation of P at the 12th line will remain null. Identifier addition for resultant (novel otherwise combined) set is done with collection of Union-Find nodes shall be aiming at each of z-clique for present k-cliques as illustrated in 2th Line [4].

4 Analysis of the Community Detection Algorithms

In this section, the authors have tried to illustrate a relative analysis of the algorithms for community detection illustrated in the above section (Table 1).

Table 1. Analysis of the community detection algorithms.

Name of the Algorithm	Advantages	Disadvantages
Dynamic SCAN	Runs fast This algorithm can be compared in terms of being modular with the algorithms that detect presence of static community It can be used with supplementary community detection algorithm for its conversion to dynamic community detection algorithms	As the size of social network has increased rapidly, this algorithm has become expensive This algorithm is not reasonable for use with static community detection approaches for analysis of the networks
Label propagation algorithm	Convenient and straightforward approach Does not require any constraints for implementation easy to understand and implement	sensitive to the random behavior in node ordering within the update rule that finally results in instability establishment of trivial solution that is acknowledged as monster community absence or sluggishness of convergence in numerous cases one-hop horizon
LPA-MNI Algorithm	High nature of segmentation within networks with unrecognized community structure Improved stabile nature than its predecessor i.e. LPA	
The Kernighan-Lin algorithm	Being a two-stage procedure, the algorithm permits for the likelihood for a sudden increment in the value of Q is not seen Even though there is reduction in value of Q, its high value shall be found afterwards in some series of swaps	Specification of sizes for the two communities is required before commencement Division of network occurs into two groups only at a time. Even though division into additional groups are achievable through repeated bisection, although there does not exist any assurance for division being its best No clue is provided regarding the conclusion of the repetitive bisection procedure i.e. the extent of communities existing within the network
Girvan and Newman algorithm	Permits for the fragmentation of network into any extra volume of communities	No guidance regarding the extent of community to which a network should be spitted Slowness of the algorithm. Worst-case run time of the algorithm is O (m^2n), or O (n^3) for sparse graphs
Clique Percolation Method (CPM) Algorithm	Storage of an accumulation of disjoint sets which will permit for the efficient union operations between them	Due to large quantities of (k- 1)-cliques, this methodology sometimes causes problem due to the inability in storing all values within the memory
CPMZ Algorithm	Consumption of lesser memory as compared to its predecessor Outstanding accurateness, scores closer to 1 in obtained in most of times	Runtime is much more

5 Discussion

Within the present section, the authors shall analyse some of the research gaps and some proposed techniques that has been discussed within the reviewed works. The researchers hypothesise that situations may be built in which no computational sequence of the k-cliques would result in an accurate response in [4]. Nevertheless, it is achievable that in numerous situations, which includes practical problems graphical representations, a particular processing sequence of k-cliques produces outcome of greater accuracy than alternative successful process. The issue of how to create such an order is brought up by this. Running the cpmz algorithm alongside more than one distinctive k-cliques sequences and comparing the results would be an additional intriguing option. Each community outputs can be compared to get a superior outcome than any of the separate runs because the cpmz communities are smoother than the actual cpm communities. Additional study on [9] might concentrate on expanding the current framework to recognise overlapping communities in which every node can affiliate with multiple neighbourhoods, that include in systems in real life. As a result of the nodes' freedom from the predefined community structures, this may also open the door for the creation of techniques that are capable of adapting to systems that are changing. A territory's political and socioeconomic landscape, as well as the internal frameworks of numerous entities like companies and governments cannot guarantee uniformity. Thus, the requirement to resolve community identification issues in diverse systems is increasing. Within the future, there is a requirement in improving the currently used strategies in addition to create fresh, effective ones that could address issues in such complex systems. A more potent community detection algorithm for weighted, directed, and dynamic networks is the main goal of ongoing research on [10]. The research in [11] and [18] demonstrates that there can be opportunity for enhancement of the structure of community's techniques' efficiency and sensibility, and numerous intriguing systems with networks await the opportunity to be analysed using these approaches

5.1 Dynamic WhatsApp Community

After it was created, WhatsApp quickly became a vital tool for communicating between various groups of people in the workplace, colleges, and universities. Participants of the community established by this messaging software participate in all aspects of life. An admin who formed the group and occasionally adds and removes members is in charge of managing the group centrally. Assume that a group of people needs to be informed urgently of something. As soon as the message is placed in the official group, everyone is immediately informed rather than having to phone each person individually. But the message is said to have been shared immediately every individual is accessible online and has viewed it. It is possible to find out who the message has been delivered to, how many people have seen it, and how many have read it. It occasionally receives updates on a regular basis. Let's say a business conclave is going to be planned, thus the team leader, Mr. Y, has set up a WhatsApp group to facilitate better and more effective communication amongst team members ($t = 0$). The administrator (Mr. Y) is adding the required team members and other individuals as needed to establish coordination ($t = 1$). The procedure results in the formation of numerous additional subgroups for every single job, keeping the team leader informed (t = 2). Against the consent of the management or the primary organiser, some team members who disagreed with the team leader left the group and later formed their own group (t = 3). In accordance with the manager's instructions (t = 4), they further unite with a few of the subgroups for greater and more effective coordination. Figure 1 shall discuss a framework based on the real life scenario.

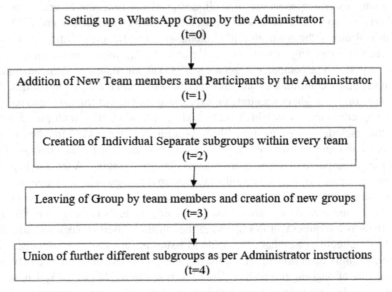

Fig. 1. An example based on the Dynamic WhatsApp Community.

6   Conclusion

Community detection algorithms are extensively used in the study of structural and topological properties of real-world networks. Recognizing the best algorithm for detection of community in a dynamic social network has been a significant area of research. This paper has discussed the various algorithms for community detection and has examined their effectiveness in terms of the advantages and disadvantages. Explanation of some real-life examples has also been provided within this paper. Authors further plans to incorporate the real-world examples into the studied algorithms and analyze the efficiency in community detection in the future.

Acknowledgments. The authors do hereby declare that there is no known competing financial interests or personal relationships that could have appeared to influence the work reported in this paper.

References

1. Fortunato, S., Hric, D.: Community detection in networks: a user guide. Phys. Rep. **659**, 1–44 (2016)
2. Khan, B.S., Niazi, M.A.: Network community detection: a review and visual survey. arXiv preprint: arXiv:1708.00977 (2017)
3. Fortunato, S., Castellano, C.: Community Structure in Graphs, pp. 490–512. Springer, New York (2012)
4. Baudin, A., Danisch, M., Kirgizov, S., Magnien, C., Ghanem, M.: Clique percolation method: memory efficient almost exact communities. arXiv preprint: arXiv:2110.01213 (2021)
5. Faust, K.: Using correspondence analysis for joint displays of affiliation networks. In: Carrington, P., Scott, J., & Wasserman, S. (eds.) Models and Methods in Social Network Analysis. Ch. 7, Cambridge University Press, New York (2005)
6. Palla, G., Derényi, I., Farkas, I., Vicsek, T.: Uncovering the overlapping community structure of complex networks in nature and society. Nature **435**, 814–818 (2005). https://doi.org/10.1038/nature03607
7. Parés, F., et al.: Fluid communities: a competitive, scalable and diverse community detection algorithm. In: Cherifi, C., Cherifi, H., Karsai, M., Musolesi, M. (eds.) Complex Networks & Their Applications VI. Studies in Computational Intelligence, vol. 689, pp. 229–240. Springer, Cham (2018). https://doi.org/10.1007/978-3-319-72150-7_19
8. Aston, N., Hu, W.: Community detection in dynamic social networks. Commun. Netw. **6**, 124–136 (2014). https://doi.org/10.4236/cn.2014.62015
9. Garza, S.E., Schaeffer, S.E.: Community detection with the label propagation algorithm: a survey. Physica A (2019). https://doi.org/10.1016/j.physa.2019.122058
10. Li, H., Zhang, R., Zhao, Z., Liu, X.: LPA-MNI: an improved label propagation algorithm based on modularity and node importance for community detection. Entropy **23**, 497 (2021). https://doi.org/10.3390/e23050497
11. Newman, M.E.J.: Detecting community structure in networks. Eur. Phys. J. B **38**(2), 321–330 (2004). https://doi.org/10.1140/epjb/e2004-00124-y
12. Xu, X., Yuruk, N., Feng, Z., Schweiger, T.: SCAN: a structural clustering algorithm for networks. In: KDD'07. ACM, pp. 824–833 (2007). https://doi.org/10.1145/1281192.1281280
13. Gregory, S.: Finding overlapping communities in networks by label propagation. New J. Phys. **12**(10), 103018 (2010). https://doi.org/10.1088/1367-2630/12/10/103018
14. Xie, J., Szymanski, B.K., Liu, X.: SLPA: uncovering overlapping communities in social networks via a speaker-listener interaction dynamic process. In: Data Mining Workshops, Washington, DC, USA, pp. 344–349. IEEE Computer Society (2011). https://doi.org/10.1109/ICDMW.2011.154
15. Leung, I.X.Y., Hui, P., Lio´, P., Crowcroft, J.: Towards real-time community detection in large networks. Phys. Rev. E **79** (6), 066107 (2009). https://doi.org/10.1103/PhysRevE.79.066107
16. Peng, H., Zhao, D., Li, L., Lu, J., Han, J., Wu, S.: An improved label propagation algorithm using average node energy in complex networks. Physica A **460**, 98–104 (2016). https://doi.org/10.1016/j.physa.2016.04.042
17. Gaiteri, C., et al.: Identifying robust communities and multi-community nodes by combining top-down and bottom-up approaches to clustering. Sci. Rep. **5**, 16361 (2015). https://doi.org/10.1038/srep16361
18. Girvan, M., Newman, M.E.J.: Community structure in social and biological networks. Proc. Natl. Acad. Sci. USA **99**, 7821–7826 (2002)
19. Newman, M.E.J.: Scientific collaboration networks: II. shortest paths, weighted networks, and centrality. Phys. Rev. E **64**, 016132 (2001)

20. Brandes, U.: A faster algorithm for betweenness centrality. J. Math. Sociol. **25**, 163–177 (2001)
21. Mitra, A., Paul, S., Panda, S., Padhi, P.: A Study on the representation of the various models dynamic social networks. In: International Conference on Communication, Computing and Virtualization (ICCCV 2016), Thakur College of Engineering and Technology, Mumbai, 27–28 February, pp. 624–631 (2016). https://doi.org/10.1016/j.procs.2016.03.079

Spanning Cactus Existence Problem on Flower Snark Graphs

Krishna Daripa[✉], Chinmay Debnath[✉], and Anushree Karmakar

Department of Computer and System Sciences, Visva-Bharati University, Siksha
Bhavan, Santiniketan 731235, West Bengal, India
krishnadaripa123@gmail.com, chinmaydebnath.rs@visva-bharati.ac.in

Abstract. A spanning cactus is a spanning substructure of a graph similar to a spanning tree of a graph. But it is more advantageous than the spanning tree in terms of reliability in network applications due to its higher edge connectivity. In genome expression analysis cactus graphs are widely used for important feature extraction and gene alignment. However, a graph may or may not contain a spanning cactus. Checking whether there exists a spanning cactus in a graph (SCEP) is an NP-Complete problem. In immediate past few years, the SCEP have been studied in various special graphs, such as Petersen graph, generalized Petersen graphs, $3 \times 3 \times 3$ grid graph, Desargues graph, Windmill graphs etc. In this article, we have presented that there does not exist any spanning cactus when the considered graph is a Flower Snark Graph.

Keywords: Minimum Spanning Tree · Cactus · SCEP · Minimum Spanning Cactus · Flower Snark Graph · NP-Completeness · Networking · Genome alignment

1 Introduction

A simple, undirected, connected graph [1–3] where each edge is contained in exactly one cycle is called a cactus graph. There are some important applications of the cactus graph, such as traffic estimation [4], genome comparisons [5–10], representation of cuts of graphs [11,12], etc. Recently, the cactus graph structures are also extensively used as the 'backbones' of communication systems and results in significant relief from failure in network connection. Cactus graphs are also used in wireless sensor networks.

Paten et al. [7] have shown that by using cactus graph we can get the best possible result for genome alignment.

There are many works of literature available on the cactus graphs in [13–20].

In a cactus graph, any two cycles may articulate on exactly one vertex. However, there is another useful graph where the edges of the graph can be contained in at most one cycle. This type of connected graph is referred to as a partial cactus [17]. This implies that a partial cactus may have bridges whereas a cactus can not. We can say that a cactus is a partial cactus which is bridgeless.

K. Dasgupta et al. (Eds.): CICBA 2023, CCIS 1956, pp. 65–71, 2024.
https://doi.org/10.1007/978-3-031-48879-5_6

Spanning Cactus Existence Problem (SCEP) and Minimum Spanning Cactus Problem (MSCP) have been studied extensively in a general graph in [13, 15, 17]. Both problems are NP-complete in undirected general graphs [15, 21, 22]. Similar result for the directed version was also proved in [16]. A polynomial-time algorithm for the Minimum Spanning Cactus Extension Problem on a complete graph was presented by Kabadi and Punnen [15] and some of the results have been improved by Datta et al. [17]. The SCEP on the Petersen graph, generalized Petersen graphs, three dimensional ($3 \times 3 \times 3$) Grid graph, Desargues graph and Windmill graphs have been presented in [19, 20, 23, 24] and [25] respectively. The recent works on the Spanning cactus existence problem are presented in Table 1.

Table 1. Recent works on the Spanning Cactus Existence problem.

Author(s)	Graph under consideration	Result
Kabadi & Punnen [15]	General graphs	NP-complete
Palbom [16]	Directed graphs	NP-complete
Debnath & Datta [20]	Petersen graph	Does not exists
Daripa [23]	Generalized Petersen graphs	Exists with only exception when $n \equiv 5 \mod 6$ for $k = 2$
Debnath & Datta [19]	$3 \times 3 \times 3$ grid graph	Always exists
Daripa [24]	Desargues graph	Always exists
Debnath, Daripa et al. [25]	Windmill graphs	Always exists

As mentioned, the SCEP for general graphs is NP-complete. However, polynomial time solutions are possible for some special graphs. However, results are known for a very few subclasses of graphs only. And researchers around the world are working on the problem on other classes of graphs. Here, in this paper, we have worked on the SCEP in Flower-snark graphs. Flower snark graphs are well known graphs and have been studied for long [26–30]. In this work, we have proved that there does not exist any spanning cactus in Flower-snark graphs. Real life application of the spanning cactus problem includes construction of reliable networks, traffic estimation, etc. This result will help solving many problems in reliable network construction, genome expression analysis, etc.

Basic definitions related to the problem, construction and properties of flower snark graphs are presented in Sect. 2. The spanning cactus existence has been studied in Sect. 3. At last, in Sect. 4, the conclusion is presented.

2   Preliminaries

If every edge of a graph is contained in at most one cycle then the graph is called as partial cactus. Whereas, if every edge is contained in exactly one cycle then the graph is called as Cactus. A subgraph G' is called a spanning cactus of a graph G if it is a cactus that spans all vertices of G [31]. Existence of multiple spanning cacti of a graph G is possible [1, 32–34]. The graphs in Figs. 2 and 3 represent two different spanning cacti of the graph in Fig. 1. However, spanning cactus may not exists in some graphs. The graph in Fig. 4 does not contain any spanning cactus.

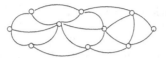

Fig. 1. A graph G.

Fig. 2. A spanning cactus SC_1 of G shown in Fig. 1.

Fig. 3. A spanning cactus SC_2 of G shown in Fig. 1.

Fig. 4. A graph having no spanning cactus.

2.1 The Y Graph

Here we define a new graph, Y graph, where there are exactly four vertices; among them, one is of degree three and the rest are all leaves. This means the Y graph is a star graph with four vertices. We label the four vertices of Y graph as Y^L, Y^R, Y^C and Y^G, where Y^C is the degree three vertex and Y^L, Y^R, Y^G all are leaves. This is depicted in Fig. 5.

Fig. 5. The Y Graph

2.2   Construction of Flower Snark Graph

The flower Snark Graph G_{FS}^n is constructed by connecting a set of n numbers Y graphs in such a manner that all Y^Gs form an $n - cycle$ and another $2n - cycle$ is formed by connecting all the Y^Ls and Y^Rs as: $(Y^{L1}, Y^{L2}, .., Y^{Ln}, Y^{R1}, Y^{R2}, .., Y^{Rn}, Y^{L1})$. The flower Snark Graph G_{FS}^5 is depicted in the following Fig. 6.

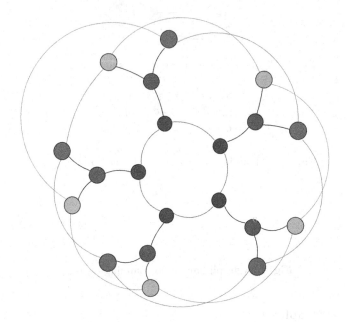

Fig. 6. A Flower Snark Graph: G_{FS}^5.

Some properties of Flower Snark Graphs are:

- Flower Snark Graph is non-hamiltonian [35].
- In a Flower Snark Graph, each of its vertices is of degree three [26].
- Flower Snark Graph contains two disjoint cycles; one is an $n - cycle$ and the other is $2n - cycle$.

3   Spanning Cactus Existence in a Flower Snark Graph

As mentioned in previous section, there does not exists any Hamiltonian cycle in Flower snark graphs. Furthermore, in a Flower Snark Graph, each of its vertices is of degree three [26]. These two important property lead us to our main result.

Theorem 1. *In a Flower Snark Graph, no spanning cactus exists.*

Proof. We can prove the nonexistence by the method of contradiction. Given Flower Snark Graph G, suppose, there exists a spanning cactus C. This means each edge of C is contained in exactly one cycle and C spans all the vertices of G. Since Flower snark graphs are non-hamiltonian [35], C is not a Hamiltonian Cycle of G. Therefore, C must contain a vertex v of degree at least four in C. But, as G is a Flower snark graph, each of its vertices has degree 3 in G [35]. As there is no vertex in G of degree more than three, this leads to a contradiction. Hence the theorem proved. □

Once we know that the underlying graph structure is a Flower snark graph, nonexistence of spanning cactus is obvious by Theorem 1 and takes only constant time. So, required time to test the nonexistence of a spanning cactus is $O(1)$ for Flower snark graphs.

4 Conclusion

Spanning cactus existence (SCEP), minimum spanning cactus, and minimum spanning cactus extension problems have found recent attention because of their applications in reliable network construction, genome sequencing, etc. Various graphs have been studied in these directions such as Petersen graph [20], 3 Dimensional grid graph [19], Desargues graph [24], Windmill graphs [25], generalized Petersen graphs [23] etc. In this work, we have studied the SCEP in Flower Snark graphs. We have proved the nonexistence of spanning cactus in the Flower Snark graph. This result will help solving many problems in reliable network construction and genome alignment. Furthermore, this result will be useful solving the SCEP in related graphs.

References

1. Harary, F.: Graph Theory. Addison-Wesley, Boston (1969)
2. West, D.B., et al.: Introduction to Graph Theory, vol. 2. Prentice Hall, Upper Saddle River (2001)
3. Deo, N.: Graph Theory with Applications to Engineering and Computer Science. Courier Dover Publications, Mineola (2017)
4. Zmazek, B., Zerovnik, J.: Estimating the traffic on weighted cactus networks in linear time. In: Ninth International Conference on Information Visualisation (IV 2005), pp. 536–541. IEEE (2005)
5. Paten, B., et al.: Cactus graphs for genome comparisons. J. Comput. Biol. **18**(3), 469–481 (2011)
6. Paten, B., et al.: Cactus graphs for genome comparisons. In: Berger, B. (ed.) RECOMB 2010. LNCS, vol. 6044, pp. 410–425. Springer, Heidelberg (2010). https://doi.org/10.1007/978-3-642-12683-3_27
7. Paten, B., Earl, D., Nguyen, N., Diekhans, M., Zerbino, D., Haussler, D.: Cactus: algorithms for genome multiple sequence alignment. Genome Res. **21**(9), 1512–1528 (2011)
8. Kehr, B., Trappe, K., Holtgrewe, M., Reinert, K.: Genome alignment with graph data structures: a comparison. BMC Bioinform. **15**(1), 1–20 (2014)
9. Nguyen, N., et al.: Building a pan-genome reference for a population. J. Comput. Biol. **22**(5), 387–401 (2015)

10. Armstrong, J., et al.: Progressive cactus is a multiple-genome aligner for the thousand-genome era. Nature **587**(7833), 246–251 (2020)
11. Fleischer, L.: Building chain and cactus representations of all minimum cuts from Hao-Orlin in the same asymptotic run time. J. Algorithms **33**(1), 51–72 (1999)
12. Dinits, E.A.: On the structure of a family of minimal weighted cuts in a graph. Studies in Discrete Optimization (1976)
13. Datta, A.K.: Approximate spanning cactus. Inf. Process. Lett. **115**(11), 828–832 (2015)
14. Ben-Moshe, B., Bhattacharya, B., Shi, Q., Tamir, A.: Efficient algorithms for center problems in cactus networks. Theoret. Comput. Sci. **378**(3), 237–252 (2007)
15. Kabadi, S.N., Punnen, A.P.: Spanning cactus of a graph: existence, extension, optimization and approximation. Discret. Appl. Math. **161**(1), 167–175 (2013)
16. Palbom, A.: Complexity of the directed spanning cactus problem. Discret. Appl. Math. **146**(1), 81–91 (2005)
17. Datta, A.K., Debnath, C.: Spanning cactus: complexity and extensions. Discret. Appl. Math. **233**, 19–28 (2017)
18. Das, K., Pal, M.: An optimal algorithm to find maximum and minimum height spanning trees on cactus graphs. Adv. Model. Optim. **10**(1), 121–134 (2008)
19. Debnath, C., Datta, A.K.: Spanning cactus existence in a three-dimensional (3 x3 x3) grid. In: Proceedings of the International Conference on Innovative Computing & Communications (ICICC) (2020)
20. Debnath, C., Datta, A.K.: A short note on spanning cactus problem of Petersen graph. In: Dawn, S., Balas, V.E., Esposito, A., Gope, S. (eds.) ICIMSAT 2019. LAIS, vol. 12, pp. 757–760. Springer, Cham (2020). https://doi.org/10.1007/978-3-030-42363-6_88
21. Aho, A.V., Hopcroft, J.E.: The Design and Analysis of Computer Algorithms. Pearson Education India (1974)
22. Cormen, T.H., Leiserson, C.E., Rivest, R.L., Stein, C.: Introduction to Algorithms. PHI Learning Pvt. Ltd., Originally MIT Press (2010)
23. Daripa, K.: Spanning cactus existence in generalized Petersen graphs. Innov. Syst. Softw. Eng. (2022)
24. Daripa, K.: Spanning cactus in desargues graph. In: Intelligent Application of Recent Innovation in Science & Technology IARIST-2K22. Accepted, Presented and Yet to be published
25. Debnath, C., Daripa, K., Mondal, R., Datta, A.K.: Spanning cactus existence, optimization and extension in windmill graphs. In: Algorithms for Intelligent Systems, International Conference on Data, Electronics and Computing (ICDEC-2022). Accepted, Presented and Yet to be published
26. Isaacs, R.: Infinite families of nontrivial trivalent graphs which are not tait colorable. Am. Math. Mon. **82**(3), 221–239 (1975)
27. Rao, K.S., Kumar, U.V.C., Mekala, A.: Rainbow connection number of flower snark graph. Int. J. Appl. Math. **33**(4), 591 (2020)
28. Sasaki, D., Dantas, S., de Figueiredo, C.M.H.: On coloring problems of snark families. Electron. Notes Discret. Math. **37**, 45–50 (2011)
29. Jothi, R.M.J., Revathi, R., Angel, D.: SSP-structure of closed helm and flower snark graph families. In: Journal of Physics: Conference Series, vol. 1770, p. 012081. IOP Publishing (2021)
30. Kratica, J., Matić, D., Filipović, V.: Weakly convex and convex domination numbers for generalized Petersen and flower snark graphs. Rev. Un. Mat. Argentina **61**(2), 441–455 (2020)

31. Pulleyblank, W.R.: A note on graphs spanned by eulerian graphs. J. Graph Theory **3**(3), 309–310 (1979)
32. Gutin, G., Punnen, A.P.: The Traveling Salesman Problem and Its Variations, vol. 12. Springer, New York (2006). https://doi.org/10.1007/b101971
33. Hobbs, A.M.: Hamiltonian squares of cacti. J. Comb. Theory Ser. B **26**(1), 50–65 (1979)
34. Kruskal, J.B.: On the shortest spanning subtree of a graph and the traveling salesman problem. Proc. Am. Math. Soc. **7**(1), 48–50 (1956)
35. Clark, L., Entringer, R.: Smallest maximally nonhamiltonian graphs. Period. Math. Hung. **14**(1), 57–68 (1983)

Analysis of Quantum Cryptology and the RSA Algorithms Defense Against Attacks Using Shor's Algorithm in a Post Quantum Environment

Sumit Biswas and Prodipto Das[✉]

Department of Computer Science, Assam University, Silchar, Assam, India
prodiptodas@aus.ac.in

Abstract. Over the course of the previous twenty years, quantum cryptanalysis has become an important topic of research. The development of two well-known algorithms one for speedier factoring and the other for quicker searching has brought about a change in the conventional technique of computation. These algorithms are responsible for the change. A great number of the algorithms that were used in the conventional way of computing were really risk-free, precise, speedy, and output-oriented. In the post-quantum environment, it is absolutely necessary to investigate the behaviour of various classical algorithms when they are under attack. The behaviour of the RSA algorithm in terms of its resilience to attacks is the subject of investigation in this work. Deciphering the RSA codes requires the application of the Shor algorithm. In order to conduct the experiment, both the Qiskit simulator and the IBM quantum environment are utilised. The amount of qubit capacity now available is the primary determinant of how simple it is to break the RSA algorithm. One can draw the conclusion that the capacity of any quantum computer to decode RSA codes is directly dependent on the number of bits used in those codes.

Keywords: RSA Algorithm · Quantum Cryptanalysis · Post Quantum Environment · Attack-Resistant Conduct · Asymmetric Cryptography · Shor's Algorithm

1 Introduction

Data is one of the most significant and valuable resources around the globe right now, especially in the modern era. The majority of decisions made by almost all firms across all industries are based on mathematics and data analysis. The key to maintaining the security and dependability of the data throughout both its management and transfer is currently critical and essential. This also requires verifying the validity of the data sources and preventing malicious changes to the original data. The methods used today to guarantee the decentralised privacy, honesty, and trustworthiness of data rely on the selected methods of encryption. "Encryption" is shorthand for "encoding" which is

K. Dasgupta et al. (Eds.): CICBA 2023, CCIS 1956, pp. 72–87, 2024.
https://doi.org/10.1007/978-3-031-48879-5_7

what cryptologists use to send secret messages or pieces of data so that only authorised individuals can access them. To accomplish secure communication between source and sink with various performances, several encryption techniques are used.

In this work, we evaluate the strengths and weaknesses of both the popular Rivest-Shamir-Adleman (RSA) encryption method and a quantum technique designed to crack RSA keys, namely Shor's algorithm, to determine if RSA would be a secure method when quantum computers become a reality with a sufficient number of accessible qubits. Section 2 introduces the related works that were used to put this concept into practice. We talk about the RSA algorithm in addition to the Shor algorithm concepts in Sect. 3. In Sect. 4, we will offer an experiment that will analyse and compare the differences between the RSA algorithm and Shor's algorithm. In Sect. 5, we talk about how our research came to a conclusion and some potential directions for further research. The information we used in our experiment to compare and contrast the two algorithms is two different prime numbers.

It is discovered that the majority of the publications here used as references had individually studied RSA and Shor's from various angles, consisting of key length, speeds of key creation, signature verification, computation, processor use, key breaking time, and qubit size. To give a general notion of which RSA key size is best right now, it is hard to say that any algorithm may be dominant in all areas. In order to determine the viability of RSA with an answer that could be simple and more thorough. In this paper, we develop a mathematical model to compare and contrast these two techniques across multiple dimensions.

2 Related Works

At the crossroads of computer science, mathematics, and physics, quantum computing is an intriguing new discipline that aims to use the strange properties of quantum mechanics to expand the possibilities of computation [1].

The Quantum Turing Machine (QTM) model defined by Umesh Vazirani and his student Ethan Bernstein in their 1997 publication on quantum complexity theory is amenable to complexity based analysis. A Quantum Fourier Transform (QFT) technique was provided in the same research publication, which Peter Shor subsequently employed in his now-famous quantum algorithm for factoring integers [2].

Vazirani and three other authors demonstrated that quantum computers cannot solve black-box search problems in less than O(N) time for large numbers of search elements. The superiority of the Grover search algorithm has been demonstrated. Further, it demonstrates that the certifier alone is not sufficient for quantum computers to perform NP-complete tasks in polynomial time [3].

The exponential speedup in which a quantum computer can solve Simon's problem compared to a classical computer is a well-established fact in the disciplines of computational complexity theory and quantum computing. The idea behind Shor's algorithm came from a quantum algorithm that could solve Simon's dilemma. These are two variants of the abelian hidden subgroup issue, for which it is now known that effective quantum methods exist. Daniel Simon [4] posed the issue within the framework of the decision tree complexity model. By demonstrating a quantum algorithm, Simon proved that his problem could be solved exponentially more quickly and with fewer queries than the best probabilistic classical approach. When compared to the exponential number of queries required by most classical probabilistic algorithms, Simon's technique stands out as a notable exception. Specifically, the Simon problem causes a partition between the two types of query complexity, polynomial time with limited error (BPP) and quantum polynomial time with bounded error (BQP). In the field of convex optimization, an oracle separation is a mathematical concept. There is a difference between this algorithm and the Deutsch-Jozsa algorithm [5], although it is comparable to the Bernstein-Vazirani algorithm [2].

Peter Shor, an American mathematician, proposed Shor's algorithm, a quantum algorithm for determining the prime factors of an integer [6]. In the next section, we will go over the specifics of Shor's algorithm.

The time complexity of Shor's algorithm with fast multiplication for factoring is shown in another article [7]. In this study, it is calculated how many quantum bits of memory are needed for fast factorization, as well as how many operations are necessary. Beckman claims that a machine with storage for $5K + 1$ qubits can factor a K-bit number to the third power of time. Shor's algorithm's bottleneck, the evaluation of the modular exponential function, may be accomplished with approximately $72 K3$ elementary quantum gates, but its implementation using a linear ion trap would require approximately $396 K3$ laser pulses.

Grover's algorithm [8] is another game-changing development in quantum computing. In $O(\sqrt{N})$ evaluations of a function, where N is the size of the function's domain, with a high probability, this quantum search technique for unstructured search could determine the one input to a black box function that always produces the same output.

Numerous works are reported in the most recent Post Quantum Cryptography (PQC) advances. Current research programs, including PQCrypto, SAFEcrypto, Crypto-MathCREST, and PROMETHEUS, are all concentrating on cryptography after quantum computers, in addition to numerous standardisation initiatives that have been established at various levels. In particular, post-quantum public-key cryptosystems are being developed by the United States government's National Institute of Standards and Technology (NIST). The current stage of this project is the second round, and the first standard draughts are anticipated somewhere between the years 2022 and 2024 [9].

With the development of the algorithm of Shor and Grover, cryptography faced difficulties in the 1990s that made it possible to break well-known algorithms such as the RSA (1978), Diffie-Hellman (2002), and Elliptic Curve Cryptography (ECC) (1985). Algorithmic approaches relying on codes, hashes, lattices, or many variables are not supported [10].

The current situation calls for a quantum resistant network platform. Along with NIST activities, the IETF (Internet Engineering Task Force) has released a Call for Participation (RFC) that can be modified to improve the widespread use of Internet Key Exchange's (IKE) quantum resistance. In a similar vein, the US Federal Information Processing Standards (FIPS) and the International Organization for Standardization (ISO) both offer programmes that check to see whether the cryptographic modules are implemented correctly and dependably in networks. The PQCRYPTO Horizon 2020 project is cooperating with ISO (Post-Quantum Cryptography for Long-Term Security). A proposed roadmap for assessments of post-quantum hardware and software modules has been created by FIPS [11].

PQC algorithms are currently the main area of interest for research teams working on quantum cryptography. Coding, ring learning with errors, and super singular isomorphy are the post-quantum algorithms' primitives for quantum-resistant cryptography [12].

Quantum Key Distribution (QKD) is a recent development in the realm of quantum cryptography and is thought to have great promise. There are numerous algorithms that have already been developed based on the Heisenberg uncertainty principle and quantum entanglement, including BB84, B92, COW04, KMB09, S13, and AK15 [13].

3   RSA Algorithm

In order to store and transmit information so that only the people for whomever it is intended can read and understand it, a procedure known as cryptography is used. Two forms of cryptography can be distinguished: symmetric cryptography and asymmetric cryptography [14].

Ron Rivest, Adi Shamir, and Leonard Adleman created RSA [15], one of the most popular public key encryption algorithms. Key encryption and digital signatures can both benefit from this method, which is based on the exceptionally difficult factoring of huge integers. The private key can be generated by combining two large prime numbers, and the product can be shared as the public key for encryption. The difficulty of decrypting a message using the public key and ciphertext is related to the difficulty of factoring a product of two large prime numbers.

3.1 RSA Key Generation, Encryption and Decryption

The RSA key generation, encryption, and decryption algorithms are 1, 2, and 3, respectively

Algorithm 1: RSA Key Generation

Input: *Prime numbers p and q, p ≠ q*

Output: RSA modulus n, e, d

Begin

     1.   *Compute $n = p \times q$*
     2.   *Compute $\varphi(n) = (p - 1) \times (q - 1)$*
     3.   *Compute $e, \gcd(\varphi(n), e) = 1, 1 < e < \varphi(n)$*
     4.   *Compute $d, de \bmod \varphi(n) = 1$*

End

Algorithm 2: Encryption with RSA

Input: RSA public key (n,e), 0 < message size (m)< n

Output: Ciphertext c

Begin

     1.   *Compute $c = m^e \bmod n$*
     2.   Return c

End

Algorithm 3: Decryption with RSA

Input: Private key d, Public key (n, e), Ciphertext c

Output: Plain text m

Begin

     1.   *Compute $m = c^d \bmod n$*
     2.   Return m

End

3.2 RSA Algorithm Time Complexity

As depicted in Fig. 1, RSA's time complexity is $O((log_2 x)^3)$. The growth rate for RSA is faster. RSA concentrates on quick and simple encryption and verification since it is simpler to use and comprehend. However, the creation, signing, and decoding of keys takes longer. The time required grows exponentially as the size of the keys [15].

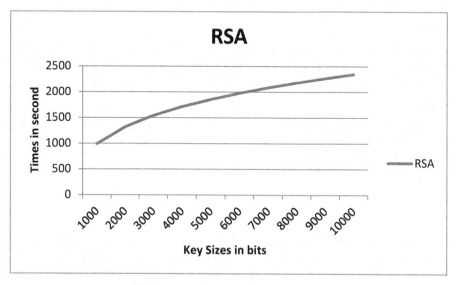

Fig. 1. RSA algorithm time complexity.

4 Shor's Algorithm

Quantum factorization with Shor's algorithm takes $O((\log N))$ space and $O((\log N)^3)$ time, for a given integer N [6]. The significance of this algorithm is it demonstrates that RSA, a common asymmetric encryption technique, could be immediately cracked when we have an enhanced an enhanced quantum computer with a larger number of qubits. The RSA algorithm is easy to crack by factoring N, yet, factoring with traditional algorithms takes more time as N increases. However, no known classical algorithm can factor N in polynomial time. In a polynomial period of time, Shor's algorithm can crack RSA. Like other quantum algorithms, Shor's method is probabilistic and, with a high probability, yields the correct solution.

Shor's Algorithm Steps:
Step 1:

Let N be the target number for factorization and it should be a multiple of two large prime numbers.

Step 2:

Pick a number at random from 1 to N. Dial this as if it were the letter 'j.

Step 3:

Determine the GCD (N,j). Euclid's algorithm for dividing might be used to figure it out. Good news if the GCD is not equal to one. Our work here is finished because the GCD is a factor of N. On the other hand, if GCD=1, then move on to step 4.

Step 4:

The goal is to identify the smallest positive integer r such that if $f(x) = j^x \bmod N$, then $f(a) = f(a + r)$
To determine r, proceed as follows:

Step 4.1:

Introduce a new variable $q = 1$.
Step 4.2:

Calculate $(q \times j) \bmod N$. If the remainder is one, continue to step 4. 3. if not, set the value of q to the remainder we obtained. Repeat this step until the remainder equals 1 and keep track of how many times the transformation was performed. Always remember to alter the value of 'q'.
Step 4.3:

r equals the number of transformations performed in step 4.2.
Step 5:

If r is an odd number, return to Step 2 and select a different value for j.

Step 6:

Define $p = remainder\ in\ \left(\frac{r}{2}\right) th\ transformation$. If $p + 1 = N$, then return to Step 2 and select a new value for j. Otherwise, proceed to Step 7.
Step 7:

What makes up N are:
$$f_1 = GCD(P + 1, N)$$
$$f_2 = GCD(P - 1, N)$$

4.1 Shor's Algorithm Time Complexity

In order to factor an integer N on a quantum computer, Shor's algorithm needs a temporal complexity that is polynomial in log N. The efficiency of Shor's method originates from the modular exponentiation by repeated squaring, which is in turn made possible by the efficiency of the quantum Fourier transform. Figure 2, depicts the temporal complexity of Shor's algorithm, which is $O((log_2 N)^3)$ for factoring a number N.

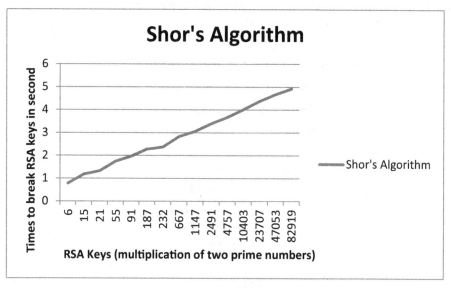

Fig. 2. Shor's Algorithm's time complexity.

5   RSA and Shor's Algorithms Evaluation

Smaller transaction sizes and improved transaction efficiency are becoming increasingly necessary due to the ongoing applications of diverse transactions in global data communication. All of these conditions have a direct connection to the transaction's chosen encryption technique. Smaller key sizes use less memory and longer encryption, decryption, and key generation times in the RSA algorithm but provide less security. In order to improve security, RSA uses keys of a larger size.

One of the most popular encryption methods, RSA, relies on the fact that it is essentially impossible to factor really large numbers. But if we could factor them, RSA would be compromised.

Large numbers can be factored using Shor's approach in polynomial time. Shor's algorithm makes it simple to find these prime numbers because the RSA algorithm is based on the multiplication of two prime numbers. The number of qubits that quantum computers have available determines which RSA key size Shor's technique can crack.

5.1 Evaluation of RSA Algorithm

To produce the two huge prime numbers p and q needed to calculate the public and private keys, we applied the prime numbers generator algorithm 4 to find the all the prime numbers between a given range and then calculate the bit size of these prime numbers using decimal to binary conversion method. For our RSA algorithm implementation, we have chosen to work with Jupyter Notebook. All letters, numbers, and special characters are encoded using the ASCII range of 0 to 126, and we've employed a variety of message widths for each RSA modulus size. A block cypher implementation of RSA can be used to encrypt massive amounts of plain text.

Algorithm 4: Prime Numbers Generator

Input: An arbitrary number (n)

Output: Prime numbers smaller than n

Begin

$$flag \leftarrow 0$$

$for\, i \leftarrow 2\, to\, n\, do$
$\quad for\, j \leftarrow 2\, to \frac{i}{2}\, do$
$\qquad if\, i\%j == 0\, then$
$\qquad\quad flag \leftarrow 1$
$\qquad\quad break$
$\qquad End\, if$
$\qquad j \leftarrow j + 1$
$\quad End\, for$
$\quad if\, flag == 0$
$\qquad print\, i$
$\quad i \leftarrow i + 1$
$End\, for$

End

5.2 Evaluation of Shor's Algorithm

Instead of using a conventional computer, we should have done the work on Shor's Algorithm using a quantum computer. On a quantum computer, the speed at which the algorithm is carried out can be increased. Because a Classical Computer is capable of managing Steps 1, 2, 3, 5, 6, and 7 with a reasonable amount of ease. Step 4, which requires determining the value of the subroutine r, presents a challenge for traditional computers because it is the most time-consuming element of the algorithm. Quantum computers, on the other hand, have a competitive advantage over. Utilizing classical computers will take an exponentially longer amount of time than using quantum computers will, which will take a logarithmically longer amount of time. As a result, quantum computing is preferable when dealing with very large quantities.

For the purposes of this investigation, We utilise the Qiskit open-source software development kit [16] to work with quantum computers on the circuit, pulse, and algorithm levels. It offers a set of tools for the creation and modification of quantum-based software, which may then be run on experimental quantum hardware through IBM Quantum Experience or on local PCs operating as simulators [17]. Scientific computing is taken care of by Anaconda, while interaction with Qiskit is carried out using Jupyter. Shor's algorithm is implemented locally by utilising the IBM QASM simulator.

Due to their size, quantum circuits with more qubits cannot be demonstrated. As can be seen in Fig. 3, a four-qubit quantum circuit is formed by combining four classical registers with four quantum registers in order to factor the number 15 into its prime components, which are 3 and 5. We are unable to factor $N > 2^4$ with only 4 qubits because $2^4 = 16$ is greater than N.

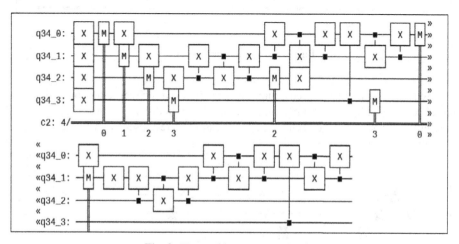

Fig. 3. Four qubits quantum circuit.

As can be seen in Fig. 4, A six-qubit quantum circuit that factors the number 21 into its prime factors, 3, using six conventional registers and six quantum registers. We are unable to factor $N > 2^6$ since $2^6 = 64 > N$, and we only have six qubits at our disposal. We are only able to factor the integers 6, 10, 14, 15, 21, 33, 35, 39, and 55 with our current quantum computer, which only has six qubits. In order to factor extremely large RSA keys, we construct quantum circuits with an increased number of qubits.

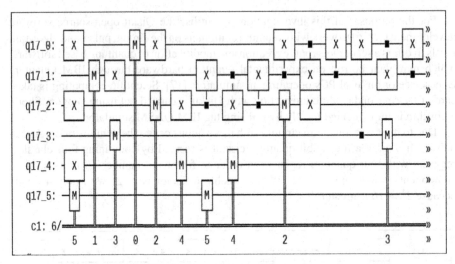

Fig. 4. Six qubits quantum circuit.

Figure 5, displays a coloured depiction of the four-qubit circuit diagram, which was visualised by making use of a matplotlib figure object in order to provide better output flexibility. The related circuit schematic for six qubits is re-presented in colour in Fig. 6, which may be found below.

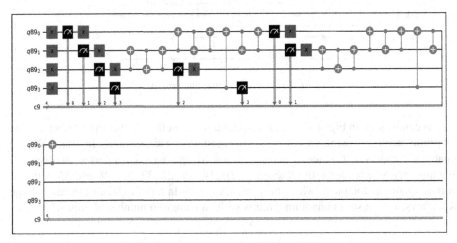

Fig. 5. Quantum circuit with five qubits.

We make use of Qiskit Aer's qasm simulator in order to simulate the quantum circuit. Our goal is to understand how the quantum circuit works. In order to get information regarding the frequency at which the various bit strings appear, it will be necessary for us to perform repeated runs over the circuit. You may gain access to the execute function by utilising the shots keyword, and once there, you will be able to set the desired amount

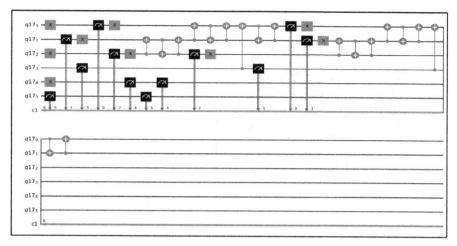

Fig. 6. Quantum circuit with six qubits.

of times that the circuit should be iterated. There are a total of 1,024 frames contained within the entirety of this work.

Figure 7, 8 illustrates the probability measurements that were taken of the performance of a four-qubit quantum circuit while it was run on both classical computers and quantum computers by utilising qiskit. Figure 9, 10 provides a visual representation of the comparable performance measurements of a six-qubit quantum circuit. Shor's method is used to factor one integer, which is displayed in binary form on the horizontal axis, and the chance of success is displayed on the vertical axis.

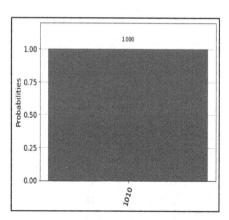

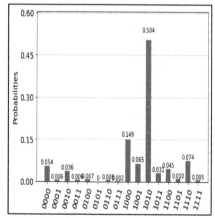

Fig. 7. Classical computer performance to measure 4-qubits quantum circuit

Fig. 8. Quantum computer performance to measure 4-qubits quantum circuit.

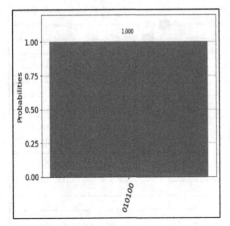

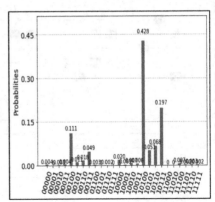

Fig. 9. Classical computer performance to measure 6-qubits quantum circuit

Fig. 10. Quantum computer performance to measure 6-qubits quantum circuit

5.3 Result Analysis

The sets of primes are listed below that were utilised in the experiment that compared these two methods. This prime number was produced via an algorithm that was designed specifically to produce prime numbers. The size of each key can be calculated by first translating the data from decimal to binary, and then back again. In the case of a binary number, the size of the key is identical to the size of the number's bits which is shown in Table 1.

Table 1. RSA modulus with a comparable key size.

P	Q	RSA Modulus (N)	Key Size
2	3	$2 \times 3 = 6$	3
3	5	$3 \times 5 = 15$	4
3	7	$3 \times 7 = 21$	5
5	11	$5 \times 11 = 55$	6
7	13	$7 \times 13 = 91$	7
11	17	$11 \times 17 = 187$	8
17	19	$17 \times 19 = 323$	9
23	29	$23 \times 29 = 667$	10
31	37	$31 \times 37 = 1147$	11
47	53	$47 \times 53 = 2491$	12
67	71	$67 \times 71 = 4757$	13
101	103	$101 \times 103 = 10403$	14
151	157	$151 \times 157 = 23707$	15
211	223	$211 \times 223 = 47053$	16
48371	50417	$48371 \times 50417 = 2438720707$	32

5.4 Comparison and Performance Analysis

Shor's algorithm requires $2^{numberofavailablequbits} > N$ to factorize N. The IBMQ QASM simulator, which can handle as many as 32 qubits, has been our tool of choice for simulations. Given that the maximum size of an RSA key is 32 bits, we are able to factor it using these qubits. How long the RSA modulus is, denoted by "N," can now be one of four distinct values (1024, 2048, 3072, and 4096). We do not have the processing capacity (qubits) necessary to break these RSA modulus codes with such incredibly huge key sizes RSA encryption and decryption time to break different sizes RSA keys are shown in Table 2.

Table 2. Comparison of RSA vs Shor's algorithm's performance.

Key Size in bits	Encryption Time in Second	Decryption Time in Second	Breaking Time in Second
3	$2.0047531127929e^{-05}$	$1.9788742065429608e^{-05}$	0.000347
4	$2.5033950805664062e^{-}05$	$2.8371810913085938e^{-05}$	0.000385
5	$3.0517578125e^{-0}$	$3.6716461181640625e^{-05}$	0.000555
6	$3.25175846256e^{-05}$	$3.695487976074219e^{-05}$	0.000860
7	$3.695487976074219e^{-05}$	$4.0531158447265625e^{-05}$	0.44
8	$3.719329833984375e^{-05}$	$5.3882598876953125e^{-05}$	0.60
9	$5.03245612458542112e^{-05}$	0.0001154226532115465	0.89
10	$7.4145411154628702e^{-05}$	0.0001726598547515984	1.20
11	0.000190215036521569	0.0008542537689208984	1.49
12	0.0008542537689208984	0.0010116100311279297	1.79
13	0.001402159847584845	0.006359577178955008	2.11
14	0.004050493240356445	0.02031731605529785	2.36
15	0.010325649515251456	0.06241798400878906	2.75
16	0.0212298478597534286	0.18036317825317383	3.14
32	1.1849319846253018741	2.8036317825317383	3.51

We see in Fig. 11, that when the key size is large, RSA encryption and decryption take longer than Shor's approach. Given enough qubits in a quantum computer, Shor's method can quickly and easily break any size RSA key. This is because Shor's algorithm works in polynomial time, while RSA's process runs in exponential time.

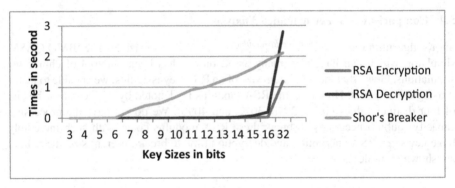

Fig. 11. Time required for RSA encryption, decryption, and Shor's algorithm to crack.

6   Conclusions and Future Directions

Encryption systems that are Quantum-proof have been studied, and they have begun to emerge as viable alternatives to RSA. As a result, the field of Post Quantum Cryptography emerged. Concerns about the safety of the RSA asymmetric cryptographic algorithm in a post-quantum setting are discussed in this study. Key generation, encryption, and decryption times all increase exponentially with a bigger key size, as do the computational resources and battery life needed to support the process. Therefore, it is impossible to indefinitely raise the RSA key size. The future of RSA is uncertain as larger-scale development of quantum computers with more qubits continues. The study of how existing cryptographic algorithms can be improved for usage in a post-quantum setting is a promising field of study.

References

1. Yanofsky, N., Mannucci, M.: Quantum Computing for Computer Scientists. Cambridge University Press, Cambridge (2008). https://doi.org/10.1017/CBO9780511813887
2. Bernstein, E., Vazirani, U.: Quantum complexity theory. SIAM J. Comput. **26**(5), 1411–1473 (1997). https://doi.org/10.1137/S0097539796300921
3. Bennett, C.H., Bernstein, E., Brassard, G., Vazirani, U.: Strengths and weaknesses of quantum computing. SIAM J. Comput. **26**(5), 1510–1523 (1997). https://doi.org/10.1137/S00975397 96300933
4. Simon,D.: On the power of quantum computation. In: 2013 IEEE 54th Annual Symposium on Foundations of Computer Science, Santa Fe, NM, USA, pp. 116-123 (1994). https://doi.org/10.1109/SFCS.1994.365701
5. Deutsch, D., Jozsa, R.: Rapid solution of problems by quantum computation. Proc. R. Soc. Lond. Ser. A: Math. Phys. Sci. **439**, 553–558 (1992)
6. Shor, P.W.: Algorithms for quantum computation: discrete logarithms and factoring. In: Proceedings 35th Annual Symposium on Foundations of Computer Science, Santa Fe, NM, USA, pp. 124–134 (1994). https://doi.org/10.1109/SFCS.1994.365700
7. Beckman, D., Chari, A., Srikrishna, D., Preskill, J.: Efficient networks for quantum factoring. Phys. Rev. A **54**, 1034 (1996). https://doi.org/10.1103/PhysRevA.54.1034
8. Grover, L.K.: A fast quantum mechanical algorithm for database search. In: Symposium on the Theory of Computing (1996)

9. Fernandez-Carames, T.M., Fraga-Lamas, P.: Towards post-quantum blockchain: a review on blockchain cryptography resistant to quantum computing attacks. IEEE Access **8**, 21091–21116 (2020). https://doi.org/10.1109/ACCESS.2020.2968985

10. Mailloux, L.O., Lewis, C.D., II., Riggs, C., Grimaila, M.R.: Post-quantum cryptography: what advancements in quantum computing mean for IT professionals. IT Profess. **18**(5), 42–47 (2016). https://doi.org/10.1109/MITP.2016.77

11. Zeydan, E., Turk, Y., Aksoy, B., Ozturk, S.B.: Recent advances in post-quantum cryptography for networks: a survey (2022). https://doi.org/10.1109/MobiSecServ50855.2022.9727214

12. Borges, F., Reis, P.R., Pereira, D.: A comparison of security and its performance for key agreements in post-quantum cryptography. IEEE Access **8**, 142413–142422 (2020). https://doi.org/10.1109/ACCESS.2020.3013250

13. Chamola, V., Jolfaei, A., Chanana, V., Parashari, P., Hassija, V.: Information security in the post quantum era for 5G and beyond networks: threats to existing cryptography, and post-quantum cryptography. Comput. Commun. **176**, C (Aug 2021), 99–118 (2021). https://doi.org/10.1016/j.comcom.2021.05.019

14. Stallings, W.: Cryptography and Network Security: Principles and Practice, 6th edn. Prentice Hall Press, USA (2013)

15. Rivest, R.L., Shamir, A., Adleman, L.: A method for obtaining digital signatures and public-key cryptosystems. Commun. ACM **21**, 2 (Feb. 1978), 120–126 (1978). https://doi.org/10.1145/359340.359342

16. Aleksandrowicz, G., et al.: Qiskit: an open-source framework for quantum computing (2019). https://doi.org/10.5281/ZENODO.2562111

17. IBM Quantum (2021). https://quantum-computing.ibm.com/

Blockchain-Enabled IoV Framework for Establishing Automated Communication Using Smart Contract

Rakhi Chakraborty[1]([✉]) [iD], Kousik Dasgupta[2] [iD], Debashis Das[3] [iD],
Sourav Banerjee[2] [iD], and Uttam Ghosh[4] [iD]

[1] Department of CSE, Global Institute of Management and Technology, Krishnagar
741102, India
waiting.rakhi@gmail.com
[2] Department of CSE, Kalyani Government Engineering College, Kalyani 741235,
India
mr.sourav.banerjee@ieee.org
[3] Department of CSE, University of Kalyani, Kalyani 741235, India
debashisdascse21@klyuniv.ac.in
[4] Department of CS and DS, Meharry Medical College, Nashville, TN, USA
ghosh.uttam@ieee.org

Abstract. A global network known as the Internet of Things (IoT) connects all sentient objects and allows inter-object communication. Internet of Vehicles (IoV) refers to the IoT-on-Wheels, wherein moving objects exchange information that could mean the difference between life and death to one another and the nearby environment to ensure highly dependable and efficient traffic flows. IoV is a method used in intelligent transportation systems to enable vehicle communications. The leading intent of IoV is to offer a safer, more efficient, and ecologically friendly transportation system. In this paper, we first look at a thorough literature review of the core notion of IoV, its evolution, its architecture, and the underlying principles of VANET technology. Many analyses on IoV have been explored to identify and categorize the current issues with adopting and deploying IoV in urban cities. A seven-layered IoV architecture is proposed, with each layer's functionality and representation is taken into account. This paper presents a blockchain-enabled IoV framework to enable trusted and disseminated communications among vehicles. In this framework, each vehicle act as a blockchain node and should be verified by smart contracts automatically. The proposed work concludes with a Blockchain-based security framework for the security and smooth functioning of IoV.

Keywords: Blockchain · Internet of Vehicles · Vehicular
Communication · Blockchain-integrated IoV · Smart Contracts ·
Automated Verification

K. Dasgupta et al. (Eds.): CICBA 2023, CCIS 1956, pp. 88–101, 2024.
https://doi.org/10.1007/978-3-031-48879-5_8

1   Introduction

The number of people using transportation in the modern world has been rising quickly. Vehicle usage has increased dramatically as a result. Consequences are that Urban countries have traffic congestion and increased accident rates as a result of this uncontrolled expansion in the number of automobiles. A novel idea called the Internet of Vehicles (IoV) was developed to meet the impending needs in the transportation sector.

The first technology advancement created to enable safe and comfortable driving was the vehicular ad hoc network (VANET), which was based on the mobile ad hoc network (MANET). Any vehicle in the system acts as a mobile node, and all additional nodes (vehicles) are linked via wireless networks and V2V [5] along with V2R [10] protocols. The VANET or vehicular ad hoc network's overall growth was slowed by problems with its limited-service area, short-lived connectivity, and inconsistent wireless connections. The development of 5G and the Internet of Technologies has made it possible to introduce the innovative idea of IoV. Recent years have seen a surge in interest in V2V, Vehicle-to-Infrastructure (V2I), and Vehicle-to-Pedestrian (V2P) research because of cutting-edge uses like autonomous driving. Besides, Vehicle-to-Everything (V2X) environment [7] has been made available.

The emergence of vehicles to the Internet of Vehicles has undergone through many innovation stages. Since the 1970s, vehicular communication has taken its first evolutionary step. In 1999, the Intelligent transportation system was introduced. 2001 marked the emergence of the Vehicular ad-hoc network (VANET). Moving forward to 2008, Internet of Vehicles has emerged as one of the main forces propelling innovation in the intelligent vehicular industry. A complete block diagram showing the different stages that lead to the development of IoV has been given in Fig. 1.

Sensors, communication, and communication rate construct the core of IoV. Many interrelated organizations, including hardware, software, networks, and communications service providers, drive this feasible. The ultimate goal of IoV is to improve vehicle maintenance while also ensuring the safety of the vehicle and its surroundings. To enable predictive analytics and corrective actions for better vehicular movement and traffic management, the IoV needs real-time insights into the motion of vehicles, traffic on the roads, and other elements. Conventional wireless communication approaches are unable to deliver the latency and availability required for the IoV infrastructure. IoV needs real-time data

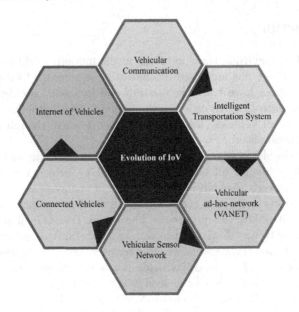

Fig. 1. The evolution of internet of vehicles.

on how vehicles are moving, how traffic is moving, and other aspects. It also needs to perform predictive analytics and prompt corrective action. Although IoV technologies have advanced significantly in recent years, they are still in their infancy and present several obstacles during functional implementation. These systems currently need to solve several challenges; the present overview critically examines the most recent progress in this field.

The remainder of the paper is organized as follows. The most recent and pertinent facts on challenges in IoV have been presented in Sect. 2. Related works are described in Sect. 3. A suggested Blockchain-enabled IoV Architecture is provided in Sect. 4. In Sect. 5, A Blockchain-based security IoV framework is implemented. Section 6 depicts a miner node selection algorithm. Finally, Sect. 7 depicts the conclusion and future work.

2   Challenges in IoV

The challenges and research potential in the IoV are described in the following Table 1.

Table 1. Challenges in IoV.

Challenges	Obstacles	Opportunities
Centralized Cloud Server	Many smart cars are currently communicating with one another and frequently attempting to reach the cloud. It is, therefore, inefficient for the IoV to use a central cloud server to manage billions of nodes and enormous amounts of data storage. A server crash could break the connection to the entire system.	Blockchain is the most effective solution for centralized organization issues in the IoV, particularly in vehicular networks, because it enables the distributed collection, processing, and storage of vehicle data in real-time. [2]
Security and Privacy	The existing IoV systems are not excluded from the never-ending issues of security threats and privacy. These security threats can be categorized based on the physical, network, and application-level challenges. The following are the security issues associated with IoV data, In-vehicle, vehicle-to-everything communication, and service platforms (cloud, edge, and fog). Multiple security vulnerabilities are connected to vehicle-to-everything communications as a result of weaknesses in the communication protocol stacks, a lack of adequate security management and detection measures, and weaknesses in the user interface and communication mode of RATs traffic management, safety applications, and other services are made possible by data on location, acceleration, speed, heading, fuel consumption, brake, driving behavior, tyre pressure, and vehicle profile, etc. The safety of the drivers and passengers would be seriously jeopardized if this data were manipulated or faked. Due to a lack of robust access control policies, authentication systems, audits, certificate management, intrusion detection mechanisms, etc., centralized cloud service platforms face several security difficulties. DoS, Sybil, DDoS, Blackhole, man-in-the-middle (MiM), Wormhole, and Greyhole are some of the well-known attacks.	A possible option is to encrypt information using biometric data, such as protecting device access with iris and face recognition or exchanging data by identifying heart rate and other biometric data. Using an authentication and key management mechanism between various entities (such as vehicles and RSUs) with fog servers, the security issue can be resolved [19]. Sybil attacks may be discovered by analysing vehicle movement patterns to choose the correct path among multiple false paths based on the vehicle's typical beginning and ending points. [16].
Limited Network Coverage	Vehicles connected to the IoV network work together to broadcast emergency messages; they also serve as service providers and publishers [1]. Typically, automobiles communicate with one another through use of Vehicular Cloud utilizing either a fixed infrastructure or mobile network. If a vehicle is outside the network coverage area, they are unable to publish their request with other vehicles. Due to their high-speed mobility in various locations, RSUs have a limited coverage area and are, therefore, ineffective for Vehicular Cloud services [14].	In lieu of fixed cloud servers, one of the proposed solutions is to use mobile brokers as service providers in the VANET environment. For instance, A public bus may act as a mobile broker considering its route incorporates a significant portion of the metropolis [13]. When a message of inquiry is conveyed to the public transport (broker) in search of best compatible package among the closest vehicles, the public transport will forward the vendor's ID (vehicle ID) to the intended vehicle in order to assist it in communicating and acquiring the service it requires. If a broker is unable to locate a compatible package, the request is routed to other closer public transport (brokers) or the RSU [11].
Heterogeneous Network & Lack of Standardization	IoV is diverse regarding data formats, core network technologies, access networks, etc. It is, therefore, complicated to deal with various data formats and interpretations. It's possible that the AI and Blockchain deployment technique employed in one IoV situation won't work in another. Proof-of-Work (PoW) is the best option for delay-tolerant non-safety applications where security is a top priority, but it is not appropriate for delay-sensitive safety applications [18].	There are numerous research opportunities to address the obstacles. Using advanced cryptographic techniques such as lattice-based and multivariate methods to make the Blockchain solution for IoV quantum secure is one feasible approach [18].

3   Related Works

Li Fan et al. identified a three-layer architecture based on the IoT's present architecture and the interactions between various technologies in the IoV Environment [8]. The Perception layer contains all integrated vehicle sensor's collected surrounding data that recognise particular events, such as environmental conditions, vehicle status, driving behaviours, etc. This main job role of this layer is the identification of network nodes via RFID(Radio Frequency Identification Card), collecting all the vehicle-human-road data using various sensors, and enabling the user to receive active updates using various OBUs (Onboard units). The Network layer facilitates multiple wireless modes of communication, such as vehicle-to-vehicle (V2V), vehicle-to-infrastructure (V2I), vehicle-to-pedestrian (V2P), and vehicle-to-sensor (V2S). It guarantees seamless connection to wireless networks, including Bluetooth, Wi-Fi, WiMax, WLAN, GSM, and 4G/LTE. Application layer is to be accountable for storing, analysing, processing, and taking decisions on various risk situations, including transportation delays, poor weather etc., using various statistical tools, storage support, and processing infrastructure.

An IoV architecture with four layers has been proposed by CISCO [9]. The layer at endpoints deals with vehicle-to-vehicle communication, software, and vehicles through 802.11p. All technologies that permit connections between each actor in the IoV are defined in the infrastructure layer. The flow-based management and policy enforcement are monitored by the operation layer. The service layer outlines the services that the various clouds (public, private, and enterprise) provide to drivers in accordance with the data center, on-demand models, or subscription. IoV permits vehicles to connect to the Internet, giving them access to several service providers.

The SAP research team has proposed a service-based architecture based on events-driven design and a service-oriented framework. [15]. Vehicle to Business Architecture has recommended two specific elements, which are as follows: 1) A platform for vehicle integration that enables effective data transfer between enterprise applications and vehicles to build a back-end system 2) A back-end integration manager is in charge of connecting the in-vehicle components.

Fangchun Yang et al. [20] proposed a four-layer architecture of IoV in the research literature that is vehicle network environment sensing and control layer, network access and transport layer, coordination computing control layer, and application layer. The environment sensing layer's job is to collect information from the environment around the vehicle, such as the object's location, the condition of the roads, and driving patterns, using RFID and sensors built into the Vehicles. It investigates the process of tracking and gathering various dynamic information about people, vehicles, and the environment using sensing technology. The network access and transport layers are accountable for supplying all required connection types, such as short-range communication (such as Bluetooth, Wi-Fi and Zibee) or cellular network (such as 4G/LTE or WiMAX) between vehicular environmental components and its connectivity to the cloud. The coordination computing control layer's main function is to store, process, and analyze the collected data to provide a convenient, safe, and risk-situation-aware environment.

According to Abdullah et al., the three primary elements of IoV are the connections, the clients and the cloud [17]. IoV's brain is the cloud, which controls several intelligent computing services. These services on the cloud-based platform connect through a trustworthy connection. The connections, the second largest component of IoV, are separated into various types by the different wireless access technologies. Clients can use cloud-based services with the help of network connections.

Kaiwartya et al. proposed a five-layer architecture consisting of a perception layer, coordination layer, AI layer, application layer, and business layer [12]. The perception layer's primary job is to gather diverse data about vehicles, equipment, the environment, and others using inexpensive and low-energy means. The coordination layer, which is the second layer, is primarily in charge of interoperability, coordination, and unification of information across various structures and among various networks (WAVE, LTE, and WiFi). The AI layer known as the IoV's brain is the third layer. Processing, storing, analyzing, and making decisions based on the information are its responsibility. This layer's primary technologies are vehicle cloud computing and big data analysis. The application layer is the fourth layer. It is responsible for providing intelligent services to users. The fifth and final layer is the business layer, which is accountable for business growth and investment through evaluating the application's impacts.

Min Chen & co-authors also proposed a five layers network architecture [3]. Acquiring and preprocessing massive data from several sources is the responsibility of the sensing layer. In contrast to the previous communication layer, the architecture's communication layer uses a hybrid cloud/edge structure to accommodate the various timescales of various applications. In the cognition layer, heterogeneous data streams are processed and analyzed by the data cognition engine using several cognitive analysis techniques (data mining, machine learning, and deep learning). Using technologies such as network function virtualization (NFV), software-defined networking (SDN), self-organized networking (SON), and network slicing, the resource awareness engine at the control layer is responsible for managing and allocating network resources.

After analyzing numerous IOV architectures that have been proposed, we have identified the following issues: 1) Earlier proposed IoV models don't consider security such as authentication, trust, and authorization; despite the fact that all communication occurs in an unsafe environment. 2) All of the collected data from various services is transferred without any preprocessing, which may cause network congestion as the number of vehicles increases. 3) They do not include a layer for choosing the most suitable network for information dissemination/transmission or service access, i.e. for integrating communication intelligence. 4) The only means of communication between drivers and passengers are the notification via various in-car equipment. To overcome these deficiencies, we propose a novel seven-layered paradigm for IoV that allows the transparent interconnectivity and data dissemination of all network components in an IoV environment. The IoV framework provides a user-vehicle interface that controls vehicle and driver interactions. In the proposed seven-layered architecture, there is a security layer for authorizing, authenticating, and accounting for each transaction between various entities of IoV. The proposed work suggests the progress of a Blockchain-based security framework for the safety and efficient operation of IoV.

4   Proposed IoV Framework

A seven-layered architecture is designed, including presentation, data acquisition, data preprocessing, network and coordination, intelligent data processing, application, and security layers. A summary of each layer's functionalities is presented in Fig. 2, which also provides a detailed description of each layer.

4.1   Presentation Layer

The layer enables direct communication with a driver through an interface for management to organize all notifications to the driver and choose the most suitable display component for the environment or event to minimize the driver's diversion. For instance, the dashboard of the vehicle may light up and generate a sound to inform the driver of a potential accident with a vehicle ahead.

4.2   Data Acquisition Layer

The various actuators and sensors that are embedded into vehicles, smartphones, RSUs, and other personal electronic devices are represented by this layer in the framework. The prime role of this layer is to collect data about humans, vehicles, and the environment through sensing technology. A large amount of data comprises the vehicle's engine conditions, speed, position, direction, travel documents related to vehicles, and acceleration. Additionally, data on the number of vehicles on the road and information on the weather's impact on traffic conditions are included.

4.3   Data Preprocessing and Edge Layer

The analysis and storage of enormous amounts of data provide a major obstacle to IoV's real-time data processing capabilities. There will be significant delays if data processing and analysis are done in one cloud computing event. So, it is necessary to process data near its original source. The edge layer performs initial filtering and analysis upon the gathered local data using an edge node, that is a physical device located nearest to the data source. It reduces network traffic and avoids the transmission of irrelevant information.

4.4   Network and Coordination Layer

This layer is characterized by a virtual global network coordination module for heterogeneous networks, such as WiFi, 4G/LTE, WAVE, and satellite networks. It is compatible with various wireless communication means, including Vehicle-to-Vehicle (V2V), Vehicle-to-Sensor (V2S), Vehicle-to-Infrastructure (V2I), and Vehicle-to-Pedestrian (V2P). By considering a number of selection criteria, including network congestion, QoS levels across different networks that are available, privacy, information relevancy, and security among others, this layer chooses the appropriate network to deliver the information over.

4.5   Intelligent Data Processing Layer

The cloud infrastructure stands in for the architecture's fifth layer. This cloud-based platform is IoV's brain. The cloud data center is in charge of storing, processing, and analyzing the collected global traffic data and decision-making built on critical analysis. One of the major issues in the IoV is service management because of the abundance of services available there. Dedicated and specialized services are needed by smart applications, which are also managed by this layer.

4.6   Application Layer

Smart applications that include everything from multimedia-based entertainment to web-based utility apps are represented by the sixth layer of the architecture and include everything from traffic safety and efficiency. One of the primary duties of this layer is to efficiently discover the services offered by the Intelligent data processing layer so that they can be combined to create smart applications for end users.

4.7   Security Layer

This transversal layer is connected to the rest of the layer directly. This layer is responsible for all security issues, including data authentication, authorization, access control, privacy, and trust. This layer provides support for different types of security attacks. Security problems in IoV typically arise during V2V and V2I communication. In terms of authentication, this layer's primary function is to find out the recognition of the vehicle and whether the RSU that is making the request to connect to the network is legitimate or not. This is important in the case that an unauthorised vehicle or illegal RSU tampers or steals the data from an authorised vehicle. Each factory-issued vehicle has a distinct serial number. The automobile's serial number and login password of the user is necessary to confirm the user's identification when they utilize the vehicle communication function. By checking the manufacturer's database of vehicle serial numbers, the security layer confirms the legality of the vehicle first. Next, the password associated with the user's login id is verified to ascertain that the inquiry originates from the vehicle's proprietor. The legal road-side-unit has a distinct identifying number as well. The legal set of RSU can connect with the vehicle once the security layer does a query against the database of road traffic management.

When a vehicle is initiated, the initialization procedure is stimulated to authenticate the vehicle with the IoV network. Each vehicle has a unique identity token and account address for verification and communication purposes. Smart contracts store each vehicle's credentials, such as identity and authorization information. Within the vehicular network's accessible zone, the data collecting layer collects all data generated by automobiles, pedestrians, and road-side units (traffic lights, car sensors, mobile devices, GPS, pollution level sensors, etc.). The edge layer performs preliminary filtering and analysis of the collected local data using an edge node. For instance, when a vehicle obtains an accident intimation, the information will be broadcasted. However, if some other vehicle gets the very same knowledge without modification, it will not re-transmit. The network and coordination layer determines the most appropriate network over which to transmit the data, taking into consideration a range of selection factors such as network congestion, QoS levels across all accessible networks, privacy, information relevancy, and security, among others. All network-transmitted data is sent to the cloud for analysis, processing, storage, and critical analysis-based decision-making. The Application layer efficiently discovers the Intelligent data processing layer's services so they can be combined to create smart applications for end users.

5 Implementation of the Proposed Framework

In this section, a blockchain-enabled decentralized vehicular communication framework is designed to establish secure communication among vehicles. There are no intermediaries' nodes required to communicate with vehicles. Vehicles can share data in a peer-to-peer (P2P) manner [6]. Each vehicle acts as a blockchain node and has all the necessary communication devices to maintain a stable network. Figure 3 shows the system model, where a vehicle can be a miner node to generate a block. The miner node can be changed periodically based on trust, performance, and computing power. The following components are taken for designing the system model.

5.1 Blockchain Network

Blockchain network is designed for vehicles to access secure and trusted services. Each participant node (i.e., vehicle) should be authenticated using a secure authentication protocol like the 2-step authentication protocol [4]. Vehicles can share data about traffic, incidents, or other necessary data. All features are available to maintain the network and function automatically using smart contracts. Smart contracts decide the miner node based the trust, performance, and computing power. Each miner node will gain an incentive wallet token for mining a block. This feature encourages vehicle nodes to participate in the mining policy.

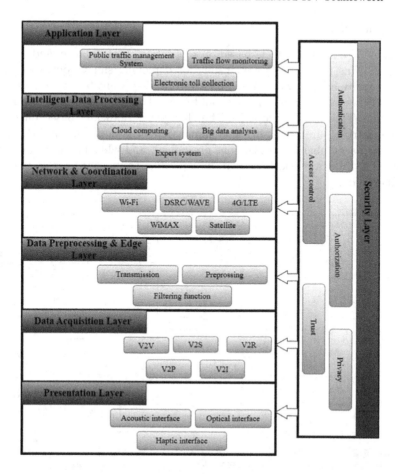

Fig. 2. Proposed seven-layered IoV framework

5.2 Vehicle Node

A vehicle node should have a sensor device(s), computing device, location device, communication device, and storage device for the requirements of the proposed model. The sensor device(s) sense objects and shares the data with the network based on necessity and requirements. The computing device computes the sensed data or received data from the network. The location device enables the current location of the vehicle. It can help another vehicle to gather knowledge about the traffic conditions of the road. The communication device can communicate with other vehicles directly through the P2P communication protocol. The storage device can store information. However, a vehicle node has a unique identifier that is required in the future for node identification. So, other vehicles can easily identify vehicles and exchange information without conflicts.

5.3   Miner Node

A miner node can be a vehicle based on reputation, performance, and computing power. This node is also responsible for deploying smart contracts. Smart contracts verify all newly registered nodes while they want to establish communication. However, the miner node should be verified by others before being the miner node. The miner node should be changed periodically based on performance and trust parameters like how many times the node becomes the miner node, which a number of transactions are mined, and what minimum time was consumed to mine a block. Based on these parameters next vehicle node will be the miner node.

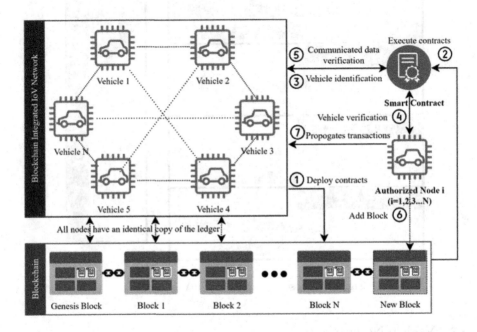

Fig. 3. System model

6   Miner Node Selection

The implementation of the proposed work is described in the following step-by-step. The vehicle authentication process is done using [4]. Therefore, the vehicular communication process will be discussed here.

6.1   Vehicle Registration as a Blockchain Node

A vehicle has to register in the blockchain network to facilitate the proposed features in the vehicular communication system. Each vehicle has an identity token to identify uniquely by others and a unique account address for communication purposes. Smart contracts also store each vehicle's details, for example, identity and authorization information and other credentials. However, an unregistered vehicle cannot join the blockchain network. Vehicles must be registered for facilitating communication or data sharing with others.

6.2 Selection of Smart Contracts Deployment and Execution Node

A vehicle node selection for the smart contract is a major part of the proposed framework. A node will be a smart contract deployment node that has the maximum trust value T_i as shown in Algorithm 1. At first, the vehicle deploys smart contracts to the blockchain. These contracts will be accessed by miner nodes to validate all nodes and their transactions before adding them to the blockchain. Smart contracts are also responsible validate the miner node before adding transactions to the blockchain.

Algorithm 1: Miner Node Selection Algorithm

---

    input : N number of vehicles, Authorization_Status (AS), addresses;
    output: V_i(i=1,2,3, ..., N)
1 Start
2 Step1: **for** *each vehicle* **do**
3 | Check the validity of addresses;
4 | Check the validity of AS;
5 **end**
6 Step2: Find such as V_i, where,
7        $T_i > T$, T=threshold of trust value to become miner node;
8        $TB_i > TB_j$ (j=1,2,3...N and j! =i), TB= total block producing no.;
9 Step3: **if** *(such V_i found in step2)* **then**
10 | $M_k=V_i$; M_k=miner node in k iteration, where k=1,2, 3, ...n;
11 | return M_k;
12 **end**
13 **else**
14 | Goto Step 2;
15 **end**
16 Step4:   Remove those nodes at k+1 iteration, who failed in step 1 at k iteration.
17 End

6.3 Miner Node Selection

Suppose, there are N number of vehicle nodes denoted as V_1, V_2, $V_3 ..., V_N$. Each vehicle should be verified before accessing vehicular communication and block production features. Vehicular communication can be done through proper verification by smart contracts. Block producer can be selected using Algorithm 1 which shows the miner node selection process through smart contracts. Each vehicle node should be authenticated to join the miner node selection process. After validation of each vehicle node, the smart contract checks whether T_i is greater than T or not, where T is the threshold of trust value to become a miner node. Therefore, the smart contract checks the maximum block-producing node in a selected time period. If found, the node will be a miner node to produce a block in k iteration, where $k = 1, 2, 3, \ldots, n$. This way miner node will be selected in the proposed framework. The complexity of miner node selection algorithm is O(N).

7   Conclusion and Future Works

The Internet of vehicles can establish communication among vehicles and other infrastructures to facilitate data communication and the exchange of information. In this paper, a seven-layered IoV framework has been designed for vehicular communication. In this context, vehicles are assumed as blockchain nodes that can communicate with each other. A miner node selection algorithm has also been proposed to mine a block by a vehicle node. The proposed framework can provide new vehicular communication automatically by employing an automated miner selection algorithm. Herein, there is a possibility to select a miner node among all vehicles periodically. Thus, vehicles will be encouraged to participate in the miner node selection process. The proposed framework signifies a new generation IoV system where roadside infrastructures are not required to facilitate smart IoV communication. Vehicles can communicate directly by defining themselves as blockchain nodes. A new model will be designed for block producing mechanism based on a significant incentive-based approach.

References

1. Ahmed, E., Gharavi, H.: Cooperative vehicular networking: a survey. IEEE Trans. Intell. Transp. Syst. **19**(3), 996–1014 (2018)
2. Chen, C., Wu, J., Lin, H., Chen, W., Zheng, Z.: A secure and efficient blockchain-based data trading approach for internet of vehicles. IEEE Trans. Veh. Technol. **68**(9), 9110–9121 (2019)
3. Chen, M., Tian, Y., Fortino, G., Zhang, J., Humar, I.: Cognitive internet of vehicles. Comput. Commun. **120**, 58–70 (2018)
4. Das, D., Banerjee, S., Biswas, U.: A secure vehicle theft detection framework using blockchain and smart contract. Peer Peer Netw. Appl. **14**(2), 672–686 (2021)
5. Das, D., Banerjee, S., Chatterjee, P., Ghosh, U., Biswas, U.: A secure blockchain enabled V2V communication system using smart contracts. IEEE Trans. Intell. Transp. Syst. **24**(4), 4651–4660 (2022)
6. Das, D., Banerjee, S., Chatterjee, P., Ghosh, U., Mansoor, W., Biswas, U.: Design of a blockchain enabled secure vehicle-to-vehicle communication system. In: 2021 4th International Conference on Signal Processing and Information Security (ICSPIS), pp. 29–32. IEEE (2021)

7. Das, D., Banerjee, S., Mansoor, W., Biswas, U., Chatterjee, P., Ghosh, U.: Design of a secure blockchain-based smart IoV architecture. In: 2020 3rd International Conference on Signal Processing and Information Security (ICSPIS), pp. 1–4. IEEE (2020)
8. Fan, L., Li, G., Yang, J., Sun, H., Luo, Z.: The design of IOV overall structure and the research of IoV key technology in intelligent transportation system. In: 2015 International Power, Electronics and Materials Engineering Conference, pp. 1079–1084. Atlantis Press (2015)
9. Flavio, B.: The smart and connected vehicle and the internet of things. WSTS, San José (2013)
10. Ghori, M.R., Zamli, K.Z., Quosthoni, N., Hisyam, M., Montaser, M.: Vehicular ad-hoc network (VANET). In: 2018 IEEE International Conference on Innovative Research and Development (ICIRD), pp. 1–6. IEEE (2018)
11. Guezzi, A., Lakas, A., Korichi, A.: A new approach to manage and disseminate data in vehicular ad hoc networks. In: Proceedings of the International Conference on Intelligent Information Processing, Security and Advanced Communication, pp. 1–4 (2015)
12. Kaiwartya, O., et al.: Internet of vehicles: motivation, layered architecture, network model, challenges, and future aspects. IEEE Access 4, 5356–5373 (2016)
13. Kerrache, C.A., Ahmad, F., Ahmad, Z., Lagraa, N., Kurugollu, F., Benamar, N.: Towards an efficient vehicular clouds using mobile brokers. In: 2019 International Conference on Computer and Information Sciences (ICCIS), pp. 1–5. IEEE (2019)
14. Meneguette, R.I., Boukerche, A., Pimenta, A.H.: AVARAC: an availability-based resource allocation scheme for vehicular cloud. IEEE Trans. Intell. Transp. Syst. 20(10), 3688–3699 (2018)
15. Miche, M., Bohnert, T.M.: The internet of vehicles or the second generation of telematic services. ERCIM News 77, 43–45 (2009)
16. Sharma, S., Kaushik, B.: A survey on internet of vehicles: applications, security issues & solutions. Veh. Commun. 20, 100182 (2019)
17. Sherazi, H.H.R., Khan, Z.A., Iqbal, R., Rizwan, S., Imran, M.A., Awan, K.: A heterogeneous IoV architecture for data forwarding in vehicle to infrastructure communication. Mob. Inf. Syst. 2019 (2019)
18. Singh, P.K., Nandi, S., Nandi, S.K., Ghosh, U., Rawat, D.B.: Blockchain meets AI for resilient and intelligent internet of vehicles. arXiv preprint arXiv:2112.14078 (2021)
19. Wazid, M., Bagga, P., Das, A.K., Shetty, S., Rodrigues, J.J., Park, Y.: AKM-IoV: authenticated key management protocol in fog computing-based internet of vehicles deployment. IEEE Internet Things J. 6(5), 8804–8817 (2019)
20. Yang, F., Li, J., Lei, T., Wang, S.: Architecture and key technologies for internet of vehicles: a survey. J. Commun. Inf. Netw. 2(2), 1–17 (2017)

Load Balancing in a Heterogeneous Cloud Environment with a New Cloudlet Scheduling Strategy

Gopa Mandal[1]([✉]), Santanu Dam[2] [ID], Kousik Dasgupta[3], and Paramartha Dutta[4]

[1] Jalpaiguri Government Engineering College, Jalpaiguri 735101, West Bengal, India
gopa.mandal@gmail.com
[2] Netaji Subhas Open University, Sector 1, Salt Lake City 700064, West Bengal, India
[3] Kalyani Government Engineering College, Kalyani 741235, West Bengal, India
[4] Visva-Bharati University, Santiniketan 731235, India

Abstract. The idea of cloud computing has completely changed the digital world in the age of the internet. Cloud computing offers a variety of cloud services, including software (Software as a Service), platforms (Platform as a Service), and infrastructure (Infrastructure as a Service). Pay-as-you-go is the primary business model used by cloud service providers (CSP). Services are offered that are in demand. Therefore, it is the only obligation of the cloud service provider to guarantee a terrific, continuous, and seamless service to its clients. To ensure an increase in service quality, load balancing is highly solicited. This paper mainly focused on task scheduling in a heterogeneous cloud environment so that no VM gets overloaded or under loaded. Users of cloud services typically submit tasks to CSPs. We mainly focused on enhancing the tasks' completion rates and turnaround times. Enhancing the overall completion time of all jobs unquestionably contributes significantly to raising system throughput. This is accomplished by assigning a specific task to a particular virtual machine so that all machine loads are nearly equal and all tasks have nearly equal priority. Finally, we compare our task scheduling algorithm by substituting the original task scheduler with the one we have proposed. We then compare the results with the load-balancing techniques currently in use. The results are quite encouraging and have significantly improved the load balancer's efficiency.

Keywords: Cloud computing · QoS · Cloudlet Scheduling · Task Scheduling · Load Balancing

1 Introduction

The "cloud" is a network of linked computers that combines multiple computing resources into one. Broadly, we can say that a network of remote servers that can be accessed via an Internet connection and store and manage information is referred to as the "cloud" [1]. The development of cloud computing in recent years has made it possible to quickly set up geographically scattered datacenters that are interconnected to provide high-quality and reliable services [2]. Cloud computing has developed into a useful paradigm for providing computational capabilities on a "pay-per-use" basis in modern times [3]. Cloud computing opens a tonne of opportunities for the development of traditional IT due to its expanding application and marketing [4]. On-demand, users who use cloud computing can access computing resources in the form of virtual machines. These virtual machines are installed in a cloud provider's datacenters. The computing resources are distributed among several cloud users, who pay for the service according to their usage. The primary objective of the clouds is to equally spread user jobs among the VMs to ensure that each VM can handle a specific number of tasks and not become overloaded. Additionally, load-balanced task scheduling has grown to be a significant problem in cloud computing. Both academics and businesspeople are now paying more attention to this issue. To supply infrastructure as a service (IaaS), Amazon EC2, a cloud service provider (CSP), uses elastic load balancing to distribute the workloads of its clients [5]. Although it is an NP-hard problem [6–9], sustaining load balancing while using a task scheduling method in the clouds. Achieving this resource allocation and efficient task scheduling has a significant impact on the system's effectiveness and efficiency. According to what we have just said, cloud computing enables users to access computing resources like storage, databases, and processing power online. Users of these services submit their job requests in the task manager module as their job requests, or "cloudlets. The task manager is employed in the following step. The task scheduler's duties include scheduling the cloudlet and assessing the resources available at any given time in the cloud [12].

Therefore, a task scheduler needs to be extremely effective to be able to analyze this demand and supply pool with the aid of a resource information server. Divide tasks among the virtual machines (VMs) using an effective job scheduling algorithm. To maximize the resource consumption of the VM. So, a fundamental necessity in a cloud computing architecture for scheduling tasks is the allocation of cloudlets to the appropriate virtual machines, or simply VMs. A module called datacenter broker (DCB) controls all aspects of the datacenter, including cloudlet distribution to virtual machines in a cloud environment. One of the most pressing issues in cloud computing is cloudlet or task scheduling. The cloudlet-scheduling problem is matching a set of provided cloudlets with a set of available virtual machines (also known as VMs) to shorten the finishing time, that is the time of completion of a given application without violating the available resources. In a cloud computing environment, multiple cloudlets are typically submitted simultaneously. To execute its Cloudlets, the Cloudlet Time Shared Scheduler employs a virtual machine to carry out a scheduling policy. In a VM, cloudlets execute in a time-shared fashion. The Cloudlet Scheduler does not consider cloudlets' priorities to define execution order. The scheduler just ignores the priorities even if they are defined. Preemption is also not considered to get resources available to the cloudlets that are waiting for their turn. It simply requires that there be no waiting cloudlet, oversimplifying the problem in this case. Here, the total processing capacity of the processor (in MIPS) is equally divided by the applications that use them. Scheduling's primary goals are to maximize resource usage and speed up the processing time of given work or tasks. The scheduler needs to be effective enough to assign VMs in a way that improves the quality of service (QoS) and makes better use of available resources.

An efficient scheduling algorithm should be able to submit a greater number of user tasks to the algorithm with less response time. The user submits a set of cloudlets (user tasks) to the broker, who distributes the cloudlets to various virtual machines running on the host. Each datacenter has hosts, and each host can be virtualized to create a number of virtual machines. In order to assign the cloudlets to VMs, the broker uses these scheduling policies. In this research work, we typically investigate a task scheduling problem that also balances the loads in a cloud environment by satisfying the QoS parameters mentioned here. Task Scheduling in Heterogeneous Cloud Environments is the primary focus of our study. Users of cloud services typically submit tasks to CSPs. We concentrated primarily on reducing the tasks' overall completion and turnaround times. Enhancing the overall completion time of all jobs unquestionably contributes significantly to raising system throughput. We concentrated on assigning a specific work to a specific virtual machine so that the loads on all machines are almost equal and that all jobs receive nearly equal priority. To prove the novelty of our proposed algorithm, we simulate it using CloudSim [11]. We found that there are two different possibilities for implementing scheduling in a cloud environment, as mentioned below.

(I) Time Shared Policy: Under the time-sharing scheduling policy, the resources are shared among the cloudlets. Each cloudlet receives resources for execution for a set period of time. After that time, the resources are released from that task and become available to different cloudlets. The Round Robin (RR) algorithm is used in this policy.

(II) Space Shared Policy: In Space Shared Policy, assigned resources are exclusive for those cloudlets. A cloudlet possessed a virtual machine until it completes execution. Execution is done on a first-come, first-served basis, so the waiting time is high.

In [12] a different version of the heuristic-based task scheduling algorithm Heterogeneous Earliest Finish Time (HEFT) was proposed. The proposed approach is also compared to other scheduling approaches and found more effective. It was also concluded that the HEFT algorithm's efficiency can be improved by selecting the best results from each approach's schedules. Although this may result in a higher cost for the algorithm, it is a trade-off between cost and performance. Nature-inspired optimization-based scheduling should be considered as a future research direction.

Our proposed algorithm is a space-shared algorithm that splits all the cloudlets and all the VMs into two categories depending on the categorizing factor. The parameters we considered were waiting time and overall turn-around time. In order to test the effectiveness of our suggested approach, we also replace the use of the conventional scheduling approach in load balancing with our proposed strategy. The outcome is encouraging and outperforms several existing strategies. The remainder of the article is structured as follows: A quick overview of our proposed scheduling strategy is provided in the next section. In the following section, we include a brief discussion of the simulation testbed. The section on result analysis compares the new strategy to the existing one. Then we look at how well the proposed algorithm works for load balancing in cloud computing by comparing it with some existing strategies.

2 Our Proposed Scheduling Algorithm

As we've already discussed, the cloud offers services to its customers in order to satisfy their needs. Therefore, once a user's job is found in the ready queue and a virtual machine is not already available, the datacenter spawns a virtual machine using a hypervisor. To determine the best virtual machine that might be available in the cloud environment, a broker algorithm is always used. If no available VMs are discovered, it must provide one. To schedule the task for VM allocation task scheduler will operate based on this concept by creating two distinct queues for virtual machines and cloudlets that are requesting resources. We put all the cloudlets into the cloudlet queue (CLQueue) as well as the VMs into another queue (VMqueue). The basic goal of our algorithm is to map cloudlets to VMS so that larger cloudlets are properly mapped to high VMs and smaller cloudlets are properly mapped to shorter VMs. To meet the basic goal we introduced the categorization coefficient (k) which was calculated by taking the mean of all cloudlet lengths available across the network. Now we'll go over the steps to figure out how 'k' is calculated.

2.1 Introduction of 'Categorizing Factor (k)'

Prior to scheduling any cloudlets, we are first determining a classification factor, also known as the "k" factor. It is necessary to our algorithm since it establishes the categories under which our cloudlets are placed and the order in which they are arranged. Because our algorithms are static, the "k" factor is something that must be calculated at the beginning and then used for the entirety of the scheduling procedure. This means that the "k" value is not subject to change. The "k"-factor is computed by taking the length of each cloudlet that is present at that time and averaging its value.

- The Categorizing Factor (k): As our cloudlet lengths are almost equally distributed over a certain range we have defined it as the average of the cloudlet's length.

$$k = \frac{\sum All\ cloudlet\ lengths}{number\ of\ cloudlets} \tag{1}$$

We attempted to strike a balance between the burst times of the cloudlets, as we deemed them to be of almost identical importance. To do this, we have to adjust the mapping of specific cloudlets to a specific category of virtual machines (VMs) so that no VMs are overloaded and none are underloaded. Therefore, we split the entire VM list into two separate lists. One list has VMs with a larger MIPS or processing power (1000 MIPS) than the other (VMs in the lower category) (600 MIPS). To link a cloudlet to a given VM category, we have established a "categorizing factor (k)". This results in larger cloudlets being assigned to higher-category VMs and smaller cloudlets being assigned to lower-category VMs. In order to mimic a real-world scenario and test the algorithms in a non-biased setting, we made a number of assumptions while selecting cloudlet lengths. The two assumptions listed below were made.

1. Over a specific range, all cloudlet lengths are evenly distributed.
2. We assumed that all cloudlets had nearly similar priorities in order to shorten the total completion time. Below is the illustration of the various length cloudlets considered in our suggested algorithm in Fig. 1.

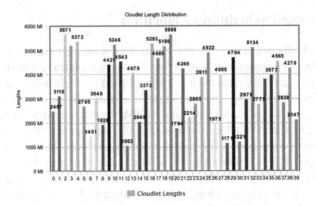

Fig. 1. Cloudlet of Different Size

Therefore, it is anticipated that the average Burst Time of the cloudlets will decrease by mapping two separate categories of VMs for various categories of cloudlets. Additionally, the overall Completion Time will increase while waiting times will be reduced. The average length of all cloudlets present at that specific moment served as the initial categorization criteria. We selected two types of VMs to represent a diverse environment (a) High Category VMs, first (Each VM has 1000 Mips) and (b) VMs of Low Category (Each VM has 600 Mips). Our process involves comparing a VM's cf High category virtual machines are assigned if it is judged to be higher than the categorization factor. If not, low-category VMs are allocated.

The following is an outline of the algorithm we've named Schedule_Cloudlet, which will be used to present our proposed approach.

ALGORITHM Schedule_Cloudlet

```
List_vm =>input ids of all  created  VM available over network
List_cloudlet=>input job ids of all cloudlets spawned over network
1.  START
2.  Create a variable cf (categorizing factor) and ini-
tialize to avg(all cloudlet lengths )
3.  Create two VM lists high_vms and low_vms
4.   for each VM v in vm_list:
5.          if v is 600: put v into low_vm
6.          else: put v into high_vms
7.   Create two variables call high_id and low_id and in-
itialize both to zero
8.  for each cloudlet c_i in cloudlet_list:
9.          if c_i < cf:
10.         assign c_i to low_vms[low_id] for execution
11.         do low_id = ( low_id + 1 ) % size(low_vms)
12.         else:
13.         assign c_i to high_vms[high_id] for execution
14.         do high_id = ( high_id + 1 ) % size(high_vms)
15. Check List_tcloudlet  is empty or not..
16.  if List_cloudlet is Empty then goto step 18
17.  else goto step 8
18. END
```

In the world of distributed computing, there is no such thing as a "perfect algorithm." Because of the needs of the users and the nature of the task shifted over time. Advantages of our novel method in our setting, however, include -

- The accurate mapping between longer cloudlets and High VM and shorter cloudlets and Low VM has been achieved since the lengths of cloudlets are uniformly distributed over a range.
- No virtual machines are overloaded, and none are going unused.
- Overall completion time is a major issue for tasks with equal priorities. Because of our algorithm, we expect a decrease in that.
- Unlike the SJF technique, sorting the cloudlets doesn't add any unnecessary processing time.

Given that our method is non-preemptive, it is important to note that no Job has exclusive CPU use for an extended length of time. As a result of our scheduling approach, we hope to reduce the variability in the peak times of individual cloudlets.

3   Simulation Environment

Measuring the success of a proposed policy during testing in the actual world has become increasingly challenging and time-consuming. As it is extremely challenging to estimate the number of simultaneous users' applications at any moment and their impact on real-world performance. As a result, simulation becomes extraordinarily beneficial for users and academics, as it permits practical feedback in an artificial world. This section provides a brief description of cloud-based simulation for supporting application-level infrastructure and services. It involves the modeling of virtualized resources on demand, which enables cloud infrastructure. To test these new concerns, a testbed that is compatible with Cloud infrastructures is necessary. Various simulators, such as CloudSim [11] and CloudAnalyst [13], are available to model real-world environments. In our work, we use the CloudSim simulator to test our proposed task scheduling algorithm. Further Cloud Analyst, a simulator developed at the University of Melbourne, has been utilized in this work to prove the novelty of the proposed algorithm in the load balancing technique by replacing the initial First Come First Serve (FCFS) scheduling approach in GA [14], SHC [15], Round Robin and FCFS.

3.1   Environment Set Up for CloudSim

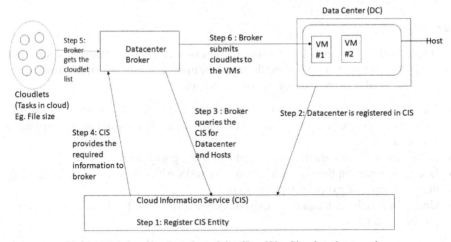

Fig. 2. High-level explanation of the CloudSim Simulator's operation

We set up a testing environment where the datacenter contained two hosts, each of them configured with 100 GB of storage, 1000 MB of accessible bandwidth, and 4 GB of RAM. Each datacentre (DC) is expected to have four CPUs capable of 10000 MIPS. We started with 10 virtual machines, and then we added more over time. The lengths of the cloudlets are dispersed over a specified range in order to imitate a real-world scenario and test the algorithms in an unbiased setting. Here, almost all cloudlets are prioritized equally (Figs. 2 and 3).

3.2   Environment Set Up for CloudAnalyst

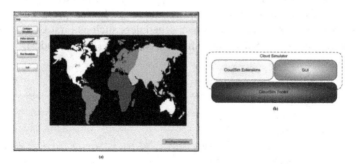

Fig. 3. CloudAnalyst snapshot (a) CloudAnalyst's user interface (b) Architecture of CloudAnalyst based on CloudSim

We selected a few current cutting-edge load-balancing techniques that are initially employed by the FCFS task scheduler to redistribute users' jobs to compare the performance of the proposed task scheduler algorithm. They start the load-balancing approach after a certain period of time when the resources are about to run out. We replace the task scheduler that was previously set up in a First Come First Serve fashion to demonstrate the novelty of our approach. For this purpose, we took CloudAnalyst while keeping the configuration of the datacenters as same as CloudSim. Though the geographic distribution of the datacenters is taken into account. We keep track of the simultaneous online users available over the network. Whereas one-tenth of users is considered offline depicted in Table 1.

Table 1.   Simulation environment set-up for CloudAnalyst

No.	User Base	Region	Online Users (Peak-hours)	Online Users (Off-peak hours)
1	UBase1	0 – N. America	4,70,000	80,000
2	UBase2	1 – S. America	6,00,000	1,10,000
3	UBase3	2 – Europe	3,50,000	65,000
4	UBase4	3 – Asia	8,00,000	1,25,000
5	UBase5	4 – Africa	1,15,000	12,000
6	UBase6	5 – Oceania	1,50,000	30,500

When we reevaluated our scheduling strategy and moved virtual machines (VMs) from the overloaded host to the underloaded host, we discovered that the proposed method provided better performance than the previous strategy. We created 25, 50, and 75 virtual machines (VMs) from a single datacenter before extending to six datacenters.

4 Result and Performance Analysis

We build 10,000 cloudlets with various job lengths and execute our proposed algorithm to examine the efficacy of the scheduling technique. To further prove our algorithm's uniqueness, we mimic several popular task schedulers such as First Come First Serve (FCFS), Shortest Job First (SJF), Max-Min, and Min-Min (Figs. 4 and 5).

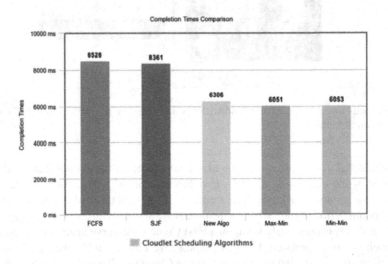

Fig. 4. Completion Time Comparison

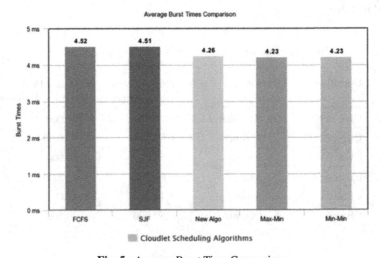

Fig. 5. Average Burst Time Comparison

Every algorithm uses two different types of time. One is the actual cloudlet execution time, while the other is the cloudlet's mapping time to a particular VM. Due to the less complicated algorithms used in FCFS, SJF, and New Algo, the mapping time is extremely short. Therefore, the next mapped cloudlet is already queued on that VM's waiting list when one cloudlet is being performed in it. There isn't any downtime. However, Max-Min and Min-Min take a long time to map because of the algorithm's high temporal complexity. As a result, there may be some idle time (little overhead) between two cloudlet executions that follow one another in the same virtual machine The overall cloudlet completion time in our CloudSim simulation ignores idle time. For this reason, we get to see that the overall completion time of the cloudlets is low but the actual simulation time of the algorithm is very high. The following changes are observed when overhead is considered, as shown in Fig. 6.

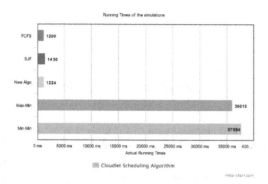

Fig. 6. Actual runtime duration of the Algorithm

The actual execution time of the algorithm (for 10000 cloudlets) is significantly longer for Max-Min and Min-Min than for New Algorithm, despite the fact that the theoretical completion time was comparable. This is because the CloudsSim simulation framework completely ignores the overhead of running the algorithm.

Running Time and Overhead Analysis of the Algorithms
We determined how long our algorithm would take to execute and found that there were M numbers of VMs available for the 'N' numbers of cloudlets. In which we demonstrated that our approach had O(N) complexity. In the following figure displays a comparison of time complexity and current policies. The comparison of the time complexities of the algorithms used here is shown in Fig. 7. The overhead graphs are shown below for the actual running times in Fig. 8.

FCFS	SJF	New Algo	Max-Min	Min-Min
O(N)	O(NlogN)	O(N)	$O(MN^2)$	$O(MN^2)$

Fig. 7. Asymptotic time complexity comparison of different algorithms

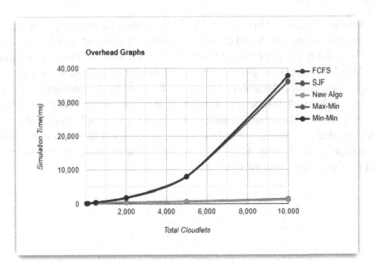

Fig. 8. The overhead graphs comparison of different algorithms

The next step entails the replacement of the conventional scheduling policy, which is utilized from the moment cloudlets are allotted to virtual machines (VMs) until the point at which all available VMs have been used completely. Lastly, we assess the efficacy of the novel scheduling policy by incorporating it into the existing approach and comparing it to standard load-balancing strategies using CloudAnalyst [13]. The findings are presented below (Tables 2, 3, 4, 5, 6, 7 and Figs. 9, 10, 11, 12, 13, 14).

Table 2. Calculation of the Average Response Time, or RT, in milliseconds across a variety of cloud configurations one Datacenter

Cloud Configuration	Datacenter Specification	GA_LBNEW	GA	LBNEW	RR	FCFS
CC1	One DC with 25 VM	327.65	329.01	329.89	330	330.11
CC2	One DC with 50 VM	327.41	328.97	329.25	329.42	329.65
CC3	One DC with 75 VM	243	244	313.56	329.67	329.44

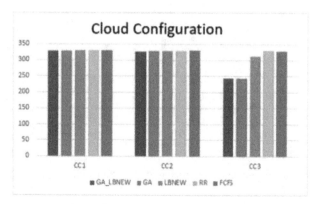

Fig. 9. Performance comparison of the proposed algorithm with Genetic Algorithm, RR and FCFS using one Datacenter.

Table 3. Calculation of the Average Response Time, or RT, in milliseconds across a variety of cloud configurations using two Datacenter

Cloud Configuration	Datacentre Specification	GA_LBEW	GA	LBNEW	RR	FCFS
CC1	Two DC with 25 VM	353.51	360.77	368.44	376.27	376.34
CC2	Two DC with 50 VM	343.31	355.72	364.15	372.49	372.52
CC3	Two DC with 75 VM	347.35	355.32	361.73	369.48	370.56
CC4	Two DC with 25,50 VM	346.31	350.58	360.72	367.91	368.87
CC5	Two DC with 25,75 VM	348.82	351.56	356.23	369.45	367.23
CC6	Two DC with 75,50 VM	348.66	352.01	354.04	356.01	361.01

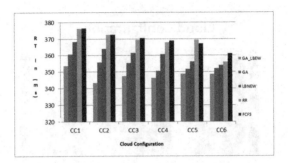

Fig. 10. Performance comparison of the proposed algorithm with Genetic Algorithm, RR and FCFS using two Datacenter.

Table 4. Calculation of the Average Response Time, or RT, in milliseconds across a variety of cloud configurations using three Datacenter

Cloud Configuration	Datacentre Specification	GA_LBNEW	GA	LBNEW	RR	FCFS
CC1	DC with 25 VM	340.73	350.32	354.92	366.17	363.34
CC2	DC with 50 VM	338.76	350.19	352.51	363.52	363.52
CC3	DC with 75 VM	342.55	346.01	353.83	360.18	361.56
CC4	DC with 25,50,75 VM	332.19	345.98	352.42	361.21	360.87

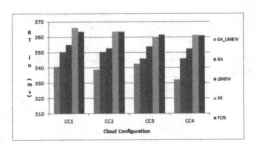

Fig. 11. Performance comparison of the proposed algorithm with Genetic Algorithm, RR and FCFS using three Datacenter.

Table 5. Calculation of the Average Response Time, or RT, in milliseconds across a variety of cloud configurations using Four Datacenter

Cloud Configuration	Datacentre Specification	GA_LBNEW	GA	LBNEW	RR	FCFS
CC1	DC with 25 VM	332.76	348.85	352.66	359.35	360.95
CC2	DC with 50 VM	335.84	345.54	343.54	356.93	359.97
CC3	DC with 75 VM	331.62	340.65	342.88	352.09	358.44
CC4	DC with 25,50,75 VM	329.63	337.88	341.91	351	355.94

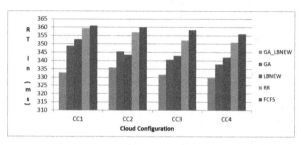

Fig. 12. Performance comparison of the proposed algorithm with Genetic Algorithm, RR and FCFS using four Datacenter.

Table 6. Calculation of the Average Response Time, or RT, in milliseconds across a variety of cloud configurations using Five Datacenter

Cloud Configuration	Datacentre Specification	GA_LBNEW	GA	LBNEW	RR	FCFS
CC1	DC with 25 VM	327.82	335.64	341.03	348.57	352.05
CC2	DC with 50 VM	321.35	326.02	329.14	339.76	345.44
CC3	DC with 75 VM	319.22	322.93	326.52	335.88	342.79
CC4	DC with 25,50,75 VM	316.41	319.98	324.6	334.01	338.01

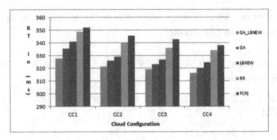

Fig. 13. Performance comparison of the proposed algorithm with Genetic Algorithm RR and FCFS using five Datacenter.

Table 7. Calculation of the Average Response Time, or RT, in milliseconds across a variety of cloud configurations using Six Datacenter

Cloud Configuration	Datacentre Specification	GA_LBNEW	GA	LBNEW	RR	FCFS
CC1	DC with 25 VM	317.89	330.54	335.61	341.87	349.26
CC2	DC with 50 VM	312.3	323.01	328.82	338.14	344.04
CC3	DC with 75 VM	308.74	321.54	327.08	333.67	339.87
CC4	DC with 25,50,75 VM	302.71	315.33	324.65	334.01	338.29

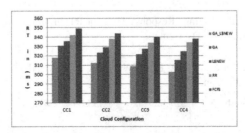

Fig. 14. Performance comparison of the proposed algorithm with Genetic Algorithm, RR and FCFS using six Datacenter.

5   Conclusion and Future Scope

We compared the implemented approach to previously tested methods. We compared completion time, burst time, and so on. The "categorizing factor (k)" of our algorithm currently, k is constant. To improve our algorithm, we may compute k in a different way. We also compared the throughputs of the algorithms and graphed their performance. When developing this method, we believed that cloudlets were evenly distributed. Not all assumptions are correct. Cloudlet lengths may be skewed. In this case, a static "k" will overutilize some VMs while underutilizing others. The priority of the job is not considered, which may not be the same in the real world. Our future research may include a wide range of learning methodologies that have the potential to improve results and must be compared to other existing strategies. We must also compute the cost effectiveness of the algorithms.

References

1. Venu, G., Vijayanand, K.S.: Task scheduling in cloud computing: a survey. Int. J. Res. Appl. Sci. Eng. Technol. (IJRASET). **8**(5), 2258–2266 (2020)
2. Lee, S., Kumara, S., Gautam, N.: Efficient scheduling algorithm for component-based networks. Future Gener. Comput. Syst. **23**(4), 558–568 (2007). ISSN 0167-739X, https://doi.org/10.1016/j.future.2006.09.002
3. Wang, W., Zeng, G., Tang, D., Yao, J.: Cloud-DLS: dynamic trusted scheduling for Cloud computing. Expert Syst. Appl. **39**(3), 2321–2329 (2012). ISSN 0957-4174, https://doi.org/10.1016/j.eswa.2011.08.048
4. Senkul, P., Toroslu, I.H.: An architecture for workflow scheduling under resource allocation constraints. Inf. Syst. **30**(5), pp. 399–422 (2005). ISSN 0306-4379, https://doi.org/10.1016/j.is.2004.03.003
5. Elastic load balancing. https://aws.amazon.com/elasticloadbalancing/. Accessed Nov 2022
6. Zhang, J., Huang, H., Wang, X.: Resource provision algorithms in cloud computing: a survey. J. Netw. Comput. Appl. **64**, 23–42 (2016)
7. Panda, S.K., Jana, P.K.: Efficient task scheduling algorithms for heterogeneous multi-cloud environment. J. Supercomput. **71**(4), 1505–2153 (2015)
8. Panda, S.K., Jana, P.K.: Normalization-based task scheduling algorithms for heterogeneous multi-cloud environment. Inf. Syst. Front. **20**(2), 373–399 (2016)
9. Li, J., Qiu, M., Ming, Z., Quan, G., Qin, X., Gu, Z.: Online optimization for scheduling preemptable tasks on IaaS cloud system. J. Parallel Distrib. Comput. **72**, 666–677 (2012)
10. Hojjat, E.: Cloud task scheduling using enhanced sunflower optimization algorithm. ICT Express **8**(1), 97–100 (2022). ISSN 2405-9595, https://doi.org/10.1016/j.icte.2021.08.001
11. Calheiros, R.N., Ranjan, R., Beloglazov, A., Rose, C., Buyya, R.: CloudSim: a toolkit for modeling and simulation of cloud computing environments and evaluation of resource provisioning algorithms. Softw. Pract. Exp. (SPE) **41**(1), 23–50 (2011). ISSN: 0038-0644. Wiley Press, New York, USA
12. Hai, T., Zhou, J., Jawawi, D., Wang, D., Oduah, U., Cresantus, B.: Task scheduling in cloud environment: optimization, security prioritization and processor selection schemes. J. Cloud Comput. **12**, 15 (2023). https://doi.org/10.1186/s13677-022-00374-7
13. Wickremasinghe, B., Calheiros, R.N., Buyya, R.: CloudAnalyst: a CloudSim-based visual modeller for analysing cloud computing environments and applications. In: Proceedings of the 24th International Conference on Advanced Information Networking and Applications (AINA 2010), Perth, Australia, pp. 446–452 (2010)
14. Dasgupta, K., Mandal, B., Dutta, P., Mondal, J.K., Dam, S.: A Genetic Algorithm (GA) based load balancing strategy for cloud computing. In: Proceedings of CIMTA-2013. Elsevier, Procedia Technology, vol. 10, pp. 340–347 (2013). ISBN 978-93-5126-672-3
15. Mondal, B., Dasgupta, K., Dutta, P.: Load balancing in cloud computing using stochastic hill climbing-a soft computing approach. In: Proceedings of (C3IT 2012). Elsevier, Procedia Technology, vol. 4, pp. 783–789 (2012)

Protocol for Dynamic Load Distributed Low Latency Web-Based Augmented Reality and Virtual Reality

T P Rohit[1]([✉])(iD), Sahil Athrij[2], and Sasi Gopalan[1]

[1] Cochin University of Science and Technology, Kalamassery, Kochi, Kerala, India
20cs078rohi@ug.cusat.ac.in, sasigopalan@cusat.ac.in
[2] University of Washington, Seattle, WA 98195, USA

Abstract. The content entertainment industry is increasingly shifting towards Augmented Reality/Virtual Reality applications, leading to an exponential increase in computational demands on mobile devices. To address this challenge, this paper proposes a software solution that offloads the workload from mobile devices to powerful rendering servers in the cloud. However, this introduces the problem of latency, which can adversely affect the user experience. To tackle this issue, we introduce a new protocol that leverages AI-based algorithms to dynamically allocate the workload between the client and server based on network conditions and device performance. We compare our protocol with existing measures and demonstrate its effectiveness in achieving high-performance, low-latency Augmented Reality/Virtual Reality experiences.

Keywords: 2D kernel · Augmented reality · Cloud computing · Dynamic load distribution · Immersive experience · Mobile computing · Motion tracking · Protocols · Real-time systems · Web-based augmented reality application

1 Introduction

The motivation for writing this paper is to address the increasing demand for computing power required to run AI-based algorithms in augmented reality (AR) applications. While these algorithms can enhance the physical world of the user by embedding virtual information seamlessly, the need for dedicated applications and hardware has always been a barrier to entry into the XR world for common users. This limitation is now being solved with the use of AI-based algorithms in place of hardware solutions (e.g. depth measurement, object tracking, etc.). However, this approach has resulted in an increased workload on consumer computing devices, which has made cloud-based solutions popular in most industries. Unfortunately, cloud-based AR/VR applications are still being left behind due to the two major barriers.

© The Author(s), under exclusive license to Springer Nature Switzerland AG 2024
K. Dasgupta et al. (Eds.): CICBA 2023, CCIS 1956, pp. 118–129, 2024.
https://doi.org/10.1007/978-3-031-48879-5_10

– Latency
– Server Cost

The common approach for solving these problems is a trade-off between quality and cost. We propose this protocol as a hybrid to attain high quality with minimal cost. In our technique only the bare minimum required amount of computing will be done on the server, that is the device will be utilized to its maximum. This allows the reduction of server costs. The protocol will also allow the allocation of load dynamically between the client and the server depending on the network conditions and device performance to attain minimum latency.

2   Related Works

2.1   Mobile Augmented Reality

In recent years, the number of applications that run Mobile Augmented Reality (MAR) [3] has drastically increased thanks to increased computational resources available on Mobile Devices. Most MAR applications can run on current high-end mobile devices, but in order to achieve an immersive experience processes such as precise object detection, realistic model rendering, smooth occlusion and accurate augmentation in real time cannot be handled by mobile devices. Further, most mid-range and low-end mobile devices are not capable of achieving admissible quality augmentation due to limited resources and battery capacity.

2.2   Cloud Based Gaming Technology

Cloud-based gaming uses mobile devices to send inputs to a remote server, which then renders and runs the game. The resulting video is streamed back to the mobile device, allowing users to play high-quality games on a variety of devices without downloading them. This makes gaming devices more flexible and allows for better performance scaling. Services like Google Stadia [2], Microsoft xCloud, Amazon Luna, Nvidia GeForce Now, and PlayStation Now all use this technology to stream games to users' devices. In research on this topic, reducing latency in the communication between the mobile device and the server is a key focus [4,13]. This approach can also be applied to developing protocols for web-based augmented reality, to dynamically manage the distribution of computing tasks between the client and server.

2.3   Web Based Augmented Reality

Creating a Web-based AR experience typically involves using a rendering library like WebGL or THREE.js, a marker tracking library such as AR.js, and APIs like WebXR to manage the AR session. However, browsers that run these libraries have limited access to device resources and may not be able to handle heavy computational tasks like markerless detection and realistic rendering. Additionally, technologies like WebXR are still relatively new and do not provide options for custom detection algorithms. To improve the performance of Web-based AR, technologies like SceneViewer by Google and ARQuickLook [19] by Apple have been developed to handle rendering, lighting, surface detection, and placement within the browser. However, these technologies are specific to certain browsers and do not offer compatibility across different browsers. Additionally, they limit developer options such as custom detection algorithms and interaction. As a result, alternative solutions such as server-based AR systems are being developed to address these limitations. [21]

3   Components of the Protocol

3.1   Client Side

The client architecture is divided into independent submodules for easy extension/modification. The client will be responsible for capturing frames from the camera feed, doing pre-processing, and optionally streaming the frames to the server. The client will also take care of displaying the final output in the desired format.

Frame Preprocessing. The raw frames captured from the video source (most likely webcam/smartphone camera) will be of varying resolution and FPS depending on the video source. In the prepossessing stage, the client ensures the captured frames are below the maximum resolution supported by the server and also limits the frame rate if necessary. In cases where the video source is underperforming the preprocessing module just forwards the stream as is. The maximum resolution and frame rate can either be obtained from the server or hardcoded in the client itself. The recommended resolution is 1280×720 at 30 FPS.

Landmark Detection. The landmark detection can happen in two modes depending on the device performance and network conditions, Low Compute Mode (LC) or High Compute (HC) mode. In LC the landmark detection is done by the server and the client merely streams the captured frames. In HC the client runs a comparatively lightweight (which can be changed by the developer) AI model to do the landmark detection and sends the detected landmarks to the server as a JSON.

3.2   Server Side

Transport Module. It is the duty of the transport module to send and received data from the client. The module uses the data type of the received data to determine whether the client is in LC or HC mode. The transport module depending on this information automatically adjusts the pipeline to continue the further process. The transport module is also responsible for spinning up as many instances of the pipeline as required to meet the client's needs. The transport module uses WebSockets to maintain consistent data communication between the client and server. To obtain maximum performance separate WebSockets running on different ports (if they are available else the same port is shared) are used for different clients.

Frame Processing. This module is an optional part of the pipeline that only runs when the client is in LC mode. The frame processing module is responsible for decompressing the received frame and doing the landmark detection. This module produces normalized landmark points that are of the same structure as the landmark points generated by the client in HC mode.

Overlay Rendering. Depending on the landmark points received (either from the client or Frame Processor) the overly has to be rendered. This involves 3D rendering and is computationally expensive and therefore is reserved for the server only. Appropriate 3d models are loaded and transformed to fit the landmarks and then rendered from the required perspective. The rendered images along with the anchor points are then passed on to the Transport module to send to the client (Figs. 1 and 2).

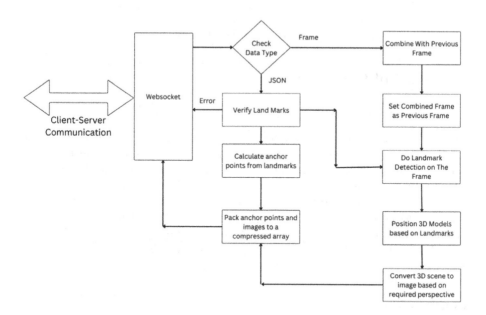

Fig. 1. Server Architecture

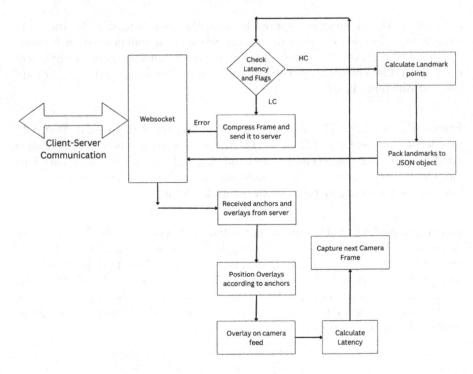

Fig. 2. Client Architecture

4   Model of Operation

4.1   Low Compute Mode

In LC mode the client device is deemed to be underpowered and the network condition is stable enough. In LC the client device doesn't do the landmark detection rather it sends the frame to the server for this task. To keep the latency low the images are compressed by the client.

Here it is very critical that the frames streamed should be of high quality since the AI needs to be able to detect landmarks from it. But streaming high-quality frames at rates near 30 FPS will require impractical bandwidth usage. The client solves this problem by using an improved inter-frame compression algorithm.

Compression

The common approach to inter-frame compression is to just compute the difference between consecutive frames and discard areas without change. Implementing this algorithm on CPU (sequential) will be $O(n^2)$ time complexity. So for an image of 720×720 pixels, it would take 518400 operations. This will slow down the process significantly. So the only viable solution is to use the GPU. In browser-based platforms, the GPU can be accessed using WebGL API. Using the WebGL shaders to perform the subtraction brings down the time complexity to practically $O(1)$. This is the approach commonly followed.

The shortcoming of this approach is that due to random noise and floating point precision issues the image difference may not always yield the required results. If there is noise in the image taking the pixel vise difference will always yield a huge number of non-zero pixels. This reduces the compression efficiency. Another caveat is that due to the floating point precision issue, the color produced in the subtracted frame will not be accurate. This hinders the reconstruction process.

Tunable Kernel and Region Of Interest. We propose an improved version of inter-frame compression that overcomes the shortcomings of the conventional method. Instead of taking the pixel-wise difference of consecutive images a kernel is used to get values for each pixel before doing the subtraction.

For pixels a_{00} to a_{nn} and b_{00} to b_{nn}
Let $k(i, j)$ be the kernel value at i^{th} column and j^{th} row of the kernel

$$d_{ij} = (b_{ij} - a_{ij}) \times k(i, j) \tag{1}$$

$$sigDiff = \sum_{i=0}^{n} \sum_{j=0}^{n} d_{ij} \tag{2}$$

$$out_{(n/2)(n/2)} = \begin{cases} 0, & \text{if } sigDiff \leq threshold \\ b_{(n/2)(n/2)}, & \text{if } sigDiff > threshold \end{cases} \tag{3}$$

Here out_{ij} is the color of the pixel at location i, j

After calculating the image difference using Eqs. 1 to 3 the pixels with values 0 are discarded. This use of kernel enables noise removal. The floating point precision error is also eliminated since the output doesn't directly depend on any result of float operations. The values of the kernel can be tuned as required to change how the noise is eliminated. The size of the kernel determines the granularity of regions of difference in the obtained image. With a larger kernel size, a more continuous part of the image will be selected whereas smaller values will select discrete scattered points/blobs (Figs. 3 and 4).

At the receiving end the frames can be reconstructed by,

$$frame = framePrev[diffFrame \neq 0] = diffFrame[diffFrame \neq 0] \tag{4}$$

That is replace all changed pixels from the previous frame with sent pixels and keep pixels from the previous frame where there is no change. It has to be noted that the change discussed here is not the pixel-wise change but rather the change after applying the kernel.

Fig. 3. Output of 33 × 33 kernel   **Fig. 4.** Output of 3 × 3 kernel

4.2 High Compute Mode

High Compute mode is selected for devices with powerful processing capacity or when network conditions are very poor. In the High Compute mode, the client-side tries to do as much computation as possible. There are two configurations for HC mode for doing landmark detection,

Region of Interest Tracking. In this method instead of detecting and tracking the landmarks directly only a region of interest is calculated and tracked. Here the logic is that if a landmark is initially found in the region bounded by a polygon P then the landmarks can change only when the pixels inside the set polygonal region change.

The client sends the first frame to the server for landmark detection. The server sends back landmark points along with the ROIs. The client keeps track of the landmark points according to the motion of ROIs.

The relative position of a particular landmark at time $t+\Delta t$ can be calculated by adding $V_c \times \Delta t$ to position of that landmark at time t

Here V_c is the velocity of the center of mass of the region enclosing that particular landmark. Where the center of mass of a region is defined as the average location of changing pixels.

Given two consecutive frames, the center of mass C can be calculated as,

$$C = (\frac{\Sigma x}{w}, \frac{\Sigma y}{h}) \tag{5}$$

w, h are the width and height of the region of interest

From this V_c will be,

$$V_c = \frac{|C(f_i) - C(f_{(i-1)})|}{\tau} \tag{6}$$

In order to reduce computation, the approximate velocity of motion can be calculated by taking the center of mass of the differential frame f'' given by,

$$f'' = f_i' - f_{(i-i)}' \tag{7}$$

$$V(f) = C(f'') \tag{8}$$

Object Detection. In this configuration, the client runs an object detection model using pre-trained weights provided by the server. The weights are collected from the server to enable hot replacement of the detection model while maintaining the expected structure of landmark points. The client is responsible for requesting this mode. So developers can opt out of setting up an environment for running a model in the front end if necessary.

4.3   Dynamic Switching

The protocol will switch between LC and HC modes depending on the computed network latency and device performance. The switching information is inferred by the server automatically based on the data type of the transmitted data. This enables the client to react to real-time events without waiting for the server's response. There are four cases for the switching,

Low Compute Latency. In this case, the time required for the device to do landmark detection on a frame is calculated. If this latency is below a threshold λ_c then Low Compute Latency is assumed. In this case, the protocol will default to HC mode. This can be overridden by the developer by using the force LC flag. This can be used if there are power consumption limitations for the device.

High Compute Latency. In this case, the time required for the device to do landmark detection on a frame is calculated. If this latency is above a threshold λ_c then High Compute Latency is assumed. In this case, the protocol will switch dynamically between LC and HC modes. This can be overridden by the developer by using the force LC flag.

High Network Latency. In this case, the round trip time for a frame is calculated. If this latency is above a threshold λ_n then High Network Latency is assumed. In this case, the protocol will switch dynamically between LC and HC modes until the conditions improve. This cannot be overridden by the developer.

Low Network Latency. In this case, the round trip time for a frame is calculated. If this latency is below a threshold λ_n then Low Network Latency is assumed. In this case, the deciding factor will be Compute-Latency. The developer can force the use of LC by setting the LC Flag.

5   Results

These results are based on the implementation of this protocol with Flask-Python as the Backend (Server) and JS Frontend (Client).

5.1   Latency

The latency was measured as the time between a frame being captured and the corresponding overlay being drawn on the live camera feed. As expected the latency increases exponentially with an increase in frame resolution. This latency is the least of computing/network latency. It is achieved by dynamically switching between LC and HC modes.

The latency encountered for lower resolution images (lower than 144 p) was found to be varying drastically so is not included in the table (Table 1).

Table 1. Latency Vs Resolution.

Resolution	Latency
1280×720	20 ms
852×480	15 ms
480×360	12 ms
256×144	10 ms

5.2   Frame Size

The average frame size in KB was calculated from a sample of 546 frames. RAW indicates the maximum size required for a frame without any compression. From the table, it is evident that our modified inter-frame compression algorithm can reach a compression ratio about three times better than JPEG compression, which is the next best option.

The compressed image size of both PNG and JPEG remained fairly stable, 108–132 KB for PNG and 47–60 KB for JPEG. The compression ratio of our algorithm varied drastically depending on the amount of motion in the transmitted frame. It was in the range of 2.49–108 KB. Here even though the maximum frame size is 108 KB it is only reached when all the pixels of the frames change (e.g. The initial frame, when switching cameras etc.). But since the probability for such a change in a normal use case is very low our algorithm is able to outperform existing methods (Table 2).

Table 2. Compression Using Each Techniques

Compression	Size
RAW	270 KB
PNG	104.40 KB
JPEG	56.22 KB
Ours	18.04 KB

6   Conclusion

In this paper, we have designed Protocol For Dynamic Load Distributed Low Latency Web-Based Augmented Reality And Virtual Reality (DLDL-WAVR) to introduce the method of dynamic load distribution between the client and the server for Augmented reality / Virtual Reality applications. The protocol was designed to be cross-platform and extremely configurable. The server architecture was proposed so as to enable it to be client agnostic. The mechanism to optimize based on network latency and device performance as well as to provide maximum quality at the lowest latency was devised. The results of the algorithm were rigorously tested and verified to match the theoretical values of the same.

The major drawback of the protocol is that it may not be able to handle large numbers of concurrent users, which can lead to performance degradation and increased latency. This is due to the lack of multiple server support in the backend. Despite these drawbacks, the DLDL-WAVR protocol has been shown to be a powerful and effective solution for dynamic load distribution in AR/VR applications, and further research is needed to address these limitations and improve its performance.

References

1. Bray, T.: The JavaScript Object Notation (JSON) Data Interchange Format. RFC **7159**(2014), 1–16 (2014)
2. Carrascosa, M., Bellalta, B.: Cloud-gaming: analysis of google stadia traffic. arXiv:2009.09786 (2020)
3. Chatzopoulos, D., Bermejo, C., Huang, Z., Hui, P.: Mobile augmented reality survey: from where we are to where we go. IEEE Access **5**(2017), 6917–6950 (2017). https://doi.org/10.1109/ACCESS.2017.2698164
4. Chen, D.-Y., El-Zarki, M.: Impact of information buffering on a flexible cloud gaming system. In: Proceedings of the 15th Annual Workshop on Network and Systems Support for Games (Taipei, Taiwan) (NetGames 2017), pp. 19–24. IEEE Press (2017)
5. (2006) Chen, J.-W., Kao, C.-Y., Lin, Y.-L.: Introduction to H.264 advanced video coding. In: Proceedings of the 2006 Asia and South Pacific Design Automation Conference vol. 2006, pp. 736–741 (2006). https://doi.org/10.1109/ASPDAC.2006.1594774
6. Fette, I., Melnikov, A.: The WebSocket Protocol. RFC **6455**(2011), 1–71 (2011)

7. Furht, B. (ed.) JPEG, pp. 377–379. Springer, Boston (2008). https://doi.org/10. 1007/978-0-387-78414-4_98
8. Furht, B., (ed.) Portable Network Graphics (PNG), pp. 729–729. Springer, Boston (2008). https://doi.org/10.1007/978-0-387-78414-4_181
9. IEEE Digital Reality 2020 (accessed September 16, 2020). Standards. IEEE Digital Reality. https://digitalreality.ieee.org/standards 13 AIVR 2021, July 23-25, 2021, Kumamoto, Japan Sahil Athrij, Akul Santhosh, Rajath Jayashankar, Arun Padmanabhan, and Jyothis P
10. Kiyokawa, K., Billinghurst, M., Campbell, B., Woods, E.: An occlusion capable optical see-through head mount display for supporting co-located collaboration. In: The Second IEEE and ACM International Symposium on Mixed and Augmented Reality, 2003. Proceedings, pp. 133–141 (2003). https://doi.org/10.1109/ISMAR. 2003.1240696
11. Kooper, R., MacIntyre, B.: Browsing the real-world wide web: maintaining awareness of virtual information in an AR information space. International Journal of Human-Computer Interaction **16**(3), 425–446 (2003). https://doi.org/10.1207/ S15327590IJHC1603_3
12. Langlotz, T., Nguyen, T., Schmalstieg, D., Grasset, R.: Next generation augmented reality browsers: rich, seamless, and adaptive. Proc. IEEE **102**(2), 155–169 (2014)
13. Lee, K., et al.: Outatime: using speculation to enable low-latency continuous interaction for mobile cloud gaming. In: Proceedings of the 13th Annual International Conference on Mobile Systems, Applications, and Services (Florence, Italy) (MobiSys 2015). Association for Computing Machinery, New York, NY, USA, pp. 151–165 (2015). https://doi.org/10.1145/2742647.2742656
14. Liu, L., et al.: Deep learning for generic object detection: a survey. arXiv:1809.02165 (2019)
15. Liu, W., et al.: SSD: single shot multibox detector. In: Leibe, B., Matas, J., Sebe, N., Welling, M. (eds.) ECCV 2016. LNCS, vol. 9905, pp. 21–37. Springer, Cham (2016). https://doi.org/10.1007/978-3-319-46448-0_2
16. Huynh, L.N., Lee, Y., Balan, R.K.: DeepMon: Mobile GPU-based Deep Learning Framework for Continuous Vision Applications. In: MobiSys, Tanzeem Choudhury, Steven Y. Ko, Andrew Campbell, and Deepak Ganesan (Eds.). ACM, pp. 82–95 (2017). http://dblp.unitrier.de/db/conf/mobisys/mobisys2017.html
17. MacIntyre, B., Hill, A., Rouzati, H., Gandy, M., Davidson, B.: The Argon AR Web browser and standards-based AR application environment. In: 2011 10th IEEE International Symposium on Mixed and Augmented Reality, pp. 65–74 (2011). https://doi.org/10.1109/ISMAR.2011.6092371
18. Olsson, T., Salo, M.: Online user survey on current mobile augmented reality applications. In: 10th IEEE International Symposium on Mixed and Augmented Reality. ISMAR 2011, pp. 75–84 (2011). https://doi.org/10.1109/ISMAR.2011.6092372
19. Oufqir, Z., El Abderrahmani, A., Satori, K.: ARKit and ARCore in serve to augmented reality. In: 2020 International Conference on Intelligent Systems and Computer Vision (ISCV), pp. 1–7 (2020). https://doi.org/10.1109/ISCV49265.2020. 9204243
20. PTCGroup: Vuforia developer portal (2020). https://developer.vuforia.com/
21. Qiao, X., Ren, P., Dustdar, S., Liu, L., Ma, H., Chen, J.: Web AR: a promising future for mobile augmented reality-state of the art, challenges, and insights. Proc. IEEE **107**(4), 651–666 (2019). https://doi.org/10.1109/JPROC.2019.2895105
22. Redmon, J. Farhadi, A.: YOLO9000: better, faster, stronger. In: 2017 IEEE Conference on Computer Vision and Pattern Recognition (CVPR), pp. 6517–6525 (2017). https://doi.org/10.1109/CVPR.2017.690

23. Rouzati, H., Cruiz, L., MacIntyre, B.: Unified WebGL/CSS scene-graph and application to AR. In: Proceedings of the 18th International Conference on 3D Web Technology (San Sebastian, Spain) (Web3D 2013). Association for Computing Machinery, New York, NY, USA, p. 210 (2013). https://doi.org/10.1145/2466533.2466568

24. Shea, R., Sun, A., Fu, S., Liu, J.: Towards fully offloaded cloud-based AR: design, implementation and experience. In: Proceedings of the 8th ACM on Multimedia Systems Conference (Taipei, Taiwan) (MMSys 2017). Association for Computing Machinery, New York, NY, USA, pp. 321–330 (2017). https://doi.org/10.1145/3083187.3084012

25. Sun, N., Zhu, Y., Hu, X.: Faster R-CNN based table detection combining corner locating. In: 2019 International Conference on Document Analysis and Recognition (ICDAR). IEEE Computer Society, Los Alamitos, CA, USA, pp. 1314–1319 (2019). https://doi.org/10.1109/ICDAR.2019.00212

26. Duong, T.N.B., Zhou, S.: A dynamic load sharing algorithm for massively multiplayer online games. In: The 11th IEEE International Conference on Networks, 2003. ICON2003, pp. 131–136 (2003). https://doi.org/10.1109/ICON.2003.1266179

27. Tao, Y., Zhang, Y., Ji, Y.: Efficient computation offloading strategies for mobile cloud computing. In 2015 IEEE 29th International Conference on Advanced Information Networking and Applications, pp. 626–633 (2015). https://doi.org/10.1109/AINA.2015.246

28. Zhou, X., Gong, W., Fu, W., Du, F.: Application of deep learning in object detection. In: 2017 IEEE/ACIS 16th International Conference on Computer and Information Science (ICIS), pp. 631–634 (2017). https://doi.org/10.1109/ICIS.2017.7960069

29. Zimmermann, C., Brox, T.: Learning to estimate 3D hand pose from single RGB images. In: IEEE International Conference on Computer Vision (ICCV) (2017). https://lmb.informatik.uni-freiburg.de/projects/hand3d/https://arxiv.org/abs/1705.01389

Dynamic Priority Based Application Offloading Strategy in Mobile Cloud Computing

Priyajit Sen[1]($\boxtimes$) (iD), Rajat Pandit[1] (iD), and Debabrata Sarddar[2] (iD)

[1] Department of Computer Science,
West Bengal State University, Barasat, Kolkata, West Bengal, India
priyajit91@gmail.com

[2] Department of Computer Science and Engineering, University of Kalyani, Kalyani, Nadia,
West Bengal, India

Abstract. Offloading an application from mobile device to nearby cloudlets is a critical task and at the same time to take the decision regarding the offloading. In paper [11], the cloudlets were selected based on the execution time. Execution time of the applications is a fixed parameter and therefore it was a static priority algorithm. In this paper, we are going to introduce the dynamic priority algorithm for the selection of the cloudlets to offload an application. Based on the type of the application, the priority will vary. The user applications will be set with the task priority and the priority parameter will be dependent on the type of the task. Thus, it will reduce the energy consumption and delay to execute an application efficiently compared to the FIFO based, round robin based, proxy server based, App-Spec cloudlet based and App-Exec cloudlet based techniques. This will also give priority to the mobile user to execute an application outside the mobile device based on various parameters for different applications. The simulation work is carried out in the university laboratory with the mobile, desktop and laptop devices.

Keywords: Dynamic Priority · Static Priority · Computation Offloading · Cloudlets · Energy Consumption · Delay

1 Introduction

Mobile Devices have flaws to execute a resource hungry application within itself and for that reason it is sometimes required to offload the application to the cloud. But, offloading the application to the cloud and getting the result back from there is time consuming and also costly. Instead of that, cloudlets that store the cache copies of data of the cloud server can take the responsibility of executing applications which are coming from the mobile devices. Cloudlets can work at high bandwidth and low latency [1]. Only if the cloudlets are not sufficient to handle the requests of the mobile user then it will be forwarded to the cloud server. Offloading has different parameters and based on that a suitable cloudlets can be chosen. Various techniques were used to choose the cloudlets and different parameters were selected for that. First Come First Serve Cloudlet selection has the problem of convoy effect as this algorithm suffers from

K. Dasgupta et al. (Eds.): CICBA 2023, CCIS 1956, pp. 130–141, 2024.
https://doi.org/10.1007/978-3-031-48879-5_11

this problem. Round Robin algorithm suffers as it is preemptive. Proxy server based cloudlet selection is not fruitful as extra time and power is required to select the proxy server [1, 2]. Application type based cloudlet selection suffers from cloudlet versatility and application execution time versatility. App-Exec Cloudlet based offloading suffers from the problem of static priority. Sometimes, offloading is partial and sometimes it is complete. A whole or complete application offloading is such a technique where the entire code is offloaded from mobile to cloudlet for its possible and early execution [3]. But, in partial offloading, the important and time consuming part of the application i.e. a part of the application is offloaded for execution [4]. Advantage of partial offloading over whole offloading is that, a partial offloading requires less time to offload, result gets available faster than the other, and it only focuses on the part which is must to offload and remaining part is executed in the mobile device. The problem of app-exec cloudlet based offloading is that its offloading parameter is task execution time but this parameter is a static parameter and for that the offloading of different types of applications are not done efficiently with this static parameter. This can be considered as a static priority algorithm. But, whenever users try to execute different types of applications then there should have different selection parameters for choosing the nearby cloudlets and offload his/her task (Fig. 1).

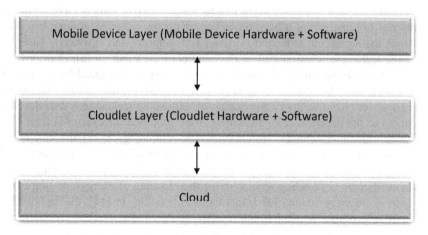

Fig. 1. Mobile Device to Cloud Server Hierarchy through Cloudlet.

In the Fig. 1, bidirectional arrows are used to show the both way communication during the offloading process. The user mobile device sends its task to the cloudlets by offloading the task and for its possible execution with minimum power requirement and delay. If the cloudlets are able to serve such request then they do so or otherwise forwards to the cloud. The reverse procedure is followed while receiving the response.

1.1 Organization of the Paper

Related works are discussed in the next portion to describe the works related to the proposed work and as a source of the problem of this research work, proposed work portion contains the algorithm, flowchart and the original proposal to deal with the problems identified in earlier cases of offloading. Experimental configuration portion is present next to explain the configuration setup to carry out the research work. Simulation result portion contains the tables and graphs to explain and compare the results of previously used algorithms and the proposed method of offloading. Conclusion and future works portion draws the conclusion of the work and the future planning of this research work.

2 Related Works

In [1], Anwesha Mukherjee et al. have introduced proxy server based offloading in multi cloudlet environment for the selection of optimum cloudlet. In [2], significant lower power consuming offloading technique is introduced with Femto Cloudlet based technique. In [3], authors have introduced cooperative code offloading method using Femto Cloudlet. In [4], authors have focused on user mobility and introduced mobility aware offloading technique for time critical applications. In [5], Priority based task caching and offloading concept is introduced by the authors. The joint optimization of offloading concept is introduced in this technique. In [6], authors have introduced a multilevel full and partial offloading technique for the selection of cloudlets which has shown the significant reduction in power consumption. In [7], Priority based fair scheduling technique is introduced by the authors of the paper. In [8], Priority-Based Servicing Task Offloading in Mobile Edge Computing is introduced by the authors. In [9], Task priority based offloading in in Edge network is introduced by the authors of the paper. In [10], Quality of Service aware offloading technique is introduced by the authors of the paper. In [11], the authors have proposed the execution time based application offloading techniques for mobile cloud computing. In [12], the authors have summarized computation offloading techniques in mobile cloud computing and mobile edge computing and their issues are discussed in the paper. In [13], the authors have introduced dynamic offloading technique for the reducing of energy consumption. It is an energy aware technique for computation offloading. In [14], the authors have introduced a technique as a solution to execute resource intensive tasks in the mobile edge computing network. This technique improves the energy utilization, energy gain, delay and others.

3 Proposed Work

An application that comes to a mobile device from the user it will check for its type, deadline, software and hardware requirement, energy availability etc. Offloading decision is taken based on these conditions. If N number of applications are present in the mobile device to offload and M number of cloudlets are available nearby for the execution of those mobile applications. If applications are classified based on type, for example a gaming user who is paying high amount will get the chance to execute his game first than the other users. The same thing will happen for other applications. The priority table is prepared below for executing different types of applications (Table 1).

Table 1. Dynamic Priority Table Based on Application Type and its Selection Parameter

Application Type	Application	Priority Type (Offloading Parameter)	Priority Value	Priority Assigned (3- High Priority, 1- LowPriority
Game	Tic-Tac-Toe	Money	Rs. 200	2
	Chess	Money	Rs. 300	3
	Tower of Hanoi	Money	Rs. 100	1
Numerical Application	Matrix Addition	Deadline	5 ms	3
	Matrix Multiplication	Deadline	10 ms	2
	Finding roots usingbisection method	Deadline	15 ms	1
Searching Elements	Linear Search	No. of elements and order	10, sorted order	1
	Binary Search	No. of elements and order	8, sorted order	2
	Interpolation Search	No. of elements and order	7, sorted and equally distributed order	3
Sorting Elements	Bubble Sort	Execution Time or Burst Time	6 ms	1
	Quick Sort	Execution Time or Burst Time	4 ms	2

We have considered three types of applications such as game, numerical application, searching and sorting process. Each of them has some sub-categories. They are different examples of that type of application. Execution Priority of each of the application is assigned dynamically based on application type and offloading parameters.

Time taken by the local device to offload a code is calculated as,

$$T_{upload} = \text{size of the code(in kb)/upload speed (in kbpms)} \qquad (1)$$

$T_{execute}$ = Time taken for the execution in the remote device.

Time taken to get the result back to the local device after processing is calculated as,

$$T_{download} = \text{size of the code (in kb)/download speed (in kbpms)} \qquad (2)$$

$$\text{Total time taken} = (T_{upload} + T_{execute} + T_{download+network\ delay}) \qquad (3)$$

Network delay is sometime negligible.

In every case, power consumption is calculated as an offloading parameter.

$$P_{upload} = \text{Average power consumption of the device(in watt per ms)} * T_{upload}(\text{in ms}) \qquad (4)$$

$$P_{execute} = \text{Average power consumption of the remote device(in watt per ms)} * T_{execute}(\text{in ms}) \quad (5)$$

$$P_{download} = \text{Average power consumption of the device (in watt per ms)} * T_{download} (\text{in ms}) \quad (6)$$

$$\text{Total Energy Consumption} = (P_{upload} + P_{execute} + P_{download}) \quad (7)$$

3.1 Proposed Algorithm

Step 1: {A1, A2,..., An} are the applications present in the mobile device to offload the {C1, C2,..., Cm} cloudlets.

Step 2: If the power of the local device is sufficient to execute the particular application then it will be executed in the local device or offloading decision will be taken.

Step 3: Application deadline will determine fSList_Level1irst whether the application will be executed in the mobile device or offloaded to the nearby cloudlet.

Step 4: If the user agrees to enhance the deadline of the application, the system will search for cloudlets to offload the task otherwise ask the user to extend the battery life of local device.

Step 5: If the application type = "Game" then
   Offloading Parameter = Money spent by the user
   Highest money paid by the user will be given the high priority to play his game.

Step 6: If the application type = "Numerical" then
   Offloading Parameter = Deadline given by the user
   The lowest deadline given by the user will get the high priority.

Step 7: If the application type = "Searching" then
   Offloading Parameter = No. of elements and order of occurrences of the elements.
Suppose, binary search requires all element to be in sorted order and at the same time if number of elements are less than the time taken to execute will also be less.

Step 8: If the application type = "Sorting" then
   Offloading Parameter = Burst Time of the application
   The lowest burst time containing application will get high priority.

Step 9: These steps will be continued until all applications are executed successfully.

Step 10: Stop

3.2 Flowchart

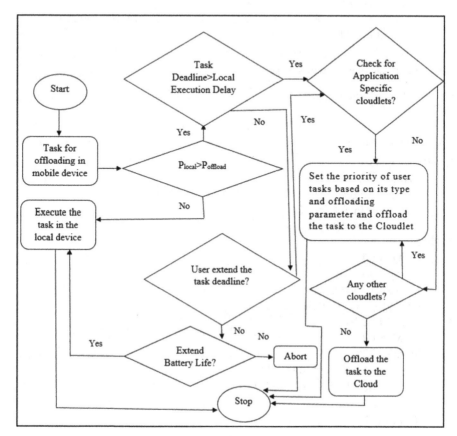

Fig. 2. Flowchart of the Proposed System

3.3 Experimental Configuration Setup

This experiment is carried out in the university laboratory with mobile devices and laptops.

3.3.1 Local Devices

1. Realme 50A
   RAM: 4 GB
   Storage: 128 .mGB
   Processor: MediaTek Helio G85
   OS: Android 11s

2. Honor 9 Lite
   RAM: 3 GB
   Storage: 32 GB
   Processor: Octa-core (4x2.36 GHz Cortex-A53 & 4x1.7 GHz Cortex-A53)
   OS: Android 8.0 (Oreo)

3.3.2   Local Device Network Speed

Download: 1.5 Mbps
Upload: 0.19 Mbps

3.3.3   Cloudlet Devices

1. HP Laptop 430
   RAM: 4 GB
   Storage: 1 TB
   Processor: Intel Core i5
   OS: Windows 10 Professional
2. HP Laptop
   RAM: 4 GB
   Storage: 500 GB
   Processor: Intel Core i3
   OS: Windows 10 Professional
3. Xiaomi 11 Lite NE.
   RAM: 8 GB
   Storage: 128 GB
   Processor: Octa-core Max 2.4 GHz
   OS: Android 11 RKQ1.210503.001

3.3.4   Cloudlet Network Speed

Download: 1.78 Mbps
Upload: 2.84 Mbps

3.3.5   Cloud Server

1. HP Laptop
   RAM: 16 GB
   Storage (SSD): 1 TB
   Processor: Intel Core i7
   OS: Windows 10

3.3.6   Internet Speed

Download: 1.78 Mbps
Upload: 2.84 Mbps

Table 2. Power Consumption of Different Types of Applications using Different Offloading Techniques

Application Type	Offloaded Process Code	Average Power Consumption (watt)				
		Round Robin approach	Proxy server based approach	Application type specific approach	App-Exec Cloudlet based Approach	Dynamic Priority Based Approach (Proposed Method)
Game	Tic-Tac-Toe	0.82	0.80	0.75	0.74	0.70
	Chess					
	Tower of Hanoi					
Numerical Application	Matrix Addition	0.51	0.50	0.484	0.456	0.45
	Matrix Multiplication					
	Finding roots using bisection method					
Searching	Linear Search	0.49	0.47	0.45	0.44	0.4
	Binary Search					
	Interpolation Search					
Sorting	Bubble Sort	0.371	0.36	0.356	0.352	0.35
	Quick Sort					

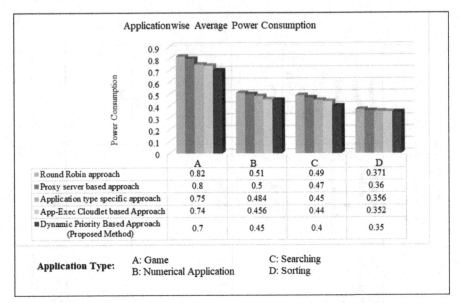

Fig. 3. Power Consumption of Different Types of Applications using Different Offloading Techniques

4 Simulation Result

(See Tables 2, 3 and Figs. 2, 3, 4).

4.1 Result Analysis

The Code size for the Tic-Tac-Toe game is 14 kb. A local device with 0.19 mbps network speed can offload the tic-tac-toe game at 0.0007 ms., when other games are considered and average delay is found, the value changes. Average power consumption of an office PC is 150 W per hour. To execute a code for 0.0007 ms, the power consumption will be 0.002 W. Average power consumption for the gaming application in round robin, proxy server, application type, application execution time and dynamic priority based approach is 0.82 W, 0.8 W, 0.75 W, 0.74 W and 0.70 W. Average power consumption for the numerical application in round robin, proxy server, application type, application execution time and dynamic priority based approach is 0.51 W, 0.50 W, 0.484 W, 0.456 W and 0.45 W. Average power consumption for the searching application in round robin, proxy server, application type, application execution time and dynamic priority based approach is 0.49 W, 0.47 W, 0.45 W, 0.44 W and 0.40 W. Average power consumption for the sorting operation in round robin, proxy server, application type, application execution time and dynamic priority based approach is 0.371 W, 0.36 W, 0.356 W, 0.352 W and 0.350 W. Average delay for the gaming application in round robin, proxy server, application type, application execution time and dynamic priority based approach is 8.52 ms, 8.30 ms, 8.18 ms, 8.14 ms and 8.10 ms. Average delay for the numerical application in round robin, proxy server, application type, application execution time

Table 3. Delays of Different Types of Applications using Different Offloading Techniques

Application Type	Offloaded Process Code	Average Delay (ms)				
		Round Robin approach	Proxy server based approach	Application type specific approach	App-Exec Cloudlet based Approach	Dynamic Priority Based Approach (Proposed Method)
Game	Tic-Tac-Toe	8.52	8.30	8.18	8.14	8.10
	Chess					
	Tower of Hanoi					
Numerical Application	Matrix Addition	7.75	7.70	7.65	7.60	7.55
	Matrix Multiplication					
	Finding roots using bisection method					
Searching	Linear Search	6.50	6.20	6.15	6.10	5.85
	Binary Search					
	Interpolation Search					
Sorting	Bubble Sort	5.45	5.35	5.25	5.25	5.20
	Quick Sort					

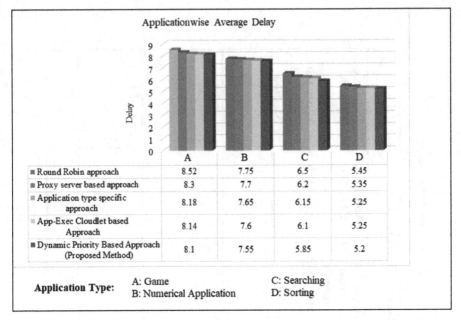

Fig. 4. Delays of Different Types of Applications using Different Offloading Techniques

and dynamic priority based approach is 7.75 ms, 7.7 ms, 7.65 ms, 7.6 ms and 7.55 ms. Average Delay for the searching application in round robin, proxy server, application type, application execution time and dynamic priority based approach is 6.50 ms, 6.20 ms, 6.15 ms, 6.10 ms and 5.85 ms. Average Delay for the sorting application in round robin, proxy server, application type, application execution time and dynamic priority based approach is 5.45 ms, 5.35 ms, 5.25 ms, 5.25 ms and 5.20 ms.

5   Conclusion and Future Works

The proposed system will give the user more usability because as per his choice and selected parameter the tasks are getting executed at the remote location. This will also enhance the energy efficiency of the mobile device. In turn, it will reduce the delay of executing applications. The tasks are executed in the secure cloudlets and hence the user applications along with the data will be kept secured. User mobility is present so that the user can give his application from anywhere and anytime. The corresponding task will be taken and executed at the remote server. The proposed system will perform better than the existing cloudlet selection strategies such as FCFS, Round Robin, Proxy Server Based Approach, Application Type, Application Execution Time Specific and Static Priority Based Approach. The proposed system is dynamic and therefore the user can change the priority of an application at runtime by varying the offloading parameters. The limitation of the work is that self-decision making feature for the priority to be set for the user tasks and based on that the selection of cloudlets is not introduced yet. Therefore, in our future work, we will consider about the dynamic cloudlet selection manager based approach to solve the problems of offloading.

Acknowledgements. We would like to extend our acknowledgement to Prof. Debashis De, Maulana Abul Kalam Azad University of Technology, West Bengal, India and Dr. Anwesha Mukherjee, Assistant Professor, Mahishadal Raj College, West Bengal, India for their guidance and support to carry out this work. We would also like to thank all faculties and researchers of West Bengal State University, University of Kalyani and Center for Mobile Cloud Computing, Maulana Abul Kalam Azad University of Technology, West Bengal, India.

References

1. Mukherjee, A., De, D., Roy, D.G.: A power and latency aware cloudlet selection strategy for multi-cloudlet environment. IEEE Trans. Cloud Comput. **7**(1), 141–154 (2016)
2. Mukherjee, A., De, D.: Low power offloading strategy for femto-cloud mobile network. Eng. Sci. Technol. Int. J. **19**, 260–270 (2016)
3. Mukherjee, A., Deb, P., De, D., Buyya, R.: C2OF2N: a low power cooperative code offloading method for femtolet-based fog network. J. Supercomput. **74**, 2412–2448 (2018)
4. Ghosh, S., Mukherjee, A., Ghosh, S.K., Buyya, R.: Mobi-iost: mobility-aware cloud- fog-edge-iot collaborative framework for time-critical applications. IEEE Trans. Netw. Sci. Eng. **7**(4), 2271–2285 (2019)
5. Nur, F.N., Islam, S., Moon, N.N., Karim, A., Azam, S., Shanmugam, B.: Priority-based offloading and caching in mobile edge cloud. J. Commun. Softw. Syst. **15**(2), 193–201 (2019). https://doi.org/10.24138/jcomss.v15i2.707
6. De, D., Mukherjee, A., Roy, D.G.: Power and delay efficient multilevel offloading strategies for mobile cloud computing. Wirel. Pers. Commun. **112**(4), 2159–2186 (2020). https://doi.org/10.1007/s11277-020-07144-1
7. Madej, A., Wang, N., Athanasopoulos, N., Ranjan, R., Varghese, B.: Priority-based Fair scheduling in edge computing. In: IEEE 4th International Conference on Fog and Edge Computing (ICFEC): Proceedings, pp. 1–10. IEEE (2020)
8. Farooq, M.O.: Priority-based servicing of offloaded tasks in mobile edge computing. In: IEEE 7th World Forum on Internet of Things (WF-IoT). IEEE (2021). https://doi.org/10.1109/WF-IoT51360.2021.9595838
9. Ullah, I., Khan, M.S., St-Hilaire, M., Faisal, M., Kim, J., Kim, S.M.: Task priority-based cached-data prefetching and eviction mechanisms for performance optimization of edge computing clusters. Secur. Commun. Netw. **2021**, 1–10 (2021). https://doi.org/10.1155/2021/5541974
10. Hosseinzadeh, M., Wachal, A., Khamfroush, H., Lucani, D.E.: QoS- aware priority-based task offloading for deep learning services at the edge. In: IEEE 19th Annual Consumer Communications & Networking Conference (CCNC). IEEE (2022). https://doi.org/10.1109/CCNC49033.2022.9700676
11. Sen, P., Pandit, R., Sarddar, D.: App-exec cloudlet based computation offloading in mobile cloud computing. In: International Conference on Applied Computational Intelligence and Analytics (ACIA-2022), NIT-Raipur, 26–27 February 2022 (2022)
12. Maray, M., Shuja, J.: Computation offloading in mobile cloud computing and mobile edge computing: survey, taxonomy, and open issues. Mob. Inf. Syst. 1–17 (2022). https://doi.org/10.1155/2022/1121822
13. Lu, J., Hao, Y., Wu, K., Chen, Y., Wang, Q.: Dynamic offloading for energy-aware scheduling in a mobile cloud. J. King Saud Univ.-Comput. Inf. Sci. **34**(6), 3167–3177 (2022)
14. Mahenge, M.P.J., Li, C., Sanga, C.A.: Energy-efficient task offloading strategy in mobile edge computing for resource-intensive mobile applications. Digital Commun. Netw. **8**, 1048–1058 (2022)

Chaotic Quasi-Oppositional Moth Flame Optimization for Solving Multi-objective Optimal DG Emplacement Problem in Radial Distribution Network

Sneha Sultana[1]([✉])(iD), Sourav Paul[1](iD), Anupriya Singh[1], Ankita Kumari[1], and Provas Kumar Roy[2](iD)

[1] Dr. B. C. Roy Engineering College, Durgapur, India
sneha.sultana@gmail.com
[2] Kalyani Government Engineering College, Kalyani, India
http://www.bcrec.ac.in

Abstract. Many scientists are still concerned about power quality and minimising system losses. By lowering distribution losses, distributed generation (DG) increases overall electricity efficiency and quality. The approach used in this work employs chaotic quasi-oppositional moth flame optimisation (CQOMFO) to determine the appropriate scale of DG in the radial distribution system, hence minimising losses, lowering voltage deviance, and improving the voltage stability index. The aforementioned technique is put to the test on three separate test systems, which include buses of 33, 69, and 118. The multi-objective function has been significantly fine-tuned in order to gain a thorough technical understanding of the CQOMFO algorithm. The results of the computer simulations produced with the assistance of the scheduled approach are contrasted with the earlier optimisation methods put forth by several authors.

Keywords: Distributed generation · radial distribution network · chaotic quasi-oppositional moth flame optimization · power loss reduction · voltage deviation reduction

1 Introduction

Electricity is transferred from the power plant to the distant consumer via a distribution network. The distribution system obtains the load demand from consumers who have requested it. The current radial distribution network (RDN) has reached the demand for high-quality electricity due to the progress of human civilization and technology. This makes the operation of the distribution system more complex, likely to fail, and discontinuous. As a result, the power system's basic goal is prevented. Additionally, the distribution system's bulk power transmission includes a considerable amount of power loss which reduces the effectuality of the power system.

© The Author(s), under exclusive license to Springer Nature Switzerland AG 2024
K. Dasgupta et al. (Eds.): CICBA 2023, CCIS 1956, pp. 142–155, 2024.
https://doi.org/10.1007/978-3-031-48879-5_12

Therefore, researchers are paying careful attention to the distribution network in order to develop answers to the existing problem of fulfilling load demand while also ensuring the dependability of the power system. Modifying or increasing the capacity of the current distribution system network may be one way to address the mentioned problems. However, it won't be a simple task, and it is also not cost-effective. Integrating DG with the current electricity grid is another highly effective and efficient method. An overview of the integration of DG is found in reference [1] and its effects on dynamic behaviour and steady-state operation. Integration of DG contributes to improved reliability and voltage profile while reducing losses of the distribution system. DGs also help with grid distribution by providing both active and reactive electricity. They also contribute to the network's future growth. To address the issue of rural electrification, in ref [1] author proposed expanding the national power system with renewable energy generation and storage. DGs also contribute to grid distribution by supplying both true and complex power electricity.

Many researchers have used analytical approaches to fix the optimal DG allocation (ODGA) problem. References [2–4] used a methodical approach to select the proper DG in the RDN to minimising system loss. In ref [5] introduced a mix-up approach that combines the sensitivity and power factor methods to select the ideal DG position and size. Installation of DG requires in RDN while accounting for loss of power at every bus it is linked to, Dulau et al. [6] recommended an enhanced version of the newton-raphson methodology. Babul et al. [7] suggested the power loss sensitivity (PLS) and non-linear programming (NLP) approaches to achieve optimum placement of the distributed network's DG with the precise size for a significant reduction in system losses. To address losses and voltage stability, Injeti et al. [8] recommended using the load flow analysis approach to address the ODGA issue in RDN.

Analytical approaches for the ODGA issue are easy to use, and have a high convergence rate, but have certain drawbacks when dealing with small-scale optimisation problems. Multi-DG in a variety of load-generation conditions makes the challenge more complex. Analytical techniques frequently deal with issues by taking into account a number of irrational assumptions that, when applied to real systems, result in incorrect output. Moreover, the probabilistic methods utilised to solve the (ODGA) problem need a significant quantity of computing data and processing power. On the other hand, meta-heuristic approaches can produce a solution to the ODGA problem that is nearly optimal when a single or several DG are taken into account, and they can do it with a sufficient level of processing capabilities and computational speed.

In recent years, metaheuristic techniques have been very popular for assessing the appropriate position of DG and its size. To locate DG location in RDN for voltage improvement and integrated power failures optimisation, reference [9–13] approach is based on partial swarm optimisation (PSO). Ahmed et al. [14] used the PSO algorithm to transform the radial segment to a loop while addressing the DG in the RDN. For solving the ODGA problem in the RDN, found in reference [15, 16] used a genetic algorithm (GA). Reference [17] developed a direct technique to estimate the ideal position and appropriate DG size in reference [18] according to a correlation of the fast voltage stability index (VSI) and simulated annealing (SA). For determining the best DG allocation with the fewest system losses, this methodology uses the GA and ds evidence theory. The recommended method was evaluated using the MATLAB and MAT-POWER software, and the results revealed that the DG's emplacement and size at a proper site impact the system breakdown and voltage profile. Sultana *et al.* [19] modified the optimisation strategy based on teaching-learning to discover the ideal DG layout by reducing power loss minimization, voltage fluctuations, and improving the voltage stability index in the system of radial distribution. In order to tackle an optimisation problem, a distribution system that uses DG with size are coupled, Nguyen *et al.* [20] address the cuckoo search technique. With a remarkable decrease in power loss, In [21] proposed the harmony search algorithm (HSA) for locating an assigned DG and an adjusting device both. In order to choose the ideal location for the DG and reduce system loss and voltage variation, Hashemabadi *et al.* [22] employed the bacteria foraging algorithm and the binary genetic algorithm. With the aim of optimising system losses, Mahdad *et al.* [23] developed the adaptive differential search algorithm (DSA), which looks for the ideal place and size for numerous DGs in presence of SVC. Concentrating on the DG's technological and monetary advantages, Injeti *et al.* [24] proposed an improved differential search method (IDSA) to overcome optimisation concerns with DG allocation and sizing. Othman *et al.* [25] improved the site of a voltage-operated DG in a balanced/unbalanced distribution system using the firefly algorithm (FA). To determine DG installation candidate nodes with minimal power loss and voltage deviation, Katamble *et al.* [26] proposed indeterminate reasoning. A hybrid imperialistic competitive algorithm (ICA) technique was presented by Poornazaryan *et al.* [27] in reference to [27] for determining the ideal position of the DG to reduce losses. For discovering the ideal DG location in RDN, In [28] introduced mixed integer conic programming (MICP), which has both higher potential with performance. To reduce loss, enhance the voltage profile, and increase stability while meeting a variety of parameters, Nguyen *et al.* [29] invented the stochastic fractal search algorithm (SFSA). Reddy *et al.* [30] proposed that the power loss index (PLI) and the whale optimisation algorithm (WOA) determine the ideal size DG for minimising losses as well as voltage profile enhancement in RDN. According to the analysis, the primary distribution system DG's voltage profile should be stabilised and the loss minimised [31], are applied in the distributed networks. PSO is a cost-effective technique for regulating the optimal design of grid-connected solar installations presented in [32]. By applying the Integer encoding genetic algorithm [33] introduced a paper on optimal capacitor placement problem economically. Tolba *et al.* [34] suggested voltage-loss-cost-index for maximum annual saving in capacitor allocation of a distribution system. This paper is based on a hybrid version of the PSOGSA optimisation algorithm. Lakshmi *et al.* in [35] employed the hybrid genetic dragonfly algorithm to determine the best position and size of the DG. The algorithm in question was tested on 15 buses and 69 bus distribution systems. Gangil used the backward forward sweep algorithm [36] to calculate real power losses, voltage profiles, and voltage stability indices for each bus in a 33-bus radial distribution network.

Furthermore, "no-free-lunch" theorem depicts that there isn't a single optimization method that works well for a variety of optimisation issues. This inspired the author to develop novel algorithm, chaotic quasi-oppositional moth flame optimization, problem of optimal DG with several objectives placement in RDN along with The potential outline's growth and the voltage stability index. In comparison to other optimization issues, CQOMFO is a relatively recent optimization algorithm that is significantly simpler and more robust. To reduce drop and improve the potential outline and stability index of the distribution system, the chaotic quasi-oppositional moth flame optimisation (CQOMFO) method was utilised in this work. The simulation results produced with the aid of MATLAB software are explained in the later part of the paper in comparison to other methods put forth by other authors. The following method is used to organize the paper. Section 2 describes mathematical formulation. Section 3 provides a description of the chaotic quasi oppositional moth flame optimization algorithm. Section 4 discusses the application of CQOMFO to the ODGA problem. Results and analysis are discussed in Sect. 5. The findings and analysis are discussed in Sect. 5. The conclusion is discussed in Sect. 6.

2   Mathematical Expression

2.1   Multi-objective Function

The employment of various decision-making criteria that are primarily focused on the optimisation of several objective functions characterises multi-objective optimisation, also known as pareto optimisation. This research focuses on how properly scaled and distributed DG can help to reduce system power outage (OF_{PLOSS}) and voltage deviance (OF_{VD}), and voltage stability index (OF_{VSI}) improvement 1 by DG that is sized and distributed optimally. The outcomes of this function with several objectives are as follows:

$$Fitness = MIN\left[OF_{PLOSS} + \varsigma OF_{VD} + \varsigma OF_{VSI}\right] \tag{1}$$

$$OF_{PLOSS} = MIN\left(P_{LOSS}\right) \tag{2}$$

$$OF_{VD} = \sum_{K=1}^{M} \left(V_K - V_{RATED}\right)^2 \tag{3}$$

$$OF_{VSI} = V_K^4 - 4\left(P_{K+1}R_K + Q_{K+1}X_K\right)V_K^2 - 4\left(P_{K+1}X_K - Q_{K+1}R_K\right)^2 \tag{4}$$

$$P_{LOSS} = \sum_{K=1}^{R}\sum_{L=1}^{R} C_{KL}\left(P_K P_L + Q_K P_L\right) + D_{KL}\left(Q_K P_L - P_K Q_L\right) \tag{5}$$

$C_{KL} = \frac{R_{KL}}{|V_K||V_L|}\cos\left(\psi_K - \psi_L\right)$, $D_{KL} = \frac{R_{KL}}{|V_K||V_L|}\sin\left(\psi_K - \psi_L\right)$, Q_K and Q_L, P_K

and P_L are the imaginary and true power of the Kth and L^{th} buses respectively, while V_K and V_{RATED} are the potential and the rated potential of Kth bus; P_{K+1} and Q_{K+1} are $K+1^{th}$ bus power i.e. true and imaginary; V_L is the Lth bus voltage, resistance, reactance of the line connection between the buses K^{th} and L^{th} respectively.

2.2 Constraints

Load Balancing Restrictions: Power produced by DG at a specific bus plus the power supplied by the substation must satisfy the demand at the bus and system losses in order to achieve power equilibrium. The load equilibrium constraints are given below:

$$P_{sub-station} + \sum_{K=1}^{R} P_{DG,K} = \sum_{K=1}^{R} P_{TD,K} + P_{LOSS} \tag{6}$$

$$Q_{sub-station} + \sum_{K=1}^{R} Q_{DG,K} = \sum_{K=1}^{R} Q_{TD,K} + Q_{loss} \tag{7}$$

Bus Voltage Capacity: For guaranteed system stability and power quality, the bus voltage must be between its maximum and minimum voltage limits as given by:

$$V_{K,MIN} \leq V_K \leq V_{K,MAX} \tag{8}$$

Restricted Voltage Angle: By the bus, the voltage angle must fall within the permitted range of angles, including maximum and minimum.

$$\delta_{K,MIN} \leq \delta_K \leq \delta_{K,MAX} \tag{9}$$

3   Optimization Technique

3.1   Moth Flame Optimization

Seyadali Mirjalili originally developed the moth flame optimization (MFO) [37] in 2015, an evolutionary population-based meta-heuristic optimization technique inspired by nature. Elegant insects like moths are quite identical to butterflies. The Larvae Stage and the Adult Stage are the two basic stages they go through during their lifetime. This algorithm is based on the particular way that moths fly at night. Moths are considered to have a special nighttime navigation system called a transverse mechanism.

By maintaining a constant tilt to the moon at night, moths fly using the aforementioned method. This technique makes sure the moths travel in a straight line even when the moon is quite distant from them. Nevertheless, when the moths are brought close to a man-made light source, they have a tendency to travel in a lethal spiral direction. Real-world issues can be resolved by using this specific behaviour.

The position coordinates vector of the moths are defined as variables and are possible solutions according to the MFO algorithm. In basic MFO, individual moths represent potential solutions, and each position is expressed as a matrix of choice variables, as shown below.

$$x = \begin{bmatrix} z_1 \\ z_2 \\ \vdots \\ z_1 \end{bmatrix} = \begin{bmatrix} z_{1,1} & z_{1,2} & \cdots z_{1,n-1} \ z_{1,n} \\ z_{2,1} & \ddots & \cdots\cdots z_{2,n} \\ \vdots & \cdots & \ddots & \cdots & \vdots \\ z_{N-1,1} & \cdots & \ddots & z_{N-1,n} \\ z_{N,1} & z_{N,2} & \cdots & z_{N,n-1} & z_{N,n} \end{bmatrix} \tag{10}$$

where, $z_i = [z_{i,1}, z_{i,2}, \ldots, z_{i,n}]$, $i \in 1, 2, \ldots, n$. The moth and the flame are the two main characters of MFO. To get the desired consequences, the moth must pass across the flame. The logarithmic spiral function, which is described in the equation below, is used to model the spiral movement of the moth.

$$z_i^{k+1} = \begin{cases} \zeta_i.e^{an}.cos(2\pi t) + f_{k_i}(k), i \leq n.fm \\ \zeta_i.e^{an}.cos(2\pi t) + f_{kn.fm}(k), i \geq n.fm \end{cases} \tag{11}$$

where, $\zeta_i = |z_i^k - f_{ki}|$ represents the distance between a moth at point z_i from its corresponding flame f_{ki}.

The MFO algorithm is seen to have a greater convergence rate in its results when compared to other meta-heuristic algorithms, which deliver better quality answers in a relatively short amount of time. After completing the aforementioned process, there is one more issue to be taken into consideration: the position refreshing of the moths with regard to various locations in the specific search space may make it more difficult to find the optimum answers. Using the mathematical formulation given below, where the number of flames is decreased with each successful repetition, this issue can be resolved.

$$N_f = round(\alpha - \beta * \frac{\alpha - \beta}{\phi}) \tag{12}$$

where N_f is the flame number, is then the maximum number of flames at the present time, β is the iteration number currently in use and ϕ is the maximum repetition number.

3.2   Quasi-Oppositional Based Learning

Tizhoosh et al. [38] introduced oppositional-based learning (OBL), a distinct soft computing concept aimed at improving numerical optimisation approaches. It seems to be one of the most effective theories in computational intelligence for solving nonlinear optimisation problems. It does this by enhancing the search capabilities of traditional population-based optimization techniques. The fundamental goal of OBL is to compare the original assumption with the opposite or reciprocal of an estimate or assumption in order to increase the possibility of obtaining a solution more quickly. The first step of the OBL algorithm is initialising the first estimate, which is generated randomly or in accordance with a certain previous overview of the outcome. The best action may be taken in any path, or at a minimum it could be the reverse. The opposing set of estimates is taken into consideration for convergence while iteratively replacing the initial estimates to improve the best option that leads to optimal results.

Opposite Number. Let, the real number be denoted by $P \in [W, X]$ and P^{0N} be its corresponding counterpart number is defined real number by:

$$P^{0N} = W + X - P \tag{13}$$

Opposite Point. Say $A = (Y_1, Y_2, ..., Y_N)$ is a point in N-dimensional space, where, $P_A \in [Y_A, Z_A], A \in 1, 2, ..., N$. The $A^0 = (Y_1{}^0, Y_2{}^0, ... Y_N{}^0)$ opposite point is defined by its components:

$$P_A{}^0 = Y_A + Z_A - P^{0N} \tag{14}$$

Quasi-Opposite Number. Suppose a real number P, in the range of $[Y, Z]$. It is said that the quasi-opposite number is:

$$P^{Q0} = rand(C, \tilde{P}) \tag{15}$$

where C is given by: $C = \frac{Y+Z}{2}$

Point Almost Opposite. Suppose a genuine number P is represented in the range $[A, B]$. The Point Almost Opposite $P_R{}^{Q0}$ is defined as:

$$P_R{}^{Q0} = rand(C_R, \tilde{P}_R) \tag{16}$$

$$\text{where } C_R = \frac{Y_R + Z_R}{2}$$

3.3   Chaotic Number

To get closer to the ideal global solution, current studies are expanding the quasi oppositional based learning (QOBL) to chaotic quasi oppositional based learning (CQOBL). A key factor in enhancing the convergence speed of a metaheuristic algorithm is the random and pseudo-repeating nature of chaos, which performs entire searches at greater speeds. Numerous chaotic maps are taken into consideration to control the MFO's parameters in the CQOMFO optimisation problem. There are a total of 10 chaotic maps chosen for a chaotic set, and each one has a unique behaviour. The starting point of this set has been determined to be 0.7 in the interval from 0 to 1. The many chaotic map behaviours help to solve the issues of local optimum and convergence speed.

4   CQOMFO Applied to Optimum DG Location Issue in RDN

CQOMFO was produced in this study by adding the concept of CQOBL into MFO.

Step 1: The system with limits was assessed for content, size of populations (P_N), the iterations number and DGs in the network that are maximally specified, and the parametric quantity of MFO.

Step 2: The DG size is created at random and is then normalised between the running limitations. In order to satisfy the following capacity restriction, DG's K^{th} value is normalised to P^K:

$$P^K = P^K_{MIN} + R^*(P^K_{MAX} - P^K_{MIN}) \qquad (17)$$

The power rating and site of all installed DGs combine to form a transmitter that reflects the initial state of each ODGA problem factor:

$$SITE_K = [POSITION_{K,1}, POSITION_{K,2}, ... POSITION_{K,N},$$
$$P_{K,1}, P_{K,2}, ... P_{K,N}] \qquad (18)$$

Starting solvent S is formed in relation to population size as follows:

$$P = [P_1, P_2, ... P_K, ... P_N] \qquad (19)$$

Step 3: Install the optimal power flow in order to detect power losses using the BIBC and BCBV matrices [35].

Step 4: Depending upon the present candidate solution in the search space, a logarithmic spiral is defining a little better solution is retained as noble solutions.

Step 5: The opposing population is produced by using the jumping rate, which is provided by:

$$\tilde{x}_1 = A + B - W \qquad (20)$$
$$\tilde{x}_i = P_i + Q_i - X_i \qquad (21)$$

Step 6: Selecting the elite individual N from the present and oppositional based populations. If the experimental value is more than the stated limit, the acquired value is set as the maximum. If the experimental value is less than the lower limit, the obtained value is assigned as the minimum.

Step 7: Until the iteration's maximum count is reached, the points from 3 to 7 are repeated.

5   Solutions and Discussion

The suggested approach CQOMFO is evaluated applied on three separate sets of test systems made up of 33, 69, and 118 buses, with a 12.66 kV operational voltage, to assess its usability and superiority in solving the MFO problem. Simulations are carried out using MATLAB (2022a) software on a PC equipped with 1.8 GHz Dual-Core Intel Core i5, 8 GB 1600 MHz DDR3. The algorithm's population size is set at 50, and its iteration count is set at 100.

5.1   33-Bus Test Radial Networks of Distributing

The CQOMFO approach is evaluated on the 33-bus test RDN, which includes 33 buses and 32 branches, as shown in Figs. 1 and 2. Reference [39] is used to calculate the true power of 3.7 MW and phantom power of 2.3 MVAR power consumption for the systems. For a 33-bus test system with CQOMFO, the voltage stability index, voltage deviation, and power loss are each 0.9701, 0.00082 p.u, and 0.10003 MW, respectively. The results from CQOMFO optimization techniques are shown in Table 1. From there, it is shown that the results obtained by CQOMFO are superior to those obtained by the other methodologies listed. The concurrent improvement of voltage stability and profile significantly contributes to the several objectives of power loss reduction.

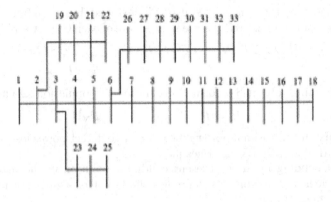

Fig. 1. Topology 33-bus radial distribution test system

Table 1. Summary of the outcomes for the 33-bus RDN

Methodology	DG ideal site	DG optimal dimension	Power Losses in (MW)	Voltage Deviance (p.u.)	Voltage Stability Index	CPU Time in Sec
GA [40]	11,29,30	1.500,4.288,1.071	0.1063	0.0407	0.9490	12.55
PSO [40]	8,13,32	1.176,0.981,0.829	0.1053	0.0335	0.9256	NA
GA/PSO [40]	11,16,32	0.925,0.863,1.200	0.10340	0.0124	0.9508	NA
TLBO [19]	12,28,30	1.1826,1.1913,1.1863	0.1246	0.0011	0.9503	12.63
QOTLBO [19]	13,26,30	1.0834,1.1876,1.1992	0.103409	0.0011	0.9530	12.55
MFO	13,29,31	1.1898,1.16897,0.96472	0.11732	0.001166	0.9300	12.45
CQOMFO	**11,29,31**	**1.0307,1.1345,1.1992**	**0.10003**	**0.00082**	**0.9701**	**12.32**

5.2   69-Bus Test Radial Networks of Distributing

The 69-bus distribution network is made up of 69 buses and 68 branches, seen in Fig. 2, were employed to test the aforementioned aim. Reference [41] is used to determine The worth of each line and corresponding actual power of 3.8 MW and phantom power of 2.69 MVAR consumption for the systems. Table 2 provides the results of the simulation for the methodology. The results are then compared with those of several authors who used various optimization techniques to derive their results. The result shows that the CQOMFO algorithm is more effective than other approaches in terms of voltage deviance 0.00041, power losses 0.0711 MW, and voltage Level of consistency 0.9831 p.u are parallel optimised.

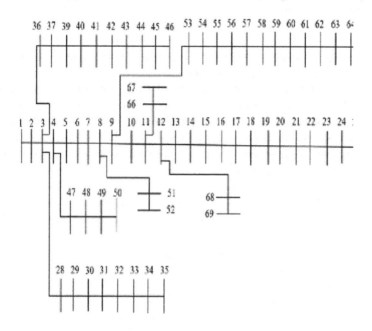

Fig. 2. Topology of the 69-bus test RDN

Table 2. Summary of the outcomes for the 69-bus RDN

Methodology	DG ideal site	DG optimal dimension	Power Losses in (MW)	Voltage Deviance (p.u.)	Voltage Stability Index	CPU Time in Sec
GA [40]	21,62,64	0.9297,1.072,0.9848	0.0890	0.0012	0.9705	NA
PSO [40]	17,61,63	0.9925,1.198,0.7956	0.0832	0.0049	0.9676	NA
GA/PSO [40]	21,61,63	0.9105,1.126,0.8849	0.0811	0.0031	0.9768	NA
TLBO [19]	13,61,62	1.0134,0.9901,1.1601	0.082172	0.0008	0.9745	15.77
QOTLBO [19]	15,61,63	0.8114,1.1470,1.0022	0.080585	0.0007	0.9769	15.71
MFO	15,61,62	0.9005,1.1002,1.03305	0.081012	0.00049	0.9770	15.33
CQOMFO	**15,61,63**	**0.8244,1.187,1.0022**	**0.0711**	**0.00041**	**0.9831**	**15.10**

5.3   118-Bus Test Radial Networks of Distributing

To demonstrate the superiority of the CQOMFO procedure, it's used to the 118 bus test system Fig. 3, which includes of 118 buses and 116 branches. The sys-

Table 3. Summary of the outcomes for the 118-bus RDN

Methodology	DG ideal site	DG optimal dimension	Power Losses in (MW)	Voltage Deviance (p.u.)	Voltage Stability Index	CPU Time in Sec
LFSA [41]	36,48,56,75, 88, 103,116	7.4673,0.7109,3.6739,2.824, 2.2979,5.0503,0.4606	0.9001885	NA	0.7561	25.29
TLBO [19]	35,48,65,72, 88, 99,111	3.2462,2.8864,2.4307,3.305, 1.9917,1.6040,3.5984	0.705898	0.0327	0.8548	20.91
QOTLBO [19]	43,49,54,74, 80, 94,111	1.5880,3.8459,0.9852,3.1904, 3.1632,1.9527, 3.60132	0.6775881	0.0233	0.8794	20.85
MFO	35,48,65,74, 85, 99,111	3.3011,2.8324,2.8743,3.2354, 1.9908,1.6421,3.5984	0.70001	0.0298	0.8599	20.55
CQOMFO	43,49,54,74, 80, 94,111	1.9803,3.535,0.6752,3.1303, 3.1631,1.19526,3.6013	0.66032	0.0111	0.8905	20.12

tem's basic parameters are 100 and 11. There are two separate phantom, actual
power requirements of 17.04 Mega-VAR and 22.70 Megawatts. The load value
for the line is obtained from [42]. The simulation results taking into consideration 7DGs at various location is displayed in Table 3. For the system under
consideration, the values for network losses, voltage deviation and stable voltage
rating are 0.66032 MW, 0.0111 p.u, and 0.8905, ideally. When compared to other
authors' suggested approaches, the result shows its effectiveness by CQOMFO.

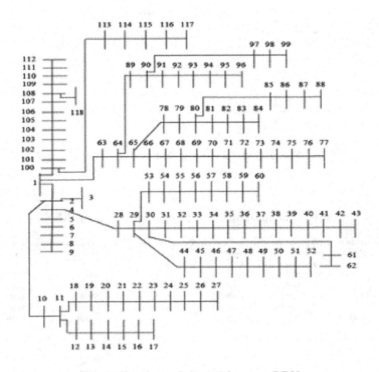

Fig. 3. Topology of the 118-bus test RDN

6   Conclusion

The study discusses MFO and CQOMFO for locating the ideal location for running DG using the appropriate RDN size for multiple-purpose optimising while also satisfying system constraints. The 33, 69, and 118 bus test systems with many DG at various sites are used for the methodological analysis. The outcomes demonstrate effectiveness of the recommended CQOMFO addresses the multi-purpose optimals DG installation issue for RDN. The outcomes demonstrate conclusively that CQOMFO intersects to higher-quality solutions while MFO offers much less satisfactory solutions when compared to CQOMFO. Results from other methodologies are compared to those that were obtained. The results show that the suggested CQOMFO achieves better outcomes in solving the CQOMFO problem with simultaneous loss optimization and improvement to the voltage profiles in the RDN.

References

1. Robert, F.C., Gopalan, S.: Low cost, highly reliable rural electrification through a combination of grid extension and local renewable energy generation. Sustain. Cities Soc. **42**, 344–354 (2018)
2. Viral, R., Khatod, D.K.: An analytical approach for sizing and siting of DGs in balanced radial distribution networks for loss minimization. Int. J. Electr. Power Energy Syst. **67**, 191–201 (2015)
3. Hung, D.Q., Mithulananthan, N., Lee, K.Y.: Optimal placement of dispatchable and nondispatchable renewable DG units in distribution networks for minimizing energy loss. Int. J. Electr. Power Energy Syst. **55**, 179–186 (2014)
4. Acharya, N., Mahat, P., Mithulananthan, N.: An analytical approach for DG allocation in primary distribution network. Int. J. Electric. Power Energy Syst. **28**(10), 669–678 (2006)
5. Mirzaei, M., Jasni, J., Hizam, H., Wahab, N.I.A., Mohamed, S.E.G.: An analytical method for optimal sizing of different types of dg in a power distribution system. In: 2014 IEEE International Conference on Power and Energy (PECon), pp. 309–314. IEEE (2014)
6. Dulău, L.I., Abrudean, M., Bică, D.: Optimal location of a distributed generator for power losses improvement. Procedia Technol. **22**, 734–739 (2016)
7. Vijay Babu, P., Singh, S.P.: Optimal placement of DG in distribution network for power loss minimization using NLP & PLS technique. Energy Procedia **90**, 441–454 (2016)
8. Injeti, S.K., Prema Kumar, N.: A novel approach to identify optimal access point and capacity of multiple DGs in a small, medium and large scale radial distribution systems. Int. J. Electric. Power Energy Syst. **45**(1), 142–151 (2013)
9. Kayal, P., Chanda, C.K.: Placement of wind and solar based DGs in distribution system for power loss minimization and voltage stability improvement. Int. J. Electric. Power Energy Syst. **53**, 795–809 (2013)
10. Zongo, O.A., Oonsivilai, A.: Optimal placement of distributed generator for power loss minimization and voltage stability improvement. Energy Procedia **138**, 134–139 (2017)

11. Tawfeek, T.S., Ahmed, A.H., Hasan, S.: Analytical and particle swarm optimization algorithms for optimal allocation of four different distributed generation types in radial distribution networks. Energy Procedia **153**, 86–94 (2018)
12. HassanzadehFard, H., Jalilian, A.: Optimal sizing and location of renewable energy based DG units in distribution systems considering load growth. Int. J. Electric. Power Energy Syst. **101**, 356–370 (2018)
13. Prakash, D.B., Lakshminarayana, C.: Multiple DG placements in distribution system for power loss reduction using PSO algorithm. Procedia Technol. **25**, 785–792 (2016)
14. Ahmed, A.H., Hasan, S.: Optimal allocation of distributed generation units for converting conventional radial distribution system to loop using particle swarm optimization. Energy Procedia **153**, 118–124 (2018)
15. Zongo, O.A., Oonsivilai, A.: Optimal placement of distributed generator for power loss minimization and voltage stability improvement. Energy Procedia **138**, 134–139 (2017)
16. Din, F.U, Ahmad, A., Ullah, H., Khan, A., Umer, T., Wan, S.: Efficient sizing and placement of distributed generators in cyber-physical power systems. J. Syst. Architect. **97**, 197–207 (2019)
17. Kanaan, H.A.M., EL-Gazaar, M.M., Mehanna, A.: Optimal location and sizing of SVC considering system losses, voltage division and system overload. J. Al-Azhar Univ. Eng. Sect. **15**(57), 1040–1051 (2020)
18. Zhao, Q., Wang, S., Wang, K., Huang, B.: Multi-objective optimal allocation of distributed generations under uncertainty based on ds evidence theory and affine arithmetic. Int. J. Electric. Power Energy Syst. **112**, 70–82 (2019)
19. Sultana, S., Roy, P.K.: Multi-objective quasi-oppositional teaching learning based optimization for optimal location of distributed generator in radial distribution systems. Int. J. Electric. Power Energy Syst. **63**, 534–545 (2014)
20. Nguyen, T.T., Truong, A.V., Phung, T.A.: A novel method based on adaptive cuckoo search for optimal network reconfiguration and distributed generation allocation in distribution network. Int. J. Electric. Power Energy Syst. **78**, 801–815 (2016)
21. Muthukumar, K., Jayalalitha, S.: Optimal placement and sizing of distributed generators and shunt capacitors for power loss minimization in radial distribution networks using hybrid heuristic search optimization technique. Int. J. Electric. Power Energy Syst. **78**, 299–319 (2016)
22. Hashemi Zadeh, S.A., Zeidabadi Nejad, O., Hasani, S., Gharaveisi, A.A., Shahgholian, G.H.: Optimal DG placement for power loss reduction and improvement voltage profile using smart methods. Int. J. Smart Electric. Eng. **1**(03), 141–147 (2012)
23. Mahdad, B., Srairi, K.: Adaptive differential search algorithm for optimal location of distributed generation in the presence of SVC for power loss reduction in distribution system. Eng. Sci. Technol. Int. J. **19**(3), 1266–1282 (2016)
24. Injeti, S.K.: A pareto optimal approach for allocation of distributed generators in radial distribution systems using improved differential search algorithm. J. Electric. Syst. Inf. Technol. **5**(3), 908–927 (2018)
25. Othman, M.M., El-Khattam, W., Hegazy, Y.G., Abdelaziz, A.Y.: Optimal placement and sizing of voltage controlled distributed generators in unbalanced distribution networks using supervised firefly algorithm. Int. J. Electric. Power Energy Syst. **82**, 105–113 (2016)
26. Katamble, S., Palled, S., Gaikwad, V., Shetty, V.: Reconfiguration of distribution system by optimal placement of distributed generator. Int. J. Sci. Eng. Res. **10**, 192–197 (2019)

27. Poornazaryan, B., Karimyan, P., Gharehpetian, G.B., Abedi, M.: Optimal allocation and sizing of DG units considering voltage stability, losses and load variations.
Int. J. Electric. Power Energy Syst. **79**, 42–52 (2016)

28. Home-Ortiz, J.M., Pourakbari-Kasmaei, M., Lehtonen, M., Mantovani, J.R.S.:
Optimal location-allocation of storage devices and renewable-based DG in distribution systems. Electric Power Syst. Res. **172**, 11–21 (2019)

29. Nguyen, T.P., Vo, D.N.: A novel stochastic fractal search algorithm for optimal allocation of distributed generators in radial distribution systems. Appl. Soft Comput.
70, 773–796 (2018)

30. Veera Reddy, V.C., et al.: Optimal renewable resources placement in distribution
networks by combined power loss index and whale optimization algorithms. J.
Electric. Syst. Inf. Technol. **5**(2), 175–191 (2018)

31. Shahzad, M., Akram, W., Arif, M., Khan, U., Ullah, B.: Optimal siting and sizing of
distributed generators by strawberry plant propagation algorithm. Energies **14**(6),
1744 (2021)

32. Kefale, H.A., Getie, E.M., Eshetie, K.G.: Optimal design of grid-connected solar
photovoltaic system using selective particle swarm optimization. Int. J. Photoen-
ergy **2021** (2021)

33. Ketut Suryawan, I., Saputra, I.D.: Optimization of capacitor placement in radial
distribution system using integer encoding genetic algorithm. In: 2020 International
Conference on Applied Science and Technology (iCAST), pp. 544–548. IEEE (2020)

34. Tolba, M.A., Zaki Diab, A.A., Tulsky, V.N., Abdelaziz, A.Y.: VLCI approach for
optimal capacitors allocation in distribution networks based on hybrid PSOGSA
optimization algorithm. Neural Comput. Appl. **31**(8), 3833–3850 (2019)

35. Naga Lakshmi, G.V., Jayalaxmi, A., Veeramsetty, V.: Optimal placement of distribution generation in radial distribution system using hybrid genetic dragonfly
algorithm. Technol. Econ. Smart Grids Sustain. Energy **6**, 1–13 (2021)

36. Gangil, G., Goyal, S.K., Srivastava, M.: Optimal placement of DG for power losses
minimization in radial distribution system using backward forward sweep algorithm. In: 2020 IEEE International Conference on Advances and Developments in
Electrical and Electronics Engineering (ICADEE), pp. 1–6. IEEE (2020)

37. Mirjalili, S.: Moth-flame optimization algorithm: a novel nature-inspired heuristic
paradigm. Knowl.-Based Syst. **89**, 228–249 (2015)

38. Tizhoosh, H.R.: Opposition-based learning: a new scheme for machine intelligence.
In: International Conference on Computational Intelligence for Modelling, Control
and Automation and International Conference on Intelligent Agents, Web Technologies and Internet Commerce (CIMCA-IAWTIC 2006), vol. 1, pp. 695–701.
IEEE (2005)

39. Kashem, M.A., Ganapathy, V., Jasmon, G.B., Buhari, M.I.: A novel method for
loss minimization in distribution networks. In: DRPT2000. International Conference on Electric Utility Deregulation and Restructuring and Power Technologies.
Proceedings (Cat. No. 00EX382), pp. 251–256. IEEE (2000)

40. Moradi, M.H., Abedini, M.: A combination of genetic algorithm and particle swarm
optimization for optimal DG location and sizing in distribution systems. Int. J.
Electric. Power Energy Syst. **34**(1), 66–74 (2012)

41. Chakravorty, M., Das, D.: Voltage stability analysis of radial distribution networks.
Int. J. Electric. Power Energy Syst. **23**(2), 129–135 (2001)

42. Zhang, D., Zhengcai, F., Zhang, L.: An improved TS algorithm for loss-minimum
reconfiguration in large-scale distribution systems. Electric Power Syst. Res. **77**(5–
6), 685–694 (2007)

Authentication and Access Control by Face Recognition and Intrusion Detection System

Indrajit Das[1,2](✉), Papiya Das[1,2], Ritabrata Roychowdhury[2], and Subhrapratim Nath[2]

[1] Department of Information Technology, Meghnad Saha Institute of Technology, Kolkata, India
indrajitdas1979@hotmail.com
[2] Department of Computer Science and Engineering, Meghnad Saha Institute of Technology, Kolkata, India
subhrapratim.nath@ieee.org

Abstract. The main worry with the rapid growth of technology has been cyber assaults. To counter these threats, sophisticated security systems have been created, however none of them function completely error-free. This study uses face detection and recognition by Haar cascade classifier and LBPH for authentication initially, and then an intrusion detection system (IDS) using machine learning algorithm like FNT and KNN can identify fraudulent behavior. The typical accuracy for face detection is 90.2%. Whereas in recognition, it can be demonstrated that LBPH performs better in both still images and video than Eigen faces with respect to detection accuracy and execution speed. With a false positive rate of 1.6%, known and unknown intrusions accuracy detected by FNT is 97.2%. The detection rates for DOS, probe, U2R, and R2L in the known intrusion classifier by KNN are 98.7%, 97.4%, 97.8%, and 96.6%, respectively, whereas the false positive rates are 0.4%, 0.0.1.45%, 2.19%, and 1.97% respectively. The proposed known intrusion mechanism is demonstrated to outperform competing methods. The percentage of intrusion detection in the unknown intrusion detected by C-means clustering is 98.6%, and the rate of false positives is 1.32%.

Keywords: Haar-cascade Classifier · LBPH · Eigenfaces · IDS · FNT · KNN · C-means clustering

1 Introduction

The Internet's integration into our daily lives has created several new opportunities in a variety of fields, including commerce, entertainment, education, and medicine. People rely largely on the Internet to conduct their daily business, which includes a variety of beneficial applications like online banking, online marketing, online advertising, online shopping, online learning, and online payment services (paying rents, bills of consumed utilities like gas, electricity, etc.). For each of these actions, highly secure Internet transmission is required. Information privacy and authentication on the Internet has been continuously bothered and endangered by invasions and unwanted access, as shown by recent trends in the cyber world. Although there are numerous effective encryption techniques that can be used to stop network breaches via the Internet for privacy, none of them

K. Dasgupta et al. (Eds.): CICBA 2023, CCIS 1956, pp. 156–170, 2024.
https://doi.org/10.1007/978-3-031-48879-5_13

provide complete performance assurance. For that purpose, in this paper first authentication is done by face recognition after that malicious activity can be detect by intrusion detection system (IDS) with the help of machine learning algorithm. Algorithms that use facial recognition are aimed to ease the burden of verification and authentication. When confirmation is required, an image of the subject's face is fed into a facial recognition machine, which is then assigned a claimed identity. The system is to either refuse the claim or accept it. Creating an IDS with a perfect track record is extremely challenging, if not impossible. There are numerous security holes in modern systems. All forms of intrusion are not yet fully understood. Intruders can be identified faster if these attacks can be detected quickly and contain the resulting harm. Consequently, improving network security requires creating an effective IDS.

1.1 Face Recognition

Face detection and identification are practical and trustworthy ways to authenticate a person's identity [1]. This element could be used in biometric identification and security techniques. Face recognition methods have been used over the years with many approaches, including the use of neural networks to recognize faces, elastic template matching [2], algebraic moments, isodensity, lines, and others. The major objective of face recognition is to teach the computer what a face looks like. Face recognition is essentially controlled by a few principles, including the nose position and how far apart each eye is. From an image or video stream, face position and size are captured, and this information is logged. Some hindrances encountered with face detection and recognition, such as convenient conditions during imaging may make it difficult to tell the foreground from the background.

This problem might be resolved by training a good template with larger and better training samples. This technique cannot tell a fake face from a real one and a face printed on paper [3]. Therefore, in this manner, a real face cannot be verified by a typical camera. The process of face recognition can be carried out after the face detection step. Face recognition has an advantage over iris or fingerprint recognition because it may be done without the subject's consent, whereas the latter two require it. The system can identify the needed face in any lighting situation based on geometry data, the subject's skin tone, and other data collected by any facial recognition algorithm. The image background can obstruct normal processing and facial recognition procedures that depend on skin tone. Post-processing could be significantly impacted if the face is not accurately separated from the image's background. Methodologies for recognizing faces based on skin tone may be preferable to others because, despite considerations like changing facial expressions, moving faces, and other such things, skin tone is unaffected by posture and size. This study compares the accuracy levels attained by the LBPH [5] and Eigenfaces [6] face recognition algorithms. Using the Haar-classifier, photos of faces (positive images) and images without faces must be used to train the classifier (negative images). If Haar-like features are discovered after the classifier has scanned an image, a face is said to have been discovered. The application of Eigenfaces by a collection of eigenvectors is one approach of face recognition. All the images needed to create a matrix are represented by the eigenfaces themselves. Comparison of the premise sets representations of faces can help with classification. Utilizing the Local Binary Patterns

Histogram (LBPH), which focuses on the description of texture aspects and represents the specifics of the facial traits displayed, is another technique for face identification.

1.2 Intrusion Detection System

IDS fundamentally acts as a security system that counters attacks produced by intruders against hosts or networks connected to the Internet. It helps with identifying and detecting the use, access, abuse, alteration, and destruction of information systems by unauthorized parties. IDSs are classified in two categories: anomaly-based detection and signature-based detection. At the point when known attacks are contrasted with a data set of significant assault marks, they can be successfully perceived under the mark-based classification. These rule-based expert systems primarily use the idea of signature matching for intrusion detection. Attack signatures list specific characteristics of the attack, which may take the form of a behavioral profile, a code fragment, or a series of system call patterns. These systems have low false positive rates and excellent detection accuracies for known intrusion types, but they are unable to identify unidentified attack patterns. The anomaly-based strategy, which is covered next, can be used to get around this scheme's requirement for routine updating and maintenance of the attack signature database. In the category that is based on anomalies, the traffic profile and usual behavior are first modeled and then updated often. An anomaly is defined as any observed departure from the regular trend. In essence, these systems encode every network connection flow as a function of several features and record this over time. An anomaly is defined as any recorded trait that signals an aberrant value for any connection flow. These systems exhibit great accuracy in identifying unknown intrusion types, but due to their inherent inability to distinguish between intrusive actions and changing typical traffic profiles, they frequently show significant false positive rates.

1.3 Classification of Attacks

Denial of Service (DoS)
This is an example of a classic attack that uses bandwidth and resource depletion. Due to the lack of services, authorized users are incapable to use the scheme. The adversaries essentially overwhelm the network with unrestricted service requests, which finally results in circumstances where services are disrupted. The offender either takes advantage of internet protocols or creates data that is forwarded to the object machine through the network in a way that reduces their resources [7].

Scanning Attacks
Here the offenders investigate and use well-known network vulnerabilities to find the weak host or system. Adversaries transmit several scan packets using tools like nmap, devil, etc. to gather crucial information and a description of the hosts; more information is provided in [8]. Open scans, stealthy scans, sweep scans, and other classifications are among the 19 that have been described here. Typically scanning incursions can be either active or passive by nature. Ipsweep, reset scan, SYN scan, and other attacks, to name

a few, are examples of potential future assaults that might be sparked utilizing these probing tactics.

R2L

It provides the opponent can transmit information to the target machine over any network. Imap attack [9], Dictionary attack, Xlock assault [10], and others are a few examples of this type of attack.

U2R

It is another illustration of a low-frequency attack category in which a series of exploits on the objective computer are utilized as a point of entry to obtain access to that machine. Attacks on Ffconfig [11], rootkits [12], loadmodules [13] are examples.

2 Literature Survey

2.1 Authentication

Mayur Surve et al. [14] created a model that captures real-time images from cameras. Then it employs several face detection and facial recognition methods. Additionally, they developed a GUI that, with a single click, can capture photos, build datasets, and include datasets. To identify the face in the image, they utilized the Haar cascade technique.

Palanivel N et al. [15] developed a system that verifies people's presence by identifying their face features and producing the attendance data themselves. To assess the features of the faces, they applied the K-means clustering algorithmic rule. The SVM approach is then used to identify the properties of the photographs. With fewer traits, it may nevertheless fulfill high identification displaying requirements.

D. Jenif et al. [16] introduced a scheme that requires image processing approaches for facial recognition. To contrast with the staved catalogue, the improved picture is used. Four modules were used to carry out the first procedure: image capture, group photo cleavage, face identification and comparison.

Automatic presence management system by face identification technique is a method that M. Kasiselvanathan et al. have developed [17]. The technology used to identify the facial features and find the face. This process utilizes the Eigen Faces algorithm. The method uses changing rules to recognize faces in addition to the area occupied by the human face.

Xiang-Yu et al. [18] overcome the issue of not having correct guidance to recognize a squat face under unlimited circumstances in predicted an identification scheme. The Haar-feature classifier has been employed to remove the attribute from the primordial database. In addition, the method is applied to the method for removing the feature. The use of facial detection can be used to achieve private recognition, according to the currently available probing technologies.

V.D.A. Kumar et al. [19] proposed a concept for facial recognition is put forth to identify people and notify the system when someone is discovered at a certain place under Surveillance cameras. A directory of all people who need to be located is kept on the server. A signal is sent to the device in charge and the presence of the suspect is monitored related to video stream by each camera when they are identified in a specific clip. Therefore, locating an individual becomes a matter of identifying face images in the video stream and comparing them to the database's already-existing photos.

The video tracking method suggested by V.D.A. Kumar et al. [20] is regarded as the most significant development for tracking and protection domain. Facial recognition in video tracking also gradually improves protection and defense. The primary goal of the paper is to explore and evaluate the various methods for facial recognition. Face detection is carried out by efficiently segmenting the face into different areas and combining its numerous traits and dependencies. VGG-face algorithm allows for accurate face recognition despite lighting differences.

The two-factor authentication technique established by R. Venkatesan et al. [21] increases the safety of conducting business online. Facial recognition and proxy detection are incorporated into this mechanism before the UPI PIN is entered. Since the method employed in this research embeds 128 feature points of the consumer's face, it increases the efficiency of the technique and greatly improves the safety and effectiveness of facial recognition. Triple DES encryption is employed during the verification of information transmission. The proposed method is more effective than previous attempts while still being easy to use due to its straightforward user interface.

2.2 Access Control

The IDS methods can be divided as Signature-based or Anomaly-based to detect intrusion.

Signature Based IDS

In high dimensional association rule mining, the relationship between related events is clearly established by the identified rules [22]. In this technique, the dataset is used to represent the logic, and the outcomes show many incursion types. This method accurately and confidently determines attack signatures. On the 1998 DARPA dataset, DR of 99.1%, 95.3%, 75.2%, and 87.1% were attained for known intrusion.

In [23], an ensemble ML strategy made up of 6 K-NN and 6 SVM classifiers is created, and the output from all 12 models is combined using 3 different methods. In the first scheme, weights generated by PSO are combined; in the 2nd scheme, local unimodal sampling is used; and in the third scheme, WMA is utilized to combine the results produced by every classifier. Compared to its rivals, the former method, LUS-PSO-WMA, delivers greater accuracy. According to the reported results, the accuracy for the Normal, Probe, DoS, U2R, and R2L kinds on the KDD'99 dataset is 83.6878%, 96.8576%, 98.8534%, 99.8029%, and 84.7615%, respectively.

Anomaly Based IDS

For creating an IDS framework using the KDD"99 dataset [24], uses the PSO-SVM approach. Here, binary PSO (BPSO), which selected the attributes from the featured dataset, and information gain are the two feature selection techniques applied. The detection rate 99.4%, 99.5%, 98.9%, and 98.7%, respectively, for DoS, Probe, R2L, and U2R types.

3 Proposed Algorithm and Methodology

The work focuses on internet security. First, a face-recognition authentication process verifies the user. After successful authentication the malicious activity will be identified by Intrusion detection system with the help of machine learning.

3.1 Authentication

The authentication process that has been proposed in this article is face detection, recognition and making of database.

Face Detection

The Haar classifier [4] was chosen because of its rapidity. It can be compared to a funnel where each area of a picture is examined utilizing a collection of classifiers called Haar Features that serve as a funnel known as the Haar Cascade. Regions of an image without faces are promptly removed by the top classifiers in the cascade.

As an optimization, the Haar features get progressively more complicated down in the cascade. If the characteristics don't resemble a face, the photos are dismissed as soon as feasible. An image in grayscale has its integral calculated by the Haar detector. Each pixel in the integral image holds the total of the intensities of all the pixels in the original image to its left and above. Equation (1) provides a mathematical illustration of the haar classifier.

$$\text{Sum}(S) = P(Q) + P(R) - P(S) - P(T) \tag{1}$$

where Q, R, S, and T: all make up the whole image P.

Three distinct categories of rectangular characteristics are each utilized by a Haar-object detector, one at a time: To find an object, use four rectangle combinations, lines, and edges. To define an object and detect it, a Haar-object detector is able to recognize several hundred square characteristics and group them into zones. Each of these features can be identified in an integral image relatively fast, and for every video frame, thousands of features are checked thousands of times.

Database Creation

The most crucial step in the procedure is database building. To find a face in a picture or video frame, utilize the Haar cascade face detector. The photograph is saved in a folder after a face has been found. The database contains the names of the people along with an id. The photos of the faces in the file are kept with the associated ids. The photographs are reduced in size and made grayscale. For the next level to function effectively, grayscale photographs make the intensities much more noticeable.

Face Recognition

Face Recognition Using LBPH

A type of visual course used for computer vision classification is called a local binary pattern. It has been discovered to be a significant determinant in texture classification. Each photo is evaluated as a framework of micro-patterns using the LBP operator. The face is then listed according to the LBP histogram, which only encrypts the details of micro-patterns. The 3×3 neighborhood is used by the original LBP to name the pixels in respect to the central pixel value. The general characteristics, such as edges, lines, and points, can be defined by a number in a certain numerical scale. Therefore, to use a set of values collected a priori, it is possible to identify objects in an image.

LBP is defined in Eq. 2 as:

$$LBP(g_d, h_d) = \sum_{q=0}^{1} 2Q_s(p_q - p_d) \tag{2}$$

where (g_d, h_d) is the center pixel and its brightness is pc, and the brightness of adjacent pixels are p_q.

w(.) is a sign function defined as:

$$w(x) = 1 \quad \text{if } x \geq 0 \text{ and}$$
$$w(x) = 0 \quad \text{otherwise} \tag{3}$$

In a histogram, the total LBPH value is shown as Eq. 4

$$G(r) = \sum_{i=0}^{p} \sum_{j=0}^{q} e(LBP_{x,y}(i, j), r), r \in (0, r) \tag{4}$$

where x is sampling points and y is the radius.

Face Recognition Using Eigenfaces

Based on Principle Component Analysis, this process (PCA) is employed in pattern recognition. The connected vectors of large dimensions are swapped out for disconnected vectors of lesser dimensions in PCA. Calculations based on the data set are also necessary. PCA is favorable because it is more effective, requires less memory, and is less sensitive to noise. Eigenfaces extract the features of the face.

Face's key segments are computed by training data. The projection of it into the area framed by the eigenfaces is used to achieve recognition. A correlation based on the eigenface's and eigenvector's Euclidian distance. The person is recognized if the distance is small enough. Conversely, if it's too large, the picture is perceived as belonging to a specific person for whom the framework needs to be developed.

The faces in the training dataset are the primary components which are first calculated. To make it easier to recognize, the predicted face onto the area created by the eigenfaces. It determines the Euclidean distance between the appropriate eigenface and its corresponding eigenvector. The face is recognized if the value is insignificant; else, it is not.

Methodology

The proposed authentication methodology is done by face detection and recognition shown in Fig. 1.

Step1: load the input picture.

Step2: Convert the RGB to Grayscale

Step3: Putting the Haar Cascade Classifier in operation.

Step4: The LBPH classifier is loaded once the cascade classifier has spotted the face.

Step5: The face in the image is separated into multiple blocks when the camera captures it.

Step6: Following that, the Histogram is determined for each block. A single vector is created by concatenating the histogram of block local binary patterns.

Step7: If there are further faces in the image, the aforementioned procedure is repeated; otherwise, LBP is used to represent face recognition.

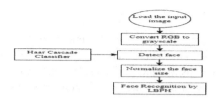

Fig. 1. Proposed Face Recognition method

3.2 Access Control

Access control is done by the Intrusion detection system. For that purpose, it utilizes a variety of ML algorithms to detect different types of intrusion like DOS, U2R, R2L and Probe. The prior probability of various classes used in Naive Bayes. In ensemble learning, the data are merged using a variety of parameters, such as voting, averaging, and stacking, to provide a final forecast. KNN calculates the distance using the Euclidean distance method to the closest neighbor throughout the learning process; in some techniques, however, the range formula is improved by contrasting it with other similar equations to get the best outcomes. Genetic algorithm applications consider the population's growth and generational makeup, and the likelihood of mutation and crossover. Fuzzy logic is incapable of recognizing patterns through machine learning and neural networks. The PSO method, which is efficiently a population-based search, is used to optimize the FNT's settings.

Considering this, it may be deduced from Fig. 2 KNN and Artificial Neural Networks employing Flexible Neural Trees (FNT) will perform better than the alternative methodologies, according to the aforementioned statistics.

K – Nearest Neighbor

It has been one of the easiest and most basic ones. It's also dependent on the learning by equivalence method and performs well even when there was hardly any prior knowledge of the data distribution. The training samples are described by 'm' dimensional numerical properties. As a result, an m-dimensional pattern space is where all the points are kept.

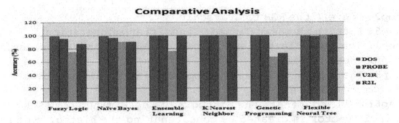

Fig. 2. A comparison of various machine learning algorithms in IDS

The pattern space for the k training attributed is examine that is relatively close to the unidentified sample while dealing with unknown data samples. Euclidean distance is what is meant by "closeness".

Flexible Neural Tree

For issue solving, a generic and improved flexible neural tree (FNT) model is suggested. It is possible to build and develop a flexible neural tree model using the specified instruction/operator sets. This method permits selection of input parameters, overlayer linkages, and multiple node initiation methods. Using evolutionary algorithms with precise instructions, a tree-structure based structure could evolve. Algorithms for parameter optimization could be used to fine-tune the parameters encoded in the structure. The suggested approach combines the two optimizations. It starts with arbitrary frameworks and accompanying parameters, tries to enhance the framework, and then adjusts the parameters whenever an improved structure is found. This cycle keeps going until a sufficient solution is right or the time limit expires (Fig. 3).

Methodology

Step1: Utilize FNT to identify known and unknown intrusions.
Step2: If Y is a recognized form of attacks, classify DOS, Probe, U2R, and R2L using the KNN method.
Step3: Otherwise for detection of unknown intrusion, pass Y to the C-means Clustering technique for cluster.
Step4: Let Zi represent the database's largest number of intrusion records across all classes.
Step5: If Zi > fixed threshold then it leaves the database and send it to the new classifier.
Step6: Include the new classifier in the known intrusion database.

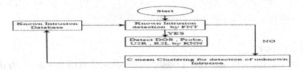

Fig. 3. Proposed Access control method

4 Experimental Result

4.1 Authentication

On a Windows 11 pc running the Intel 5th generation operating system, the experiment was carried out using Python IDLE 3.7. The processor ran at a 2.2 GHZ frequency. Information was kept in a SQLite 3 database. Images of a face are shown in Fig. 4's first row in several perspectives. The next column proves that the pictures were recognized appropriately.

Fig. 4. Face Detection in various poses [25]

Both still photos and video recordings were used in the face detection method. The cropped face regions are illustrated in Fig. 5.

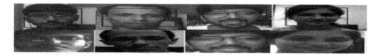

Fig. 5. Cropping detected faces [25]

The learner algorithm is used to these clipped faces in order to prepare it for face recognition. LBPH algorithms are used to do face recognition. Figure 6 demonstrates the results obtained using the LBPH algorithms.

Fig. 6. Recognized Faces [25]

A range of face photos and videos (from 1 to 2000) were used in the investigation. The Haar cascade classifier's face detection average efficiency is 90.2%, which is shown in Fig. 7. The graph in Figs. 8, 9, 10, and 11 displays a comparison of the outcomes utilizing both the Eigenfaces and LBPH algorithms. The average face recognition rate of still images for LBPH and Eigenfaces are 81.2% and 73.4% respectively. Whereas the face recognition rate of video for LBPH and Eigenfaces are 88.6% and 77.2% respectively. The execution time of still images for LBPH and Eigenfaces are 0.084 s and 0.247 s respectively. Whereas the execution time of video for LBPH and Eigenfaces are 0.255 s and 0.394 s respectively.

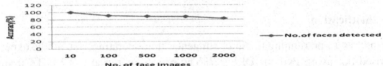

Fig. 7. Face detection accuracy

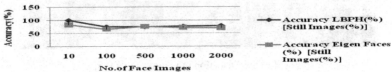

Fig. 8. A comparison of face recognition techniques (Still Image)

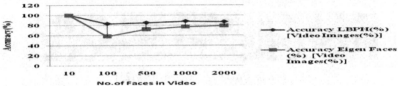

Fig. 9. A comparison of face recognition techniques (Video)

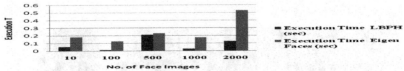

Fig. 10. Comparative analysis of Execution time (Still Image)

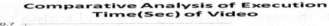
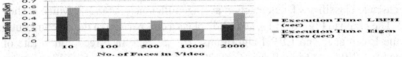

Fig. 11. Comparative analysis of Execution time (Video)

4.2 Access Control

First level classifier, which uses FNT classifier and classifies known and unknown attack identifiers, has a detection rate of 97.2% overall and a FPR of 1.6%. The known intrusion classifiers are trained to divide attacks into four categories using the KNN algorithm. According to the results provided in Fig. 12, DoS, Probe, U2R, and R2L are detected at rates of 98.7%, 97.4%, 97.8%, and 96.6%, respectively, while False Positive Rates are 0.4%, 0.1.45%, 2.19%, and 1.97% (Fig. 14). Figure 13 displays the results of a comparison between the proposed method and another approach. The C-Means clustering approach is used to perform clustering on the unidentified incursion. The C-Means clustering algorithm's distance threshold is crucial. A lower range requirement will group evidence into a huge amount of minimal groups, whereas a larger range barrier is unclear for grouping similar types of invasions collectively. In the experiment, a new classifier's training began when the number threshold reached 160. The findings indicate that the unknown intrusions with a detection rate of 98.6% and a false positive rate of 1.32%. The aforementioned conclusion was calculated using the following Eqs. 5, 6 and 7.

$$Detection\, Rate\, (DR) = TP/(TP + FN) \tag{5}$$

$$Efficiency = (TP + TN)/(TP + TN + FP + FN) \tag{6}$$

$$FNR = FN/(FN + TP) \tag{7}$$

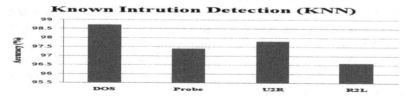

Fig. 12. Known Intrusion detection (KNN)

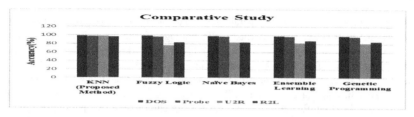

Fig. 13. Comparative analysis of Known Intrusion detection

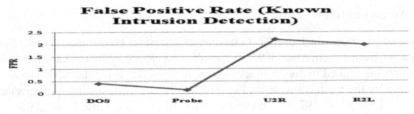

Fig. 14. FPR (Known Intrusion detection)

5 Conclusion

As technology has developed, many cyber-attacks have become a big worry. Therefore, the security, privacy, and availability of information sent through the Internet are all at danger. This paper has explored many potential attacks, including Denial of DoS, probe, R2U, and U2R. IDS system is utilized for access control, while facial recognition technique is employed for authentication. The average accuracy of the Haar cascade classifier for detecting faces is 90.2%. Whereas in recognition, it can be shown that LBPH outperforms Eigen faces in terms of detection accuracy and execution speed in both still images and video. Lighting, facial expression, and camera angle are just a few of the many variables that might throw off a face recognition system. Therefore, in the future, the job will be handled by a finger vein authentication system. The key advantage of adopting finger vein systems for safety and dependability is that they are unique and hidden beneath the skin. A comparison of several of the examined works' relatively best-performing Ml algorithms shows that the FNT and KNN algorithm has the maximum incursion accuracy. The access control model put out in this research has a false positive rate of 1.6% and a detection rate of 97.2% for known and unknown intrusion done by FNT. The detection percentages in the widely used intrusion classifier for DOS, Probe, U2R, and R2L are 98.7%, 97.4%, 97.8%, and 96.6%, respectively, with false positive rates of 0.4%, 0.1.145%, 2.19%, and 1.97%. Which is done by KNN. The accuracy of intrusion detection using C mean clustering in an unknown intrusion classifier is 98.6%, and the percentage of false positives is 1.32%.

References

1. Wang, Z., Gao, F.: An embedded parallel face detection system based on multicore processor. In: IEEE 2nd Advanced Information Technology, Electronic and Automation Control Conference (IAEAC), pp. 2684–2688 (2017). ISBN: 978-1-4673-8979-2
2. Ji, P., Kim, Y., Yang, Y., Kim, Y.S.: Face occlusion detection using skin color ratio and LBP features for intelligent video surveillance systems. In: Federated Conference on Computer Science and Information Systems (FedCSIS), pp. 253–259 (2016). ISBN: 978-8-3608-1090-3
3. Li, T., Hou, W., Lyu, F., Lei, Y., Xiao, C.: Face detection based-on depth information using HOG-LBP. In: 6th International Conference on Instrumentation and Measurement, Computer, Communication and Control, pp.779–784 (2016). ISBN: 978-1-5090-1195-7
4. Thiyagarajan, B.V., Mayur, A., Ravina, B., Akilesh, G.: LBP-Haar multi-feature pedestrian detection for AutoBraking and steering control system. In: International Conference on Computational Intelligence and Communication Networks (CICN), pp. 1527–1531 (2015). ISBN: 978-1-5090-0077-7

5. Faudzi, S.A.A.M., Yahya, N.: Evaluation of LBP – based face recognition techniques. In: International Conference on Intelligent and Advanced Systems (ICIAS), pp. 1–6 (2014). ISBN: 978-1-4799-4653-2

6. Turk, M., Pentland, A.: Eigenfaces for recognition. J. Cogn. Neurosci. **3**(1), 71–86 (1991)

7. Kumar, D.: Ddos attacks and their types. In: Network Security Attacks and Countermeasures, p. 197 (2016)

8. Bou-Harb, E., Debbabi, M., Assi, C.: Cyber scanning: a comprehensive survey. IEEE Commun. Surv. Tutor. **16**(3), 1496–1519 (2014)

9. Manadhata, K., Wing, J.M.: An attack surface metric. IEEE Trans. Softw. Eng. **37**(3), 371–386 (2011)

10. Singh, S., Silakari, S.: A survey of cyberattack detection systems. Int. J. Comput. Sci. Netw. Secur. **9**(5), 1–10 (2009)

11. Rostamipour, M., Sadeghiyan, B.: Network attack origin forensics with fuzzy logic. In: 2015 5th International Conference on Computer and Knowledge Engineering (ICCKE), pp. 67–72. IEEE (2015)

12. Edge, C., O'Donnell, D.: Malware security: combating viruses, worms, and root kits. In: Enterprise Mac Security, pp. 221–242. Apress, Berkeley (2016). https://doi.org/10.1007/978-1-4842-1712-2_8

13. Bahl, S., Sharma, S.K.: A minimal subset of features using correlation feature selection model for intrusion detection system. In: Satapathy, S.C., Raju, K.S., Mandal, J.K., Bhateja, V. (eds.) Proceedings of the Second International Conference on Computer and Communication Technologies. AISC, vol. 380, pp. 337–346. Springer, New Delhi (2016). https://doi.org/10.1007/978-81-322-2523-2_32

14. Surve, M., Joshi, P., Jamadar, S., Vharkate, M.: Automatic attendance system using face recognition technique. Int. J. Recent Technol. Eng. (IJRTE). IEEE **9**(1) (2020)

15. Palanivel, N., Aswinkumar, S., Balaji, J.: Automated attendance systems using face recognition by K-means algorithms. In: International Conference on System Computation Automation and Networking. IEEE (2019)

16. Jenif, D., Souza, W.S., Jothi, S., Chandrasekar, A.: Automated attendance marking and management system by facial recognition using histogram. In: 5th International Conference on Advanced Computing & Communication Systems (ICACCS). IEEE (2019)

17. Kasiselvanathan, M., Kalaiselvi, A., Vimal, S.P., Sangeetha, V.: Smart attendance management system based on face recognition algorithm. Int. J. Pure Appl. Math. **120**(5), 1377–1384 (2018)

18. Li, X.-Y.: Face recognition supported HOG and quick PCA rule. In: Euro China Conference on Intelligent Data Analysis and Applications (2017)

19. Kumar, V.D.A., Ashok Kumar, V.D., Malathi, S., Vengatesan, K., Ramakrishnan, M.: Facial recognition system for suspect identification using a surveillance camera. Pattern Recognit. Image Anal. **28**, 410–420 (2018)

20. Kumar, V.D.A., Ramya, S., Divakar, H., Rajeswari, G.K.: A survey on face recognition in video surveillance. In: International Conference on ISMAC in Computational Vision and Bioengineering, pp. 699–708 (2018)

21. Venkatesan, R., Anni Princy, B., Kumar, V.D.A., Raghuraman, M., Gupta, M.K., Kumar, A.: Secure online payment through facial recognition and proxy detection with the help of Triple DES encryption. J. Discr. Math. Sci. Cryptogr. **24**(8), 2195–2205 (2021)

22. Brahmi, H., Imen, B., Sadok, B.: OMC-IDS: at the cross-roads of OLAP mining and intrusion detection. In: Advances in Knowledge Discovery and Data Mining, pp. 13–24. Springer, New York (2012)

23. Aburomman, A.A., Reaz, M.B.I.: A novel svm-K-NN-pso ensemble method for intrusion detection system. Appl. Soft Comput. **38**, 360–372 (2016)

24. Saxena, H., Richariya, V.: Intrusion detection in KDD99 dataset using SVM-PSO and feature reduction with information gain. Int. J. Comput. Appl. **98**(6), 25–29 (2014)
25. Das, I., Sarkar, A., Singh, S., Sawant, S.K.: Authentication and secure communication by Haar Cascade classifier, eigen face, LBP histogram and variable irreducible polynomial in (2^8) finite field. In: 2021 Devices for Integrated Circuit (DevIC), Kalyani, pp. 536–540 (2021)

A Novel Trigonometric Mutation-Based Backtracking Search Algorithm for Solving Optimal Power Flow Problem Considering Renewable Energy Sources

Sriparna Banerjee[1]($^\boxtimes$) (iD), Provas Kumar Roy[1,2] (iD), and Pradip Kumar Saha[2] (iD)

[1] Kalyani Government Engineering College, Kalyani, India
sriparnabhattacharya8@gmail.com
[2] Jalpaiguri Government Engineering College, Jalpaiguri, India

Abstract. Renewable energy sources (RESs)−based optimal power flow (OPF) problem that imposes a higher degree of uncertainty and non-linearities into the solution process is a great concern for the power system researchers. In the present work, to improve the convergence rate of the orthodox backtracking search algorithm (BSA), a highly intelligent trigonometric mutation−based BSA (TMBSA) is proposed. The proposed technique is used to minimize highly non-linear, non-convex, and uncertainty-induced power generation costs for thermal power units along with highly intermittent wind energy (WE) and tidal energy (TDE). Further, the power generation cost objective is considered with the valve-point loading effect and prohibited operating zones (POZs) to make the research work more pragmatic. To confirm the superiority of the proposed technique, simulation work is performed on a RESs-based modified IEEE 30−bus test system, and the results are compared with the BSA. The result analysis clearly shows that the proposed TMBSA outperforms the BSA in terms of delivering more high−quality, accurate results with a faster convergence speed while solving the uncertainty−based OPF problem.

Keywords: OPF · TMBSA · Valve-point loading effect · Prohibited Operating zone · WE · TDE

1 Introduction

The OPF problem ensures reliable power system operation by obtaining optimal power system parameter settings [1,2]. The OPF problem takes into account various objectives such as fuel cost, emission level, and so on, subject to various system constraints [1]. Researchers have been combining thermal power plants with RESs like wind energy and tidal energy because of the growing threat of global warming and the depleting supply of fossil fuels [2]. However, the intermittent characteristics of WE and TDE make it difficult for the researchers to

K. Dasgupta et al. (Eds.): CICBA 2023, CCIS 1956, pp. 171–185, 2024.
https://doi.org/10.1007/978-3-031-48879-5_14

solve the RESs−based hybrid OPF problem due to the presence of different significant intermittency introduced by RESs [3]. In [3,4], the researchers solved a WE−based OPF problem while accounting for WE uncertainties. Other OPF problems were solved in [3,5] using a WE−TDE−based power system for various power system objectives.

Metaheuristic techniques are crucial for solving complex optimization problems because of their potent problem-solving abilities. The researchers have long been resolving power system optimization problems by utilizing metaheuristic techniques with a derivative−free simple algorithmic structure based on the behavioural characteristics of nature−inspired phenomena [6,7]. According to [8], and [9], metaheuristic techniques significantly aid in getting quality OPF problem solutions.

The BSA [10] is a metaheuristic technique with a single control factor and a simple mathematical structure, but it is slow to converge because it uses historical population data to reach the global optimal point [11]. The current work introduces a highly sophisticated mechanism known as trigonometric mutation [12] to improve the BSA's exploitation ability, resulting in a fast convergence characteristic. The proposed technique is termed as TMBSA. Furthermore, the proposed TMBSA's performance is validated on WE and combined WE−TDE integrated modified IEEE 30−bus power system for power generation cost optimization. The results are compared with the conventional BSA from both an analytical and statistical point of view to demonstrate the superiority of the proposed TMBSA.

However, the main contribution of the current work is to improve the exploitation ability and convergence speed of the orthodox BSA by integrating trigonometric mutation operation. Utilizing the probabilistic approach, the uncertainties of WE and combined WE−TDE are estimated. The proposed technique is applied to minimize the power system's generation cost, which is significantly uncertain due to the presence of WE and combined WE−TDE with the thermal power unit. The remainder of the paper is divided into sections, the first containing the problem formulation. Section 3 describes the solution methodology, Sect. 4 discusses the results, and Sect. 4 concludes the entire work performed.

2   Optimization Problem

To reduce the generation cost of the thermal unit, WE, and combined WE-TDE integrated power system, an OPF problem is formulated and solved in this work. A generalized formulation of the OPF objective function is discussed below [8].

$$Minimize\ Obj\_func(x, u) \tag{1}$$

$$Subject\ to\ g(x, u) = 0 \tag{2}$$

$$h(x, u) = 0 \tag{3}$$

where $g(x, u)$ and $h(x, u)$ are the equality and inequality constraints for the OPF objective, respectively. A detailed description of these constraints is included in [8].

This section modelled the objective function of the optimisation problem, which included thermal power units and highly uncertain WE and TDE. The uncertain characteristics of WE and TDE are then estimated using a probabilistic paradigm. Furthermore, the formulated OPF problem's operating constraints are stated in this section's last part.

2.1   Total Cost for Active Power Generation with Valve-Point Loading and Prohibited Operating Zones

The total cost objective (Obj_1) for the active power generation is given by the following equation that includes generation cost corresponding to the thermal generator, wind power unit (WPU), and wind−tidal unit (WTDU).

$$Obj\_1 = \sum_{i=1}^{n_{GB}} f(P_{g,i}) + \sum_{i=1}^{n_{WPU}} C\_W_i + \sum_{i=1}^{n_{WTDU}} C\_WTD_i \tag{4}$$

where n_{GB}, n_{WPU}, and n_{WTDU} are the number of thermal generators, wind power units, and wind−tidal units.

The valve−point loading effect that resulting in a highly nonlinear and non−smooth power generation cost is a practical phenomenon related to the operation of the multi-valve system of thermal generating unit. Due to the physical constraints of power plant components, a thermal or hydel power unit may have POZs bringing discontinuities into the generator's input−output characteristics [3]. Each thermal generator with $(Z-1)$ POZs is formulated using the following approach.

$$P_{g,i,z}^{l} \leq P_{g,i} \leq P_{g,i,z}^{u} \ \forall i \in z=1,2,...,Z \tag{5}$$

where $P_{g,i,z}^{l} = P_{g,i}^{MIN}$ and $P_{g,i,z}^{u} = P_{g,i}^{MAX}$. $P_{g,i}^{MIN}$ and $P_{g,i}^{MAX}$ correspond to the lower and upper limit of the active power generation for the ith thermal generator, and Z is the number of prohibited zone corresponding to the thermal generator.

The cost for the ith thermal generator is formulated below, considering the of the valve−point loading effect and POZs to incorporate the realistic effect of the practical power system [2].

$$f(P_{g,i}) = \left((\sum_{i=1}^{n_{GB}} \alpha_i + \beta_i P_{g,i} + \gamma_i P_{g,i}^2 + \left| m_i \times \sin(n_i \times (P_{g,i}^{min} - P_{g,i})) \right| \right) (\$/h)$$

$$\tag{6}$$

where α, β, and γ represent fuel cost coefficients for the ith thermal generator. m and n are the valve−point loading coefficients for the ith thermal generator.

Modeling of Wind Power Generation Cost Considering Intermittency

Direct Cost: The direct cost for the ith WPU is given by the following expression [2].

$$C\_W_{d,i} = d_{w,i}P_{w,i} \tag{7}$$

where $i = 1, 2, .., n_{WPU}$. $d_{w,i}$ indicates the direct cost coefficient for the ith WPU, and $P_{w,i}$ is the scheduled power corresponding to the ith WPU.

Overestimation Cost: When the scheduled power is more than the available wind power, then the overestimation cost is considered, as shown below for the ith WPU [3].

$$C\_W_{o,i} = o_{w,i} \int_0^{P_{w,i}} (P_{w,i} - wp)f(wp)dwp \tag{8}$$

where $o_{w,i}$ is the overestimation cost coefficient for the ith WPU and $f(wp)$ is the probability density function (PDF) of the ith WPU output.

Underestimation Cost: If the available wind power is more than the scheduled power, then underestimation cost is formulated as stated below [3].

$$C\_W_{u,i} = u_{w,i} \int_{P_{w,i}}^{P_{w,r,i}} (wp - P_{w,i})f(wp)dwp \tag{9}$$

where $u_{w,i}$ is the underestimation cost coefficient for the ith WPU, and $P_{w,r,i}$ is the rated output power for the ith WPU.

Total Cost: The total cost of wind power generation corresponds to the ith WPU is given below [3].

$$C\_W_i = C\_W_{d,i} + C\_W_{o,i} + C\_W_{u,i} \tag{10}$$

Modeling of Intermittent Characteristic of Wind Power: The intermittent velocity v_w of wind can be modeled using the Weibull PDF as shown below.

$$f(v_w) = \left(\frac{k}{c}\right)\left(\frac{v}{c}\right)^{(k-1)} e^{-(v/c)^k} \quad 0 < v < \infty \tag{11}$$

where c and k are the scale and shape parameter of the Weilbull PDF.

After integrating Eq. (8), the cumulative distribution function (CDF) of v_w is obtained as shown below.

$$F(v_w) = 1 - e^{-\left(\frac{v_w}{c}\right)^k} \tag{12}$$

Considering the linear model of the wind turbine output power curve the relationship between wind power (wp) and v_w is established in the below$-$mentioned expression [13].

$$wp = \begin{cases} 0 & v_w < v_{in}, v_w > v_{out} \\ P_{w,r} \dfrac{(v - v_{in})}{(v_r - v_{in})} & v_{in} \leq v_w \leq v_{out} \\ P_{w,r} & v_r \leq v_w \leq v_{out} \end{cases} \tag{13}$$

where v_{in}, v_r and v_{out} refer to the cut$-$in, rated, and cut$-$out velocity in miles/h or miles/second of the wind, correspondingly.

Modeling of Wind-Tidal Power Generation Cost Considering Intermittency

Direct Cost: The formula of the direct cost for the ith wind$-$tidal unit (WTDU) is expressed by the following expression [3].

$$C\_WTD_{d,i} = \sum_{i=1}^{n_{WTD}} d_{WTD,i} P_{WTD,i} = \sum_{i=1}^{n_{WTDU}} d_{w,i} P_{w,i} + \sum_{i=1}^{n_{WTDU}} d_{TD,i} P_{TD,i} \tag{14}$$

where n_{WTDU} is the number of WTDU, n_{TDU} is the number of tidal units (TDU), $d_{WTD,i}$ indicates the direct cost coefficient for the ith WTDU, $P_{WTD,i}$ is the scheduled power corresponding to the ith WTDU, $d_{TD,i}$ indicates the direct cost coefficient for the ith TDU, and $P_{TD,i}$ is the scheduled power corresponding to the ith TDU.

Overestimation Cost: The overestimation cost for the ith WTDU is calculated by the following formula [3].

$$C\_WTD_{o,i} = \sum_{i=1}^{n_{WPU}} C\_W_{o,i} + \sum_{i=1}^{n_{TDU}} C\_TD_{o,i} \tag{15}$$

The overestimation cost for the ith TDU is expressed below.

$$C\_TD_{o,i} = o_{TD,i} \int_{0}^{P_{TD,i}} (P_{TD,i} - P_{av,TD,i}) f(P_{TD}) dP_{TD} \tag{16}$$

where $o_{TD,i}$ refers to the overestimation cost coefficient for the ith TDU, $P_{av,TD,i}$ is the available power for the ith TDU, $f(P_{TD})$ signifies the PDF of $P_{TD,i}$.

Underestimation Cost: The underestimation cost for the ith WTDU is computed by the following expression [3].

$$C\_WTD_{u,i} = \sum_{i=1}^{n_{WPU}} C\_W_{u,i} + \sum_{i=1}^{n_{TDU}} C\_TD_{u,i} \tag{17}$$

The underestimation cost for the ith TDU is shown below.

$$C\_TD_{u,i} = u_{TD,i} \int\limits_{P_{TD,i}}^{P_{TD,r,i}} (P_{av,TD,i} - P_{TD,i})f(P_{TD})dP_{TD} \qquad (18)$$

where $u_{TD,i}$ refers to the underestimation cost coefficient for the ith TDU, $P_{TD,r,i}$ is the rated power for the ith TDU.

Total Cost: The total cost for the ith WTDU is given below.

$$C\_WTD_i = C\_WTD_{d,i} + C\_WTD_{o,i} + C\_WTD_{u,i} \qquad (19)$$

Modeling of Intermittent Characteristic of Tidal Power: The tidal discharge rate (Q_{TD}) in (m^3/sec) and P_{TD} are two random variables. Q_{TD} can be modelled by the Gumbel PDF [3], as shown below.

$$f(Q_{TD}) = \frac{1}{\psi} \exp\left(\frac{Q_{TD} - \zeta}{\psi}\right) \exp\left[-\exp\left(\frac{Q_{TD} - \zeta}{\psi}\right)\right] \qquad (20)$$

where ψ $(=24.52)$ is the scale parameter and ζ $(=220)$ is the location parameter. P_{TD} as a function of Q_{TD} is expressed below.

$$P_{TD} = \eta Q_{TD} \rho g h_{TD} \qquad (21)$$

where η $(=0.85)$ is the efficiency of the TDU, ρ $(=1025 \, kg/m^3)$ is the density of water, g $(=9.81 \, m/s^2)$ signifies the acceleration of the gravity, h_{TD} $(=3.2 \, m)$ is the pressure head caused by the level difference between high and low tide.

2.2   OPF-Constraints

Equality Constraints

$$a) \sum_{i=1}^{n_{GB}} P_{g,i} = P_d + P_{loss} \qquad (22)$$

$$\sum_{i=1}^{n_{GB}} Q_{g,i} = Q_d + Q_{loss} \qquad (23)$$

where $P_{g,i}$ and $Q_{g,i}$ are the active and reactive power for the ith generator bus, P_d and Q_d correspond to the total active and reactive power demand of the system, respectively, and P_{loss} and Q_{loss} refer to the total active and the reactive power loss of the power system considered.

Inequality Constraints

$$b)P_{g,i}^{MIN} \leq P_{g,i} \leq P_{g,i}^{MAX}; \; i = 1, 2, ..., n_{GB} \tag{24}$$

$$Q_{g,i}^{MIN} \leq Q_{g,i} \leq Q_{g,i}^{MAX}; \; i = 1, 2, ..., n_{GB} \tag{25}$$

where $Q_{g,i}^{MIN}$ and $Q_{g,i}^{MAX}$ are the minimum and maximum limits of the reactive power for the ith thermal generator.

$$c)V_{g,i}^{MIN} \leq V_{g,i} \leq V_{g,i}^{MAX}; \; i = 1, 2, ..., n_{GB} \tag{26}$$

where, $V_{g,i}^{MIN}$ and $V_{g,i}^{MAX}$ refer to the minimum and maximum limits of the bus voltage for the ith thermal generator.

$$d)V_{l,i}^{MIN} \leq V_{l,i} \leq V_{l,i}^{MAX}; \; i = 1, 2, ..., n_{LB} \tag{27}$$

where n_{LB} corresponds to the load bus number, $V_{l,i}^{MIN}$ and $V_{l,i}^{MAX}$ are the minimum and maximum limits for the ith load bus.

$$e)S_{l,i} \leq S_{l,i}^{MAX}; \; i = 1, 2, ..., n_{Tl} \tag{28}$$

where $S_{l,i}^{MAX}$ is the maximum loading limit of the ith power transmission line, and n_{Tl} is the number of the power transmission line.

$$f)T_{c,i}^{MIN} \leq T_{c,i} \leq T_{c,i}^{MAX}; \; i = 1, 2, ..., n_{rt} \tag{29}$$

where the limiting values of the tap−setting for the ith regulating transformer is $T_{c,i}^{MIN}$ and $T_{c,i}^{MAX}$ and n_{rt} refers to the number of the regulating transformer.

$$g)Q_{c,i}^{MIN} \leq Q_{c,i} \leq Q_{c,i}^{MAX}; \; i = 1, 2, ..., SC \tag{30}$$

where the ith shunt compensator has the lower and upper limiting values of $Q_{c,i}^{MIN}$ and $Q_{c,i}^{MAX}$, SC is the number of shunt compensators.

$$h)0 \leq P_{w,i} \leq P_{w,r,i}; \; i = 1, 2, .., n_{WPU} \tag{31}$$

$$i)Q_{w,reac}^{MIN} \leq Q_{w,reac,i} \leq Q_{w,reac}^{MAX}; \; i = 1, 2, .., n_{WPU} \tag{32}$$

where $Q_{w,i}$ is the reactive power for the ith DFIG connected WPU, with lower and upper limits of the reactive power producing capability $Q_{w,reac}^{MIN}$ and $Q_{w,rea}^{MAX}$, respectively.

$$j)0 \leq P_{TD,i} \leq P_{TD,r,i}; \; i = 1, 2, .., n_{TDU} \tag{33}$$

3   Proposed Methodology

The proposed methodology to be used for addressing the considered optimization problem is described in this section. We will first briefly go over the traditional BSA's working procedure. The idea behind the proposed modification to improve the BSA's performance is then discussed.

3.1   Backtracking Search Algorithm (BSA)

BSA is a metaheuristic technique that uses three popular genetic operations, *i.e.*, selection, mutation and crossover. Using the mentioned operations, the BSA will find the trial population. At the final step of the BSA, a greedy selection is considered between the trial population and the present population to select the fittest population as the output solution. The following five key processes are involved in the BSA to find the global best solution.

I.Initialization: This process randomly initializes the initial population $Pop_{i,j}$, as shown below.

$$Pop_{i,j} \tilde{} U(LOW_j, UP_j) \tag{34}$$

where $i = 1, ..., P$ and $j = 1, ..., D$. P indicates the population size and D indicates the total number of the control variables, UP and LOW signify upper and lower ranges of the control variables, and U is the uniform probability distribution function.

II.Selection-I: In this process, the historical population known as the old population is generated in the following way.

$$Pop_{i,j}(old) \tilde{} U(LOW_j, UP_j) \tag{35}$$

As per the BSA, the $Pop(old)$ is updated considering the "if−then" logic at the beginning of each iterative step in the following way.

$$if\ a > b\ then\ Pop(old) := Pop\,|a, b\tilde{}U\,(0,1) \tag{36}$$

where a and b are two random numbers.

III.Mutation Strategy: Here, the initial trial population is formed by the following equation.

$$Mutant_{i,t+1} = Pop_i + F_i * (Pop_i(old) - Pop_i) \tag{37}$$

where $F = 3.c$ and $c\tilde{}N(0,1)$ (N is the standard normal distribution function).

IV.Crossover: In this process, the final formation of the trial population T is done. The initial form of the T is $Mutant$ as generated in the previous step. Two key steps are involved in this process. In first step, a binary integer−valued matrix map considering a dimension of $P \times D$, is formed. In the second step, depending upon the values of each entries of the binary map, T is updated with Pop.

V.Selection-II: This process conducts a greedy selection scheme. The T_i which has better fitness value, update the corresponding Pop_i. If the fitness of best population of Pop, *i.e.*, Pop_{best} is less than the fitness of the global best population (G_{best}) obtained so far, then the G_{best} is updated with Pop_{best} and the updated G_{best} is displayed as the output of the optimization problem.

A detailed description of the BSA can be found in [10].

3.2 Trigonometric Mutation-Based Backtracking Search Algorithm (TMBSA)

The BSA uses the information from the old or historic population thus the promising neighbouring region of the existing solution may get unvisited causing poor exploitation leading slow convergence speed of the BSA. Hence to mitigate the drawback of the BSA, a novel trigonometric operation−based mutation technique, that replaces the orthodox mutation strategy (Eq. (37) of the BSA in a probabilistic manner, is incorporated in the proposed TMBSA.

As per our proposed mutation operation, a hyper-geometric triangle is formed in the search space, and the individual to be mutated is considered the center point of that triangle. As a matter of fact, three random individuals, *i.e.*, $r1$, $r2$, and $r3$ of the *Pop*, which are mutually independent, are selected as the three vertices to form the hyper−geometric triangle in the search space of the proposed TMBSA. Basically, our proposed mutation is biased towards the vertices of the hyper−geometric triangle due to the presence of the objective function values of the three vertices. In this context, it must be mentioned that, in the proposed mutation strategy, the target vector, which is equivalent to the center point of the hyper−geometric triangle, is added with three weighted differential vector terms for keeping the balance between convergence speed and robustness of the proposed TMBSA. However, the proposed TMBSA selects from the trigonometric mutation scheme based on the mutation probability (M_{pf}). If M_{pf} (=0.05) is less than d (uniformly distributed random number with a range 0-1), then the proposed TMBSA opts for the trigonometric mutation else, the orthodox mutation, as given in Eq. (37)), is executed. M_{pf} controls to maintain the proper balance between the convergence speed and the global search ability of the proposed TMBSA. The mathematical expression for the proposed mutation strategy to update the Mutant of the $(t+1)^{th}$ iteration is given below.

$$Mutant_{i,t+1} = \left(\frac{Pop_{r1,t} + Pop_{r2,t} + Pop_{r3,t}}{3} \right) + (f_2 - f_1)\left(Pop_{r1,t} - Pop_{r2,t}\right)$$
$$+ (f_3 - f_2)\left(Pop_{r2,t} - Pop_{r3,t}\right) + (f_1 - f_3)\left(Pop_{r3,t} - Pop_{r1,t}\right)$$

$$(38)$$

where

$$f_1 = |fit(Pop_{r1,t})|/f' \tag{39}$$

$$f_2 = |fit(Pop_{r2,t})|/f' \tag{40}$$

$$f_3 = |fit(Pop_{r3,t})|/f' \tag{41}$$

$$f' = |fit(Pop_{r1,t})| + |fit(Pop_{r2,t})| + |fit(Pop_{r2,t})| \tag{42}$$

where $fit(Pop_i)$ function calculates the objective value of the corresponding *Pop*.

The flowchart of the proposed TMBSA is shown in Fig. 1.

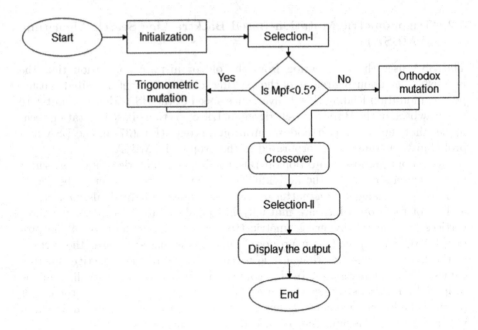

Fig. 1. Flowchart of the proposed TMBSA

4   Result Analysis

To authenticate the strength of the proposed TMBSA, it is applied to minimize the power generation cost objective considering the valve−point loading effect and POZs, of WPU and WTDU integrated modified IEEE 30−bus power system and the simulation results are compared with the BSA. The simulation is executed in Matlab 2018b. After carrying out 30 independent simulation runs for the considered objective, the best result is obtained when $Pop=30$; hence the present simulation work is done with same size of Pop. The iteration count is 100 for the present paper.

To house the RESs in the considered power system, some modifications are done. Two WPUs are connected with the bus number 5, replacing the corresponding thermal generator. One WPU and TDU are combined to form WTDU and integrated with bus number 8. The cost coefficients for the thermal generator, WPU, and TDU, as well as the valve−point loading, are collected from [3]. The rest of the data for the considered test system can be found in [3].

Minimization of Power Generation Cost with Valve-Point Loading Effect and Prohibited Operating Zones, Considering Wind and Wind-Tidal Integrated Power System: The power generation cost considering the valve−point loading effect and POZs is minimized by the proposed TMBSA for a wind and wind−tidal integrated power system. The simulation results for this case are presented in Table 1. Whereas Table 2 shows the objective values and CPU times. Table 2 verifies that our proposed metaheuristic technique produces more accurate and high−quality results than the BSA. Thus it is established that the proposed mutation operation greatly aids the proposed TMBSA to exploit the potential solution space. However, in Fig. 2, the minimized objective values for the proposed TMBSA and BSA are graphically represented. It is evident from Fig. 2 that the proposed TMBSA minimized the objective function up to a greater extent than the BSA. Table 2 and Fig. 3 prove that the CPU time required to process TMBSA−OPF is less than BSA−OPF, thus confirming the fact that our proposed modification successfully helps the proposed TMBSA to operate computationally faster than the BSA. Further, it is clearly verified from Fig. 4 that the proposed modification significantly improves the convergence speed of the proposed TMBSA than the BSA.

Table 1. OPF outcomes for wind-tidal integrated power system, obtained by considered metaheuristic techniques.

Control variables	Technique	
	TMBSA	BSA
$P_{g,1}$ (MW)	100.66	100.14
$P_{g,2}$ (MW)	41.55	40.77
$P_{w,5}$ (MW)	40.87	40.79
$P_{WTD,8}$ (MW)	24.34	23.11
$P_{g,11}$ (MW)	20.11	21.14
$P_{g,13}$ (MW)	24.21	21.07
$V_{g,1}$ (p.u.)	1.01	1.03
$V_{g,2}$ (p.u.)	1.02	1.02
$V_{g,5}$ (p.u.)	1.04	1.04
$V_{g,8}$ (p.u.)	1.05	1.02
$V_{g,11}$ (p.u.)	1.02	0.99
$V_{g,13}$ (p.u.)	1.02	1.01
$T_{c,11}$ (p.u.)	1.07	0.99
$T_{c,12}$ (p.u.)	1.06	1.01
$T_{c,15}$ (p.u.)	1.03	0.98
$T_{c,36}$ (p.u.)	1.04	1.0123
$Q_{c,1}$ (MVAR)	0.026	0.0279
$Q_{c,2}$ (MVAR)	0.022	0.0098

Analysis of Load Bus Voltage Profile: The profile of load bus voltage obtained by the proposed TMBSA is shown in Fig. 5. It is confirmed from Fig. 5 that the proposed technique maintains a flat voltage profile for the smooth operation of the power system.

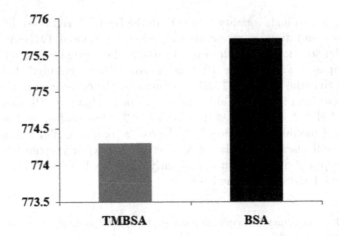

Fig. 2. Comparative representation of objective-value.

Table 2. Comparison between OPF-objective and CPU time obtained by the considered metaheuristic techniques for wind-tidal integrated power system.

Technique	Wind cost ($/hr)	Wind-Tidal cost ($/hr)	Thermal cost ($/hr)	Total cost ($/hr)	CPU time (sec.)
TMBSA	62.001	10.029	702.259	774.289	16.147
BSA	61.781	11.623	702.317	775.721	17.329

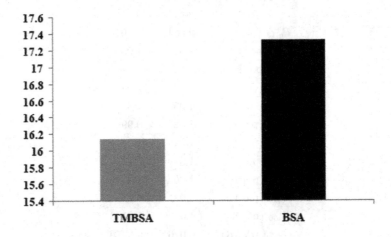

Fig. 3. Comparative representation of CPU time.

Statistical Investigation of OPF-Output: Table 3 represents the best, average, worst, and standard deviation (SD) values for the TMBSA−OPF and BSA−OPF. The results shown in Table 3 explicitly confirm that the statistical robustness of the proposed TMBSA is more than the BSA. However, from the box plots displayed in Fig. 6 it is evident that in the case of the proposed TMBSA the overall spread of the minimized objective values obtained by the

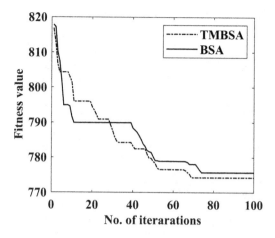

Fig. 4. Convergence profiles for different techniques.

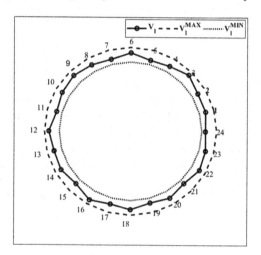

Fig. 5. Load bus voltage profile for TMBSA-OPF.

Table 3. Statistical outcomes (30 runs) of considered metaheuristic techniques for wind-tidal integrated power system.

Technique	Best	Average	Worst	SD
TMBSA	774.289	774.527	774.791	0.168
BSA	775.721	776.039	776.523	0.196

different independent runs is less than what is obtained by the BSA, thus confirming the statistical efficacy of our proposed technique.

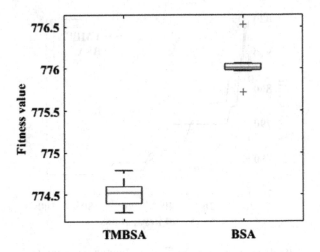

Fig. 6. Box plots for different techniques.

5   Conclusion

This work formulates an OPF problem for the WE and WE−TDE integrated power system to minimize power generation cost objective taking into account the valve−point loading effect and POZs. A trigonometric mutation−based BSA, i.e., TMBSA, is proposed to solve the RESs−based OPF problem with significant uncertainties and nonlinearities. According to the analytical and statistical analysis of the results, the proposed modification significantly improves the proposed technique's performance in obtaining a more accurate, quality, statistically robust solution and speedy convergence profile than the orthodox BSA to deal with uncertain, nonlinear, and complex OPF problems.

References

1. Trivedi, I.N., Jangir, P., Parmar, S.A., Jangir, N.: Optimal power flow with voltage stability improvement and loss reduction in power system using moth-flame optimizer. Neural Comput. Appl. **30**(6), 1889–1904 (2018)
2. Abbasi, M., Abbasi, E., Mohammadi-Ivatloo, B.: Single and multi-objective optimal power flow using a new differential-based harmony search algorithm. J. Ambient Intell. Humaniz. Comput. **12**(1), 851–871 (2021)
3. Duman, S., Wu, L., Li, J.: Moth swarm algorithm based approach for the ACOPF considering wind and tidal energy. In: Hemanth, D.J., Kose, U. (eds.) ICAIAME 2019. LNDECT, vol. 43, pp. 830–843. Springer, Cham (2020). https://doi.org/10.1007/978-3-030-36178-5_72
4. Kaymaz, E., Duman, S., Guvenc, U.: Optimal power flow solution with stochastic wind power using the Lévy coyote optimization algorithm. Neural Comput. Appl. **33**(12), 6775–6804 (2021)

5. Fernandes, I.G., Pereira, F.B., Gomes, T.L., Sá, B.F.: An optimal power flow approach including wind and tidal generation. In: IEEE PES Innovative Smart Grid Technologies Conference-Latin America (ISGT Latin America), pp. 1–6. IEEE (2019)
6. Warid, W.: Optimal power flow using the AMTPG-Jaya algorithm. Appl. Soft Comput. **91**, 106252 (2020)
7. Kaur, M., Narang, N.: An integrated optimization technique for optimal power flow solution. Soft Comput. **24**, 10865–10882 (2020)
8. Abusorrah, A.M.: The application of the linear adaptive genetic algorithm to optimal power flow problem. Arab. J. Sci. Eng. **39**(6), 4901–4909 (2014)
9. Akbari, E., Ghasemi, M., Gil, M., Rahimnejad, A., Andrew Gadsden, S.: Optimal power flow via teaching-learning-studying-based optimization algorithm. Electric Power Compon. Syst. **49**(6–7), 584–601 (2022)
10. Civicioglu, P.: Backtracking search optimization algorithm for numerical optimization problems. Appl. Math. Comput. **219**(15), 8121–8144 (2013)
11. Zhao, W., Wang, L., Wang, B., Yin, Y.: Best guided backtracking search algorithm for numerical optimization problems. In: Lehner, F., Fteimi, N. (eds.) KSEM 2016. LNCS (LNAI), vol. 9983, pp. 414–425. Springer, Cham (2016). https://doi.org/10. 1007/978-3-319-47650-6_33
12. Fan, H.Y., Lampinen, J.: A trigonometric mutation operation to differential evolution. J. Glob. Optim. **27**(1), 105–129 (2003)
13. Agwa, A.: Interior search optimization algorithm for modeling power curve of wind turbine. Int. J. Renew. Energy Res. (IJRER) **10**(3), 1349–1358 (2020)

Qualitative and Quantitative Analysis of Modifications in Playfair Cipher

Anubhab Ray$^{(\boxtimes)}$, Kartikeya Singh, Aditya Harsh, Shubham Thorat, and Nirmalya Kar

Department of Computer Science and Engineering, NIT Agartala, Agartala, India
rayanubhab@gmail.com, nirmalya@ieee.org

Abstract. Security in digital world has become a paramount issue, even more so in the post pandemic world when the digital footprint of the world has increased. Multiple encryption techniques are used to ensure the same. Certain famous classical ciphers which were in prevalent use during ancient times are now not robust enough to keep up with security requirements of modern world. This paper analyses the different modifications proposed to one such cipher i.e., Playfair Cipher and how these modifications enhance it's performance thus making it usable in modern world.

Keywords: encryption · decryption · playfair cipher · cryptography

1 Introduction

In the post pandemic era, the digital footprint of the world has increased as a result of professional settings like institutions and industries adopting remote work. With this increase in internet traffic data security is needed more than ever. Data Encryption refers to the transformation of a given message into a structure that makes it indecipherable to anyone without a secret key. This technique ensures the message is read by only the intended recipient thus ensuring privacy and safety of both parties.

In the current world when the transfer of data has become a big part of everyday life, encryption is more important than ever to ensure the protection of private information, sensitive data, and enhancing the security of both sender and receiver. Cryptography [1] is one such technique. Cryptography is essentially a process of conversion of plain text into indiscernible text and vice-versa. By doing so, it is ensured that the message can only be read by intended recipient and sender. Cryptography has various applications ranging from preventing data theft and ensuring user security to user authentication. Cryptography is divided into two categories: symmetric and asymmetric. The classical cipher [2] techniques like Hill Cipher [3], Playfair Cipher, etc. while used in ancient times are now obsolete can't be employed because of complexity of today's protocols.

However, modified version of some of these classical ciphers [4] can be used in modern world as they are stronger and can sustain certain attacks. They can

K. Dasgupta et al. (Eds.): CICBA 2023, CCIS 1956, pp. 186–195, 2024.
https://doi.org/10.1007/978-3-031-48879-5_15

be employed in a resource constrained environment where computation speed and size requirements play a vital role. In this paper we will discussing the modifications proposed to one of the most widely known encryption algorithms i.e., the Playfair cipher and how these modifications affect it's performance. We tried to do a qualitative and quantitative analysis of modifications in playfair cipher and how these changes affect it's performance and analyse the attacks possible.

2   Motivation and Objective

The enduring popularity of the classic Playfair cipher has prompted researchers and practitioners to subject it to both qualitative and quantitative analyses. Such multifaceted investigations offer valuable opportunities to thoroughly examine the cipher's advantages and disadvantages, as well as identify ways to enhance its security and performance. By exploring the cipher from a variety of angles, researchers can gain a deeper understanding of its underlying principles and assumptions, uncover vulnerabilities that can be exploited by attackers, and develop novel modifications to bolster its security. Moreover, quantitative analysis empowers researchers to rigorously test the cipher's effectiveness against a range of attacks, providing insights into its practicality, efficiency, and resilience. In combination, qualitative and quantitative analyses are essential tools for ensuring that the classic Playfair cipher continues to serve as a valuable cryptographic system in an ever-changing digital landscape [5].

Our goal is to research the different variations of the well-known Playfair cipher, a classical cryptography technique. We want to examine the adjustments made by earlier researchers to increase the complexity and security of the algorithm. We want to obtain a greater grasp of the approaches used to accomplish the desired result by understanding these techniques. We intend to build our own algorithm in the future using this information.

3   Literature Survey

3.1   Traditional Playfair Cipher

Playfair cipher [6] algorithm is one of the most renowned symmetric encryption algorithms. It is dependent on the 5 × 5 matrix which is created by inputting the given key into the matrix row-wise, left to right first and then using all the other alphabets to fill the rest of the matrix in chronological order. The encryption is carried out in following steps:

1. Termination of white space in the given plaintext and then grouping the letters into groups of two. The two grouped letters must be distinct, if two letters in a group happen to be same, an additional "X" is inserted between them to maintain aforementioned condition. In the case of length of plaintext being odd, a "X" is concatenated at the end of the plaintext.

2. The resulting groups of two characters, are then taken one by one and encrypted with respect to their position in the matrix.
   - The characters immediately to their right take the place of the two characters if they happen to lie in the same row of the matrix. If a character is last in the row it is replaced by first.
   - In a similar manner, in case the two characters are located in the same column of the matrix, they are substituted with the characters located just below them. When the character is positioned at the last slot of the column, it is substituted with the first character
   - If the two plaintext characters are neither in same row nor same column, they are replaced by character in their own row and in the column of the other character in the pair of two.

Playfair cipher, however has some major disadvantages:

- The plaintext can only contain 25 upper case alphabets (with I and J considered one character), lower case characters are not handled.
- Encrypted text when decrypted contains extra characters, like X which is added when the given pair has the same characters or the plaintext's length is odd. Thus adding to the confusion.
- Since the matrix purely constitutes upper case letters, plaintext with numbers, special characters and lower case letters are not handled.
- Whitespace in the plaintext is ignored and hence cannot be handled.

3.2 Discussion on the Modifications of Playfair Cipher

It is evident from the discussion that the traditional playfair cipher cannot be employed in most cases of real world application. Hence many modifications have been proposed to the traditional playfair cipher over the years along with it being used with other encryption techniques to improve on its core functionality. Some of the commonly used modifications which can be used to overcome the limitations of Playfair Cipher are given in Fig. 1.

The methodology proposed by Marzan et al. [7] aims to tackle the security problem of the playfair cipher by encrypting and decrypting the key. Using a 16×16 matrix along with the aforementioned method, the intent is to overcome the shortcomings of both symmetric and asymmetric keys with the use of XOR operations, two's complement followed by bit swapping. First sender enters both plaintext and the key, the key is used to convert plaintext into ciphertext. The key's security is then ensured by encrypting key by converting ASCII characters into decimal, converting decimal into binary, applying 2's compliment, XOR and bit swapping. The result ciphertext and the original ciphertext are both sent to receiver and decrypted to get the intended message.

Albahrani et al. [8] presented a method for encrypting images using a combination of diffusion and modified Playfair cipher. Their approach employs two cross-chaotic maps to generate a 16×16 Playfair matrix as the encryption key. To encrypt an input bitmap image, it is first divided into red, blue, and green

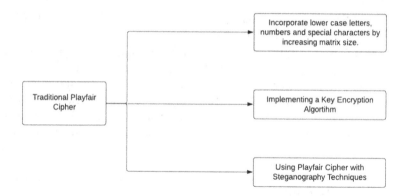

Fig. 1. Playfair Cipher Possible Modification

color matrices. The two cross-chaotic maps are then iterated to generate random numbers in the range of [0 to Number of Rows] and [0 to Number of columns], which are used to encrypt each of the color matrices using the Playfair matrix. The resulting image is further divided into 16×16 blocks and each block is encrypted as a separate Playfair matrix. The proposed method is capable of encrypting all types of inputs, including alphanumeric and special characters. Additionally, the encrypted image exhibits a low correlation coefficient, indicating that statistical attacks are unlikely to reveal any useful information to an attacker. Furthermore, the algorithm demonstrates remarkable resilience against differential attacks as even a minor change to the original image results in significant modifications in the encrypted counterpart.

In [9] the authors seek to combine the advantages of 3D Playfair Cipher and PVD method. 3D Playfair Cipher is easy to implement and has reliable encoding and lossless fat compression while PVD helps algorithm hide more info without causing distinguishable distortions between original and stego image. Maximum hiding of bits and falling of problem are addressed by treating each RGB pixel pair on RGB cover image as three distinct pixel pair. It is observed that the Peak signal to noise ratio (PSNR) and data hiding capacity are better in the proposed method than just using original PVD method, 1.023 times and 1.333 times respectively.

Siswanto et al. [10] suggest using cryptography and LSB (Least Significant Bit) steganography in combination to ensure safety of a message. The text message is first encrypted with playfair cipher method and the resultant ciphertext will be embedded om 8-bit grayscale digital image using steganography. Using both Cryptography and Steganography in combination helps user maintain confidentiality of a message. The Mean Square Error (MSE) and Peak Signal to Noise Ratio showed normal results. MSE is valued between the original image and the manipulated image. Based on the result of the study, there's no notable difference in the stego image containing secret message from the plain image.

The methodology proposed by Patil et al. [11] aims to address modern day attacks by proposing security improvements in existing models. RSA, steganography and RMPS keyless transposition is used in tandem with playfair cipher for encryption and decryption. The traditional 5×5 playfair matrix is replaced by 19×4 matrix to accommodate more characters. Sender encrypts the Playfair cipher using recipient's public key which employs RSA algorithm. Then RMPS keyless transposition and LSBS is used to encrypt the message and insert it into image and send it to receiver. Then the exact reverse process of encryption is applied in decryption. The resulting method can withstand Brute-Force, Frequency analysis, Replay attack and Man in the middle attack due to it's various properties.

4   Result and Analysis

The following aspects have been considered for the evaluation of the cryptographic algorithms:

4.1   Brute Force Attack

In a cryptographic assault known as a "brute force", the attacker tries every key combination and password combination until they find the one that works. In other words, until they discover the one that unlocks the ciphertext or allows them access to the system, the attacker thoroughly tests every potential answer.

When there is no other way for the attacker to decrypt the data, such as when the encryption key is unknown or the password is challenging to figure out, brute force attacks are frequently utilised. Despite their potential effectiveness, brute force attacks can be time-consuming and computationally demanding, especially for longer keys or passwords. Generally, if the size of key space is less than 2^{128} it is considered vulnerable [5].

The calculation of the projected duration for a brute force attack is as follows:

$$\frac{\text{Number of character set}^{\text{length of key}}}{\text{Encryption/Second(EPS)}}$$

4.2   Frequency Analysis Attack

A frequency analysis attack exploits predictable patterns in certain encryption schemes that substitute one letter or symbol for another based on a fixed pattern. By analyzing the frequency of letters or symbols in a ciphertext, an attacker can infer the substitution pattern used and eventually decipher the message. To protect against frequency analysis attacks, encryption schemes can be designed to avoid predictable patterns, use more complex substitution rules, or use polyalphabetic ciphers with multiple substitution rules [11].

4.3   Avalanche Effect

The avalanche effect serves as a means to test the randomness of a cryptographic system. A desirable characteristic of an encryption algorithm is that even a minor modification to either the plaintext or the key should bring about a considerable change in the resulting ciphertext. If an algorithm fails to demonstrate a strong avalanche effect, it could be vulnerable to attacks such as known plaintext or chosen-plaintext, where an attacker can potentially predict the input from the given output.

The avalanche effect is calculated as:

$$AE(\%) = \frac{\text{No. of Changed Bits in Cipher text}}{\text{Total no. of Bits in Cipher text}} \times 100$$

Generally, if the avalanche effect is greater than 50% the cryptosystem is considered to be secure [12]. The following metrics are used to measure avalanche effect in a cryptosystem:

4.3.1   Mean Squared Error (MSE)

Mean Square Error (MSE) is a commonly used measure of the difference between an estimator or predictor and the true value of what is being estimated or predicted. It is often used in statistical analyses and machine learning to evaluate the performance of a model or algorithm. The MSE is calculated by taking the average of the squared differences between the predicted and actual values. The formula for MSE is:

$$MSE = \frac{1}{H \times W} \sum_{i=0}^{H-1} \sum_{j=0}^{W-1} | \, C(i,j) - P(i,j) \, |^2$$

where C(i,j) and P(i,j) denotes the pixels at the ith row and j^{th} column of H X W cipher and plain image respectively. Normally, If $MSE > 30dB$ then it is considered to be secure enough and no relationship can be established easily between the two images [13].

4.3.2   Number of Pixel Change Rate (NPCR)

The NPCR value is determined by the number of pixels in the original and processed images that have the same location. A higher NPCR score signifies that there has been an abrupt alteration of the position of pixels in the image. The NPCR score should ideally be 99.6094% [13]. NPCR is calculated as:

$$NPCR(\,\% \,) = \frac{\sum_{i=1}^{H} \sum_{j=1}^{W} D(i,j)}{H \times W} \times 100$$

where, H and W are the height and width of the image respectively and D(i, j) is defined such that D(i, j) = 0, if C1(i, j) = C2(i, j); else D(i, j) = 1.

4.3.3 Unified Averaged Changed Intensity (UACI)

The UACI score is a measure of the average difference in intensity between two cipher images c1 and c2. The value of UACI should ideally be: 33.46% [8]. The formula for calculating UACI is:

$$\text{UACI(\%)} = \frac{1}{H \times W} \sum_{i,j} \frac{\mid C1(i,j) - C2(i,j) \mid}{255} \times 100$$

A high UACI/NPCR value is typically interpreted as a strong resistance to differential attacks (Tables 1 and 2).

The tables presented above offer a comprehensive comparison and analysis of different variations of the Playfair cipher that have been proposed by several authors. These variations suggest diverse strategies for enhancing the cipher's security and effectiveness, which has undergone several modifications over time. By studying these improvements, we can gain insights into the strengths and weaknesses of the Playfair cipher and explore ways to enhance it further. This analysis can be valuable in reinforcing current cryptographic systems and ensuring the confidentiality of sensitive information.

Table 1. Comparative analysis

Ref	Encryption technique	Complexity	Avalanche effect	Drawbacks
[11]	4 × 19 playfair matrix and RSA for encryption, RMPS keyless transposition followed by LSB steganography	Medium (Matrix size is 4 × 19, so a little slower as compared to traditional 5 × 5. The usage of RSA, steganography and RMPS keyless transposition adds to the complexity)	Weak (< 50%)	Can be broken by Man-in-the-middle attack as standard RSA is used risking the security of the public Key
[10]	Encryption using 5 × 5 playfair cipher method followed by LSB steganography	Medium (In Comparision to 16 × 16 matrix it will be fast but all characters won't be included)	Weak (MSE < 30 dB)	i) Large overhead to hide a very tiny amount of information using LSB. ii) When embedding the message in more than one LSB, the image quality may decrease depending on how many pixels are changed. So it is not robust.
[9]	3D 4 × 4 × 4 matrix is used for encryption, size is reduced by altering 8 digit ASCII code's binary form to it's corresponding 6 digit form followed by PVD steganography to conceal the message.	High (Lengthy algorithm that involves encoding using 3D 4 × 4 × 4 matrix, compression followed by hiding)	Weak (MSE < 30 dB)	i) Might be computationally complex ii) PVD displays a greater disparity between the original pixel values of the image allowing for more alteration.
[8]	Using two cross-chaotic maps a 16 × 16 Playfair matrix is produced. Image is divided into numerous blocks of size 16 × 16 bytes each which is encrypted using different playfair matrices.	High (Chaotic system is used for generating 16 × 16 byte playfair matrix corresponding to each image block)	Strong (The values of NPCR & UACI are in proximity to the optimal values.)	i) Original message cannot be retrieved from the enciphered text in many cases ii) Third party can access the information in the arrays, in case they get the algorithm. iii)Unless cipher text and plain text are in the same row or column they have a reciprocal relationship.
[7]	Use of 16 × 16 cipher matrix, XOR operations, two's complement followed by bit swapping	Medium (Improved performance significantly and processing time of the algorithm is linearly proportional)	Strong (around 53.7% on an average)	The proposed playfair cipher algorithm might not be highly optimised for implementation in software applications

Table 2. Analysis of different types of attacks on the modified playfair algorithm

Ref.	Brute force attack	Frequency analysis attack
[11]	Very difficult to carry out(Key domain size is 73! which is a very large number)	Although difficult but can be broken (Chance of occurrence is 0.013 as compared to 0.0385 in traditional cipher which is a significant improvement)
[10]	Can be broken(Key domain size is 25! Which is less than 2^128)	Weak resistance. Can be deciphered using modern techniques
[9]	Difficult as the attacker must find in 4096(64 × 16 × 4) trigraphs	A character's likelihood of appearing in 3D Playfair matrix is $1/16 \times 1/4 = 1/64(0.0156)$. Thus frequency analysis attack is difficult to carry out but chance of attack still persists
[8]	Might be regarded to be safe from brute force attack because of the large size of search space: $256 \times 256 = 65{,}536$	The likelihood of occurence is 0.0039(1/256) which is comparatively less when compared to traditional cipher making frequency analysis a more durable employment.
[7]	Good resistance (estimated 43.2 billion years required to crack a key containing 10 characters)	Randomness analysis of the algorithm indicated that the binary sequence is arbitrary. Thus difficult to decipher by analyzing the frequency of zeroes and ones [14]

5 Conclusion

After analysing different kinds of modification to Playfair Cipher, we came to conclusion that their security is not too high but can be employed in specific circumstances due to easy and low cost implementation. Playfair Cipher was in wide use during ancient period but due to increasing security requirements it became easily breach-able and thus unfit to use. We analysed few of the modifications to the Playfair cipher proposed in the last few years to strengthen it. The modified versions can be used in certain implementations due to their increased performance and low cost implementation thus, making it employable in modern day scenario.

References

1. Pandey, M., Dubey, M.: Survey paper: cryptography the art of hiding information. Int. J. Comput. Eng. Technol. **2**, 3168–3171 (2013)
2. Chhabra, P.: A survey on classic cipher in cryptography. Int. J. Innov. Res. Sci. Eng. Technol. **6** (2017). https://doi.org/10.15680/IJIRSET.2017.0605020
3. Rahman, M.N.A., Abidin, A., Yusof, M.K., Usop, N.: Cryptography: a new approach of classical hill cipher. Int. J. Secur. Appl. **7**(2), 179–190 (2013)
4. Majumder, R., Datta, S., Roy, M.: An enhanced cryptosystem based on modified classical ciphers. In: 2022 8th International Conference on Advanced Computing and Communication Systems (ICACCS), vol. 1, pp. 692–696 (2022). https://doi.org/10.1109/ICACCS54159.2022.9785033
5. Ahmad, J., Ahmed, F.: Efficiency analysis and security evaluation of image encryption schemes. IJENS **12**, 18–31 (2012)

6. Deepthi, R.: A survey paper on playfair cipher and its variants. Int. Res. J. Eng. Technol. **4**, 2607–2610 (2017)
7. Marzan, R.M., Sison, A.M.: An enhanced key security of playfair cipher algorithm. In: ICSCA 2019: Proceedings of the 2019 8th International Conference on Software and Computer Applications, pp. 457–461 (2019). https://doi.org/10.1145/3316615.3316689
8. Albahrani, E.A., Maryoosh, A.A., Lafta, S.H.: Block image encryption based on modified playfair and chaotic system. J. Inf. Secur. Appl. **51**, 102445 (2020). https://doi.org/10.1016/j.jisa.2019.102445
9. Kaur, G., Verma, H., Singh, R.: Dual steganography approach using 3D playfair cipher and pixel value differencing method. SSRN Electron. J. (2020). https://doi.org/10.2139/ssrn.3526694
10. Siswanto, A., Wahyuni, S., Arta, Y.: Combination playfair cipher algorithm and LSB steganography for data text protection, pp. 125–129 (2019). https://doi.org/10.5220/0009144501250129
11. Patil, R., Chaudhari, P.R., Dindorkar, M.R., Bang, S.V., Bangar, R.B.: Improved cryptography by applying transposition on modified playfair algorithm followed by steganography (2021)
12. Kshiteesh, R.B., Koundinya, U.R., Varun, R., Ajina, A., Prathima, G.: A review on challenges and latest trends on cyber security using text cryptography. In: Proceedings of the 3rd International Conference on Integrated Intelligent Computing Communication and Security (ICIIC 2021), pp. 194–201 (2021). https://doi.org/10.2991/ahis.k.210913.024
13. Ahmed, N., Asif, H., Saleem, G.: A benchmark for performance evaluation and security assessment of image encryption schemes. Int. J. Comput. Netw. Inf. Secur. **8**, 18–29 (2016). https://doi.org/10.5815/ijcnis.2016.12.03
14. Marzan, R.M., Sison, A.M., Medina, R.P.: Randomness analysis on enhanced key security of playfair cipher algorithm. Int. J. Adv. Trends Comput. Sci. Eng. 1248–1253 (2019). https://doi.org/10.30534/ijatcse/2019/34842019
15. Modupe, A., Adedoyin, A., Titilayo, A.: A comparative analysis of LSB, MSB and PVD based image steganography. Int. J. Res. Rev. **8**, 373–377 (2021). https://doi.org/10.52403/ijrr.20210948
16. Wang, Y.: A classical cipher-playfair cipher and its improved versions. In: 2021 International Conference on Electronic Information Engineering and Computer Science (EIECS), pp. 123–126 (2021). https://doi.org/10.1109/EIECS53707.2021.9587989
17. Rajeswari, S., Ramya, N., Saranya, K.: Avalanche effect based variants of playfair cipher for data security. Int. J. P2P Netw. Trends Technol. (2017)
18. Tunga, H., Mukherjee, S.: A new modified playfair algorithm based on frequency analysis. Int. J. Emerg. Technol. Adv. Eng. **2** (2012)
19. Yadav, M., Dhankhar, A.: A review on image steganography. Int. J. Innov. Res. Sci. Technol. **2**, 243–248 (2015)
20. Oladipupo, E.T., Abikoye, O.C.: Modified playfair cryptosystem for improved data security. Comput. Sci. Inf. Technol. **3**, 51–64 (2022). https://doi.org/10.11591/csit.v3i1.p51-64
21. Hamad, S., Khalifa, A., Elhadad, A., Rida, S.: A modified playfair cipher for encrypting digital images. J. Commun. Comput. Eng. **3**, 1 (2014). https://doi.org/10.20454/jcce.2013.731
22. Shakil, T., Islam, M.: An efficient modification to playfair cipher. ULAB J. Sci. Eng. **5**, 26 (2014)

23. Sankpal, P.R., Vijaya, P.A.: Image encryption using chaotic maps: a survey. In: 2014 Fifth International Conference on Signal and Image Processing, pp. 102–107 (2014). https://doi.org/10.1109/ICSIP.2014.80

24. Salunkhe, J., Sirsikar, S.: Pixel value differencing a steganographic method: a survey. Int. J. Comput. Appl. **975**, 8887 (2013)

25. Mathur, S.K., Srivastava, S.: Extended 16x16 play-fair algorithm for secure key exchange using RSA algorithm. Int. J. Future Revolution Comput. Sci. Commun. Eng. **4** (2018)

26. Anshari, M., Mujahidah, A.: Expending technique cryptography for plaintext messages by modifying playfair cipher algorithm with matrix 5 x 19. In: 2019 International Conference on Electrical Engineering and Computer Science (ICECOS), pp. 10–13 (2019). https://doi.org/10.1109/ICECOS47637.2019.8984560

27. Ahmed, A.M., Ahmed, S.H., Ahmed, O.H.: Enhancing 3D-playfair algorithm to support all the existing characters and increase the resistanceto brute force and frequency analysis attacks. In: 2017 International Conference on Current Research in Computer Science and Information Technology (ICCIT), pp. 81–85 (2017). https://doi.org/10.1109/CRCSIT.2017.7965538

28. Liu, L., Wang, J.: A cluster of 1D quadratic chaotic map and its applications in image encryption. Math. Comput. Simul. **204**, 89–114 (2023). https://doi.org/10.1016/j.matcom.2022.07.030

29. Sai D, J., Krishnaraj P, M.: Cryptographic interweaving of messages. Int. J. Data Inform. Intell. Comput. **2**(1), 42–50 (2023). https://doi.org/10.5281/zenodo.7766607

Single Electron Tunneling Based Threshold Logic Unit

Anup Kumar Biswas[✉]

Department of Computer Science and Engineering, Kalyani Government Engineering College, P.S.-Kalyani, Nadia, West Bengal 741235, India
akbcse456@gmail.com

Abstract. In the present era, electronic goods should be of high operating speed, high fan-out, minimum cost, least power consumption, and maximal component density of integration. These attributes are essentially required in technology, business, engineering, science and manufacturing. All those attributes can be fulfilled by using the circuits based on the tunneling of electron(s) through Single Electron Transistors (SETs) and Logic Gates following the Threshold logic. A Threshold logic gate (TLG) with multiple inputs is represented. With the help of it inverter, logic AND, OR, XOR, 4 × 1 Mux and their respective threshold logic gates are also depicted. And finally a Threshold Logic Unit (TLU) is drawn with some of its simulated inputs/outputs. How much power consumed by a logic gate/circuit, how much time it takes to execute (i.e. latency), and how many components required for constructing a circuit are provided in the chapter 13. An electron bears the charge adequate to keep an information in a Single Electron tunneling based device (SED). Energy needed for execution of an operation in the SED based circuits is very low when compared with CMOS-based circuits. TLG would be a best and fine candidate that satisfies the requirements needed to implement a more complex circuit. When an extremely low noise device is essential, TLG must be an extreme entity for the implementation of logic devices/modules. The fastness of the TLG-based circuit is very close to an electronic speed as an electron tunnels through the system with speed of an electron in metal. Delay versus capacitance and delay versus error probability are graphically depicted. The operating/switching speeds for the device(s)/module(s), their fan-out etc. are also cited in the related sections.

Keywords: Logic unit · Tunneling circuit · Coulomb blockade · threshold gate · processing delay

1 Introduction

Scientists, engineers or technologists in any section realize that ever decreasing size of transistors in the field of semiconductor and the corresponding increasing in the transistor-density facilitates different improvements, where the semiconductor based designs are involved. Eventually, one day such improvement would draw to a close. For the purpose of ascertain of further reduction of feature scale/size, we have found out successor technologies that have greater scaling potential. Such a technology like

© The Author(s), under exclusive license to Springer Nature Switzerland AG 2024
K. Dasgupta et al. (Eds.): CICBA 2023, CCIS 1956, pp. 196–218, 2024.
https://doi.org/10.1007/978-3-031-48879-5_16

single electron tunneling which is being investigated deeply by the researchers. As the single electron tunneling based devices need only a single electron to give an information whether the output is high or low, so researchers will be inspired to involve themselves in this research field. As the execution of logic operation is performed on the basis of the tunneling movement of a single electron under the applied input signals, and an electron consumes a small amount of energy (meV) to tunnel through the channel, the situation is interesting. This makes us interested in and draws attention of us. So the situation provides us the best motivation to do the present job.

Linear Threshold Gates (LTGs) and Single Electron tunneling devices (or SEDs) can fulfill the capabilities of managing the travelling of a single electron through a tunnel junction. The charge in a single electron is enough to keep the information in a SED. Depending upon the principle of single electron tunneling, any logical gates can be implemented. Keeping away the classical CMOS based device, we have been interested in implementing a logic unit by using TLGs.

A SED is an entity by which all types of logic gates–universal and non-universal, sequential and combinational circuits and further complex circuits are implemented. It is a powerful technique by which a circuit can be implemented using less number of components in comparison with CMOS gates. In a SED, tunneling events happen when an electron pass through the junction of a tunnel circuit under the control of bias voltage and input signals coupled to the islands through very small capacitances (aF). The objectives of this work are (i) to make a new set logic family and more complex sequential and combinational circuits by using the tunnel junction and "Multiple-input single-output threshold logic gate", (ii) to construct a circuit unit which requires a small amount of power to execute the operation, and (iii) As the operation is done by using only an electron, there must not be any collision between any two electrons. Hence it would be a noise free operation.

Without the FET or CMOS based logic circuits, a new technique is introduced to make the logic gates like Inverter, OR, AND, XOR and a more complex circuit–4 × 1 multiplexer. And their use greatly contributes to make a threshold logic unit (TLU) which becomes a part of an ALU in a central processing unit (CPU) of a computer system. All the related gates/circuits are implemented and provided in sections starting from Sects. 5–11.

2   Literature Review

Instead of BJT, FET or CMOS based logic gates, a new invention called single electron logic circuits is introduced first and these logic circuits are verified with the help of simulation [21]. On the basis of the single electron tunneling phenomena, a single electron transistor (SET) is invented and based on the SET, Binary-decisiondiagram (BDD) devices are created. In the BDD circuit, the structure of BDD is an uprooted binary-tree. When an electron tunnels from the root node towards a leaf node, this leaf node influenced by the electron provides the logic 1 and the other leaf node not influenced by a tunneling electron gives the logic 0 [20, 22–24]. Some authors are interested in developing Complementary digital logic using the *blockade mechanism* of the island of a SET called "Coulomb-blockade" [25]. Single electron devices (SEDs) on the basis of

SET are constructed and these devices are used in different applications [11]. A linear threshold gate having n-number of inputs and a single output is constructed. In this case only one tunnel Junction-Capacitor and some true capacitors are required to build it (i.e. a threshold gate) [10]. Here the critical voltage of the tunnel Junction-Capacitor plays the important role. If the junction voltage of a threshold gate exceeds the critical voltage, then only the output goes 1(high). Study in different attributes like power consumption, switching delay and required component numbers for a circuit/gate is comparable with [26].

With the continuation and progress of the field of computation, multimedia, space communication, medical, and agriculture the devices required to implement their requirements should be speedier. To increase the speed of a system, the system should be modified by high speed based basic components. Single electron tunneling based circuit is a candidate that fulfil the requirements of demand of a speedy system. All the researchers involved in the research field of tunneling circuit and threshold logic are hopeful that the single electron based device will be in small size, low cost, less power consumption, high concentration, less operation delay and Ultra-low noise. In some SET-based papers, more complex circuits implemented.

The technology of single-electron [1–4, 8, 15, 16] is made basically depending on two facts (i) Coulomb blockade [18, 19] and (ii) single electron tunneling events. Single electron tunneling circuits may be considered as a promising candidate for future VLSI circuits with respect to its high integration density, very low power consumption, reducing node capability, very small size, and rich functionality. Initial state of the development was Binary Decision Diagram [7, 20]. Then comes single electron tunneling based transistor [5, 6, 11, 12]. Based on this transistor we have been able to implement different logic gates. Next comes single electron tunneling based threshold gates [10]. Now we are in this position. In the development of the logic gates, different approaches have been adopted but the pattern remains the same. Recently a research has been done where the influence of variability is examined on SET into the SET-Based Circuits [17] and an improvement has been observed regarding operational temperature. So, the development is a continuation process. Progress of CMOS after BJT or JFET, SET after CMOS, Single electron threshold gate after SET is happening. With the progress, switching/processing speed is also increased, weight is decreased, module density is increased, and noise is decreased [6, 7].

Based on threshold gates, a logic unit is implemented where the structure of this circuit is on capacitances–tunnel capacitance and junction capacitances, but in the classical logic gates the structure is on the basis of transistor(s). In these two cases though the approaches are different but the patterns are the same.

3   A Tunnel Junction with a True Capacitor

In Fig. 1 is a Tunnel Junction-Capacitor set, made up of a junction capacitance C_j and a real capacitance C_c in series. A small black shaded circle island lies between the true capacitor and the tunnel junction. We will refer to this island as a **node** of that circuit having more n –number of electrons. Tunneling events happen through the tunnel junction only when electrons are forced to leave the node. If $n = 0$, it indicates no charge is available at present on the island. This situation tells us the story that, in reality, the island holds as many electrons so many protons, i.e. the island maintains balance condition electrically. A negative value of n indicates n-number of electrons are kept away from the surface of the island. Well-known that an electron contains a negative charge $(-1.602 \times 10^{-19} C)$. The value of $n < 0$ tells more positive charge available on the junction island. Similarly, when value of $n > 0$, it shows that more electrons are added to the island, in other words, more negative charges exist there.

We can express critical or internal voltage V_c for the tunnel junction by the equation [8, 9] given below:

$$V_C = \frac{e}{2(C_C + C_j)} \tag{1}$$

According to the sign convention as shown in Fig. 1, the total voltage (V_j) across the junction can be expressed as:

$$V_j = \frac{C_c V_{in}}{C_C + C_j} + \frac{ne}{C_C + C_j} \tag{2}$$

The first term, in Eq. (2), is caused by the fact that the input voltage V_{in} is divided capacitively for two capacitances C_j and C_C in series. Whereas the 2nd term $\frac{ne}{C_C + C_j}$ is the voltage expression due to $n-$ number of extra electron(s) existing on island, divided by the total capacitance $s(C_j + C_C)$ *present* in between the input and ground. In Fig. 1, the voltage V_{out} at the island with respect to the ground is given below:

$$V_{out} = \frac{C_j V_{in}}{C_C + C_j} - \frac{ne}{C_C + C_j} \tag{3}$$

The circuit must be in a stable state providing that the conditional equation $|V_j| < V_C$ is satisfied, and this conditional expression can be translated by proper substitutions of values V_C and V_j in Eqs. (1) and (2) respectively, into the following relation:

$$\frac{-e - 2ne}{2C_c} < V_{in} < \frac{e - 2ne}{2C_c} \tag{4}$$

So, for any analogue voltage V_{in} in Fig. 1, the circuit gets a stable state if the conditional relation in Eq. (4) is satisfied for an integer value of n. Assuming the circuit is in a stable state, then the voltage V_{in} is slowly being enhanced or decreased. In our observation we initially feel a corresponding enhance or decrease of V_{out} on account of the capacitive division in the Fig. 1. However, the V_j called the junction voltage will obtain a point/position in which the absolute value of it is more than the value of V_C, as a result an electron is passed through the junction and goes towards a direction which bears comparatively high voltage. At this point, for any $(+)V_{in}$, the electron were residing on the island, of course, tunnel away from this island (node), living an abrupt increase of the voltage of the island concerned. In the same away when a negative input V_{in} is *applied*, an electron from the junction must tunnels towards the island, supporting a sudden decrement of voltage in the island node.

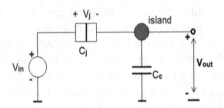

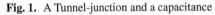

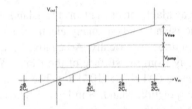

Fig. 1. A Tunnel-junction and a capacitance

Fig. 2. Junction characteristics of a tunnel-junction

The transfer characteristics for the input-output relation is shown in Fig. 2. In this figure, a sudden change of the output voltage is identified and written as $V_{jump} = \frac{e}{C_C + C_j}$, along with the voltage part V_{in} is capacitively divided on the capacitance Cc over the ranges or the input voltage, indication a stable state $V_{rise} = \frac{eC_j}{(C_C + C_j)C_C}$. The ratio of V_{jump} and V_{rise} is equal to $\frac{V_{jump}}{V_{rise}} = \frac{\frac{e}{C_C + C_j}}{\frac{eC_j}{(C_C + C_j)C_C}} = \frac{C_c}{C_j}$ which being the transfer function of this circuit and is shown in Fig. 2 as a staircase if $V_{jump} >> V_{rise}$ i.e., $C_c >> C_j$.

4 Threshold Logic Gate with Multiple Input

A TLG [1–5, 10, 11] with multiple inputs is made up of a tunnel junction with capacitance C_j and its internal resistance R_j shown in Fig. 3. Two levels of multiple input-signals V_k^P s and V_l^n s are directly joined to two different positions marking as 'q' and 'p' respectively, in which each of the input signals V_k^P is capacitively joined to "q" through their respective capacitances $C_k^P s$; and each input signals V_l^n (bottom), is capacitively connected to the position "p" through their respective capacitors C_l^n s. Supply voltage V_b is capacitively coupled with "q" through a capacitance C_b as well. The capacitor C_j is directly coupled with point "p" which is capacitively coupled with the ground through the coupling capacitor C_0. A TLG can also be implemented in cooperation with a particular function t(x) expressed with the help of the signum function V(x) in (6) and it is a dependent function of the Eq. (5) also

$$t(x) = sgn\{V(x)\} = \begin{cases} 1, & when\ V(x) \geq 0 \\ 0, & when\ V(x) < 0 \end{cases} \qquad (5)$$

$$V(x) = \sum\nolimits_{k=1}^{n} (w_k \times x_k) - \varnothing \qquad (6)$$

where $x_k \to k^{th}$-input (logic); and $w_k =$ respective k^{th}-integer weight; k=1,2,3...,n

Here $\sum_{k=1}^{n} (w_k \times x_k)$ being inputs-weighted sum and it is compared with $\varnothing$, called threshold value. When sum $\sum_{k=1}^{n} (w_k \times x_k) \geq \varnothing$ is satisfied, output of TLG will be logical "1", otherwise logical "0" is the output. The input signal vector $\{V_1^P, V_2^P, V_3^P, \ldots, V_k^P\}$, when weighted with their respective capacitance vector$\{C_1^P, C_2^P, C_3^P, \ldots, C_k^P\}$, are summed up with$V_j$. On the other hand, when input signals vector $\{V_1^n, V_2^n, V_3^n, \ldots, V_l^n\}$ (*in bottom*) are considered to be weighted with the capacitor vector$\{C_1^n, C_2^n, C_3^n, \ldots, C_l^n\}$, they are subtracted from V_j.

For enabling tunneling action, the critical voltage V_c is taken as in consideration, since V_c functions as the *intrinsic threshold* voltage regarding the junction of the tunneling circuit. The supply potential V_b joined to junction capacitance through a capacitor, C_b, is used to govern the gate threshold $\varnothing$. A tunneling happens, whenever an electron travels from position 'p' to 'q' as marked by a red arrow in Fig. 3.

The following notations and expressions will be used for the rest of our discussion and finding out the capacitance values.

$$C_\Sigma^P = C_b + \sum_{k=1}^{g} C_k^P \tag{6a}$$

$$C_\Sigma^n = C_0 + \sum_{l=1}^{h} C_l^n \tag{7}$$

$$C_T = C_\Sigma^P C_j + C_\Sigma^P C_\Sigma^n + C_j C_\Sigma^n \tag{8}$$

If all voltage sources are directly *coupled with/connected to* the ground in Fig. 3, the circuit is considered to be made up of three capacitances, C_Σ^P, C_Σ^n and C_j, connected in series. C_T in Eq. (8) is thought of the sum of products (SOP) of all 2-terms of the 3 capacitances C_j, C_Σ^P and C_Σ^n.

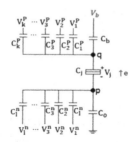

Fig. 3. Multiple input single output threshold logic gate. (Color figure online)

Here two types of capacitances should be considered: (i) C_j called tunnel junction capacitance and (ii) the capacitance of the rest part circuit called equivalent capacitance C_e. The critical voltage also called threshold voltage V_c for the tunnel junction are measured [1–4, 10] as

$$V_c = \frac{e}{2(C_j + C_e)} \tag{9}$$

$$= \frac{e}{2[C_j + (C_\Sigma^P || C_\Sigma^n)]}$$

$$= \frac{e}{2 * [C_j + \frac{(C_\Sigma^n)(C_\Sigma^P)}{(C_\Sigma^n + C_\Sigma^P)}]}$$

$$= \frac{(C_\Sigma^n + C_\Sigma^P)e}{2*[C_j(C_\Sigma^n + C_\Sigma^P) + (C_\Sigma^n)(C_\Sigma^P)]}$$

$$= \frac{(C_\Sigma^n + C_\Sigma^P)e}{2C_T} \tag{10}$$

In consideration with the fact that the voltage of the junction is V_j, a tunneling phenomenon comes to happen through this tunnel junction whenever the condition (11) is fulfilled.

$$|V_j| \geq V_c \tag{11}$$

It is transparent, when the condition $|V_j| < V_c$ happens, there will no tunneling through the junction. In this situation the tunneling circuit remains in a particular state called–*stable state*. We can also write for the function V(x) as [9, 10]

$$C_T V(x) = C_\Sigma^n \sum_{k=1}^{g} C_k^P V_k^P - C_\Sigma^P \sum_{l=1}^{h} C_l^n V_l^n - 0.5*(C_\Sigma^n + C_\Sigma^P)e + C_\Sigma^n C_b V_b \tag{12}$$

$$S(x) = C_\Sigma^n \sum_{k=1}^{g} C_k^P V_k^P - C_\Sigma^P \sum_{l=1}^{h} C_l^n V_l^n - \varnothing \tag{13}$$

$$\text{and } \varnothing = 0.5*(C_\Sigma^n + C_\Sigma^P)e - C_\Sigma^n C_b V_b \tag{14}$$

5 Buffer/Inverter

The buffer/inverter [1, 3, 4, 8–10] complements itself i.e. inverts its own input as depicted in Fig. 4(d)–(e). Inverter is constructed using two SETs (SET1 and SET2) connected in series. There are two same input voltages V_{in} and V_{in} being coupled to the two different islands the SET1 (upper) and SET2 (lower) [1–3, 9, 10] respectively through two capacitors C_1 and C_2 with same values. The islands of SET1 and SET2 bear the sizes of 10 nm diameter of gold. The capacitances of two islands are taken less than the value of 10^{-17} F. The output terminal V_0 emerging from a point in between SET1 and SET2 is connected directly to the ground through another capacitance C_L. The capacitor C_L is taken for the purpose of putting down charging effects.

The parameters for an inverter are chosen as: $V_{g2} = \frac{q_e}{10C}, V_{g1} = 0, C_L = 9C, t_4 = \frac{1}{10}C$, $t_3 = \frac{1}{2}C, t_2 = \frac{1}{2}C, t_1 = \frac{1}{10}C, C_1 = \frac{1}{2}C, C_2 = \frac{1}{2}C, C_{g1} = C_{g2} = \frac{17}{4}C, R1 = R2 = 50$ KΩ. In the present situation, the capacitance value of C would be 1aF.

The characteristics of the inverter is as: - when the input V_{in} is zero, the output V_0 is logic high; and when the input signal is logic high V_{in} the output V_0 is logic low. To get this target, previously we must set $V_{g1} = 0V$ and V_{g2}=16 mV. At present, the common input voltage V_{in} is connected for both SET1 and SET2. SET1 is in conduction mode, i.e. electron tunneling happens, if V_{in} is set to low and SET2 must be in Coulomb

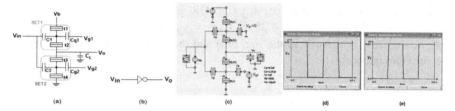

Fig. 4. (a) Buffer; (b) Symbol. (c) Buffer simulation set. (d), (e) Buffer input and output

blockade [2–6, 11] at that particular time meaning there is no electron tunneling through SET2. This situation helps connect the terminal point V_0 to V_b; and we have the output voltage 1 (high). The steady current flow through an inverter is really restricted to by Coulomb blockade. When high V_{in} ($=$ logic 1) is applied, it causes '*the charge induced on the islands for the SET1 and SET2*' to shift by only a fractional part of an electron charge (-1.602×10^{-19}) and necessitates SET1 in Coulomb blockade whereas SET2 is set in conducting mode. Therefore, V_0 is transformed from logic high to low. Hence the circuit shown in Fig. 4(a) performs the operation of an inverter.

In this case, we have taken logic "0" = zero Volt, logic "1" = $\frac{q_e}{10C}$ Volt.

When simulated, the value of $C=1$ auto Farad (aF) is taken and Logic "1" = $\frac{1.602 \times 10^{-19}}{10 \times 10^{-18}} = 0.1 \times 1.602 \times 10^{-2} = 16.02 \times 10^{-3} = 16.02$ mV $\cong$ 16 mV.

6 Threshold Logic OR Gate

For the finding out the threshold logic equation of OR gate we assume OR(P,Q) = sgn$\{w_P.P + w_Q.Q - \varnothing\}$. For constructing a desired threshold-based logic OR, at the beginning we represent the Table 1 for an OR gate, thereafter we must compare the coefficient w_P and w_Q of variables P and Q respectively with $\varnothing$(*threshold*).

Table 1. Truth table of threshold logic OR

Sl. No.	P	Q	F(P,Q)	$\varnothing$	Eqn. no.
1	0	0	0	$0 < \varnothing$	(i)
2	0	1	1	$w_Q \geq \varnothing$	(ii)
3	1	0	1	$w_P \geq \varnothing$	(iii)
4	1	1	1	$w_Q + w_P \geq \varnothing$	(iv)

For the 4 conditional equations in Table 1, when $w_P=1$, $w_Q=1$ and $\varnothing=0.5$, all 4 conditional equations in the above table are satisfied. Hence, one set of solution set is $sw_P=1$, $w_Q=1$ and $\varnothing=0.5$. Based on this solution set, the equation for OR gate regarding threshold logic is written in (15) and its TLG is depicted in Fig. 5(a).

$$OR(P, Q) = sgn\{P + Q - 0.5\} \qquad (15)$$

The parameters required to construct an OR gate, are as $C_1^n = C_2^n = 0.5aF$, $C_3 = 11.7aF$, $C_{b1} = C_{b2} = 4.25aF$, $C_{g1} = C_{g2} = 0.5aF$, $C_L = 9aF$, $C_0 = 8aF$, $R_j = 10^5\Omega$, $V_s = 16\,mV$ in the Fig. 5(b) and the output we have is presented in Fig. 5(c) through 5(e).

$$P \quad Q \quad \boxed{\begin{array}{c}1\\0.5\\1\end{array}} \quad P+Q$$
OR
(a)

Fig. 5. (a) A threshold based OR. (b) Simulation set of OR gate, (c)–(e) input-output result of an TLG based OR gate

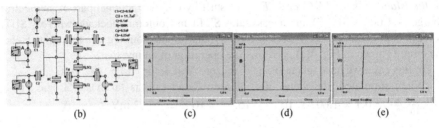

(b)   (c)   (d)   (e)

Fig. 5. (*continued*)

7 Threshold AND Gate

When an AND threshold logic gate is intended to depict, the Table 2 related to AND gate is drawn. The different coefficient values w_P and w_Q for variables P and Q consecutively are compared with the threshold $\varnothing[1, 2, 3, 4]$. Having solved the 4 inequalities in 5th column for the Table 2, a set of solution $w_P = 1$, $w_Q = 1$ and $\varnothing = 2$ is obtained.

And based on this, the expression for threshold logic of an AND gate is presented in Eq. (16) and the TLG of Eq. (16) is shown below in Fig. 6(a).

$$AND(P, Q) = sgn\{P + Q - 2\} \tag{16}$$

For AND gate implementation parameters $C_1^n = C_2^n = 0.5aF$, $C_{b1} = C_{b2} = 4.25aF$, $C_{g1} = C_{g2} = 0.5aF$, $C_L = 9aF$, $C_0 = 8aF$, $R_j = 10^5\Omega$ are accepted. The simulation set is presented in Fig. 6(b), after simulating the input-output results are given in Fig. 6(c)–(e).

8 3-Input AND Gate Based on Threshold Logic

To draw a 3-in threshold AND gate, Table 3 is depicted. Since an AND gate is positive logic and NAND is negative logic, we should accept all the weights w_P, w_Q, w_Q of variables "P, Q and R" for 3-in AND gate. *the value of* $\varnothing$ is positive. After investigating

Table 2. Truth table of 2-input threshold AND

Sl. No.	P	Q	F(P,Q)	$\varnothing$	Eqn. no.
1	0	0	0	$0 < \varnothing$	(i)
2	0	1	0	$w_B < \varnothing$	(ii)
3	1	0	0	$w_A < \varnothing$	(iii)
4	1	1	1	$w_B + w_A \geq \varnothing$	(iv)

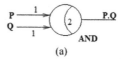

(a)

Fig. 6. (a) A threshold AND with threshold value 2. (b) A threshold AND Gate. (e) Output result of 2-input AND gate; where (c) and (d) are inputs

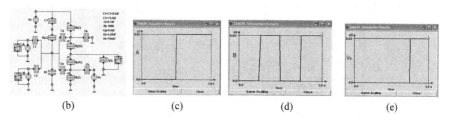

Fig. 6. (*continued*)

we have a set of values $w_P = 1, w_Q = 1, w_R = 1$ and $\varnothing = 2.5$ (or any value in the range $2 < \theta \leq 3$) those satisfy all the conditional expressions in the 6th column of the Table 3. Hence, 3-input AND gate threshold logic expression would be

$$AND(PQR) = sgn\{w_P.P + w_Q.Q + w_R.R - \varnothing\}$$

$$= sgn\{P + Q + R - 2.5\} \tag{17}$$

A simulation set for 3-input AND gate and its results are depicted below in Fig. 7(a) and (b).

9 2-Input Threshold XOR

The logic expression for an XOR is written as $Y = (P.\overline{Q} + \overline{P}.Q)$, here P and Q are two input variables. Space plot diagram of XOR of 2-variables in 2D space is shown in Fig. 8. From Fig. 8, we see that there is no linear separating line that can divide the colorless bubbles and green bubbles and into two separate groups. As a result, the Boolean logic function of the XOR is not linearly separable. So, we would not be able to construct directly a TLG representing the equation $Y = P.\overline{Q} + \overline{P}.Q$.

Table 3. Truth table of 3-input AND

Sl. No.	P	Q	R	PQR	$\varnothing$
1	0	0	0	0	$0 < \varnothing$
2	0	0	1	0	$\varnothing > w_R$
3	0	1	0	0	$\varnothing > w_P$
4	0	1	1	0	$\varnothing > w_Q + w_R$
5	1	0	0	0	$\varnothing > w_P$
6	1	0	1	0	$\varnothing > w_P + w_R$
7	1	1	0	0	$\varnothing > w_P + w_Q$
8	1	1	1	1	$w_P + w_Q + w_R \geq \varnothing$

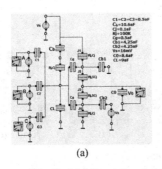 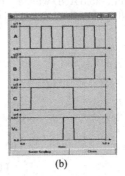

(a)   (b)

Fig. 7. (a) 3-Input threshold AND; (b) Input-output graph

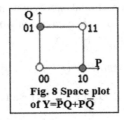

Fig. 8 Space plot of Y=$\overline{P}$Q+P$\overline{Q}$

For giving the Boolean function $Y = P.\overline{Q} + \overline{P}.Q$ by means of a threshold logic, first, we should assume $R = P.\overline{Q}$ and then express it in the form of threshold-based Eq. (18) below.

$$R = sgn\{P + \overline{Q} - 2\} \tag{18}$$

It is known that $Q + \overline{Q} = 1$ or $\overline{Q} = -Q + 1$, substituting this $\overline{Q} = -Q + 1$ for Eq. (18) and we get Eq. (19).

$$R = sgn\{P - Q - (1)\} \tag{19}$$

Fig. 8. (a) Threshold gate of P = P$\overline{Q}$. (b) Threshold gate of A.$\overline{B}$ using 2-buffers

Table 4. Truth table of Eq. (19)

Sl. No.	P	Q	R
1	0	0	0
2	0	1	0
3	1	0	1
4	1	1	0

Table 5. Truth table of $\overline{R}$

Sl. No.	P	Q	$\overline{R}$	$\varnothing$
1	0	0	1	$0 \geq \varnothing$
2	0	1	1	$W_Q \geq \varnothing$
3	1	0	0	$W_P < \varnothing$
4	1	1	1	$W_P + W_Q \geq \varnothing$

We would like to find out the inverting expression of P, so that it calculates $\overline{R} = \overline{P}$ + Q. After investigating all the conditional expressions give in Table 5 (in 5th column), we are able to write the expression of $\overline{R}$ = sgn {$-$ P +Q $-$ (−0.5)}.

The values of the parameters required to implement the threshold logic of $\overline{R}$, will be like: input "0" = 0 V, logic "1" = 16 mV and other parameters like C = 1aF, $C_1^P = C_1^n = 0.5C$ where C = 1aF, $C_b = 10.24aF$, $C_L = 9aF$, $C_j = \frac{1}{4}aF$, $C_0 = 9.5C = 9.5aF$, $R_j = 0.1$ MOhm, $V_b = 0.95e/C = 15.2$ mV($ase/C = 160$ mV) *which is close to* 16 mV, so $V_b = V_s = 16$ mV.

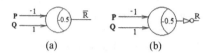

Fig. 9. (a) Threshold logic gate of $\overline{R}$, (b) of R

Now we are to convert the Boolean expression Y = P.$\overline{Q}$ + $\overline{P}$.Q into threshold logic form. We assume R = P.$\overline{Q}$., So Y = R + $\overline{P}$.Q. Say

$$Y = R + \overline{P}.Q \qquad (20)$$

If we wish to obtain logic gate based on threshold logic for the Eq. (20), we should give the Table 6 using the Table 4. Now we are able to solve the inequalities to get the weightage values in 5th col. of Table 6.

Table 6. Truth table of Eq. (20)

Sl. No.	P	Q	R	Y	$\varnothing$
1	0	0	0	0	$0 < \varnothing$
2	0	1	0	1	$W_Q \geq \varnothing$
3	1	0	1	1	$W_P + W_R \geq \varnothing$
4	1	1	0	0	$W_P + W_Q < \varnothing$

After solving the conditional equations in Table 6, we can gate a solution set $\{W_P, W_Q, W_R; \varnothing\} = \{-1, 1, 2; (1)\}$. Now the XOR expression of Y is given as

$$Y = Sgn\{-P + Q + 2R - (1)\} \tag{21}$$

The TLG for the Eq. (21) is depicted below in Fig. 10. For correct operation, we are to fix an inverter in series to get an XNOR that is shown also in Fig. 10. If we again add another inverter in series we must get an XOR gate shown in Fig. 10 as well.

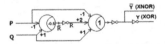

Fig. 10. XOR/XNOR gate of two inputs

10 Finding Out the Threshold Circuit Parameters of an XOR/XNOR Gate

We can describe the following approach:

$$Y = sgn\{-P + Q + 2R - (1)\} \tag{21}$$

Comparing Eqs. (6), (7) and (8), we observe the following relation for the weights

$$2C_{\sum}^P C_1^n = 2C_{\sum}^n C_1^P = C_{\sum}^n C_2^P$$

Assuming $C_{\sum}^P = C_{\sum}^n$ then we have

$$C_1^n = C_1^P = 0.5C_2^P = \frac{1}{2}C \text{ (assume)}$$

Assuming $C_{\Sigma}^P = 10C$, $C_{\Sigma}^n = 10C$, from Eq. (6)

$$C_{\Sigma}^P = C_b + \sum_{k=1}^{g} C_k^P$$

$$10C = C_b + 0.5C + 1C \Rightarrow C_b = 8.5C$$

From Eq. (7), $C_{\Sigma}^n = C_0 + \sum_{l=1}^{h} C_l^n$

$$10C = C_0 + 0.5C \Rightarrow C_0 = 9.5C$$

When an electron passes through the junction as marked by a red arrow from position "p" to the position "q" in Fig. 11, there will have an effect of enhancing the charge on the node position "q" by an amount equal to "-e" and this in term changes the voltage V_q at point "q" by a small amount δV_q, ($\delta q_{charge} = -e$) equal to $\frac{(C_j + C_{\Sigma}^n)e}{C_T}$. This voltage change will also effect on the voltage output by an amount $V_0(\delta q_{charge} = -e)$ equal to $\frac{-(C_j)e}{C_T}$. In the same way, there will be an effect of voltage on the point "p" and the voltage change will be equal to $\delta V_0(\delta p_{charge} = +e) = \frac{(C_j + C_{\Sigma}^P)e}{C_T}$. Total voltage effect on the output when an electron goes towards the red arrow direction will be

$$\delta V_0(1e) = V_0\left(\delta q_{charge} = -e\right) + \delta V_0(\delta p_{charge} = +e)$$

$$= \frac{-(C_j)e + (C_j + C_{\Sigma}^P)e}{C_T} = \frac{e(C_{\Sigma}^P)}{C_T} \tag{22}$$

Putting the parameter values we got above into the Eq. (22), the effective output voltage will be as below.

$$\partial V_0(1 \text{ electon}) = \frac{eC_{\Sigma}^P}{C_{\Sigma}^P C_j + C_{\Sigma}^P C_{\Sigma}^n + C_j C_{\Sigma}^n} = \frac{10e}{(10 \times 0.25 + 10 \times 10 + 0.25 \times 10)C}$$

$$= \frac{10e}{105C} = 0.095e/C \tag{23}$$

From the Eq. (23) the output voltage $= \frac{10e}{105C} = 0.095e/C$ is considered "1" when electron tunnels and the output voltage $=$ "0" when no electron tunnels.

Since the voltage logic levels and the corresponding weights of the input signals are assigned and assumed to be fixed, we will be interested in finding out the exact threshold value $\varnothing$.

The threshold in a circuit is thought to be the critical voltage (V_c). The tunneling rate of in a circuit is directly proportional to the difference of the two voltages V_c *and* V_j that is $V_j \sim V_c$ and which coincides with the value of $V(x)$.

For the purpose of compromising the marginal values in Vin (input voltage) and maximizing $V(x)$, we put $\varnothing = 1$.

All the parameter values contributing to measure $V(x)$ are taken in their ratios. The same ratios are accepted for $\varnothing$. Assuming that $C_{\sum}^{n} \times C_{2}^{P} = 1$, and $0.095\ e/C \cong 0.1\ e/C$ which represents high logic, the threshold voltage $\varnothing$ [7–9] is given as per the ratio i.e.,

$$\varnothing = 1 \times C_{\sum}^{n} \times C_{2}^{P} \times 0.1e/C \tag{24}$$

Substitute this value to the equation below [14].

$$\varnothing = \frac{1}{2} * (C_{\sum}^{n} + C_{\sum}^{P})e - C_{\sum}^{n} C_b V_b \tag{25}$$

The value of $C_{\sum}^{n} C_{2}^{P}$ is used to represent the weight of value 1 and the value of $0.095\ e/C \cong 0.1\ e/C$ is used to indicate an input logic value equal to 1. Substituting these values to the Eq. (23)

$$1 \times C_{\sum}^{n} C_{2}^{P} \times 0.1e/C = \frac{1}{2} * (C_{\sum}^{n} + C_{\sum}^{P})e - C_{\sum}^{n} C_b V_b \tag{26}$$

$$\Rightarrow 1 \times 1 \times 1C \times 0.1e = 0.5(10C + 10C)e - 10C \times C_b V_b$$

$$\Rightarrow V_b = 0.99e.$$

$$\text{Hence } C_b V_b = 8.5C \times 0.99e/C = 0.84e \tag{27}$$

If we wish to take a lesser or larger value of V_b, the value of C_b would be inversely decreased or increased as the product of the two equal to 0.84e, i.e. $C_b V_b = 0.84e$. Given that $C_b = 8.5C$ then $V_b = 15.81$ mV.

We must add an additional capacitance C_g between the point q and ground in Fig. 11 to balance the required input voltage(s), satisfying the equation

$$C_g = 8.5C - C_b \tag{28}$$

Using the parameter's ratio for cases discussed above, we have verified the design of **XOR**. For simulation purpose we have to take the values as given below:

Input logic "0" $= 0$ V, Input logic "1" $= 16$ mV and other parameters like C = 1aF, $C_{1}^{P} = C_{1}^{n} = 0.5C$ where C $= 1$aF, $C_b = 10.24aF$, $C_L = 9aF$, $C_j = \frac{1}{4}aF$, $C_0 = 9.5C = 9.5aF$, $R_j = 0.1$ MOhm, $V_b = 0.95e/C = 15.2$ mV$(ase/C = 160$ mV$)$ which is close to 16 mV, so $V_b = V_s = 16$ mV.

11   A 4:1 Multiplexer Based on TLG

A (4 : 1) Multiplexer has four inputs (A,B,C,D), one output (P) and two selection or control lines C_0 and C_1. Based on threshold logic linear diagram, we have drawn a (4 × 1) Multiplexer in Fig. 12(a). By selecting the two control lines C_0 and C_1, one of the four variables A, B, C or D can be chosen and this chosen value is projected at the output terminal. The input-output relationship along with control signals is shown in Fig. 12(b).

Here we need 3 components to make the 4:1 Multiplexer like: (i) an inverter (ii) a single 3-input AND gate and (iii) a single 4-input OR gate. After measuring different required parameters for a single 4-input OR gate and a single 3-input AND gate based on TLG we have constructed the 4:1 Multiplexer depicted in Fig. 13 below.

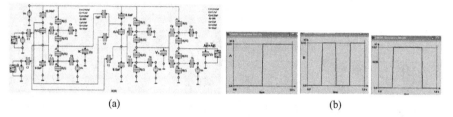

(a)   (b)

Fig. 11. (a) XOR (A,B) simulation set. (b) Input output Simulation result for (a)

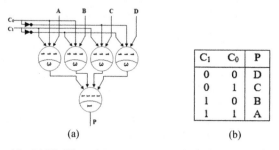

C_1	C_0	P
0	0	D
0	1	C
1	0	B
1	1	A

(a)   (b)

Fig. 12. (a) TLG based 4:1 Multiplexer. (b) Functional Diagram

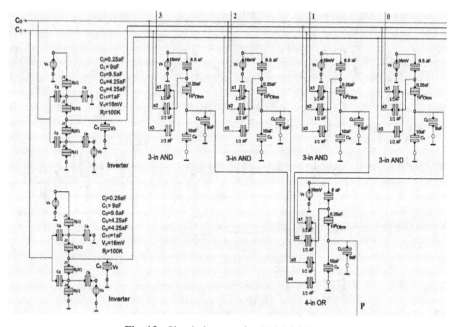

Fig. 13. Simulation set of a 4:1 Multiplexer

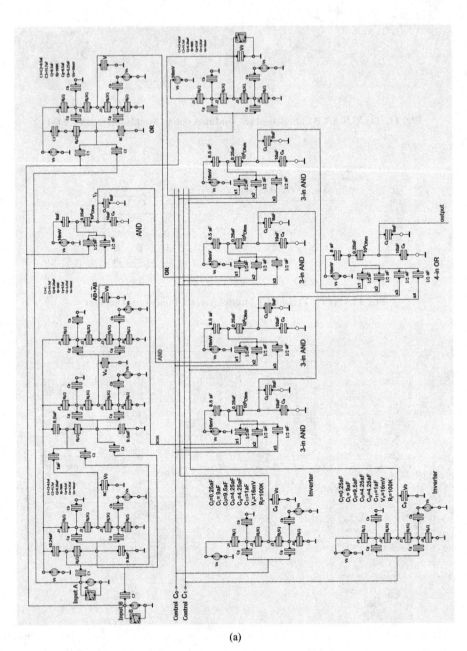

(a)

Fig. 14. (a) Logic Unit Simulation set. (b) Simulation result of Fig. 14

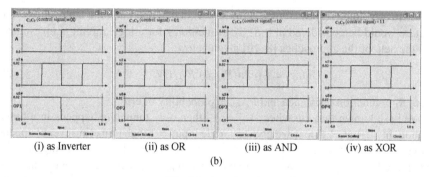

(i) as Inverter	(ii) as OR	(iii) as AND	(iv) as XOR

(b)

Fig. 14. (*continued*)

12 Circuit of a Logic Unit

In association with the 4:1 Multiplexer, one XOR gate, one AND gate, one OR gate and one Inverter, we have been able to implement a logic unit in Fig. 14 having 2 inputs A and B, 2 control lines C_0 and C_1 and one output line. The simulation set and its input-output relationship graphs are depicted respectively in the Fig. 14(a) and (b) below.

The numerical (logical) relationship of input/output is shown below in Table 7.

Table 7. Truth table of logic unit

control C_0C_1	Input (A, B)	Selected gate	output
0 0	(0,0), (0,1), (1,0), (1,1)	Inverter ($\overline{A}$)	1, 1, 0, 0
0 1	(0,0), (0,1), (1,0), (1,1)	OR	0, 1, 1, 1
1 0	(0,0), (0,1), (1,0), (1,1)	AND	0, 0, 0, 1
1 1	(0,0), (0,1), (1,0), (1,1)	XOR	0, 1, 1, 0

13 Discussion

In our present work, we have implemented some threshold logic gates like Inverter, OR, AND, and XOR, in addition, a 4 $\times$ 1 Multiplexer and a more complex circuit called a Logic Unit are implemented. Their possible circuits and simulated waveforms are also included in due places. In addition to them, their threshold logic gates have also been depicted by analyzing their different linear separable logic equations.

Fastness or speed for the perspective analysis of respective circuits should be analyzed and discussed. For the purpose of finding out the processing delay of the circuit discussed in previous sections we must include C_j and V_c called junction capacitance *and* critical voltage respectively. For our experimental operation the atmospheric temperature would be considered at $0\ K$. The time-delay for a logic circuit is investigated with the help of the approaches [8–10] given below:

$$\text{Delay} = -(e|\ln(P_{error})|R_t)/(|V_j| - V_c) \quad (29)$$

where R_t = junction resistance and P_{error} = probability of error

We have known that the when $|V_j| > V_c$ then only tunneling happens in a tunnel junction. In a 2-in OR gate if we give any logic input $= 1$ then tunneling event happens, giving junction voltage $V_j =11.8$mV and the V_c voltage $= 11.58$ mV. Taking the error probability $P_{error} = = \frac{1}{10^{12}}$ and $R_t =$ junction resistance $= 0.1$M Ohm we have the delay $= 0.07281\ |\ln(P_{error})| = 1.675$ ns. In the same process for any logic gates or circuits, the delay can be measured. For some gates, the delays are calculated and they are provided in a tabular form in the Table 8.

At the time of a tunneling event, the total energy existing in a circuit changes. The difference between the two energy levels (i) before the tunneling and (ii) after the tunneling is given in following Eq. (30).

$$\Delta E = E_{before\ tunnel} - E_{after\ tunnel}$$

$$= -e(V_c - |V_j|) \quad (30)$$

This is the total amount of tunneling energy exhausted during the event of tunneling in any circuit where tunneling event happening.

We can provide the processing delay time versus junction capacitance curve in Fig. 15(a) and processing delay versus error probability of switching in the Fig. 15(b).

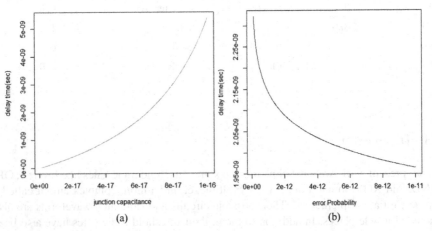

(a)   (b)

Fig. 15. (a) Variation curve: delay time versus Jn capacitance. (b) Variation curve: delay time versus error probability

The elements number applied to a circuit/ gate, switching energy consumed by the circuit and switching delays can be counted, (by the methodology used for Boolean gates). All the respective calculated parameters are given in the Table 8 for different gates/circuits.

Table 8. Truth table of delay time & switching energy

Sl. No.	Elements no.	For Gate/circuit	Delay time nano-sec	Switching Energy meV
1	09	Single inverter	$0.022|\ln(P_{error})|$	10.4
2	14	NOR	$0.072|\ln(P_{error})|$	10.7
3	14	OR	$0.062|\ln(P_{error})|$	10.8
4	14	NAND	$0.080|\ln(P_{error})|$	10.7
5	14	AND	$0.062|\ln(P_{error})|$	10.8
6	15	3-input AND	$0.104|\ln(P_{error})|$	11.58
7	15	3-input NAND	$0.072|\ln(P_{error})|$	11.58
8	29	2-input XOR	$0.102|\ln(P_{error})|$	21.2
9	15	3-input OR	$0.104|\ln(P_{error})|$	11.58
10	15	3-input NOR	$0.104|\ln(P_{error})|$	11.55
11	16	4-input OR	$0.118|\ln(P_{error})|$	12.35
12	52	4x1-MUX	$0.210|\ln(P_{error})|$	39.74
13	110	Logic unit	$0.312|\ln(P_{error})|$	84.07

The Table 9 is provided for comparing the proposed study in Table 8 with existing literature [26].

Table 9. Truth table of area, delay time & switching energy

Gate/circuit	Area	Delay	Switching Energy
2-input OR	14	$0.062\ |\ln(P_{error})|$ ns	10.8 meV
2-input NAND	14	$0.080\ |\ln(P_{error})|$ ns	10.7 meV
R-S latch	24	$0.098\ |\ln(P_{error})|$ ns	21..1 meV
D latch	38	$0.16\ |\ln(P_{error})|$ ns	31.9 meV
D flip-flop	76	$0.16\ |\ln(P_{error})|$ ns	63.8 meV

The number of elements and how much energy consumed by the respective circuits are shown by the vertical bars against the individual gates in Fig. 16.

Next, we have given the comparative study concerning switching delay of single electron Transistors (SET) and TLGs in Table 10.

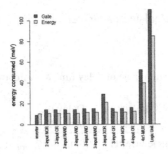

Fig. 16. Consumed energy of gates versus gate elements

Table 10. Truth table of SET-based and TLG-based circuit

Sl. No.	For which Gate/circuit	SET-based delay nano-sec	TLG-based delay nano-sec
1	inverter	8	0.60
2	NOR	4	1.67
3	OR	4	1.71
4	NAND	4	2.21
5	AND	4	1.71
6	3-input AND	8	2.87
7	3-input NAND	8	1.98
8	2-input XOR	4	2.81
9	3-input OR	8	2.87
10	3-input NOR	16	2.87
11	3-input AND	8	2.87
12	3-input NAND	16	2.26
13	4-input OR	16	2.87
14	4 × 1-MUX	22	5.74
15	Logic Unit	38	8.61

Different threshold logic gates and circuits have different processing delays. For instance, 2-input OR gates have switching delay $0.062|\ln(P_{error})|$ ns, 3-input AND gate has $0.104|\ln(P_{error})|$ ns, and 4x1-MUX has $0.208|\ln(P_{error})|$ ns and so on.

By taking the probability error $(P_{error}) = \frac{1}{10^{12}}$, the time delay after which the first most output of Logic Unit will deliver is $= 0.312(|\ln(P_{error})|) = 7.7529087$ ns. i.e., after every 7.7529087ns, the next output will be accepted from the Logic Unit. Hence, the output rate will be $\frac{1}{7.7529087} = 0.12898 \times 10^9 = 128.9$ MHz.

Somebody shall be interested about the delays of SET and CMOS -based circuit. The delays for logic gate like NOR, NAND, AND, OR, XOR of CMOS is 12 ns [13, 14], but that for a SET [10, 11] it is 4 ns [5–13].

14   Conclusion

With the improvement of engineering, science and technology, the demand of high speed electronic goods along with the fundamental logic components of gates, should be of high speed. On the basis of SET or TLG, the speed of a circuit can be increased with respect to CMOS. In this work, we discussed a tunnel junction characteristic curve, multi-input single-output threshold logic gate, some logic gates like 2-input AND, OR, XOR, 3-input AND etc. 4×1 Multiplexer, and a logic unit which is used in an Arithmetic Logic Unit (ALU). A logic family of gates can be fabricated or constructed from the conception of a linearly TLG. Almost all the circuits /gates presented in this work are verified and the results are shown in due places with the help of SIMON. Number of elements (n) required in logic gates or more complex circuits, their processing delay time, power consumed by them are discussed and given the values in different tables. We have found that the fan-out/speed a TLG is two-fold faster than the SET based logic circuits. The merits of the single electron tunneling based circuits are (i) performance of such device is increased as the density of components in space very high, (ii) Power consumption is low in meV, (iii) Speed of operational execution is close to electronic speed and (iv) Construction of threshold tunneling circuits can be made as scalable to the levels of molecules. Future scope: In reality, the circuit atmosphere is kept at low temperature (in 0 K) which is very crucial job in present situation. To overcome this trouble researches should involve themselves to make such single electron circuits being operated at atmospheric temperature close to 20 °C. One possible suggestion to overcome this demerit is to use both FET and single electron tunneling threshold gate when the variability of them are introduced [17]. When succeeded, we would be able to implant a huge number of different modules in a compact-form within a small volume with high component density. Changing the quantum dot position, the temperature level can be improved close to atmospheric temperature, though it is under investigation. When possible, a new horizon will open in front of technological world.

The capacitance value of C is chosen as 1aF for "multiple inputs and one output based single electron tunneling logic gates" in this paper, and accordingly the logic input voltage is found to be 16 mv. Somebody can intentionally change the value of C, then values of all input voltages are to be altered accordingly. The value of all input voltages V_k^p (upper) and V_l^n (lower) in Fig. 3 are 16 mV for all values of (p,k) and (n,l) respectively.

References

1. Biswas, A.K.: Measuring of an unknown voltage by using single electron transistor based voltmeter. Semiconduct. Phys. Quant. Electron. Optoelectron. **24**(3), 277–287 (2021). ISSN:1605-6582 (On-line)
2. Biswas, A.K.: Application of single electron threshold logic gates and memory elements to an up-down Counter. Int. J. Creat. Res. Thoughts **9**(6) (2021). ISSN:2320-2882
3. Biswas, A.K.: Implementation of a 4n-bit comparator based on IC Type 74L85 using linear threshold gate tunneling technology. Int. J. Eng. Res. Technol. **10**(05), 299–310 (2021). ISSN:2278-0181

4. Biswas, A.K.: State transition diagram for a pipeline unit based on single electron tunneling. Int. J. Eng. Res. Technol. **10**(04), 325–336 (2021). ISSN:2278-0181
5. Biswas, A.K.: Design of a pipeline for a fixed-point multiplication using single electron tunneling technology. Int. J. Eng. Res. Technol. **10**(04), 86–98 (2021). ISSN:2278-0181
6. Biswas, A.K., Sarkar, S.K.: An arithmetic logic unit of a computer based on single electron transport system. Semiconduct. Phys. Quant. Electron. Opt-Electron. **6**(1), 91–96 (2003)
7. Biswas, A.K., Sarkar, S.K.: Error detection and debugging on information in communication system using single electron circuit based binary decision diagram. Semiconduct. Phys. Quant. Electron. Opt. Electron. **6**, 1–8 (2003)
8. Korotkov, A.N.: Single-electron logic and memory devices. Int. Electronics **86**(5), 511–547 (1999)
9. Lageweg, C., Cotofana, S., Vassiliadis, S.: Single electron encoded latches and flip-flops. IEEE Trans. Nanotechnol. **3**(2), 237–248 (2004)
10. Lageweg, C., Cotofana, S., Vassiliadis, S.: A linear threshold gate implementation in single electron technology. In: IEEE Computer Society VLSI Workshop, p. 93 (2001)
11. Likharev, K.: Single-electron devices and their applications. Proc. IEEE **87**, 606–632 (1999)
12. Tucker, J.R.: Complementary digital logic based on the Coulomb-blockade. J. Appl. Phys. **72**(9), 4399–4413 (1992)
13. Millman, J., Halkias, C.C.: Integrated Electronics- Analog and Digital Circuits and Systems, 2nd edn. McGraw Hill Education
14. Millman's Electronic Devices & Circuits 4th edn (English, Paperback, Jacob Millman)
15. Asahi, N., Akazawa, M., Amemiya, Y.: Single electron logic device based on the binary decision diagram. IEEE Trans ED. **44**(7), 1109–1116 (1997)
16. Asahi, N., Akazawa, M., Amemiya, Y.: Single electron logic systems based on binary decision diagram. IEICE Trans. Electron. **1**, 49–56 (1998)
17. Amat, E., Bausells, J.: Exploring the influence of variability on single-electron transistors into SET-based circuits. IEEE Trans. Electron. Devices **64**, 12 (2017)
18. Durrani, Z., Irvine, A., Ahmed, H.: Coulomb blockade memory using integrated single-electron transistor/metal–oxide–semiconductor transistor gain cells. IEEE Trans. Electron Devices **47**, 2334–2339 (2000)
19. Korotkov, A., Likharev, K.: Single-electron-parametron-based logic devices. J. Appl. Phys. **84**(11), 6114–6126 (1998)
20. Asahi, N., Akazawa, M., Amemiya, Y.: Single electron logic system based on the binary decision. IEICE Trans. Electron **E81**, 1 (1998)
21. Kuwamura, N., Taniguchi, K., Halnaguchi, C.: Simulation of single electron logic circuits. IEICE Trans. **J77**(5), 221–228 (1994)
22. Asahi, N., Akazawa, M., Ainelniya, Y.: Binary -decisiondiagram device. IEEE Trans. Electron Devices **42**(11), 1990–2003 (1995)
23. Asahi, N., Akazawa, M., Alneniya, Y.: Single-electron logic device based on the binary decision diagram. IEEE Trans. Electron Devices **44**(7), 1109–1116 (1997)
24. Biswas, A.K., Sarkar, S.K.: An arithmetic logic unit of a computer based on single electron transport system. Semiconduct. Phys. Quant. Electron. Optoelectron. **6**(1), 91–96 (2003). PACS: 85.35.Gv
25. Tucker, J.R.: Complementary digital logic based on the Coulomb-blockade. J. Appl. Phys. **72**(9), 4399–4413 (1992)
26. Lageweg, C.: Single electron encoded latches and flip-flops. IEEE Trans. Nanotechnol. **3**(2), 237–248 (2004)

EDGE-Based Image Steganography

Bikram Mondal[(✉)] and Bivas Ranjan Dutta

Indian Institute of Technology, Hauz Khas, Delhi 110016, India
bikrammondal1947@gmail.com

Abstract. Steganography is a technique of hiding information in another data. In image steganography, the secret message is embedded inside one digital image. The most significant traffic comes from images on the internet, so hiding the data in images is most suitable. A digital image is represented as a grid of pixels, and generally, images have a large number of pixels, so a large amount of data can be hidden inside an Image. It is done so that there is less distortion with the image. The secret message is embedded in the image so that the human eye cannot detect it. Edge of Image means a sudden change in the image pixels. It captures the boundary present in some images, so edges are the most suitable place to hide the data in an image. In this paper, we will do some qualitative and quantitative analysis of various edge-based steganography methods, and we will compare this with the existing steganography methods available.

Keywords: Steganography · Digital image · Edge detection · Steganalysis

1 Introduction

Steganography has a very long history. This word means writing something in a covered thing. In modern times, steganography uses digital images, video, network traffic, and many more things to hide secret messages [9]. The principle of steganography says that it does not change the structure of the data, while in cryptography, the message is changed in another form.

In Cryptography, the main goal is to keep the message secret from any third party so that they cannot get the message's contents or cannot modify the message. But if the attacker knows that a secret message is transmitting through a channel, then he will try to decrypt the message using a different algorithm and may be able to get the contents of the message. we can overcome the cryptographic system's shortcomings by hiding the secret message's existence. This process is called as Steganography.

Security system is divided into two branches: message hiding and message alteration. Steganography comes under the message hiding part as we are not changing the form of data. Figure 1 will show the branches or divisions of system security [10, 14].

The process of detecting whether a digital medium contains secret information or not is known as Steganalysis.

There are two other methods in the message hiding part, along with steganography [11, 15]. In watermarking, we are concerned about the ownership of the image, and in

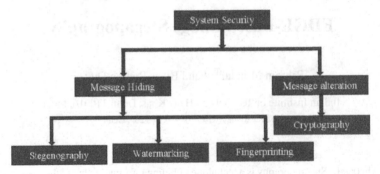

Fig. 1. Branches of system security.

fingerprinting, we give some distinct mark in the medium so that when anyone misuses the medium, the owner can take action against that. This method enables the ownership of and security of intellectual property. Any digital medium can be used as a steganography cover object to hide the hidden message. The medium with more degree of redundancy is preferred as cover objects [12]. A bit is called a redundant bit; if we change the bit, then the change in the file becomes minimal or negligible. Images consist of pixels, and each pixel is of 8 bits (generally). The pixel value can vary from 0–255. Now, if the last one or two least significant bits are modified of some pixels, then it is almost impossible for the human eye to detect the changes. So, the secret message can be embedded in the least significant one or two bits of some pixels of the image, and the attacker will not be able to guess that there is a secret message inside the image. Security of Image Steganography depends on the selection of the pixels. Now, noisy pixels are better options for hiding messages, and as the edge pixels are noisy, it is better to select the edge pixels for hiding information.

Figure 2 shows the most used digital objects that are used for steganography.

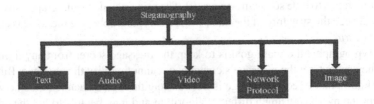

Fig. 2. Digital mediums used for steganography.

Text steganography is used at a very ancient age. Now it is not used so often because it has less redundancy. The often-used techniques for text steganography are the count of a capital letter, white spaces or tabs, and many more. In audio steganography, one popular technique is called masking. In masking, we use one phenomenon, which says that one low but the audible sound becomes not audible if we use another high-frequency sound. The digital formats used for audio steganography are AVI, WAVE. Using discrete wavelet Transformation (DWT), we can alter the pixels of images in the video file so that human eyes cannot detect the change. Network steganography can be done using the unused header bits of different networking protocols such as TCP, UDP, ICMP, and many more. Image pixel can be used as a cover to hide the information in image steganography.

As the internet explodes exponentially, the attackers become more sophisticated and have much computation power. We need to focus more on internet security. The recent studies, we see lots of development going on this topic, and edge-based steganography is a very new field of research.

In this paper, our main objective is

- To find the edges present in the cover image
- To embed the confidential data according to the edge value
- To perform some statistical analysis of our work with existing steganography techniques using quantitative metrics such as RMSE, SSIM, CC, ERGAS and PSNR.

2   Background and Related Work

Recently much research is going on image steganography, as a significant portion of network traffic contains images and videos. Because of a lot of redundant bits, hiding data becomes more easily. The process of image steganography is explained in Fig. 3.

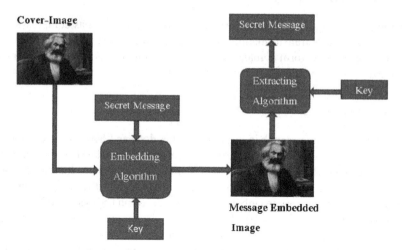

Fig. 3. Work flow of Image Steganography.

Broadly image steganography can be divided into two parts. One is the transform domain, and another is the spatial domain technique. Figure 4 shows the different techniques present in both transform and spatial domains.

2.1 Spatial Domain

In these methods, the pixel values of an image are changed. An LSB-based method is the most straightforward technique one can use, where the LSB of a pixel change so that the noise is minimal. From this technique, we are doing Edge-based Steganography methods.

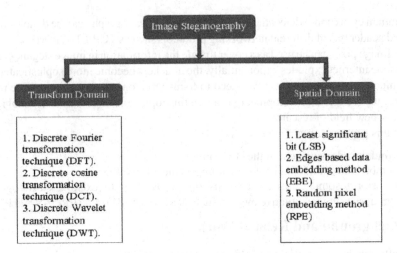

Fig. 4. Different techniques of image steganography.

2.2 Transform Domain

On the internet, images go through various transformations, such as compression, saturation, etc. For these transformations, there is a chance of data loss. However, if we embed data using Transform domain steganography methods, the chance of losing data is minimized.

2.3 Related Work

There is various similar research in this topic. [1] has done an LSB-based steganography technique where they divided the image by range and generated a key to hide the message. The secret key can take five grey label values, and each label states the number of bits that are changed in the LSB of any pixel. In [2], we can see that they have taken normal texture and edge information to embed the message based on LSB values of that portion. They choose k-bits of LSB to embed the message. The value of k varies with respect to the image region. They have embedded the information in the noise-prone areas for good spectral and spatial resolution. [3] suggest some interesting concept of random pixel embedding method, where the message is embedded in different arbitrary portions of the image. It shares the key in the LSB of a pixel. The main disadvantage of this method is that, as for randomness, the image quality will compromise, and we can get a distorted image. In [4], they have found the dark portion of the image and embedded the data in that dark area. This method is computationally heavy because it needs to find the dark area of the image, which takes lots of time. In the paper [5], the author has used image texture analysis. It divides the image into two parts; normal texture and complex texture. The simple texture portion embeds the data using 3 bits red,2 bits green, and 3 bits blue LSB of pixels of that area, whereas, in the complex texture domain, it has used 4 LSB embedding technique. [6] proposed a machine learning-based technique to hide the secret message. The algorithm that they have used was OPAC and generic algorithm. [7]

has enhanced the spectral quality of an image by applying the LSB embedding method. He has applied a generic algorithm to set the parameters of the objective function for getting the best result. [8] has used a hybrid version of the LSB-based method and Huffman coding to embed messages. [13] proposed a new image steganography using generative Adversarial Network (GAN) and they have adopted three strategies in data embedding: cover modification, cover selection, and cover synthesis. [16] proposed a security model for IoV by integrating encryption and steganography. They have shown efficiency of 0.86 ms, PSNR of 78.58%, and valanche effect of 58.81%. In the paper [17], they proposed an integrated integer Wavelet transformation technique with genetic algorithm to produce high quality stego image. [18] has shown that generative adversarial networks (GAN) have improved their performance of image steganography. [19] has embed the secret information in the image using difference of Gaussians edge detection.

3   Problem Statement and Proposed Solution

3.1   Problem Statement

Our main goal is to find a generic algorithm that can.

- hide the secret information inside the edges of an image.
- retrieve the information from the stego image.

Finally, we have compared our steganography method with all other existing steganography methods.

3.2   Proposed Solution

We can divide the solution into two parts: the sender-side algorithm and the receiver-side algorithm. But before applying these algorithms, we must assume that the secret key and the no of bits used for length information are shared between the sender and the receiver during the handshake phase. We have used one Edge detection technique. The algorithm 1 is explaining the edge detection technique.

Algorithm 1 edge detector `(Image, length)`

1: `low ← 1`

2: `high←255`

3: `ans ← -1`

4: while `low < high` do

5:     `mid ← (low+high)/2`

6:     `cannyImage ← CannyDetector (Image, mid, 255)`

7:     `count ← no of edge pixels in cannyImage`

8:     if `count < length` then

9:         `high ← mid-1`

10:     else

11:         `low ← mid+1`

12:         `ans ← mid`

13:     end if

14:     end while

15: `cannyImage ← CannyDetector(Image, ans, 255)`

16: return `cannyImage`

3.2.1 Sender Side Algorithm

We have one secret message and one carrier image. The secret message is hidden inside the edges of the carrier image. So, the LSBs of the first fixed no of pixels are substituted with the message length information bits. We need to store the length information of the message so that we can ignore the extra edge pixels and will be able to retrieve the original message.

Then the edges of the carrier image are detected. There are various edge detection algorithms like Canny edge detection, Sobel edge detection, Laplacian edge detection, etc. We have used Canny edge detection algorithms to detect edges.

Now, as the message length varies, the no of edge pixels should also vary dynamically to accommodate the message bits. It is achieved by varying the threshold; the higher threshold value results in fewer edges, whereas the lower threshold value results in more edges. As we know the length of message bits, we have applied a binary search algorithm to find out the correct threshold value so that the no of edge pixels is just greater than or equal to the no of message bits. Once the threshold is fixed, edges pixels are collected.

After detecting edge pixels, we have used the secret key to embed the message bits by shuffling the edge pixels and then replacing the least significant one bit with the original message bits. Now, this stego image is sent over the channel. The working flow for the sender side is shown in Fig. 5.

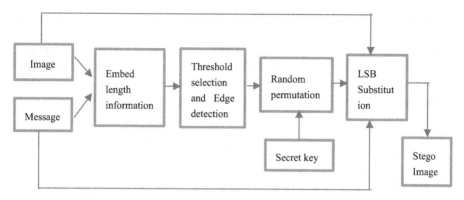

Fig. 5. Working flow of proposed algorithm for the sender side.

Algorithm 2 is describing the whole algorithm.

Algorithm 2 **Sender Code** (Image, Message)

1: // l is the no of bits used for length information and key is the secret
key (preshared)

2: Act_len ← actual length of message

3: len_bin ← Act_len in binary with l bits.

4: for first l pixels of Image do

5: Substitute LSBs with len_bin

6: end for

7: Canny image ← edge detector (Image, Act_len + l)

8: Edge index ← Edge pixel position from the Canny image

9: for i in Message do

10: find the pixel index from Edge index by shuffling using
key.

11: substitute LSB of the pixel of Image at retrieved
pixel index with i

12: end for

13: return Image

3.2.2 Receiver Side Algorithm

We have only the stego image. The secret message is extracted from the edges of the stego image. So, the length of the message is retrieved from the LSBs of the first fixed number of pixels. Then the edges of the stego image are detected using the same approach. On the receiver side also, binary search is applied to fix the threshold for the Canny edge detection algorithm.

After detecting edge pixels, we have used the same secret key to shuffle the edge pixels and then retrieve the message bits from the least significant one bits of the edge pixels. The extra pixels are ignored. The working flow for the receiver side is shown in the Fig. 6.

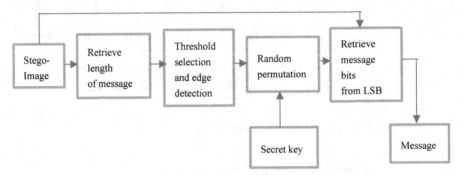

Fig. 6. Working flow of proposed algorithm for the receiver side.

Algorithm 3 is explaining whole receiver algorithm.

Algorithm 3 **Receiver Code** (Stego Image)

1: // l is the no of bits used for length information and key is the secret key(preshared)

2: for first l pixels of stego Image do

3:    retrieve message length from the LSBs and store in length

4: end for

5: Canny image ← edge detector (Stego Image, length+l)

6: Edge index ← Edge pixel positions from the Canny image

7: Message ← empty string

8: for i in range length do

9:    find the pixel index from Edge index by shuffling using key

10:   retrieve LSB of the pixel of Stego Image at retrieved pixel index and add to Message

11: end for

12: return Message

4   Evaluation

For the analysis, and output generation, certain setup and requirements are required. The following are the requirements for the same:

- Editor: Spyder (Anaconda-3)
- Operating System: Windows (Version: 10)
- Coding Language: Python 3.9.0
- RAM: 8 GB
- Processor: Intel(R)-CoreTM-i5-L16G7–3.0 GHz.

When Steganography comes into the picture, Steganalysis also comes side by side. After developing a steganography method, we should check whether the attacker can detect the existence of a secret message inside an image or not using any steganalysis method. There are various steganalysis methods like visual Steganalysis, statistical Steganalysis, non-structural Steganalysis, and many more. Mean Square Error (MSE), Root mean Square Error (RMSE), Structural Similarity Index Measure (SSIM) are some of the visual steganalysis methods. Statistical Steganalysis includes histogram-based analysis, chi-square analysis, etc. Subtractive Pixel Adjacency Matrix (SPAM), Spatial-rich model are nonstructural Steganalysis.

We have evaluated using some of the steganalysis methods like

- Root means Square Error (RMSE).
- Structural Similarity Index Measure (SSIM).
- Correlation Coefficient (CC).
- Peak signal-to-noise ratio (PSNR).
- Relative dimensionless global error (ERGAS)

Correlation Coefficient is the statistical term that is used to describe the degree in which the two coordinate moves with one-another. If each coordinate moves in the same direction, then it is said to have a positive correlation.

$$CC = \frac{\sum_i (ri - rm)(fi - fm)}{\sqrt{\sum_i (ri - rm)^2 (fi - fm)^2}} \tag{1}$$

In the above equation, r_i and f_i are indicating intensity details of ith pixel in the original (R) and the stego image (F) respectively and rm and f_m signify the mean intensity values of the referenced and the fused image respectively.

The root mean square error can help to define that how much relatable our result will be from the original image. The accuracy is inversely proportional to this error that means lower the error value will be, the more the accuracy it will gain.

$$RMSE = \sqrt{\frac{\sum_{i,j=1}^{mn}(R_{ij} - F_{ij})^2}{mn}} \tag{2}$$

Here in Eq. 2, R_{ij} and F_{ij} represent intensity information of $(i, j)^{th}$ pixel of R and F separately. This m and n denote total number of the rows and the columns of F respectively. Lower value of RMSE is desirable. Theoretically it should be 0.

The term Peak signal-to-noise ratio (PSNR) is a method for the calculation of ratio between the maximum power of a signal and the power of debasing noise that affects the quality of its output image. It is calculated by the following Eq. 3.

$$PSNR = 10 * \log_{10} \left(\frac{P^2}{\frac{\sum_{i,j=1}^{mn}(R_{ij}-F_{ij})^2}{mn}} \right) \tag{3}$$

In the Eq. 3, P is $(2^b) - 1$ and b is the absolute number of bits that has been utilized to represent a pixel of the R. High value of PSNR is desirable. ERGAS is one of the most favored global quantitative image quality methods for comparing images.

$$ERGAS = 100 \times \frac{hr}{lr} \sqrt{\frac{1}{n} \sum_{i=1}^{n} \left(\frac{RMSEi}{\mu i} \right)^2} \tag{4}$$

For this Eq. 4, hr and lr indicate the spatial resolution of input image and output images respectively. The total number of bands of input image is N. RMSEi denotes the RMSE and μi denotes the mean of i th spectral band of PAN-sharpened image. As ERGAS value depends on RMSE, less value of ERGAS specifies standard quality of the output image.

SSIM evaluate the similarity between intensity in the local pattern 5.

$$SSIM(R, F) = \left(\frac{2\mu_R\mu_F + C_1}{\mu_R^2 + \mu_F^2 + C_1} \right) \left(\frac{2\sigma_{RF} + C_2}{\sigma_R^2 + \sigma_F^2 + C_2} \right) \tag{5}$$

Here, K_1 and K_2 are constants. L is the maximum intensity value and C_1, C_2 are two constants given by $(K1L)^2$ and $(K2L)^2$ respectively.

For evaluating the paper, we have used an image of resolution (300,332,3). The image has three bands. Each band represents some color combination of image. For each band there are 300 rows and 332 columns.

We have used the following message to hide inside image.

"This is the front page of the Simple English Wikipedia. Wikipedias are places where people work together to write encyclopedias in different languages. We use Simple English words and grammar here. The Simple English Wikipedia is for everyone! That includes children and adults who are learning English. There are 207,214 articles on the Simple English Wikipedia. All of the pages are free to use. They have all been published under both the Creative Commons Attribution/Share-Alike License 3.0 and the GNU Free Documentation License. You can help here! You may change these pages and make new pages. Read the help pages and other good pages to learn how to write pages here. If you need help, you may ask questions at Simple talk. This is the front page of the Simple English Wikipedia. Wikipedias are places where people work together to write encyclopedias in different languages. We use Simple English words and grammar here. The Simple English Wikipedia is for everyone! That includes children and adults who are learning English. There are 207,214 articles on the Simple English Wikipedia. All

of the pages are free to use. They have all been published under both the Creative Commons Attribution/Share-Alike License 3.0 and the GNU Free Documentation License. You can help here! You may change these pages and make new pages. Read the help pages and other good pages to learn how to write pages here. If you need help, you may ask questions at Simple talk. This is the front page of the Simple English Wikipedia. Wikipedias are places where people work together to write encyclopedias in different languages. We use Simple English words and grammar here. The Simple English Wikipedia is for everyone! That includes children and adults who are learning English. There are 207,214 articles on the Simple English Wikipedia. All of the pages are free to use. They have all been published under both the Creative Commons Attribution/Share-Alike License 3.0 and the GNU Free Documentation License. You can help here! You may change these pages and make new pages. Read the help pages and other good pages to learn how to write pages here. If you need help, you may ask questions at Simple talk."

Our main objective of the paper is to compare edge-based image steganography and comparison with other famous existing methods. For comparison purpose we have taken the following methods.

- Least significant bit (LSB).
- Random pixel embedding method (RPE).
- Wavelet-based method.

In LSB methods, for each band we can change the LSB of pixel values using the key and receiver can get the message by taking LSB of pixel values, where sender have stored the message.

In RPE method, we randomly take any pixel value and store the message bits into that portion (Figs. 7 and 8).

(a) Original Image   (b) Stego image in edge based steganography

Fig. 7. Data Images for edge-based steganography.

(a) Stego image of lsb based method.

(b) Stego image of RPE based method.

(c) Stego image of wavelet-based method

Fig. 8. Stego Images for reference work.

The following Table 1 shows the results after applying different steganalysis methods over different steganography methods.

Table 1. Results of different steganalysis metrics.

Algorithms	Difference steganalysis metrics				
	CC	RMSE	SSIM	ERGAS	PSNR
Edge Based	0.998	0.000	1.000	0.000	1.000
LSB Based	0.997	0.001	0.999	0.001	0.610
RPE Based	0.955	0.027	0.890	0.000	0.370
Wavelet-based	0.999	0.020	0.977	0.005	0.792

5 Conclusion and Future Work

In this paper, we have analyzed the difference between cryptography and Steganography, why Steganography is used, various techniques of Steganography, various techniques of image steganography, comparative study on various steganography algorithms. We have implemented Edge-based image steganography, and it has compared with other existing algorithms like LSB based method and RPE based method and, finally, we have done some steganalysis to test the strength of our implemented steganography algorithm. We have done lots of quantitative and qualitative analysis to find out, which steganography methods will give best results, and see how much our edge-based technique will perform. After doing all the methods, we can see that our implemented method is better than reference methods. The quality of stego image is very good and it will be difficult for any adversary to detect whether an image is original image or stego image. We have only used Canny Edge detector to detect the edge but in future, we will do exhaustive research on various edge detection techniques and give the best steganography method. For reference method we have only taken LSB method and RPE method, but in future we will use many more complex steganography algorithms like Neural Network based algorithm, Discrete Cosine based algorithm, Discrete Wavelet based algorithms and many more algorithms to test our model. In future we will also use some statistical steganalysis methods to test our model.

References

1. Jain, Y.K., Ahirwal, R.R.: A novel image steganography method with adaptive number of least significant bits modification based on private stego-keys. Int. J. Comput. Sci. Secur. (IJCSS), vol. 4 (2010) March 1
2. Yang, H., Sun, X., Sun, G.: A high-capacity image data hiding scheme using adaptive LSB substitution. J. Radioengineering 18(4), 509–516 (2009)
3. Madhu Viswanatham, V., Manikonda, J.: A novel technique for embedding data in spatial domain. Int. J. Comput. Sci. Eng., IJCSE 2 (2010)
4. Motameni, H., Norouzi, M., Jahandar, M., Hatami, A.: Labeling method in steganography. World Academy of Science, Engineering and Technology, France (2007)
5. Hamid, A.M., Kiah, M.L.M.: Novel approach for high secure and high-rate da-ta hidden in the image using image texture analysis. Int. J. Eng. Technol.
6. Tseng, L.-Y., Chan, Y.-K., Ho, Y.-A., Chu, Y.-P.: Image hiding with an improved genetic algorithm and an optimal pixel adjustment process. In: 2008 Eighth International Conference on Intelligent Systems Design and Applications, pp. 320–325. IEEE (2008)
7. Khodaei, M., Faez, K.: Image hiding by using genetic algorithm and lsb substitution. In: International Conference on Image and Signal Processing, pp. 404–411. Springer (2010)
8. Than, S.S.M.: Secure data transmission in video format based on LSB and Huffman coding. Int. J. Image Graph. Signal Process. 12(1), 10 (2020)
9. Johnson, N.F., Jajodia, S.: Exploring steganography: seeing the unseen. Computer 31, 26–34 (1998)
10. Cheddad, A., Condell, J., Curran, K., Mc Kevitt, P.: Digital image steganography: survey and analysis of current methods. Signal Process. 90, 727–752 (2010)
11. Morkel, T., Eloff, J.H.P., Olivier, M.S.: an overview of image steganography. In: Proceedings of the Fifth Annual Information Security South Africa Conference (ISSA2005), Sandton, South Africa, June/July 2005

12. Hussain, M., Hussain, M.: A survey of image steganography techniques. Int. J. Adv. Sci. Technol. **54**, May 2013
13. Liu, J., et al.: Recent advances of image steganography with generative adversarial networks. National Key Research and Development Program of China, vol-8, pp. 60575–60595 (2020)
14. Mandal, P., Mukherjee, I., Paul, G., Chatterji, B.N.: Digital image steganography: a literature survey. Inf. Sci. **609** (2022)
15. Kaur, S., Singh, S., Kaur, M., et al.: A systematic review of computational image steganography approaches. Arch. Comput. Methods Eng. **29**, 4775–4797 (2022)
16. Rathore, M., et al.: A novel trust-based security and privacy model for Internet of Vehicles using encryption and steganography. Comput. Electr. Eng. **102** (2022)
17. Sabeti, V., Sobhani, M., Hasheminejad, S.M.H.: An adaptive image steganography method based on integer wavelet transform using genetic algorithm. Comput. Electr. Eng. **99** (2022)
18. Martín, A., Hernández, A., Alazab, M., Jung, J., Camacho, D.: Evolving Generative Adversarial Networks to improve image steganography. Expert Systems with Applications, vol. 222 (2023)
19. Patwari, B., Nandi, U., Ghosal, S.K.: Image steganography based on difference of Gauss ans edge detection. Multimed. Tools Appl. (2023)

Theories and Applications to Data Analytics

Classification of Microstructural Steel Images Using an Attention-Aided Transfer Learning Network

Shib Sankar Sarkar[1]([✉]), Md. Salman Ansari[1], Kalyani Mali[2], and Ram Sarkar[3]

[1] Department of Computer Science and Engineering, Government College of Engineering and Textile Technology Berhampore, Berhampore, India
shib_sankar_sarkar@yahoo.co.in
[2] Department of Computer Science and Engineering, University of Kalyani, Kalyani, India
[3] Department of Computer Science and Engineering, Jadavpur University, Kolkata, India

Abstract. Steels serve as the most widely-used structural metallic materials in industrial practice. Steels have a wide variety of microstructures and mechanical properties. The microstructure of a metal and its physical properties are highly correlated. Manual Microstructure analysis and characterization tasks require deep expertise in this field, and it is a time-consuming process. Contemporary machine vision and machine learning techniques facilitate autonomous microstructure recognition with a high degree of accuracy. To this end, the main objective of this research is to develop a Deep Convolutional Neural Network (DCNN) model based on inductive transfer learning with an attention module for steel microstructural image classification. This attention network, which has been learned in a supervised manner, precisely selects a subset of feature maps with meaningful and discriminative information. In this paper, several regularization schemes have also been investigated with this model. Experimental results show that the proposed model outperforms the baselines by a significant margin.

Keywords: Microstructure · transfer learning · regularization · attention

1 Introduction

In a variety of image classification tasks, DCNNs have demonstrated exceptional performance with an error rate that is comparable to that of a human. The development of data-driven models for object recognition, localization, and classification applications is largely influenced by traditional computer vision approaches.. However, the recent development of deep learning networks with a large variety of architectures has introduced considerable improvements in the performance of computer vision applications.

Microstructures of metals play a crucial role in structural material selection, quality control in material processing, or safety consideration. Hence, an automated and reliable microstructure recognition system is very important to understand the process-microstructure-property relationship and material selection. To learn the specifics of

K. Dasgupta et al. (Eds.): CICBA 2023, CCIS 1956, pp. 235–244, 2024.
https://doi.org/10.1007/978-3-031-48879-5_18

the microstructure of metals, 2D micrographs or digital images captured by light optical microscopy (LOM) or scanning electron microscopy (SEM) at various scales are typically utilized. In comparison to the natural images, like images available on the ImageNet database, microstructural images are complex due to the presence of different complicated textures generated under different processing conditions.

Simple traditional computer vision or machine learning approaches require image processing, suitable feature descriptors, and an efficient classifier to render robust classification results. A lot of research work with these traditional machine learning methods on microstructural classification operated on LOM or SEM images has successfully shown its excellence [1–4]. In contrast, deep learning-based methods map the inputs to the target output. These models basically try to correct itself using a learning process over some epochs by comparing the model's output to ground truth in order to optimize the mapping function. Deep learning based methods have established its efficacy in material science applications for quantitative microstructure analysis [5], microstructure recognition [6, 7], microstructure segmentation [8, 9], surface defects [10], to predict the chemical composition and processing history [11], etc.

Deep learning can be considered as a learning of an ordered set of representations, such as low, mid and high-level features extracted from images. More layers, in theory, should improve the levels of features. However, He et al. [12] have shown that if we continue increasing the number of convolution layers on top of activations, the training process will ultimately stop learning new things. Deep networks are hard to train because of the "vanishing gradient" problem. Hence, researchers have introduced the concept of skip connections. Skip connection is defined as the identity mapping where the input from the previous layer directly connects the output layers of the next layer. This is an alternate path for the gradient to flow. A pre-trained Convolutional Neural Network (CNN) model referred to as the Residual Net (ResNet) has proven its merit in image recognition. Therefore, this type of transfer learning network represents a suitable candidate to apply for the recognition of microstructure images. However, the associated drawback of deep learning models is the requirement of data in large quantities. Transfer learning helps in this context to learn with a limited volume of data. But with the transfer learning method, instead of blindly transferring the expertise from one domain to another, some regularization methods are sometimes useful to assess the significance of the features.

In this research work, a transfer learning-based network with a regularization method is proposed to recognize the microstructure of metals from a diverse set of complex microstructure images. The model has been experimented with using a wide variety of microstructural data samples and compared to some recent regularization methods in the domain of transfer learning. The experimental results show that this attention network is capable of significantly outperforming leading-edge regularization techniques.

2   Background

In traditional machine learning, the learning process takes place using the knowledge from the existing domain, and in this case, it is assumed that the distribution of the training and test data sets is the same and that they both come from the same feature space. While in transfer learning, the learning process utilizes the knowledge from any other domain, may be in a different feature space or with different data distribution. According on the domain and task parameters during the transfer, Pan et al. [13] have demonstrated many forms of transfer learning processes. A domain corresponds to the feature space and its marginal probability distribution. The domains can be differentiated either in terms of feature space or in terms of marginal distributions. For a specific domain, a task corresponds to a label space and its predictive function.

Inductive transfer learning is an approach used to transfer knowledge from a source model to a related target model in order to enhance the learning capability. This procedure is adopted for tasks where the dataset contains a little volume of data to train the model from scratch. Various techniques have been adopted by researchers to effectively use transfer learning with pre-trained deep neural network models. A few iterations of training are employed to optimize the parameters of a pre-trained model to adapt to the new data. Fine-tuning is the most widely used technique in transfer learning that increases the performance by unfreezing the entire model or part of it and rebuilding the target model with the new dataset at a very low learning rate. However, this process may involve some potential issues. During the fine-tuning, some parameters may be shifted from its starting value with a margin which may create a loss in the initial knowledge. Deep neural networks often have millions of parameters. But when the pre-trained model is trained with a relatively small-sized target dataset, the model may become prone to over-fitting due to improper initialization of these parameters. Regularization techniques are intended to prevent overfitting. There are different ways to regularize a deep learning based model. A simple regularization approach is to add another term - weight decay to the loss function. When this regularized loss function is minimized, the optimization algorithm tries to decrease both the original loss value and the squared value of weights. This type of regularization approach is known as L^2- regularization. It is applied during the training period but generates no additional operations for prediction during testing the model. This regularization method's major goal is to maintain the model's weights as low as possible. The reference formula is as follows:

$$Cost\,function = Loss + \lambda * \sum \|w\|^2 \tag{1}$$

where λ indicates the regularization parameter and it is optimized to achieve a better model. The standard L^2-regularization is useful for the transfer learning model to tune parameters towards the origin. But in some cases, it is observed that it yields suboptimal results for the target task, because during this process, a few parameters may be tuned far from their initial values. Li et al. [14] have proposed another regularization approach, called L^2-SP regularization to prevent overfitting and to prevent the forgetting problem. Here, the term "SP" implies the Starting Point of this fine-tuning process. In this approach, they have taken into account the beginning point of the fine-tuning process in this method, and they also advise employing a penalty that encodes an explicit inductive bias in favor of the trained model. But in these methods, the regularizer restricts the divergence of parameters of the source and target networks but does not consider the behavior of the networks with the training dataset.

Deep neural networks are highly configurable, layered architectures with various hyperparameters that learn different features at different layers. Yosinski et al. [15] experimentally quantify the generalizability versus specificity of these types of information in different layers of the architecture. The initial layers have been seen to learn general features similar to Gabor filters and color blobs. Later layers pick up on features that are extremely specific to a given dataset or task. That can be also observed by the visualization.

Li et al. [16] have developed a regularization method, namely Deep Learning Transfer using Feature Map with Attention (DELTA) for transfer learning networks. This regularization approach includes the behavior of the networks with the training dataset. By employing the starting point as references (SPAR), this strategy aims to maintain the target model's outer layer outputs. Instead of focusing on the difference in weights, this approach concentrates on some layers which carry more significant information. Our proposed network is inspired by the DELTA network.

The focus of this paper is to explore the attention network to regularized transfer learning model for recognizing the microstructure of metals. As far as we currently know, these are the first results on the classification of microstructural images using an attention network and also compare the results that have been achieved by some recent regularization techniques.

3 Methodology

ResNet 101 [12] architecture is used as the source and target models in our prescribed classification framework. The final output layer of the target network is dropped, and two sets of four additional layers—a linear layer, a rectified linear unit (ReLU), Dropout, and a linear layer—are added. The ReLU is used to introduce non-linearity to the network, and its output is the same as the input if it is positive, otherwise, the output sets to zero. The last layer contains a classifier with a Softmax activation function. Such an alteration of the network is very useful to minimize the training loss. Figure 1 shows the proposed architecture for microstructure image classification.

The objective of this architecture is to adjust the network behaviors and regulate a few layers of the target model to perform equivalently to the source model. Our aim is to readjust the behavior of the network and influence a few of the layers of the target network to perform identically to the source network. The remaining layers of the target network are left as trainable layers. We have considered filters of four such trainable layers (the last layer of each of the 4-blocks of the target network) to which we should pay more attention. To realize such weights of the feature maps, we have considered a supervised attention method with a back-propagation learning approach. This method pays more attention to those features that generate features with semantics-rich and discriminative information. The regularization of the behavior of the source and target networks is computed by calculating the distances between the feature maps of the outer layer outputs of these networks. The Euclidean distance is used here as a distance metric.

Let w denote the multidimensional parameter vector that includes all parameters of the target network, and w' represents the parameters of a pre-trained source network. The incorporated regularizer λ'(w,w',x) in our network estimates the distance between the behaviors of these two networks (source & target) for input image x. In this case, the transfer learning problem is represented as follows:

$$\min_{w} \sum\nolimits_{i=1}^{n} L(t(x_i, W), y_i) + \sum\nolimits_{i=1}^{n} \lambda'(w, w', x_i, Y_i, t) \qquad (2)$$

The second term of Eq. 2 describes the total difference between these two models over the training dataset with n numbers of input images using the model t. The regularizer λ/(w, w/, x_i, y_i, t) is regularizing the behavioral differences of network t using a supervised attention method with the back propagation variable selection for each labelled sample (x_i, y_i) in the dataset. The schematic representation of our proposed network is depicted in Fig. 1.

To normalize the behavior of the model, the distance between the feature maps generated at the outer layers of the source and target networks is taken into consideration. Mathematically, the behavioral regularizer for this model is calculated as

$$\lambda'(w, w', x_i, y_i, t) = \sum\nolimits_{j=1}^{N} (W_j(t, w', x_i, y_i) \cdot$$
$$\left\| FMap_j(t, w, x_i) - FMap_j(t, w', x_i) \right\|_2^2 \qquad (3)$$

where the first term indicates the assigned weight to the jth filter $(1 \leq j \leq N)$ for the ith image($1 \leq i \leq n$) and the second term indicates the Euclidean distance (marked as ||•||) between the two feature maps $FMap_j(z, w/, x_i)$ and $FMap_j(z, w, x_i)$ extracted from the source and target networks respectively.

We have taken into account a filter's weight as a performance indicator. By removing the filter (i.e., the filter set to zero), if the network causes a higher performance loss, then the filter corresponds to a greater capacity of discrimination ability. For a labelled input image (x_i, y_i), the network sets the weight of the jth channel by calculating the empirical losses with and without the jth channel in the following manner:

$$W_j(t, w/, x_i, y_i) = softmax(L\left(t\left(x_i, w'^0\right), y_i\right) - L(t(x_i, w/), y_i)) \qquad (4)$$

The first term of this Eq. 4 refers to the empirical loss with parameter w'^0 by setting all elements of the jth filter to zero and the second term refers to the empirical loss with parameter w' for the same filter. The Softmax function is used to normalize the result so that the weights are always positive.

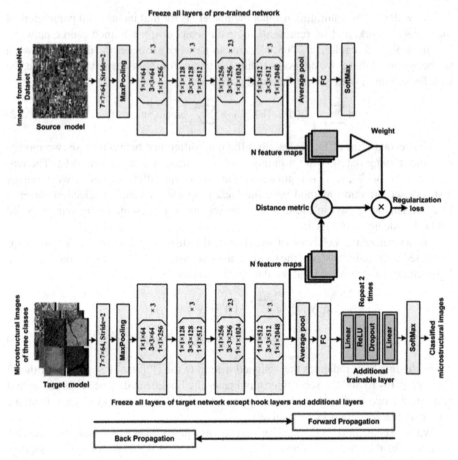

Fig. 1. Proposed network for microstructure classification

4   Results and Discussion

This section shows the classification outcomes that were attained after carefully applying the regularization strategy to the transfer learning network. The five-class microstructural image dataset of the ultra-high carbon steel (UHCS) used in this work is collected from the openly accessible website at http://uhcsdb.materials.cmu.edu [17]. In order to provide additional samples, each of the original samples is split into smaller sub-images of size 128×128. The scale bars and text that appear at the bottom of images are not considered input data in order to prevent any interference with the feature extraction process. The two groups produced from the microstructural imaging dataset are the training set and the test set. In this instance, training uses 80% (1600 images) of the dataset, whereas testing uses 20% (400 images) of the remaining dataset. Table 1 provides information about the microstructure image dataset that has been utilized in this study.

Table 1. Details of the Microstructural dataset.

Type of micrographs	# of micrographs	# of cropped images
Martensite	34	238
Network	208	208
Pearlite	121	121
Spheroidite	367	367
Spheroidite_widmanstätten	80	160

The classification accuracy of each regularization method gradually increases throughout the course of training and stabilizes after 20 training epochs, as illustrated in Fig. 2. Similarly, the training loss gradually decreases with the increase of training times and finally stabilizes at a less interval. Table 2 contains a list of the parameter settings applied to the suggested network.

Table 2. The parameters of the experimental model

Parameter	Value
Output layer size	5
Batch size	32
Optimizer	Stochastic Gradient Descent (SGD)
Learning rate	0.001
Epoch number	100

The confusion matrix presented in Fig. 2(d) shows a graphical summary of the classification performance of each class predicted by the transfer learning network with attention. We notice that our model can successfully classify each image in the test dataset for martensite, but it misclassifies only one image (0.02%) of network, one image (0.04%) of pearlite, seven images (0.09%) of spheroidite, and two images (0.6%) of spheroidite_widmanstätten types of microstructures.

After 100 epochs of training, Precision, Recall, F-value and Support values of our model are measured and the outcomes are listed in Table 3. In this projected architecture, the regularization method with attention performs better than the other two regularization methods. The comparative study of the regularization methods with the other two commonly used regularization methods is shown in Fig. 3.

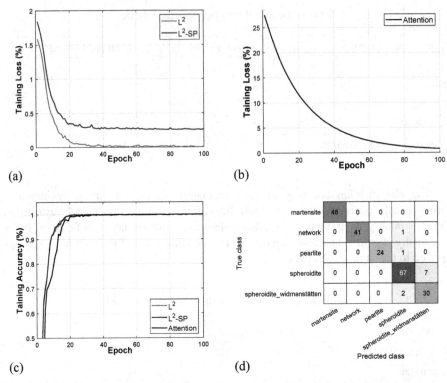

Fig. 2. Train loss, training accuracy of different methods, and confusion matrix of the proposed model: (a-b) The training loss for different regulization methods on the training set. (c) The accuracy of different regulization methods on the training set. (d) A confusion matrix representing the microstructural classification using the proposed model.

Table 3. Classification report on the test set

Class	Precision	Recall	F1-score	Support
martensite	1.00	1.00	1.00	48
network	1.00	0.98	0.99	42
pearlite	1.00	0.96	0.98	25
spheroidite	0.94	0.91	0.92	74
spheroidite_widmanstätten	0.81	0.94	0.87	32

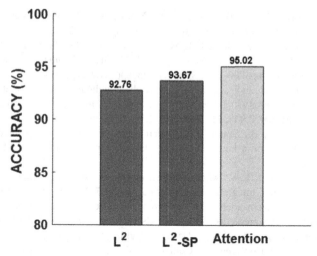

Fig. 3. Comparative results in terms of test accuracy with different regularization methods.

5 Conclusion

The present work deals with the classification of different microstructures of steel. Results are demonstrated on different micrographs of martensite, network, pearlite, spheroidite, and pheroidite_widmanstätten microstructures of low-carbon steels. The regularization technique used in the architecture considered here successfully regulates the behaviors of the target model. The used regularization method of this model is also compared with some standard regularization methods like L^2 and L^2-SP, and the results confirm that this regularization technique achieves better results in terms of classification accuracy. This transfer learning network, which is aided by an attention mechanism, has been found to be effective for microstructural image classification. Future work in this area can be an attention-based model with a reduction of the dimensionality of features by selectively processing only a small subset of the feature maps. Another plan is to use few-shot learning-based approaches as the availability of the annotated data is limited.

References

1. DeCost, B.L., Holm, E.A.: A computer vision approach for automated analysis and classification of microstructural image data. Comput. Mater. Sci.. Mater. Sci. **110**, 126–133 (2015)
2. Sarkar, S.S., Sheikh, K.H., Mahanty, A., Mali, K., Ghosh, A., Sarkar, R.: A harmony search-based wrapper-filter feature selection approach for microstructural image classification. Integrating Mater. Manuf. Innov. **10**(1), 1–19 (2021)
3. Khan, A.H., Sarkar, S.S., Mali, K., Sarkar, R.: A genetic algorithm based feature selection approach for microstructural image classification. Exp. Techn., 1–13 (2021)
4. Chowdhury, A., Kautz, E., Yener, B., Lewis, D.: Image driven machine learning methods for microstructure recognition. Comput. Mater. Sci.. Mater. Sci. **123**, 176–187 (2016)
5. Durmaz, A., et al.: A Deep Learning Approach for Complex Microstructure Inference (2021)

6. Azimi, S.M., Britz, D., Engstler, M., Fritz, M., Mücklich, F.: Advanced steel microstructural classification by deep learning methods. Sci. Rep. 8(1), 1–14 (2018)

7. Sarkar, S.S., Md Ansari, S., Mondal, R., Mali, K., Sarkar, R.: Classification of Microstructural Image Using a Transfer Learning Approach. In: Emerging Technologies in Data Mining and Information Security, pp. 203–211. Springer, Singapore (2021)

8. DeCost, B.L., Lei, B., Francis, T., Holm, E.A.: High throughput quantitative metallography for complex microstructures using deep learning: a case study in ultrahigh carbon steel. Microsc. Microanal.. Microanal. 25(1), 21–29 (2019)

9. Stuckner, J., Harder, B., Smith, T.M.: Microstructure segmentation with deep learning encoders pre-trained on a large microscopy dataset." npj Computational Materials 8, no. 1 (2022): 200

10. Kitahara, A.R., Holm, E.A.: Microstructure cluster analysis with transfer learning and unsupervised learning. Integrating Mater. Manuf. Innov. 7(3), 148–156 (2018)

11. Farizhandi, A.A., Kazemzadeh, O.B., Mamivand, M.: Deep learning approach for chemistry and processing history prediction from materials microstructure. Sci. Rep. 12(1), 1–14 (2022)

12. He, K., Zhang, X., Ren, S., Sun, J.: Deep residual learning for image recognition. In: Proceedings of the IEEE Conference on Computer Vision and Pattern Recognition, pp. 770–778 (2016)

13. Pan, S.J., Yang, Q.: A survey on transfer learning. IEEE Trans. Knowl. Data Eng. 22(10), 1345–1359 (2009)

14. Xuhong, L.I., Grandvalet, Y., Davoine, F.: Explicit inductive bias for transfer learning with convolutional networks. In: International Conference on Machine Learning, pp. 2825–2834. PMLR (2018)

15. Yosinski, J., Clune, J., Bengio, Y., Lipson, H.:How transferable are features in deep neural networks? arXiv preprint arXiv:1411.1792 (2014)

16. Li, X., et al.: Delta: Deep learning transfer using feature map with attention for convolutional networks. arXiv preprint arXiv:1901.09229 (2019)

17. DeCost, B.L., Hecht, M.D., Francis, T., Webler, B.A., Picard, Y.N., Holm, E.A.: UHCSDB: UltraHigh carbon steel micrograph database. Integrating Mater. Manuf. Innov. 6(2), 197–205 (2017). https://doi.org/10.1007/s40192-017-0097-0

Feature Selection Approaches in Online Bangla Handwriting Recognition

Bubai Das[1]([envelope]), Shibaprasad Sen[2], Himadri Mukherjee[1], and Kaushik Roy[1]

[1] TISA Lab, Department of Computer Science, West Bengal State University,
Kolkata, India
bubaidas1111@gmail.com

[2] Department of Computer Science and Engineering (AI-ML), Techno Main Salt
Lake, Kolkata, India

Abstract. Any feature selection technique aims to identify a smaller subset of essential characteristics from a larger collection by eliminating those that are redundant, noisy, or irrelevant. Feature selection techniques have proven to be a major ground-breaking technique to save computing time while strengthening prediction accuracy and data interpretation and better cognition of data in machine learning as well as pattern recognition algorithms. In the present experiment, we have compared four well-known feature selection techniques, Harmony Search, Krill Herd Algorithm, Principal Component Analysis and mRMR Algorithm when applied on the feature set produced by combining the frechet distance and distance-based features (256-dimension feature vector). The experiment has been performed on a 10000 online handwritten Bangla character database. The experimental outcome metrics and the analysis of the performances with respect to the percentage of dimensionality reduction and achieved accuracy are presented in a nutshell.

Keywords: Online Handwriting Recognition · Feature Selection · Bangla Handwriting · Classifier comparison

1 Introduction

Handwriting is one of the traditional ways through which people can communicate with each other. Research on handwriting recognition has become a major study subject because of its numerous applications. It has led to the development of numerous programmes that scan postal addresses, bank cheque amounts, forms, etc. Signature identification/verification is another example of such an application. Online and offline techniques are the two basic ways that handwritten input is recognized. In the offline technique, recognition is performed on the images that are generated using an optical scanner by scanning the handwritten input images. Whereas, in online mode, written data is recorded as timely ordered stroke sequences by tracking the movement of a digital pen-tip or finger-tip on a pressure-sensitive surface. Here, a stroke represents a set of ordered pixel

K. Dasgupta et al. (Eds.): CICBA 2023, CCIS 1956, pp. 245–258, 2024.
https://doi.org/10.1007/978-3-031-48879-5_19

points collected without lifting the pen. The recognition of handwritten input in online mode is more advantageous/easy compared to offline mode due to the following reason. An overview of the developments in offline handwriting recognition is presented in [35].

- In online recognition procedure, by utilising a pen and paper instead of a keyboard, people have the choice to submit their information in a manner that resembles their typical writing habits.
- In offline mode, when an image is scanned, there can be some extraneous noise. Therefore, as a first step, it's crucial to employ methods that eliminate that noise. On the other hand, when doing online recognition, the data is obtained straight from the input device, so there's no risk of adding noise to the data.
- The online recognition process provides vital dynamic writing order information. In the recognition phase, this information plays an important role, however, the same ordered information cannot be obtained from the images in offline recognition. Recognition of online handwriting methodologies has been introduced over many years. It has been increasing more enthusiasm because of the accessibility of personal digital assistance, and computerized scratchpads at an affordable price. Today, these technologies are commonly used worldwide encouraging organizations to develop their multiple languages support products. The organization of the manuscript is as follows: Sect. 2 describes a few of the past works done in this domain. Section 3 describes a short description of the feature extraction procedure used to identify online handwritten Bangla characters [1]. Section 4 highlights the working procedure of the feature selection methodologies applied in the current experiment. The detailed outcomes after the application of the mentioned optimization techniques applied on the feature set mentioned in [1] have been discussed in detail in Sect. 5. Finally, we conclude in Sect. 6.

2   Literature Review

Feature engineering plays an important role to solve any pattern recognition problem whatever procedure we adopt by using machine learning or deep learning approach. Features (relevant and useful information) are extracted from the objects using different techniques and fed to the different classifiers for recognition. In handwriting recognition also feature engineering has great impact. A moderate number of research works for character and word level are available in English [2,4], the research in regional languages like Gurumukhi, Devanagari, Bangla still is in infant stage. This section highlights a few important feature extraction techniques adopted by different researchers for recognizing online handwritten characters specially in Bangla script. Garain et al. have highlighted the recognition performance for two popular Indian scripts, Devanagari and Bangla by implementing the concept of human motor functionality [3] and achieved **97.29%** and **96.34%** accuracy respectively. Bhattacharya et al. in [25] used direction-code-based features for the recognition of Bangla symbols and obtained promising results. Bag et al. [26] experimented with handwritten Bangla characters recognition in a 2D plane without considering the writing direction. In [27,30,31], authors have used extracted features from constituent strokes of the characters using sequential and dynamic information, local and global shape information (distance-based and Zone-Based Path Traversal feature) to recognize the constituent strokes. The character is then predicted by matching stored stroke sequences. Sen et al. used hausdroff distance based feature [28], structural and topological features [29] to recognize online Bangla characters holistically. Shin et al. [33] have used feature extraction and feature selection to recognize handwritten characters to categorize people by age, such as adults and children, using their handwriting.

Authors in [32] have introduced stroke-level features by accounting the curvature, curliness, inclination, etc. SVM classifier was used for classification purpose. From the above mentioned works anyone can find that authors have not only tried to extract good features for recognition but also combines different features for better prediction. However, due to this attempt a lucrative growth in dimensionality of features has been observed in turn. The increase of dimensionality results in higher feature space that leads to increased utilization of computational memory and augments the computation time of the recognition engine. To lower the feature vector dimension without loss of major information, optimization techniques have been proven an efficient solution [5–7]. Begum et al. [34] have concentrated on real-time and context-free handwriting data analysis using a feature selection approach for user authentication using digital pen-tablet sensor data. A reasonable amount of research publications are present in the literature to reduce feature dimension for offline character, numerals, digits as well as various scripts like English, Gurumukhi, etc., [8–10]. These optimization techniques have been inspired mainly by biological processes, bacteriologic adaptation, electron flow and electrical conductivity (Electimize algorithm), and many other genetic algorithms. Authors through [12–15] have reported the detailed surveys on different feature optimization techniques for EC (Evolutionary Computing) algorithms like PSO (Particle Swarm Optimization), GA (Genetic Algorithm). A few renowned feature optimization works on online handwriting recognition for various scripts are also mentioned in this section. Liwicki et al. Have evaluated both online and pseudo offline features in order to determine which are essential and which aren't suitable for tracking to recognize online handwritten whiteboard notes written in English [16]. In their experiment, they have shown that an optimized feature vector of having only five feature attributes produces almost similar recognition accuracy than that of original feature vector considering all 25 feature attributes. Huang et al. have proposed an efficient feature selection model to recognize UNIPEN dataset samples by using an improved sequential floating search method in [17]. Vijayasenan et al. have presented a system [18] for online handwritten Tamil character recognition based on feature selection technique using PCA. Sundaram et al. have shown the usefulness of using 2D-PCA in [19] to recognize online handwritten Tamil characters. Prasad et al. [20] have used PCA for feature optimization towards developing a writer-independent online handwritten Kannada character recognition system for hand-held devices. The same authors in [21] have used PCA based online handwritten Hindi characters recognition on mobile devices. Sen et al. have used a krill herd algorithm-based approach to identify the relevant features from the initial feature vector for efficient recognition of handwritten Bangla characters [22]. There has been experiments with feature reduction in the avenue of handwritten character or digit recognition but most of them are concentrated on Roman and other scripts. Development in Bangla is very limited in this context. So far our knowledge, only one research publication is present in the literature that has used KH technique to reduce the feature set towards online handwritten Bangla character recognition [22]. To bridge this gap, in the present work, we have presented a detailed view to the researchers working in this language about the working procedure and performance of few feature selection techniques applied in online handwritten Bangla character recognition. In the present experiment, we have passed the feature set (256-attributed) produced in the experiment [1] through four popular feature selection procedures namely, HS, KH, PCA, and mRMR to search for reduced/optimized feature vector that can produce almost similar recognition accuracy to recognize online handwritten Bangla characters. The optimization in turn helps to reduce the space to store the feature attributes and also reduces the time taken to build the model by the same classifiers. In this paper, we have presented a detailed analysis of the effectiveness of produced optimized feature vectors in terms of length vs. achieved accuracy produced through the just mentioned feature selection procedures.

3   Feature Extraction Procedure

In the present study, the used input feature set is a combination of FD (Frechet distance) and distance-based features. This section provides a brief overview of the mechanism to extract those features. Both the features try to measure the shape of the character sample.

3.1   FD Based Feature

FD based features are generally used to find/measure the similarity between two curves and this concept has been used by the authors to generate powerful feature vector in [1] To find FD based features, authors have divided the character sample into N X N zones firstly as shown in Fig. 1.

Then the Euclidian distance between curves from one zone to every other zones is measured by evaluating the FFD and BFD values using Eq. (1). FFD (X, Y) and BFD (Y, X) represents the forward and backward frechet distances from zone X to zone Y and vice versa.

$$Min_{p,q}[maxD(X(p) - Y(q))]$$
$$Fw(X,Y) = \begin{cases} p[0,N] \leftarrow p[0,1] \\ q[0,M] \leftarrow q[0,1] \end{cases} \tag{1}$$

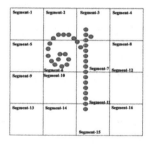

Fig. 1. Character image when 16 segments.

where p and q specify the number of object pixels associated with zone X and Y. D (X(p)-Y(q)) denotes the Euclidean distance between pixel p from zone X to pixel q belong to zone Y. According to Eq. 1, from each pixel in X, the distances of all the pixels in Y have been measured and, the maximum values are noted. The minimum of all such maximum measurements is considered as the FFD (X, Y). In a similar way, BFD (Y, X) has been computed.

Finally, the frechet distance- FD (X, Y) is considered as the minimum of FFD (X, Y) and BFD (Y, X) as mentioned in Eq. (2).

$$FD(X, Y) = min(FFD(X, Y), BFD(Y, X)) \qquad (2)$$

Authors have shown that the FD-based technique generates $N * (N - 1)/2$ feature attributes [1]. In the present experiment, we have considered the 120-attributed feature vector generated by dividing the character sample into 16 blocks.

3.2 Distance-Based Features

To extract Distance-based features, the characters are segmented into K parts. Then the distance from each segmentation point to every other points have been measured and served them as the features for their experiment [1]. Looking into the shape similarity between several basic characters of Bangla script, some local information have been extracted from the samples by using this procedure. This information in turn produce discriminating features. In this experiment, 136-dimensional feature vector was generated. In this feature extraction approach, the characters are divided into K number of segments. Then the distance from each segmentation point to every other points have been measured and served them as the features for their experiment [1]. Looking into the shape similarity between several basic characters of Bangla script, some local information have been extracted from the samples by using this procedure. This information in turn produces discriminating features for recognition the recognition of handwritten Bangla characters. Sen et al. have shown that this feature extraction technique produces $(N*(N+1))/2$ number of features [1]. For the current work, all character samples are divided into 16 segments and thus producing 136-element feature vector (Fig. 2).

Fig. 2. Illustration of distance based feature computation.

Therefore, in the present work, a 256-element (120+136) feature vector has been produced by combining FD and distance based features that undergo through mentioned four feature selection procedure for feature reduction purpose.

4 Applied Feature Selection Algorithms

As mentioned in Sect. 1, FS (feature selection) algorithms can play an important role towards recognition of different complex patterns. FS algorithms attempt to find a small feature subset from the original feature vector that contains the most relevant/strong feature attributes to describe the pattern. The reduction of feature attributes in turn reduces the time taken by the different machine learning algorithms to train the model and thus helps to reduce the overall complexity of the model. The elimination of weaker/redundant features reduces the problem of overfitting and thus may also improve the recognition accuracy if right subset is choosen. From the literature, it has been observed that FS problem can be solved in three different approaches namely, filter-based, wrapper-based and embedded methods.

Filter-based methods tries to evaluate the feature attribute without involving any machine learning algorithms. It relies solely on the intrinsic characteristics of the given input [23]. In this approach, features are gets ranked firstly on the basis of some criteria that may be independent of each other or by accounting the feature space. Finally, the optimized feature set is obtained by considering the feature attributes having highest rankings.

In wrapper-based feature selection procedure, a candidate feature subset of the entire input feature set is created firstly and then using this feature subset, trained the model by involving machine learning algorithm. Based on the importance, feature attributes may be added/removed from the considered feature subset. The importance of features can be measures by considering the performance measure that depends on the type of problem. These methods follows greedy algorithm. These procedures are computationally expensive, and sometimes impractical in the case of exhaustive search. In contrary, an embedded based model embeds feature selection within a specific machine learning algorithm.

This section briefly describes the working methodology of two filter-based (PCA, mRMR) and two embedded (HS, KH) feature selection procedures that are used in the present experiment to optimize the feature set [1].

4.1 Harmony Search (HS)

HS is a phenomenon-mimicking metaheuristic algorithm introduced by Geem et al. [11]. This technique is a special case of the well-established ES (Evolution Strategies) algorithm which is inspired by the improvisation process of jazz musicians. HS is considered as one of the mostly used feature reduction technique used in many applications like handwriting recognition, facial expression recognition [24] domains.

The overall complexity of the search process is decreased by HS algorithm. This technique has the ability of escaping local solutions while recognising multiple solutions. A large number of solutions are generated at random (referred to as Harmony memory). A novel approach is then created by utilising all of the possibilities in the harmony memory, and if it is determined that it is more effective than the worst solution, the worst solution is substituted in the harmony memory by the improved solution.

The parameters used in the current experiment include harmony memory size (HMS), consideration rate (HMCR) pitch adjustment rate, and iteratons The HMS specify the number of feature subsets The parameter, HMCR helps to take decision that how much of the previous solution will stay the same in the new one. Its value lies in the range of $[0, 1]$ and in the present experiment this value is initialized to 0.7. In this experiment, PAR helps to select a feature randomly on the basis of cosine similarity measurement. It lies in the range $[0.1, 0.5]$ and for experimental purpose, after exhaustive trials, we have fixed the value of it to 0.3. At the beginning of the proposed HSA algorithm, all the parameter values are randomly initialized. The experimental values of the number of iterations and HMS have been set to 20 and 15 respectively. In the initialization phase, we have randomly selected m number of feature subsets and placed in HMS. The selected feature subsets are 80% to 90% of the original feature vector in terms of dimension.

4.2 Krill Herd Algorithm (KH)

Gandomi et al. have proposed this algorithm and demonstrated that this feature selection procedure can produce promising outcomes [19]. The KH feature selection algorithm is a meta-heuristic algorithm that uses a Lagrangian model and crossover to solve optimisation issues based on the herding patterns of krill individuals in nature [19]. This meta-heuristic algorithms mainly follows two steps, a) a combination of random search or exploration and b) local search or exploitation. In the exploration step, a good candidate solution set is selected by running the basic KH algorithm. This selected solution set is then tuned by involving LMC (local mutation and crossover) operator in the exploitation step in search of enhancing the overall efficiency and reliability when solving global numerical optimization problems.

4.3   Principal Component Analysis

The PCA is a useful multivariate technique as well as powerful technique. The purpose of this technique was to explore and compact data in machine learning and data analysis. In a high dimensional data set it effectively detects similarities and identifies patterns. Owing to incoherence of the dataset, high-dimensional data collection is very difficult to handle. This inconsistencies increase the computational time and hinder the data method. Thus, It allows the technique of dimensional reduction in order to turn the data collection into a lower dimensional without missing any essential details. The key principle is to minimize dimensions by converting large data sets into a vector space. It first sorts the data in order the variance and extract the components that nit only adds values to the data but also helps to minimize any repetition of information was present in the database. It uses eigenvectors based method to extract the key variance from data. This lowers the scale of the initial databases by allowing higher demonstrative views or by decreasing storage as low size databases is computing requirements also reduces variables, which can be represented in just a few main components using mathematical projection. It is connected to an analysis of the element which incorporates more domain-specific inferences for the underlying structure. It generates a predictive model that is used for the data analysis discovery method, which will boost the predictive model accuracy.

Standardizing the details we are doing at first. Standardization requires extending the database to a comparable set with both the variables and their values. It is possible to quantify as:

$$Z = \frac{V - M}{S}, \tag{3}$$

where V = Variable value M = Mean S = standard deviation

The PCA is a useful multivariate technique as well as a powerful technique. This technique is aimed at data exploration and compression in machine learning and data analysis. Efficiently, it identifies correlation and finding a pattern in a high dimensional data set. High dimensional data set is extremely complex to process due to inconsistency in the dataset. These inconsistencies increase the computational time and make the data process more complex. Thus, dimensional reduce technique is enabled so that it can transform the dataset into lower dimensional without loss of any important information.

Next, to evaluate the Principal component, we calculate the eigenvectors (v) and Eigen values (λ) in the covariance matrix. Eigenvectors are such vectors that do not modify their path if a linear transformation is done on them. While the values of Eigen clearly mean the scalars of the element of the eigenvector's. The Principal components are the new collection variables obtained from the original set of variables. They contain and have much of the information distributed between the original variables. Consequently it arranged the most important value on its own in a descending order and discarded the least informative details where the first key elements where the highest eigenvalues is most significant and form first principal components. Reorganize the initial datasets with the final principal component, which is the largest and most relevant data in the database.

4.4   mRMR Algorithm

In feature selection problems, we aim to find the foremost subset of features optimally so that it best characterizes the statistical property of a target classifying variable. The proposed technique selects a subset of the best features that helps in not only reducing the number of features but also keep classification accuracy as par. The feature selection algorithm does not rely only on the selection of best features but also it depends on the relative information. This is because these features may overlap giving rise to high redundancy among selected features though individually they are very good features. As we know we can't form a team merely by selecting the best eleven players but if have to select those players they mutually compensate each other. Therefore, selecting the subset is very important that not only include highly relevant features but minimize the redundancy among the selected features which can be achieved using correlation among selected features. Minimal redundancy and maximum relevance (mRMR) algorithm use correlations among the features to select the best set of features. This algorithm not only emphasizes on preserving the most relevant features but at the same time it minimizes the redundancy among the selected features. However, the best subset set is selected using an appropriate model which also optimizes the classification rate. This is achieved by selecting a highly correlated features and it ranks in order of their relevance. Therefore the selected features are not only mutually distinct to each other but marginally closer to the classification performance.

Maximal relevance

This technique is frequently used to pair with the minimum redundancy feature set. The selected featured have the largest mutual information I individually along with target class c. For the completion of feature set X, the subset S has m number of features x_i $i \subset m$ in a selected number of feature set that has the highest relevance criterion which satisfied the maximal mean value for all mutual information value among class c and independent feature xi in the subset. The Relevance of features (D) is in set s of m features is calculated as mention below, whereas I stand for mutual information.

Minimal Redundancy

Features may be chosen mutually, which are distant from each other, while still having an immense correlation to classifying variable. Maximal relevance identifies the material which is relevant but redundant and mRMR deal with this type of problem by removing those redundant subsets.

The criterion bringing together which are above mention two constraints knows as minimal redundancy - maximal relevance. In this technique, Forward-searching algorithm is used in subsets S of m features which are grown up iteratively. Applying a greedy algorithm in each iteration single feature is select and determines whether it add to the feature set or leave. An incremental search is performed in which X feature is added to the preceding subset of m-1 features in each step. This following condition is repeated until the optimal feature is not achieved.

5   Results and Discussions

This section describes the various outcomes observed after application of the above mentioned four FS algorithms on the feature set mentioned in [1]. This section also highlights the obtained optimized feature set and its recognition effectiveness The original/input 256-element feature vector is the combination of FD (120) and distance-based features (136). In this experiment, we have tested the classification accuracy of the original 256-element feature vector by involving all the classifiers mentioned in [1] with few more added classifiers like IBK and Random forest. This original feature vector produces the highest 99.29% recognition accuracy by involving Random forest classifier. The original 256-element feature vector is then passed through the mentioned four feature optimization techniques (HS, KH, PCA, and mRMR) to find optimized feature vectors. Table 1 reflects the length of reduced feature vectors obtained by these optimization techniques along with recognition performances shown by MLP, SVM, Logistic, NaiveBayes, IBK, and Random forest classifiers. It has been observed that the original feature vector (256 elements) is reduced to 119, 116, 77, 192, 256 element feature vector by applying HS, KH, PCA, and mRMR feature selection algorithms respectively. Except 2nd column, each entry of Table 1 also highlights the recognition accuracy achieved by the particular classifier on the reduced feature set along with the percentage of change in recognition accuracy and feature dimension with respect to the original feature vector.

Table 1. Recognition performances of the different classifiers on the reduced feature set produced by applying KH, HS, PCA, mRMR feature selection algorithm

Classifier (feature dimension)	Original feature vector	Optimized feature vector by (% change in accuracy & feature dimension)			
		KH	HS	PCA	MRMR
	−256	−116	−119	−77	−192
MLP	98.25	97.95	98.3	98.81	98.79
		(0.3%, 54.69%)	(−0.05%, 53.52%)	(−0.56%, 69.92%)	(−0.54%, 25%)
SVM	98.91	98.83	98.95	98.98	99.01
		(0.08%, 54.69%)	(−0.04%, 53.52%)	(−0.07%, 69.92%)	(−0.1%, 25%)
Logistic	98.95	98.68	98.55	97.44	98.49
		(0.27%, 54.69%)	(0.4, 53.52%)	(1.51%, 69.92%)	(0.46, 25%)
Naive Bayes	92.75	91.32	90.95	95.92	93.5
		(1.43%, 54.69%)	(1.8%, 53.52%)	(−3.17%, 69.92%)	(−0.75%, 25%)
IBK	95.65	95.52	96.27	98.44	96.76
		(0.13%, 54.69%)	(−0.62%, 53.52%)	(−2.79%, 69.92%)	(−1.11%, 25%)
Random forest	99.29	99.17	99.21	98.38	99.28
		(0.12%, 54.69%)	(0.08%, 53.52%)	(0.91%, 69.92%)	(0.01%, 25%)

Table 2 reflects the best performing classifier and achieved recognition accuracy for all the reduced feature sets generated by applying the above mentioned four feature optimization techniques. This table highlights that Random forest classifier outperforms other classifiers for all cases except for the feature vector produced by PCA. SVM classifier produces best recognition performance as 99.28% on the optimized feature set produced by applying PCA which is marked bold in Table 2.

Table 2. The best performing classifier along with achieved recognition accuracy for all the feature sets produced by applying HS, KH, PCA, and mRMR feature selection algorithm

Feature vectors	Classifier	Accuracy (in %)
Original feature vector	Random forest	99.29
Optimized feature vector by KH	Random forest	99.17
Optimized feature vector by HS	Random forest	99.21
Optimized feature vector by PCA	SVM	99.28
Optimized feature vector by MRMR	Random forest	99.28

Table 3 provides an insightful analysis of the percentage of change in recognition accuracy and reduction of feature attributes for all the reduced feature set with respect to the original feature vector. From this table, it has been observed that the applied HS, KH, PCA, and mRMR algorithm reduces the original feature vector by 53.52%, 54.69%, 69.92% and 25% respectively and for those reduced feature sets, the recognition accuracy has been reduced by 0.08%, −0.62%, −3.17%, and −1.11% respectively. Looking into this table, it can be said that the feature set produced after applying mRMR algorithm can generate almost the same recognition accuracy by reducing the original feature vector by 25%. In turn, the PCA algorithm finds the optimal feature set by reducing almost 69.92% feature attributes from the original feature vector but degrades the recognition accuracy by 0.31%. After performing exhaustive analysis, it has been observed that the major disadvantage of using embedded methods is the associated effort. In turn, the potential advantage of using such methods is that they are inexpensive in terms of computation. Filter-based procedures can process thousands of features within seconds and the features that are selected can be used with any machine learning algorithm. Filtering techniques are effective for eliminating the correlated features, duplicate, constant, and irrelevant characteristics.

After observing and analyzing the different outcomes obtained, it can be concluded that for the lightly weighted system where recognition accuracy plays a most important role than that of time and space required to build the model, we can use the mRMR feature selection algorithm. Whereas, in the system where time requirement is most important, we can use PCA for feature reduction purposes.

Table 3. Percentage of reduction in the number of feature attributes for all the produced reduced feature vectors after applying HS, KH, PCA, and mRMR optimization algorithms and also the percentage of reduction in recognition accuracy with respect to the original feature vector

Optimization algorithms	% reduction in	
	feature reduction	in accuracy
KH	54.69	0.08
HS	53.52	−0.62
PCA	69.92	−3.17
MRMR	25	−1.11

6   Conclusion and Future Directions

This paper highlights the performance of various approach to optimize the feature vector generated by combining Frechet Distance and distance-based features [1] using different feature selection techniques KH, HS, PCA and MRMR. The paper also analyzes the different outcomes in terms of achieved accuracy vs. features reduction. This analysis will definitely help the researchers in this domain to choose appropriate feature selection techniques according to the requirement. In future, we will try to experiment with other popular feature optimization algorithms to explore the merits and demerits, modify the used optimization algorithms to generate more powerful reduced feature set by exploring initialization step, fitness criteria and also tuning different parameters. We are planning to experiment with these optimization techniques for other scripts and offline too.

References

1. Sen, S., Chakraborty, J., Chatterjee, S., Mitra, R., Sarkar, R., Roy, K.: Online handwritten Bangla character recognition using Frechet distance and distance based features. In: Sundaram, S., Harit, G. (eds.) DAR 2018. CCIS, vol. 1020, pp. 65–73. Springer, Singapore (2019). https://doi.org/10.1007/978-981-13-9361-7_6
2. Zafar, M.F., Mohamad, D., Othman, R.M.: On-line handwritten character recognition: an implementation of counterpropagation neural net. In: Proceedings of World Academy of Science, Engineering and Technology (2005)
3. Garain, U., Chaudhuri, B.B., Pal, T.T.: Online handwritten Indian script recognition: a human motor function based framework. In: Proceedings of the 16th International Conference on Pattern Recognition, pp. 164–167 (2002)
4. Connell, S.D., Jain, A.K.: Template-based online character recognition. Pattern Recogn. **34**(1), 1–14 (2001)
5. Langley, P., Blum, A.L.: Selection of relevant features and examples in machine learning. Artif. Intell. **97**, 245–271 (1997)
6. Isabelle, G., Elisseff, A.: An introduction to variable and feature selection. J. Mach. Learn. Res. **3**, 1157–1182 (2003)

7. Jain, A., Guyon, D.Z.: Feature selection: evaluation, application, and small sample performance. IEEE Trans. Pattern Anal. Mach. Intell. **19**(2), 153–158 (1997)
8. Zhang, B., Fu, M., Yan, H.: A nonlinear neural network model of mixture of local principal component analysis: application to handwritten digits recognition. Pattern Recogn. **34**(2), 203–214 (2001)
9. Fischer, A., Bunke, H.: Kernel PCA for HMM-based cursive handwriting recognition. In: Jiang, X., Petkov, N. (eds.) CAIP 2009. LNCS, vol. 5702, pp. 181–188. Springer, Heidelberg (2009). https://doi.org/10.1007/978-3-642-03767-2_22
10. Singh, P., Verma, A., Chaudhari, N.S.: Devanagri handwritten numeral recognition using feature selection approach. Int. J. Intell. Syst. Appl. **6**(12), 40–47 (2014)
11. Geem, Z.W., Kim, J.H., Loganathan, G.V.: A new heuristic optimization algorithm: harmony search. Simulation **76**(2), 60–68 (2001)
12. Xue, B., Zhang, M., Browne, W.N., Yao, X.: A survey on evolutionary computation approaches to feature selection. IEEE Trans. Evol. Comput. **20**(4), 606–626 (2016)
13. Dash, M., Liu, H.: Feature selection for classification. Intell. Data Anal. **1**(1–4), 131–156 (1997)
14. Oh, I.S., Lee, J.S., Moon, B.R.: Hybrid genetic algorithms for feature selection. IEEE Trans. Pattern Anal. Mach. Intell. **26**(11), 1424–1437 (2004)
15. Huang, C.L., Wang, C.J.: A GA-based feature selection and parameters optimization for support vector machines. Expert Syst. Appl. **31**(2), 231–240 (2006)
16. Liwicki, M., Bunke, H.: Feature selection for HMM and BLSTM based handwriting recognition of whiteboard notes. Int. J. Pattern Recognit Artif Intell. **23**(5), 907–923 (2009)
17. Huang, B.Q., Kechadi, M.: A fast feature selection model for online handwriting symbol recognition. In: 5th International Conference on Machine Learning and Applications, pp. 251–257 (2006)
18. Deepu, V., Madhvanath, S., Ramakrishnan, A.G.: Principal component analysis for online handwritten character recognition. In: Proceedings of 17th International Conference on Pattern Recognition, pp. 327–330 (2004)
19. Sundaram, S., Ramakrishnan, A.G.: Two dimensional principal component analysis for online tamil character recognition. In: Proceedings of 11th International Conference Frontiers in Handwriting Recognition, pp. 88–94 (2008)
20. Prasad, G.K., Khan, I., Chanukotimath, N.R., Khan, F.: On-line handwritten character recognition system for Kannada using principal component analysis approach: for handheld devices. In: World Congress on Information and Communication Technologies, pp. 675–678 (2012)
21. Prasad, G.K., Khan, I., Chanukotimath, N.: On-line Hindi handwritten character recognition for mobile devices. In: Proceedings of International Conference on Advances in Computing, Communications and Informatics, pp. 1074–1078 (2012)
22. Sen, S., Mitra, M., Bhattacharyya, A., Sarkar, R., Schwenker, F., Roy, K.: Feature selection for recognition of online handwritten Bangla characters. Neural Process. Lett. **50**, 2281–2304 (2019)
23. Ferreira, A.J., Figueiredo, M.A.T.: Efficient feature selection filters for high-dimensional data. Pattern Recognit. Lett. **33**(13), 1794–1804 (2012)
24. Saha, S., et al.: Feature selection for facial emotion recognition using cosine similarity-based harmony search algorithm. Appl. Sci. **10**(8), 2816 (2020)
25. Bhattacharya, U., Gupta, B.K., Parui, S.K.: Direction code based features for recognition of online Handwritten characters of Bangla. In: International Conference on Document Analysis and Recognition, pp. 58–62 (2007)

26. Bag, S., Bhowmick, P., Harit, G.: Recognition of Bengali handwritten characters using skeletal convexity and dynamic programming. In: International Conference on Emerging Application of Information Technology, pp. 265–268 (2011)

27. Roy, K.: Stroke-database design for online handwriting recognition in Bangla. Int. J. Mod. Eng. Res. **2**, 2534–2540 (2012)

28. Sen, S., Sarkar, R., Roy, K., Hori, N.: Recognize online handwritten Bangla characters using Hausdorff distance based feature. In: 5th International Conference on Frontiers in Intelligent Computing: Theory and Application, pp. 541–549 (2016)

29. Sen, S., Bhattacharyya, A., Singh, P.K., Sarkar, R., Roy, K., Doermann, D.: Application of structural and topological features to recognize online handwritten bangla characters. ACM Trans. Asian Low-Resour. Lang. Inf. Process. **17**(3), 1–16 (2018)

30. Sen, S., Shaoo, D., Mitra, M., Sarkar, R., Roy, K.: DFA-based online bangla character recognition. In: Chandra, P., Giri, D., Li, F., Kar, S., Jana, D.K. (eds.) Information Technology and Applied Mathematics. AISC, vol. 699, pp. 175–183. Springer, Singapore (2019). https://doi.org/10.1007/978-981-10-7590-2_13

31. Sen, S., Sarkar, R., Roy, K.: An approach to stroke-based online handwritten bangla character recognition. In: Proceedings of the Advanced Computing and Systems for Security, pp. 153–163 (2017)

32. Ghosh, R.: A novel feature extraction approach for online Bengali and Devanagari character recognition. In: International Conference on Signal Processing and Integrated Networks, pp. 483–488 (2015)

33. Shin, J., et al.: Important Features Selection and Classification of Adult and Child from Handwriting Using Machine Learning Methods (2022)

34. Begum, N., et al.: User Authentication Based on Handwriting Analysis of Pen-Tablet Sensor Data Using Optimal Feature Selection Model (2021)

35. Ruiz-Parrado, V., Heradio, R., Aranda-Escolastico, E., Sánchez, A., Vélez, J.F.: A bibliometric analysis of off-line handwritten document analysis literature (1990–2020). Pattern Recogn. **1**(125), 108513 (2022)

Predicting Disease-Associated Genes Through Interaction and Ontology-Based Inference Technique

Syed Alberuni[✉][iD] and Sumanta Ray[iD]

Department of Computer Science and Engineering, Aliah University, Kolkata 700156,
West Bengal, India
syedalberuni12@gmail.com, sumanta.ray@aliah.ac.in

Abstract. This article proposed a new framework to predict novel
disease-associated genes. First, we have compiled a gene-disease network
from an existing gene-disease association database. Next, we associated
gene ontology and protein interaction networks with the compiled gene-
disease network. The prediction is based on the three statistical hypothesis, we have deduced from the topological structure of the compiled
network. The first two hypothesis represents the association between the
functional similar genes with the disease classes. The third hypothesis
infers the association between the genes with disease class. The prediction is made based on the conclusions of these three hypotheses. Statistical tests are conducted to prove the three hypothesis. The results
show 400 high-confidence gene-disease associations. The predictions are
validated using a literature study and statistical test. The predictions
are demonstrated by using several visualization techniques.

Keywords: human Disease Network · Disease Associated Genes
Prediction · Gene Ontology · Semantic Similarity

1 Introduction

Human Disease Network is one of the very important fields of research for computational biology [17,20]. The complex structure analysis of the Human Disease Network (HDN) is one of the most difficult fields of computational biology
research [6]. A human disease network is represented as a network constructed
from human disorders/diseases of their genetic origins or other features [19].
It may be demonstrated as the map of human disease associations which refers
mostly to the disease genes. In HDN, two diseases node are connected if they have
at least one commonly associated gene. HDN usually derives from the bipartite
networks which consist of both disease and gene information [4]. Understanding the key mechanisms of this complex network is very important to know the
phenotype similarity among several diseases [5]. The majority of human diseases
are topically complex as they are often associated with not just one gene, but a

K. Dasgupta et al. (Eds.): CICBA 2023, CCIS 1956, pp. 259–272, 2024.
https://doi.org/10.1007/978-3-031-48879-5_20

set of genes [10]. One of the basic difficulties in finding out the genetic causes of complex diseases is that various disease cases could be caused by distinct genetic perturbations [3]. It is reported that humans have a similar number of genes to a worm [15]. In addition, if a disease is caused by a combinatorial effect of many mutations, the individual effects of each mutation might be small and thus hard to discover [3].

A comprehensive study of disease similarities is important to find out the root cause of the disease. This will provide us with different new ideas and solutions to the cause of diseases and will play a key role in the diagnosis and treatment of these complex diseases. A lot of research has been done and it's still going on. There exist several approaches which predict and analyze disease similarities by applying data mining and text mining approaches. For example, in [10] a network of disease phenotypes is built by performing a text search approach to group common clinical terms. Goh et al. [6] first gave the idea about the human-disease network which provides a network of disease and disorders genes that are associated with a known association of gene diseases. Using this data Bandyopadhyay et al. [1] proposed an approach to identify disease-related protein complexes within the human protein-protein interaction network. In [9] a new frame is introduced to find out the similarity between two specific tissue or disease networks by counting graphlets on multiple labels. In [13] the gene association of novel diseases is predicted using the RWR algorithm and the functional similarity between protein complexes. Bhattacharjee et al. [2] proposed a new framework for comparing the topological structure of PPI networks based on proteins associated with the disease. Duc-Hau Le and Vu-Tung Dang [11] proposed a method to predict new genes associated with Alzheimer's disease through an ontology-based disease similarity network. Yang et al. [18] developed a method called HerGePred where a heterogeneous network of diseases and genes is built to predict disease-associated genes.

2   Proposed Method

In this section, the workflow of the framework is described (see Fig. 1). The predictions are based on the three main hypothesis which is demonstrated in the Fig. 1.

2.1   Dataset Preparation

The database of disease-gene interactions is downloaded from Goh et al. [6]. A bipartite network is used to model the dataset, with one set of nodes representing disease/disorder class and the other set of nodes showing associated genes [2]. The disease class and related genes were obtained from the Online Mendelian Inheritance in Man (OMIM) [7], a database of human disease genes and phenotypes. All the diseases/disorders are classified into 22 categories and their associated genes are shown in Fig. 2. These data are used to map disease-associated proteins in the human PPI network downloaded from

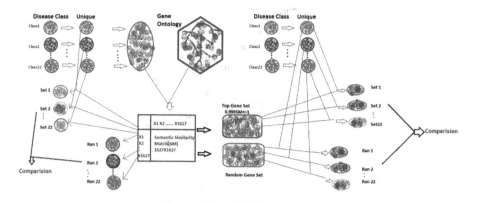

Fig. 1. This diagram demonstrates the workflow of the prediction process

Human Protein Reference Database (HPRD: http://www.hprd.org/download). From the Gene Ontology(GO) Consortium (http://www.geneontology.org/), GO data from these selected proteins were collected.

There are several methods used to compute semantic similarity matrices like Resnik's measure, Lin's measure, Calculation of funSim and Relevance Similarity measure [14]. Here we have used the Relevance Similarity measure to compute the semantic similarity matrix. We have used 22 classes for human diseases/disorders. Genes associated with 22 human disorders/diseases are collected in a single set and finally, we computed the unique set of this gene set. 3830 genes are found to be unique among 7070 total genes. Then we fetched the data from the Gene Ontology dataset common with a unique disease dataset and we finally got the final dataset. Using the Relevance Similarity measure we computed the semantic similarity matrix of the final dataset and got a 1627×1627 Similarity Matrix and named it SM.

2.2 Three Hypothesis

We have the following three assumptions, which are mentioned below-

- *Hypothesis-1: Genes associated with 22 disease classes have significantly higher semantic similarity values.*
- *Hypothesis-2: Functionality similar genes are associated with the same group of disease/disorders class.*
- *Hypothesis-3: Diseases having phenotype similarity higher are expected to be associated with the same set of genes.*

The Wilcoxon Rank-Sum Test. Wilcoxon rank-sum test is a non-parametric version of the two-sample t-test which is utilised to compare two independent samples to know whether the two tested samples have equal variance or spread [8].

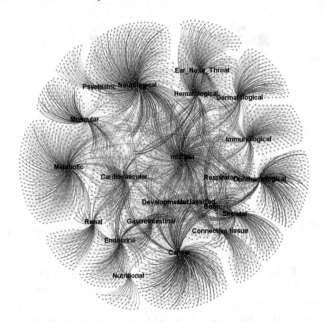

Fig. 2. Graphical representation of the human disease network where one set of nodes represents diseases/disorder class and the other set of nodes represents associated genes. Here red and grey nodes represent the disease classes and disease-associated genes respectively, while the edges represent the interaction between disease classes and their associated genes. (Color figure online)

Here we have shown the successful results of three assumptions proved. We have computed the rank-sum value also to check whether our assumption can be a true hypothesis.

Hypothesis-1: Gene Associated with 22 Disease Classes Have Significantly Higher Semantic Similarity Values. To prove this hypothesis, the common genes between the semantic similarity matrix and unique genes for all disease classes are computed using the intersect function in Matlab. Then, we fetched the similarity scores of these common gene sets and calculated the mean value for all 22 sets. Next, we randomly selected values equal to the size of common genes for each disease class 300 times and computed the mean value for all 22 classes across all the random sets. Finally, we calculated the rank-sum value and compare all the sets with their random values which are equal to $1.4360e-08$. The rank-sum value obtained is very less, which validates our hypothesis to be a true hypothesis.

The experimental results for hypothesis 1 are shown in Table 1, and the bar graph 3 compares the actual values for all the disease classes with their random values. The highest actual value is 0.8759 for the Nutritional disease class, and the highest random value is 0.5852 for the ear nose and throat.

Table 1. Experimental result of hypothesis 1

Sl no.	Disease Class	Actual Values	Random Values
1	Bone	0.8037	0.5785
2	Cancer	0.7624	0.5732
3	Cardiovascular	0.743	0.5734
4	Connective Tissue	0.7602	0.5770
5	Dermatological	0.721	0.5744
6	Development	0.8201	0.5772
7	Ear Nose Throat	0.7424	0.5852
8	Endocrine	0.7676	0.5735
9	Gastrointestinal	0.749	0.5831
10	Hematological	0.7134	0.5733
11	Immunological	0.7949	0.5739
12	Metabolic	0.7142	0.5723
13	Multiple	0.6297	0.5726
14	Muscular	0.7123	0.5751
15	Neurological	0.6901	0.5743
16	Nutritional	0.8759	0.5811
17	Ophthalmological	0.6946	0.5754
18	Psychiatric	0.7452	0.5797
19	Renal	0.6724	0.5774
20	Respiratory	0.7798	0.5785
21	Skeletal	0.7992	0.5765
22	Unclassified	0.7765	0.5754

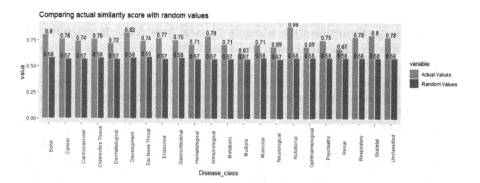

Fig. 3. Bar graph showing proof of Hypothesis 1. The actual values for all 22 disease classes are depicted in orange, while the corresponding random values are shown in cyan. As demonstrated, the actual values for all 22 disease classes are higher than their respective random values. (Color figure online)

Table 2. The intersection of each disease with the Actual Top Gene set and Random Gene set

Sl No	Disease Class	Top Gene Set	Random Gene Set
1	Bone	63	53.5733
2	Cancer	346	276.7500
3	Cardiovascular	190	145.7733
4	Connective Tissue	79	73.22
5	Dermatological	100	78.42
6	Development	117	88.48
7	Ear Nose Throat	30	28.9933
8	Endocrine	178	139.43
9	Gastrointestinal	43	31.9967
1	Hematological	200	164.7433
11	immunological	160	126.47
12	Metabolic	244	186.3600
13	Multiple	72	59.6467
14	Muscular	303	250.6733
15	Neurological	118	102.2067
16	Nutritional	289	262.98
17	Ophthalmological	38	27.67
18	Psychiatric	116	109.9933
19	Renal	59	48.7467
20	Respiratory	71	67.50
21	Skeletal	57	42.3633
22	Unclassified	85	78.3833

Hypothesis-2: Functionality Similar Genes Are Associated with the Same Group of Disease/Disorders Class- We proved this hypothesis, we formed a gene set with a very high similarity score. For this purpose, a very high threshold value of .999 to 1 is set to fetch genes from SM i.e. genes associated with these values are fetched and a set of genes is formed using all these genes having a high similarity score. We computed the uniqueness of these genes and we get a set of 1089 genes having scored from .999 to 1. Next, we wanted to find out what are disease classes highly associated with these genes, for this purpose we have computed the common genes for all diseases with this gene set of high threshold values and named it as the Top gene set. Then to find out the common genes between the high-score gene set and each disease class we computed the intersection of each disease with the high-score gene set. Again the process is repeated for 300 random gene sets of the same size as the size of the top gene set. The experimental result for hypothesis 2 is shown in Table 2. Then we calculated the rank-sum value which is equal to 7.7559e−18, which is again very small and so we conclude this hypothesis to be the true hypothesis.

Graph representing Intersection of each disease with the actual Top gene set verses Random gene set

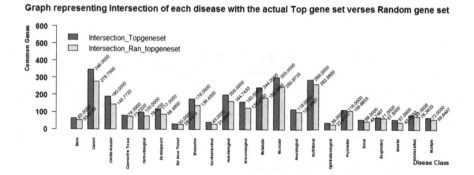

Fig. 4. Bar Graph showing the proof of hypothesis 2

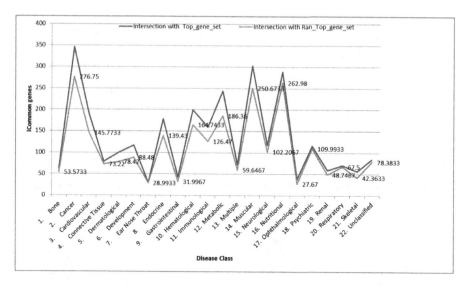

Fig. 5. Line Graph showing the proof of hypothesis 2

For a better understanding of the result, we have drawn a bar plot and a line graph to compare the values for all 22 with their actual and random values (Fig. 5).

From the Fig. 4 it is clearly shown that actual scores are higher in the actual set compared to the random set. Cancer has the highest Actual similarity score equal to 346 and also we can see that ear_nose_throat has the lowest value which is equal to 30, when it intersects with the top gene set, Which means cancer contains a higher number of high score protein and ear_nose_throat contain less number of higher score protein. For random sets also cancer has a higher score which is equal to 276.75 and Ophthalmological has a lower score which is equal to 27.67.

Hypothesis-3: Disease Having Phenotype Similarity Higher Are Expected to Associate with the Same Set of Genes- We proved this hypothesis by plotting a bar graph and comparing the result of the bar graph. Before the bar graph, we obtained some results to be used in the bar graph which is shown in Table 3. We have used the previous result where we computed similarity scores between all disease pairs and computed a bar graph with actual values of these similarity pairs with their random values side by side.

The experimental result for hypothesis 3 is shown in Fig. 6. From the figure, it can be shown that actual scores are higher in the actual set compared to the random set.

Table 3. Four higher similarity score pair with their Actual values and their Random values

Sl No	Disease pair	Actual Values	Random Values
1	Bone_Skeletal	74	32.72
2	Endocrine_Multiple	381	345.27
3	Gastrointestinal_Respiratory	75	11.34
4	Metabolic_Neurologiacl	453	395.73

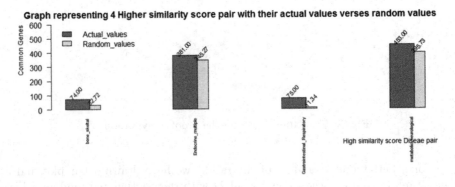

Fig. 6. Bar graph for proof of hypothesis 3

3   Experimental Result

In this section, we have shown the experimental result for predicting disease-associated Protein-Protein Interaction Networks. For this, we have used the clustering technique to get 30 clusters of top gene sets obtained previously. Clustering was formerly described as an unsupervised method for analysing data.

3.1   Clustering of Top Gene Dataset

For the prediction part, we have used our Top Gene dataset obtained earlier. Here We have used K-Means clustering to divide the dataset into 30 clusters.

K-means is a very efficient method and is commonly used for clustering purposes [12]. It is commonly used to partition a set of samples into k groups in an unsupervised way. It proceeds by selecting k initial cluster centers and then iteratively refining them [16].

Firstly we obtained 30 clusters and then we compared each cluster with all 22 disease classes and computed the common genes among them i.e. for cluster 1 we computed the common gene between cluster one and all 22 disease classes and stored the result. After that, we selected the disease which contain the maximum number of common genes. The process was repeated 30 times for all 22 disease classes with 30 clusters. All 30 cluster with respective disease class is shown in Table 4.

3.2   Predicted Interactions

We fetched the index of similarity score associated with these common genes from Semantic Similarity Matrix and also the index of similarity score of genes of the respective cluster which are not common to the respective disease class. We computed a similarity matrix with these two indexes and from the matrix, we obtained the maximum values associated with all common genes from the uncommon genes. Finally, we concluded that these genes with higher similarity scores with common genes of cluster and respective disease class are likely to be present in the same disease class or may likely have similar behaviour. Here also the process is repeated for all 30 clusters.

Here we are showing an illustration of our total prediction part in Fig. 7. In the figure, the process is shown where a disease class has the maximum number of common genes with the respective cluster. Common genes of cluster Y and Disease class X are shown separately for better illustration. Here we have seen from common genes an arrow pointing towards uncommon genes and a gene is selected which has the highest similarity score with these common genes, Which predicts that there is a high chance of the presence of these genes and there is also a chance that they may pose similar properties.

Based on the 30 identified clusters 420 protein predictions are made between human proteins and the disease class. Figure 8 shows the predicted network. As can be seen from Fig. 8 disease class 'Cancer' shows the highest degree (105)

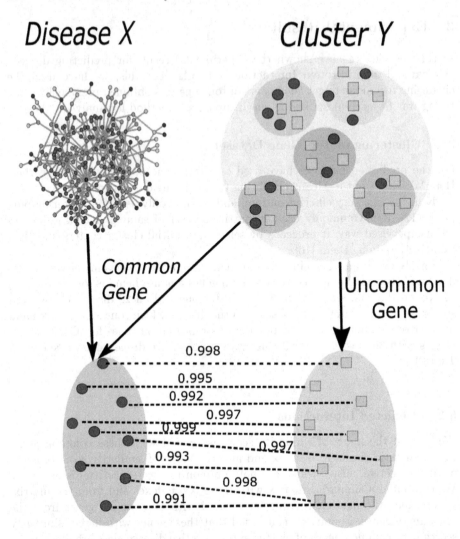

Fig. 7. The figure shows an example of a human disease class interacting with the predicted gene. Cluster Y consists of proteins/genes interacting with known and unknown disease classes.

in the predicted network. Here we predict disease class 'Cancer' interacted with some human proteins are FANCE, GIF, PDGFRL, PRPF31, AIRE, BACH1, BCL7A, DLX3, EWSR1, LRPPRC, MAML2 etc. Disease classes 'Metabolic' and 'Neurological' have 92 and 89 predicted interactions with a human protein, whereas disease classes 'Cardiovascular' and 'Ophthalmological' have the lowest number of predicted interactions with the human protein. In Table 5 we show the number of predicted proteins that interacted with disease class.

Table 4. Table Showing Disease with maximum No of the gene in each cluster

Cluster No	Disease Name with Max No of Genes	No of common genes
1	Cancer	9
2	Hematological	30
3	Hematological	20
4	Multiple	9
5	Neurological	28
6	Neurological	28
7	Multiple	13
8	Cancer	19
9	Metabolic	27
10	Ophthalmological	19
11	Cancer	40
12	Multiple	2
13	Neurological	56
14	Ophthalmological	6
15	Multiple	17
16	Multiple	16
17	Metabolic	19
18	Cancer	69
19	Cancer and Multiple	39
20	Multiple	6
21	Cancer	58
22	Neurological	16
23	Metabolic	17
24	Multiple	6
25	Metabolic	28
26	Neurological	10
27	Neurological	6
28	Metabolic	37
29	Metabolic	12
30	Cardiovascular	17

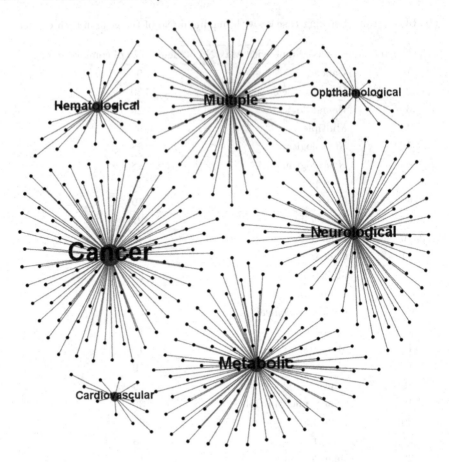

Fig. 8. Figure shows predicted association between human disease class and genes/proteins

Table 5. Number of predicted proteins with 7 disease classes

Sl. NO.	Disease Class	Number of predicted proteins
1	Cancer	105
2	Hematological	28
3	Multiple	79
4	Neurological	89
5	Metabolic	92
6	Ophthalmological	15
7	Cardiovascular	11

4   Conclusions and Future Scope of Research

In this paper, we have proposed a framework to predict novel gene-disease associations based on topological properties of the associated protein-protein interaction and gene ontology networks. Three statistical hypotheses are made from the topological characteristics of the compiled network that demonstrate the relationship among the functionally similar genes with several disease classes. We have utilized a public dataset from Goh et al. [6] which contains 22 disease classes. We have demonstrated the correlation between functionally similar genes in the 22 disease classes. The association is proved with a strong statistical hypothesis. Future Analysis and Proper investigation of the predicted interactions may reveal novel insight into the fundamental structure of disease-gene association.

References

1. Bandyopadhyay, S., Ray, S., Mukhopadhyay, A., Maulik, U.: A multiobjective approach for identifying protein complexes and studying their association in multiple disorders. Algorithms Mol. Biol. 10(1), 1–15 (2015)
2. Bhattacharjee, D., Hossain, S.M.M., Sultana, R., Ray, S.: Topological inquisition into the PPI networks associated with human diseases through graphlet frequency distribution. In: Shankar, B.U., Ghosh, K., Mandal, D.P., Ray, S.S., Zhang, D., Pal, S.K. (eds.) PReMI 2017. LNCS, vol. 10597, pp. 431–437. Springer, Cham (2017). https://doi.org/10.1007/978-3-319-69900-4_55
3. Cho, D.Y., Kim, Y.A., Przytycka, T.M.: Chapter 5: network biology approach to complex diseases. PLoS Comput. Biol. 8(12), e1002820 (2012)
4. Emmert-Streib, F., Tripathi, S., Simoes, R.D.M., Hawwa, A.F., Dehmer, M.: The human disease network: opportunities for classification, diagnosis, and prediction of disorders and disease genes. Syst. Biomed. 1(1), 20–28 (2013)
5. Goh, K.I., Choi, I.G.: Exploring the human diseasome: the human disease network. Brief. Funct. Genomics 11(6), 533–542 (2012)
6. Goh, K.I., Cusick, M.E., Valle, D., Childs, B., Vidal, M., Barabási, A.L.: The human disease network. Proc. Natl. Acad. Sci. 104(21), 8685–8690 (2007)
7. Hamosh, A., Scott, A.F., Amberger, J.S., Bocchini, C.A., McKusick, V.A.: Online mendelian inheritance in man (OMIM), a knowledgebase of human genes and genetic disorders. Nucleic Acids Res. 33(suppl_1), D514–D517 (2005)
8. Hossain, A., Willan, A.R., Beyene, J.: An improved method on Wilcoxon rank sum test for gene selection from microarray experiments. Commun. Stat.-Simul. Comput. 42(7), 1563–1577 (2013)
9. Huang, D.W., et al.: The David gene functional classification tool: a novel biological module-centric algorithm to functionally analyze large gene lists. Genome Biol. 8(9), R183 (2007)
10. Kanehisa, M., Goto, S., Furumichi, M., Tanabe, M., Hirakawa, M.: KEGG for representation and analysis of molecular networks involving diseases and drugs. Nucleic Acids Res. 38(suppl 1), D355–D360 (2010)
11. Le, D.H., Dang, V.T.: Ontology-based disease similarity network for disease gene prediction. Vietnam J. Comput. Sci. 3(3), 197–205 (2016)

12. Morissette, L., Chartier, S.: The k-means clustering technique: general considerations and implementation in mathematica. Tutorials Quantit. Methods Psychol. **9**(1), 15–24 (2013)
13. Pržulj, N.: Biological network comparison using graphlet degree distribution. Bioinformatics **23**(2), e177–e183 (2007)
14. Schlicker, A., Domingues, F.S., Rahnenführer, J., Lengauer, T.: A new measure for functional similarity of gene products based on gene ontology. BMC Bioinform. **7**(1), 1–16 (2006)
15. Valencia, A., Pazos, F.: Computational methods for the prediction of protein interactions. Curr. Opin. Struct. Biol. **12**(3), 368–373 (2002)
16. Wagstaff, K., Cardie, C., Rogers, S., Schrödl, S., et al.: Constrained k-means clustering with background knowledge. In: ICML, vol. 1, pp. 577–584 (2001)
17. Wu, X., Jiang, R., Zhang, M.Q., Li, S.: Network-based global inference of human disease genes. Mol. Syst. Biol. **4**(1), 189 (2008)
18. Yang, K., et al.: HerGePred: heterogeneous network embedding representation for disease gene prediction. IEEE J. Biomed. Health Inform. **23**(4), 1805–1815 (2018)
19. Zhang, X., et al.: The expanded human disease network combining protein-protein interaction information. Eur. J. Hum. Genet. **19**(7), 783–788 (2011)
20. Zhou, X., Menche, J., Barabási, A.L., Sharma, A.: Human symptoms-disease network. Nat. Commun. **5**(1), 1–10 (2014)

An Automatic POS Tagger System for Code Mixed Indian Social Media Text

Nihar Jyoti Basisth, Tushar Sachan, Neha Kumari, Shyambabu Pandey(✉), and Partha Pakray(✉)

Department of Computer Science and Engineering, National Institute of Technology Silchar, Silchar, Assam, India
shyambabu21_rs@cse.nits.ac.in, partha@cse.nits.ac.in

Abstract. For a range of Natural Language Processing (NLP) applications, including Sentiment Analysis, Sarcasm Detection, Information Retrieval, Question Answering, and Named Entity Identification, text derived from multiple users' posts and what they comment on social media constitute significant information (IR). All such applications require part-of-speech (POS) tagging to add tag information to the raw text. Code-mixing, a social media user's natural desire to submit content in multiple languages, presents a difficulty to POS tagging. In addition, sophisticated and freestyle writing increases the intricacy of the issue. For POS tagging of Code-Mixed Indian social media text, a supervised algorithm using Hidden Markov Model (HMM) with the Viterbi algorithm has been developed to address the problem. The suggested system has been trained and tested using publicly accessible social media text in Indian languages (ILs), particularly Bengali, Telugu, English, and Hindi. On the basis of the F-measure, the accuracy of the system-annotated tags have been assessed.

Keywords: Parts-of-speech tagging · Code-mixing · Hidden Markov Model · Viterbi algorithm · Social media text · Natural Language Processing

1 Introduction

The massive digital transformation of social media in recent decades has led to the rise in the study and analysis of natural languages. Different categories of people frequently use multiple social media platforms for their individual issues and interests, ranging from personal to professional. Personal posts are primarily distinguished by the viewpoint and outlook of the author, whereas promotional postings incorporate product marketing and customer feedback. Additionally, examining the sentiments in posts helps further evaluate such user-generated texts. In summary, social media post [17] content is an essential input for numerous NLP [15] applications.

© The Author(s), under exclusive license to Springer Nature Switzerland AG 2024
K. Dasgupta et al. (Eds.): CICBA 2023, CCIS 1956, pp. 273–286, 2024.
https://doi.org/10.1007/978-3-031-48879-5_21

With India being one of the most linguistically diverse countries in the world, people can read and write two or more languages. It has been observed that social media users tend to express their knowledge, emotions and even feedback using more than one language. This leads to the generation of code-mixed languages. This multilingual content is generally noisy with grammatically incorrect texts, unknown abbreviations, and non-standard spellings. The already existing sentiment analysis algorithms are well-developed for monolingual content but fail to achieve better accuracy for code-mixed data.

Assigning lexical class markers or part-of-speech (POS) to every corpus word is another data pre-processing component. This POS tagging is a primal task of NLP in order to develop linguistic rules and derive patterns for further applications such as Named Entity Recognition (NER), question-answering, sentiment analysis, and machine translation. POS tagging applications are broadly classified into three categories- rule-based, statistical, and hybrid tagging [12]. In a rule-based approach, handwritten rules are incorporated to assign POS tags to the words. But, these rules eventually fail when an unknown word is encountered. The way statistical tagging work is on the basis of the most frequently used tags for a word in annotated training data. Based on their probabilities, POS tags are assigned to unannotated text. The combination of the above-stated approaches, where probabilistic features are applied to pre-existing rules is known as hybrid tagging.

Let us look at an example:

a) bhaiya where r u. i can't spot u b) He later boarded up that peeping spot

As we can see the word *spot* acts as two different parts of speech, i.e. *noun* in sentence 2 and as a *verb* in sentence 1.

This paper demonstrates a statistical model- HMM to learn the information about the tag-set and word-tag frequencies for training. The size of the dataset is 1000, for each of the language pairs of the code-mixed datasets used for training the model. The Viterbi algorithm is incorporated with HMM to get high accuracy of POS taggings of sentences.

The structure of the paper is as follows: Section 2 consists of related works and an understanding of the models used, their outcomes, and drawbacks. The code-mixed dataset is described in Sect. 3. These datasets are classified into two types- coarse grained and fine grained. We explain the working of our supervised model using HMM and Viterbi algorithm; hence predicting the best possible POS tags, in Sect. 4. The results of three different language pairs viz Eng-Hindi, Eng-Bengali, and Eng-Telugu are discussed in Sect. 5, comparing them with the baseline, using a few examples. Further to the discussion, we conclude the paper with the possibilities of improving accuracy using a Quantum-based HMM in Sect. 7.

2   Literature Survey

POS Tagging has always been one of the important implementations of Computational Linguistic Domains and NLP. While several POS taggers have already achieved considerable accuracy with single and code mixed languages.

A POS tagging using a CRF++ (Conditional Random Field) of three Indian social media mixed text languages [11]- Hindi, Tamil, and Bengali achieved the highest accuracy of 75%. It adopted standard learning approaches so that the model would work well with scarce data.

Unsupervised transformation-based learning and hidden Markov model taggers were compared using the same corpus and lexicons in Banko and Moore's comprehensive evaluation of various unsupervised part-of-speech tagging techniques [4]. With supervision, the model produced cutting-edge outcomes without requiring the time-consuming training process that other high-performing models do.

Two unsupervised methods for multilingual POS tagging were used. One of them directly combined the tag sequences of two different languages into a single sequence, and the other used latent variables instead, to take into account the multilingual context. Both methods used Markov Chain Monte Carlo sampling techniques [16]. It was predicated on the notion that POS tags with comparable functionality would be used similarly.

Another POS tagger with Bidirectional Long-Short Term Memory (bi-LSTM) models, CRF, and Auxiliary loss [20] was reported in 2016 for morphologically complex languages. This model has trained 22 languages, suggesting that for label corruptions and training data size, bi-LSTMs are less sensitive as compared to previous knowledge and results.

A POS Tagging for English and Hindi Code Combinations according to reports, the accuracy of fine grained and coarse grained tag sets on Twitter and Facebook chat messages was 64.9% and 72%, respectively [13]. In order to compare how well four machine learning algorithms (Conditional Random Fields, Naive Bayes, Sequential Minimal Optimisation, and Random Forests) performed against a set of language-specific taggers, various features of word-internal and word context information were used.

Another published model looked at a language recognized, normalization, back-transliteration, and POS tagging of code mixed English-Hindi social media content [26]. Facebook forums were utilized to collect this data and then organized into a multi-level annotated corpus. The outcomes demonstrated that Hindi transliteration and language identification are two significant issues that affect the accuracy of POS tagging. Additionally, in all situations, Hindi POS tagging showed lower word-level accuracy than English POS tagging. This was mostly caused by the transliteration module's faults, which were brought on by the fact that the transliteration does not account for spelling contractions.

In their improved statistical POS tagging method for Telugu and Hindi that they proposed, Phani Gadde and Meher Vijay Yeleti [10] showed that the accuracy of TnT (Trigrams'n'Tags) was lower than the accuracy of the CRF. However, the only features used by CRF are prefix and suffix data. Therefore, since adding prefixes and suffixes did not significantly improve accuracy, the model could not be efficiently used with TnT. However, compared to the earlier approaches, the model improved Hindi by 1.85% and Telugu by 0.725.

Separate training sets for Bengali, Hindi and Tamil were parts-of-speech tagged using an HMM and rule-based chunking [3]. With the unannotated Bengali, Hindi, and Telugu test sets, the chunking method demonstrated accuracy rates of 80.63%, 71.65%, and 53.15%. The rule-based chunking method was created for Bengali, and after that, the same chunker was used to analyze test data in Hindi and Telugu. Additionally, a confusion matrix was used to analyze the POS tagger's errors for the Bengali development test set. Language rules were used to resolve the remaining ambiguities.

Ekbal et al., [8] in 2007 used Hidden Markov Model and a rule-based chunker and trained it on Telegu, Bengali, and Hindi on 2 different sets: development sets and unannotated sets. The work showed average accuracy in unannotated sets; 67.49%, 76.87% and 77.73% for each language respectively. The accuracy increased significantly for Development sets; 63.93%, 82.05% and 90.9% respectively.

A POS tagging model with a Twitter Corpus [22] for English-Hindi code mixed data was presented using LSTM Recurrent Neural Networks and Conditional Random Field (CRF) for a sequence labeling task. It achieved an average accuracy of 90.2% and 82.15% using CRF and LSTM models respectively. However, this model suffered lower performance for POS tag categories such as adverbs and adjectives, in which sets of grammatical rules for English and Hindi are different.

Shyambabu et al., [19] have implemented a Quantum LSTM-based method for the POS tagging of Mizo language. Mizo language is one of the Indian languages which is spoken in Mizoram, a state in the North East region of India. In a report from 2020 [6], POS tagging using the approach of quantum computing was proposed. Their experiment showed that the performance of QSLTM is not satisfactory as of now. The quantum gate level runnable with ZX-calculus optimization was also demonstrated, and the implementation target was kept in the context of noisy intermediate-scale quantum systems (NISQ). Additionally, while not having been implemented, this plan is anticipated to be quite accurate.

3   Dataset Description

Viterbi Algorithm-based HMM-based POS Tagger solution was trained and tested using publicly available test and train data from the NLP tools competition at ICON 2016. The dataset primarily consists of three code mixed Indian language-pairs[1]: Hindi and English language pair, Bengali and English language pair, and Telugu-English language pair with data from Twitter, Facebook, and WhatsApp. The number of sentences in each dataset is shown below (Table 1):

---

[1] http://amitavadas.com/Code-Mixing.html.

Table 1. Dataset Size

Language Pair	Source	Number of sentences
English - Hindi	Facebook	2001
English - Bengali	Facebook	728
English - Telegu	Facebook	1428
English - Hindi	WhatsApp	1264
English - Bengali	WhatsApp	474
English - Telugu	WhatsApp	998
English - Hindi	Twitter	1264
English - Bengali	Twitter	464
English - Telugu	Twitter	1588

Multiple tags have been used with each tag belonging to some category. These categories are further classified into multiple types which are shown in Fig. 1, along with some examples.

A kind of data analysis known as coarse-grained data analysis concentrates on a text's general structure and content at the sentence or paragraph level. This method's main objective is to determine the prevailing language or languages present in the text. Through statistical analysis and machine learning algorithms that look at features like word frequency, sentence structure, and syntax, this can be accomplished. For instance, the coarse-grained analysis would identify the primary language or the language that is used more frequently as the dominant language in a text that had sentences in both English and Hindi. It can be helpful to employ coarse-grained analysis for tasks like language identification [2], topic classification [14], and text summarization [1].

On the other hand, fine-grained data analysis focuses on specific linguistic features within a text at the word or phrase level. This approach aims to identify patterns of code-switching, loanwords, and other language structures within the text. Fine-grained analysis typically involves more complex linguistic analysis techniques such as part-of-speech tagging and named entity recognition. For example, in a sentence like "Mere friends ki party mein maine bahut dance kiya", fine-grained analysis would identify "mere" as an adverb, "friends ki" as a possessive noun phrase, "party" as a common noun, and so on. Fine-grained analysis can be useful for tasks such as sentiment analysis, language modeling, and machine translation.

Both coarse-grained and fine-grained data analysis are important for developing effective natural language processing systems. Coarse-grained analysis can help to identify the dominant language or languages in a text, which is crucial for developing language-specific models for downstream NLP tasks. Fine-grained analysis, on the other hand, can help to identify specific linguistic structures and patterns within the text, which can be used to build more accurate and reliable models for tasks such as machine translation and sentiment analysis. In many cases, both coarse-grained and fine-grained analysis are used in conjunction to build robust NLP models that can handle the complexity and diversity of real-world language use.

In summary, coarse-grained and fine-grained data analysis are two different approaches to data analysis in natural language processing. While coarse-grained analysis focuses on the overall structure and content of a text at the sentence or document level, the fine-grained analysis focuses on specific linguistic features within the text at the word or phrase level. Both approaches are important for developing accurate and reliable NLP models that can handle the complexity and diversity of real-world language use.

Category	Type	Description
Noun (G_N)	N_NN	Common Noun
	N_NNV	Verbal Noun
	N_NST	Spatio-temporal
	N_NNP	Proper Noun
Pronoun (G_PRP)	PR_PRP	Personal
	PR_PRL	Relative
	PR_PRF	Reflexive
	PR_PRC	Reciprocal
	PR_PRQ	Wh-Word
Verb (G_V)	V_VM	Main
	V_VAUX	Auxiliary
Adjective (G_J)	JJ	Adjective
Adverb (G_R)	RB_ALC	Locative Adverb
	RB_AMN	Adverb of Manner
Demonstrative (G_PRP)	DM_DMD	Absolute
	DM_DMI	Indefinite
	DM_DMQ	Wh-word
	DM_DMR	Relative
Quantifier (G_SYM)	QT_QTF	General
	QT_QTC	Cardinal
	QT_QTO	Ordinal
Particles (G_PRT)	RP_RPD	Default
	RP_NEG	Negation
	RP_INTF	Intensifier
	RP_INJ	Interjection
Residual (G_X)	RD_RDF	Foreign Word
	RD_SYM	Symbol
	RD_PUNC	Punctuation
	RD_UNK	Unknown
	RD_ECH	Echo Word
Conjunction, Pre- & Postposition	CC	Conjunction
	PSP	Pre-/Postposition
Numeral	&	Numeral
Determiner	DT	Determiner
Twitter-Specific (Gimpel et al. 2011) (G_X)	@	At-mention
	~	Re-Tweet/discourse
	E	Emoticon
	U	URL or email
	#	Hashtag

```
@bionicsix1      univ   @
@phanerozoic11   univ   @
@pari_cious      univ   @
bohut      hi    QT_QTF
achay      hi    JJ
ayay       hi    V_VM
-          univ  RD_SYM
Mixed      en    JJ
dabay      hi    N_NN
Wala       hi    RP_RPD
mix        en    N_NN
n          en    CC
maida      hi    N_NN
.          univ  RD_SYM
Apna       hi    PR_PRL
hee        hi    RP_RPO
koi        hi    DM_DMI
taste      en    JJ
bana       hi    V_VM
liya       hi    V_VAUX
:)         univ  E
|
listening  en    V_VM
to         en    RP_RPO
Ishq       hi    N_NNP
Wala       hi    RP_RPO
Love       en    N_NN
(          univ  RD_SYM
From       en    PSP
"          univ  RD_SYM
Student    en    N_NN
```

```
@bionicsix1      univ   @
@phanerozoic11   univ   @
@pari_cious      univ   @
bohut      hi    G_SYM
achay      hi    G_J
ayay       hi    G_V
.          univ  G_X
Mixed      en    G_J
dabay      hi    G_N
Wala       hi    G_PRT
mix        en    G_N
n          en    CC
maida      hi    G_N
.          univ  G_X
Apna       hi    G_PRP
hee        hi    G_PRT
koi        hi    G_PRP
taste      en    G_J
bana       hi    G_V
liya       hi    G_V
:)         univ  E
listening  en         G_V
to         en    G_PRT
Ishq       hi    G_N
Wala       hi    G_PRT
Love       en    G_N
(          univ  G_X
From       en    PSP
"          univ  G_X
Student    en    G_N
of         en    PSP
the        en    DT
Year       en    G_N
"          univ  G_X
)          univ  G_X
```

Fig. 1. Tags used in the dataset, along with examples

4   Methodology

Subsection 4.1 describes the implementation of a supervised bi-gram model for training purposes. The following Subsects. 4.2 and 4.3 explain the working of HMM to identify the POS of the used dataset using a dynamic programming approach- Viterbi algorithm.

4.1   Supervised Model

A POS Tagger using a supervised model, labeled training data is used, that takes the form

$$x^{(1)} : y^{(1)}...x^{(m)} : y^{(n)} \rightarrow i$$

where x^1 is the input word and y^1 is its corresponding POS tag. We are training the model to learn the optimal hypotheses for a function such that $f: X \rightarrow Y$ which should correctly be able to map a hidden word x to its tag: $f(x)$.

From equation i, it is clear that our learning algorithm should seek out the tag "textit" "in" Y for which "textit" "$P(y|x)$ is maximal. This is granted that the term "textit" "x" is a word in the code mixed sentence.

4.2   HMM

HMM [7] is the name of the stochastic technique used for POS tagging. It is widely used in bioinformatics, reinforcement learning, handwriting analysis, partial discharges, musical score interpretation, and temporal pattern identification.

Let us consider an example (Fig. 2):

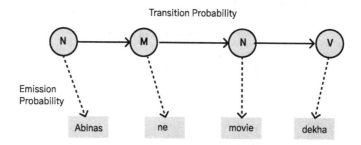

Fig. 2. Transition and Emission Probability

In this example, we have considered only 3 POS tags, i.e. Noun, Model, and Verb.

The possibility of a specific sequence, such as whether a noun would be followed by a model, a model by a verb, and a verb by a noun, is measured by the transition probability [7]. The Transition Probability is the name given to this likelihood. For a certain sequence to be accurate, it should be high.

The probability that the word Mary is a noun, can is a model is emission probability [7].

Now let us try to calculate the above-discussed probabilities for the following sentences:

– Paritesh Kumar ne Diya Dekha
– Diya Paritesh se Milegi
– Kya Diya kahani dekhegi?
– Paritesh ne kahani dekha

Let us have a look at their respective tags:

Paritesh	Kumar	ne	Diya	Dekha
Noun	Noun	Model	noun	verb

Diya	Paritesh	se	Milegi
Noun	Noun	Model	Verb

Kya	Diya	Kahani	Dekhegi?
Model	Noun	Noun	Verb

Paritesh	ne	Kahani	Dekha
Noun	Model	Noun	Verb

To calculate the emission probabilities let's divide each occurrence by the sum of its appearances. Thus, we shall create a counting table as follows (Table 2):

Table 2. Table showing the emission probability

Words	Noun	Model	Verb
Paritesh	8/18	0	0
Diya	4/18	0	0
ne	2/18	3/4	0
Kahani	2/9	0	1/4
se	0	1/4	0
dekhegi	0	0	1/4

To calculate transition probability, two new tags: [s] to denote the start of a sentence and [e] to denote the end of the sentence are added.

Next, we construct the table below by dividing each word in a row by the total number of times the tag appeared (Table 3).

After obtaining the transition and emission probability, a new sentence Paritesh ne Diya Sherlock is considered.

Table 3. Transition probability

	Noun	Model	Verb	[e]
[s]	3/4	1/4	0	0
Noun	1/9	3/9	1/9	4/9
Model	1/4	0	3/4	0
Verb	4/4	0	0	0

Just by taking into account the three POS tags we have listed, 81 distinct tag combinations are possible. The odds of all 81 possibilities can be calculated in this situation, it seems. However, the challenge looks impossible to do when the aim is to tag a longer text and all of the POS tags in the Penn Treebank [25] project are taken into account. All the 81 combinations have been shown below (Fig. 3).

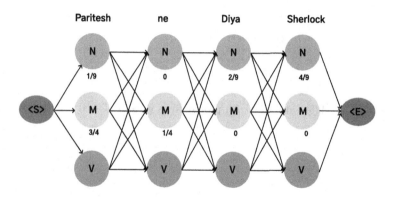

Fig. 3. Possible combinations

The following step entails removing all edges and vertices with probability zero, as well as any vertices that do not lead to the endpoint.

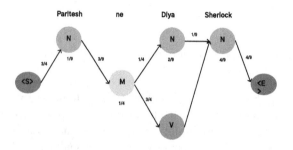

Fig. 4. Endpoint paths where probability is not zero

4.3   Viterbi Algorithm

The Viterbi algorithm [9], also knows as the Viterbi route is a DP (dynamic programming) approach for determining the greatest a posteriori probability estimate of the most likely sequence of hidden states in the context of Markov information sources and HMM. The dynamic program approach stores the previous result thus preventing further calculating the same thing over again [23].

From the above example, two paths are seen leading to the result (Fig. 5).

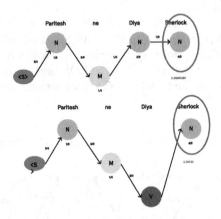

Fig. 5. The two different paths with probabilities greater than 0 reaching endpoint

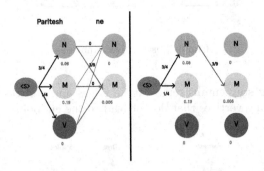

Fig. 6. Mini paths with respect to the path shown in Fig. 4

In Fig. 6 all pathways are seen leading to a node having their probabilities assessed, and any edges or paths with lower probability costs are removed. Additionally, some nodes with probability zero may not have any edges associated with the nodes because all of the pathways have probability 0. The below graph is shown calculating the odds of each path that lead to a node (Fig. 7).

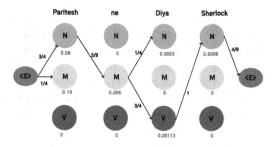

Fig. 7. Nodes labeled with their probabilities

Fig. 8. Best path according to Viterbi Algorithm

Since each state has only one incoming edge, it is traced backward from the end to obtain the best path. This gives the path that is displayed below (Fig. 8).

This algorithm only suggests one path as opposed to the prior algorithm's two suggestions. Thus, Viterbi Algorithm is a very good and efficient approach to making an inference, or prediction, to the hidden states given the model parameters are optimized and given the observed data [21].

5 Result

The Code Mixed dataset has three different language pairs viz Eng-Hindi, Eng-Bengali, and Eng-Telegu collected from three different social media sources namely Twitter, Facebook, and Whatsapp. For the experiment, there are two kinds of tagsets fine and coarse grained. In our experiments, the Code Mixed data has been split in the ratio 80:20 for train and test data.

Table 4. Table showing comparison between our results & Pakray et al.

Language	Facebook				Twitter				Whatsapp			
	Coarse Grained		Fine Grained		Coarse Grained		Fine Grained		Coarse Grained		Fine Grained	
	Our	Pakray et al	Our	Pakray et al	Our	Pakray et al	Our	Pakray et al	Our	Pakray et al	Our	Pakray et al
Bengali	93.84	83.25	78.42	76.55	89.70	84.35	82.75	81.74	90.23	75.56	87.27	72.37
Hindi	83.82	76.62	85.23	64.81	88.60	76.04	82.74	68.11	87.77	85.64	74.91	81.06
Telugu	93.70	79.89	90.27	72.90	79.65	78.25	77.44	72.46	78.82	75.06	80.45	72.26

The accuracy of the fine and coarse grained dataset has been compared with Pakray et al., [18] and the result in percentage is shown in Table 4. Comparing it with the baseline [18] we can see a clear improvement in accuracy. The difference in algorithm may be due to the use of the Viterbi algorithm.

According to the results of our investigation, Table 4 illustrates that coarse grained data is substantially more accurate than fine grained data. The ambiguity of the tag assigned to the terms in the training dataset may be the cause of this discrepancy. We have seen that different annotations have been assigned to the same word for its various appearances in the fine grained training dataset, and this pattern is true for many of the terms.

Example: Bengali word keno has been annotated as a Demonstrative word i.e. G_PRP 23 times and as Pre- & Postposition 3 times in its occurrence of 26 times in the Hindi Facebook Coarse grained training data

The same word has been annotated as PR-PRQ 12 times and as PSP 11 times in the Fine grained training data.

Below we can see an example where all the tags have been tagged correctly:

```
Or : CC chela : N_NN der : PSP campus : N_NN e : PSP
boycott : N_NN koro : V_VM    sobai : PR_PRP
```

Below is an example where all the tags were tagged wrong in a single sentence:

```
Oi : PSP loktar : Pr_PRP theke : N_NN sabdhan : RP_RDP . : PUN
Expected:
Oi : N_NNP loktar : N_NN theke : PSP sabdhan : N_NN . : PUN
```

This ambiguity results in a decreased emission probability than expected and thus results in lower accuracy.

We have observed the execution of 1.0657×10^{-4} second in our program.

6   Conclusion

Social media sites are now saturated with loud, code mixed content from multilingual users. The parts of speech of the data that have been code mixed need to be tagged with their proper POS tags in order to be used effectively in NLP applications to overcome the difficulty.

For the purpose of POS tagging of heterogeneous and noisy code mixed data, an HMM based POS Tagger utilising the Viterbi Algorithm has been designed and evaluated using code mixed social media material from Indian languages. The effectiveness of the HMM based POS Tagger, particularly for coarse grained data, is demonstrated by the system's outcomes and accuracy for diverse language pairs.

7   Future Work

The use of heuristics to restrict the search space of plausible tag sets, Quantum Machine Learning for training and testing, and raising the number of occurrences in the training dataset are some crucial perspective alterations that are anticipated to improve current evaluation scores [5].

Our future work consists of the implementation of a Quantum-based Hidden Markov Model (QHMM) [24] POS tagger on code mixed datasets. We will try to run QHMM on a simulator as well as actual quantum devices. This work shall help many future applications in various fields including, and not limited to realistic chatbots communicating naturally in codemixed language, or help to properly annotate Indian social media texts for better understanding and proper applications like sentiment analysis, hate speech detection and many more.

This work shall help many future applications in various fields including, and not limited to realistic chatbots communicating naturally in codemixed language, or help to properly annotate Indian social media texts for better understanding and proper applications like sentiment analysis, hate speech detection and many more.

Acknowledgement. The work presented here is a part of experiments being conducted under the Research Project Grant Ref. No. N-21/17/2020-NeGD supported by MeitY Quantum Computing Applications Lab (QCAL) and Amazon-braket. We also extend our gratitude to the Department of CSE, NIT Silchar, and the Center for Natural Language Processing for their support.

References

1. Allahyari, M., et al.: Text summarization techniques: a brief survey. arXiv preprint arXiv:1707.02268 (2017)
2. Ambikairajah, E., Li, H., Wang, L., Yin, B., Sethu, V.: Language identification: a tutorial. IEEE Circuits Syst. Mag. **11**(2), 82–108 (2011)
3. Bandyopadhyay, S., Ekbal, A.: HMM based POS tagger and rule-based chunker for Bengali. In: Advances in Pattern Recognition, pp. 384–390. World Scientific (2007)
4. Banko, M., Moore, R.C.: Part-of-speech tagging in context. In: COLING 2004: Proceedings of the 20th International Conference on Computational Linguistics, pp. 556–561 (2004)
5. Biamonte, J., Wittek, P., Pancotti, N., Rebentrost, P., Wiebe, N., Lloyd, S.: Quantum machine learning. Nature **549**(7671), 195–202 (2017)
6. Bishwas, A.K., Mani, A., Palade, V.: Parts of speech tagging in NLP: runtime optimization with quantum formulation and ZX calculus. arXiv preprint arXiv:2007.10328 (2020)
7. Eddy, S.R.: Hidden Markov models. Curr. Opin. Struct. Biol. **6**(3), 361–365 (1996)
8. Ekbal, A., Mondal, S., Bandyopadhyay, S.: POS tagging using HMM and rule-based chunking. Proc. SPSAL **8**(1), 25–28 (2007)
9. Forney, G.D.: The Viterbi algorithm. Proc. IEEE **61**(3), 268–278 (1973)
10. Gadde, P., Yeleti, M.V.: Improving statistical POS tagging using linguistic feature for Hindi and Telugu. In: Proceedings of ICON (2008)
11. Ghosh, S., Ghosh, S., Das, D.: Part-of-speech tagging of code-mixed social media text. In: Proceedings of the Second Workshop on Computational Approaches to Code Switching, pp. 90–97 (2016)

12. Hasan, F.M., UzZaman, N., Khan, M.: Comparison of different POS tagging techniques (n-gram, HMM and Brill's tagger) for Bangla. In: Elleithy, K. (ed.) Advances and Innovations in Systems, Computing Sciences and Software Engineering, pp. 121–126. Springer, Dordrecht (2007). https://doi.org/10.1007/978-1-4020-6264-3_23

13. Jamatia, A., Gambäck, B., Das, A.: Part-of-speech tagging for code-mixed English-Hindi Twitter and Facebook chat messages. In: Proceedings of the International Conference Recent Advances in Natural Language Processing, pp. 239–248 (2015)

14. Lee, K., Palsetia, D., Narayanan, R., Patwary, M.M.A., Agrawal, A., Choudhary, A.: Twitter trending topic classification. In: 2011 IEEE 11th International Conference on Data Mining Workshops, pp. 251–258. IEEE (2011)

15. Nadkarni, P.M., Ohno-Machado, L., Chapman, W.W.: Natural language processing: an introduction. J. Am. Med. Inform. Assoc. 18(5), 544–551 (2011)

16. Naseem, T., Snyder, B., Eisenstein, J., Barzilay, R.: Multilingual part-of-speech tagging: two unsupervised approaches. J. Artif. Intell. Res. 36, 341–385 (2009)

17. Nave, M., Rita, P., Guerreiro, J.: A decision support system framework to track consumer sentiments in social media. J. Hospitality Market. Manag. 27(6), 693–710 (2018)

18. Pakray, P., Majumder, G., Pathak, A.: An HMM based POS tagger for POS tagging of code-mixed Indian social media text. In: Mandal, J.K., Sinha, D. (eds.) CSI 2018. CCIS, vol. 836, pp. 495–504. Springer, Singapore (2018). https://doi.org/10.1007/978-981-13-1343-1_41

19. Pandey, S., Dadure, P., Nunsanga, M.V., Pakray, P.: Parts of speech tagging towards classical to quantum computing. In: 2022 IEEE Silchar Subsection Conference (SILCON), pp. 1–6. IEEE (2022)

20. Plank, B., Søgaard, A., Goldberg, Y.: Multilingual part-of-speech tagging with bidirectional long short-term memory models and auxiliary loss. arXiv preprint arXiv:1604.05529 (2016)

21. Shinghal, R., Toussaint, G.T.: Experiments in text recognition with the modified Viterbi algorithm. IEEE Trans. Pattern Anal. Mach. Intell. 2, 184–193 (1979)

22. Singh, K., Sen, I., Kumaraguru, P.: A Twitter corpus for Hindi-English code mixed POS tagging. In: Proceedings of the Sixth International Workshop on Natural Language Processing for Social Media, pp. 12–17. Association for Computational Linguistics, Melbourne, Australia (2018). https://doi.org/10.18653/v1/W18-3503. https://aclanthology.org/W18-3503

23. Sniedovich, M.: Dynamic Programming, vol. 297. CRC Press (1991)

24. Srinivasan, S., Gordon, G., Boots, B.: Learning hidden quantum Markov models. In: International Conference on Artificial Intelligence and Statistics, pp. 1979–1987. PMLR (2018)

25. Taylor, A., Marcus, M., Santorini, B.: The Penn treebank: an overview. In: Abeillé, A. (ed.) Treebanks, vol. 20, pp. 5–22. Springer, Dordrecht (2003). https://doi.org/10.1007/978-94-010-0201-1_1

26. Vyas, Y., Gella, S., Sharma, J., Bali, K., Choudhury, M.: POS tagging of English-Hindi code-mixed social media content. In: Proceedings of the 2014 Conference on Empirical Methods in Natural Language Processing (EMNLP), pp. 974–979 (2014)

Scrutinization of Text, Images and Audio Posts on Social Media for Identifying Fake Content

Neelakantam Pavani[1](✉) and K. Shyamala[2]

[1] Department of CSE, UCE, Osmania University, Hyderabad, Telangana, India
mee_pav@yahoo.com
[2] Department of CSE, Osmania University, Hyderabad, Telangana, India

Abstract. Social media platforms play a major role in dissemination of information across the world. The users of social media platforms like Twitter, Facebook, whatsapp etc. are exposed to enormous number of posts on various topics. It becomes infeasible for the users to decide the credibility of each message. As per Datareportal April 2023 global overview, there are 4.8 billion social media users equating to 59.9% of the world's population. As per PEW Research Center, 2021 report "About half of the Americans get news from Social Media" as opposed to TV, news platforms, or the newspaper. The Fake content posted on Social Networks purporting to be authentic information has misleading effect on the readers. Therefore, it is very vital to detect false information posted on social media before it proliferates around the world. This paper addresses three types of fake content: Text, Image and Audio. This work presents a framework which is a fusion of three models to identify fake text, audio and images. Best techniques like Error Level Analysis, CNN for identifying fake images; Gensim, NLP for detecting phony Text content and Librosa, MFCC for detecting fraudulent audio content are identified and used. The proposed work achieved an accuracy of 94.9% for text, 87.0% for image and 99.8% for audio with minimum number of epochs.

Keywords: CNN · ELA · MFCC · NLP · Librosa · Gensim

1 Introduction

1.1 Social Media

The use of Social Networks is increasing day by day. The availability of mobiles at cheaper costs, availability of internet at affordable prices even in remote areas, is multiplying the usage of social Networks. The availability of applications like photo editing tools in mobiles has lead to easier and faster creation of fabricated data. The increase in usage of Social Networks has expedited the spread of debunked information around the world. The dissemination of unreliable information and misleading content in social networks is faster than authentic information [1]. Everyone wants to be the first to spread new information, lack of time to verify the authenticity, religious reasons, lack of awareness and lack of knowledge are some of the reasons that add to the faster spread of fake content on social networks.

K. Dasgupta et al. (Eds.): CICBA 2023, CCIS 1956, pp. 287–300, 2024.
https://doi.org/10.1007/978-3-031-48879-5_22

This work proposes a model to detect forged content and identify the authentic text, images and audio posts on Social Networks. Figure 1 shows the types of content examined in this paper.

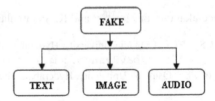

Fig. 1. Types of posts analyzed

1.2 Types of Fraudulent Posts

Misleading content can be categorized based on the context, time and place it is posted. The consequences of the phony posts vary in the degree of their effect. A post is considered to be fake [2] when:

Fabricated content is posted.

Content about a past event reposted in another event.

Wrong evidences are posted for current events.

Posts which blame any person or institution for an event occurred.

Few examples of fraudulent posts on social media are shown in Fig. 2.

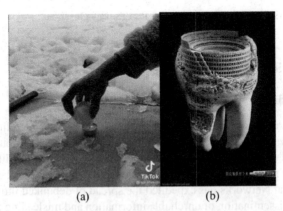

(a)   (b)

Fig. 2. (a) In 2021 amid the snowstorms, videos of burning snow to prove it fake snow went viral in TikTok and Twitter to defame the government. (b) is an advertisement that is digitally created by an art studio in Shanghai which was falsely forwarded as a carving of the Coliseum made on human tooth [3].

By thorough literature survey, the paper identifies the best possible techniques to identify phony text, image and audio posts. The work presents a combination of best techniques with an optimum CNN model developed separately for Text, Image and Audio posts. The paper aims to get best accuracy for each type of post with minimum computational power. This work restricts to general English language posts.

This paper is organized as follows: Sect. 2 summarizes the existing research to detect fraudulent content, Sect. 3 describes the proposed model and methodologies to detect fraudulent text posts, tampered audio posts and fake image posts. Section 4 presents the Experimental Setup, which describes the results obtained by applying the identified framework with different datasets of text, image and audio posts. Section 5 presents the conclusion and future scope and compares the results of the proposed model with the existing models on popular datasets.

2 Related Work

Many literature works have been published to discern between real and fake posts on social media. Some of such works are described in this section. Rezende et al. [4] developed a model to detect fake images. The proposed work performed Transfer Learning using ResNet-50 by transferring the weights of 50 layers of ResNet-50 that is already trained on ImageNet dataset. The pre-processed images were taken as input to the model to extract bottle-neck features. The model proposed three distinct CNN models: one original ResNet50, second obtained by stacking a softmax layer on top of ResNet architecture, and third with SVM classifier on the top. Experiments were performed with 2000 epochs on 9700 images from publicly available *Tokuda et.al* (CG and PG images) dataset. SVM classifier with Deep CNN achieved better accuracy of 94.05%.

Muhammed Afsal Villan et al. [5] developed the entire system using java programming language to identify phony images. The proposed work used Metadata analysis, Error Level analysis (ELA) along with CNN model to detect fake images. Metadata - extractor library is used to extract metadata of images and analysed using a tag searching technique. The final result was obtained by combining Meta data analysis and neural network results. The partial CASIA dataset with 4000 real and fake images gave 83% accuracy. Bhuvanesh Singh et al. [6] used a framework to extract textual and visual features of social media posts. The work used Error Level Analysis (ELA) followed by EfficientNetB0 model for fake image detection. Text feature learning was done by RoBERTa. The features learned from text and images are given as input to Efficient-NetB0 model and final classification is obtained by fusion of the results. CASIA dataset is used with 7492 real and 5124 fake images, MediaEval dataset with 193 real and 218 fake images and Weibo dataset are used and accuracy of 87.13, 85.3% and 81.2% respectively.

Christina Boididou et al. [2] developed a model to detect fake text posts. The proposed work included two independent classification models for training data. One model trains using User based features and the other model trains using Tweet based features. The User based features were obtained from count of friends, count of followers, account age, number of tweets posted, and friend-follower ratio. The Tweet-based features included: length of text, number of words, special characters used, emotional words used, language specific slang words of (English, German, Spanish). Two models CL_1, CL_2 were built and classification was performed with Linear Regression and Random Forest classifiers. Verification Corpus dataset of 6225 Real and 9404 fake tweets was used and an accuracy of 94.4% was obtained using Linear Regression and 90.9% accuracy was obtained using Random Forest. Sawinder Kaur et. al. [7] presents a method to combine Machine Learning models depending on false positive rate in identifying fraudulent textual posts. The phony features of text were accurately extracted using three techniques, TF-IDF (Term Frequency-Inverse Document Frequency), HV (Hash Vectorizer) and CV (Count Vectorizer). Experiments were performed on twelve Classifiers and three datasets. The datasets used were obtained from News Trends, Reuters websites and Kaggle consisting of 14658 real and 15629 fake news articles. The work concludes that Passive aggressive classifier with TF-IDF gave better accuracy of 94.7%.

Korshunov, P et al. [8] identified audio-visual inconsistencies in the videos. Audio manipulations were identified in the speech of the person in video, Mouth movements of frontal faces were considered for videos. MFCCs were used to extract audio features. Experiments were performed on various classifiers and compared results obtained from each to identify the best classifier. Empirical analysis was performed on Support Vector Machine (SVM), Gaussian Mixture Model (GMM), MultiLayer Perception (MLP) and Long Short-Term Memory (LSTM). VidTIMIT -10, AMI-977, and GRID -1000 videos of 3 s were used as datasets and achieved 99% accuracy. Bismi Fathima Nasar et. al. [9] proposed automatic detection of fake images, video, and audio. The images were first processed and sent as input to deep learning model to detect fraudulent content. The framework consists of four modules: Data Preparation, Image Enhancement module, CNN Model Generation module, and Testing module. OpenCV is used to convert video posts into sequence of frames, Matplotlib is used to convert audio posts into spectrogram images which are then enhanced using Librosa; finally, trained and tested using CNN. The datasets used were VidTIMIT, DeepfakeTIMIT and Face Forensics++ datasets and achieved 99%, 85% and 90% respectively.

Tianyun Liu et al. [10] proposed two models to detect fake audio. One model is combination of Support Vector Machines (SVM) and Mel-frequency Cepstral Coefficient (MFCC) features and second is a specially designed Convolutional Neural Network (CNN). MFCC coefficients are extracted from the training set as features to train two SVM classifiers to identify fake audio. For the second classifier, the test stereo audio is fed into two trained CNN models and the results are combined to distinguish the authenticity of stereo audio. A fusion of results from two classifications is used to get the final result. Datasets used are FILM and MUSIC achieving 99% for CNN algorithm.

3   Proposed Work

The focus of the proposed work is to achieve optimum accuracy to identify phony text, image and audio posts. Deep Learning Techniques, Error Level Analysis on images [5, 13]; Gensim for pre-processing and feature extraction of text posts; Librosa package [9, 12] and Mel-Frequency Cepstral Coefficients (MFCCs) [8, 10, 12] for audio classification are used in this work. A separate CNN model has been developed to identify fraudulent Text, Image and Audio posts by adding best combination of layers learnt from existing literature and by tuning hyper-parameters.

Data Pre-preprocessing. To improve accuracy in classification of content, the input should be preprocessed. The proposed work uses different techniques for preprocessing the text, image and audio datasets. The textual data is preprocessed using Natural Language Processing before it is input into CNN model. Gensim is used to extract semantic topics from posts. Images are first converted to grayscale images and are changed to a uniform size, then images are converted to ELA [5, 13] images by Error Level Analysis, because the features of ELA images make the task of identifying fabricated images very easy. Raw audio consists of noise, thus it is pre-processed using Librosa.

Feature Extraction. Textual data is pre-processed, by removing stop words, tokenizing and padding the data. The audio features are extracted using Mel Frequency Cepstral Coefficients (MFCCs) [8, 10, 12] which quickly present the overall characteristics of the audio. Pre-processing of images include transforming images into uniform size, color and performing Error Level Analysis. Figures 3 and 4 present a flowchart depicting the step by step approach for Text and Audio pre-processing.

Fig. 3. Text classification   **Fig. 4.** Audio classification

Build, Train and Test Using CNN. Convolution Neural Network(CNN) [4, 6] is a Deep Learning technique that takes data of various categories as input and extracts distinct features that help in classifying them. Experiments were performed by adding and removing layers to get the best possible combination of layers of the CNN's to train and validate the images, audio and text. Finally a Test Dataset is input to the CNN models to predict and classify the input as Real or Fraudulent. The proposed work aims to detect fraudulent text, images or audio posts in social networks like facebook, twitter, whatsapp etc. by making confident predictions. The fraudulent content should be identified and blocked immediately to avoid the rapid dissemination of the content and stop its damage to the society.

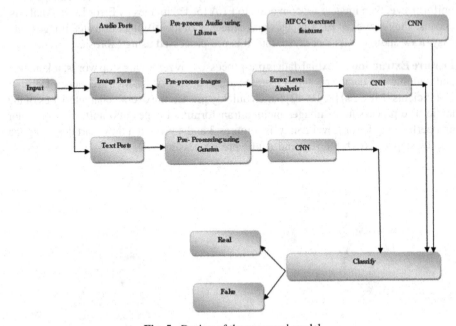

Fig. 5. Design of the proposed model

Figure 5 represents the overall design of the proposed system. The procedure followed to detect fraudulent text, image and audio posts is depicted in the design. The CNN models for each kind of post are different.

3.1 Textual Data Classification

This paper uses Gensim developed by Radim Rehurek for text processing. Gensim (Generate Similar) is an open source library, an unsupervised modeling and natural language processing library written in python used to extract semantic topics from documents. In text pre-processing, the textual data is cleaned and prepared for processing in neural networks. First step is to remove the stop words and words with two or lesser characters as they do not contribute to define any meaning to the text, then the remaining words are tokenized using the simple_preprocess() function of gensim. Then pad_sequences() method is used to bring all the items in the sequence to a constant length, some items of bigger length are also truncated to the same size and returns a list of tokens after tokenizing and normalizing.

The pre-processed textual data is given as input to CNN to train, validate and test the data. For Textual data CNN requires a special layer called Embedding layer. An

Embedding layer is used in Natural Language Processing. Textual data is converted into numbers for input into neural networks. One-hot encoding is used to convert words into numbers by creating dummy features for each word, but this is not feasible in terms of space and efficiency. Embedding layer converts each word into a fixed length vector with real values and reduces dimensions. Long Short-Term Memory (LSTM) [8, 11] is good to identify order dependencies in sequence prediction problems. Bidirectional LSTMs trains two LSTMs on input sequence instead of one, where the second sequence is a reversed copy of the original input sequence. This improves the efficiency of the model. The proposed CNN model for text classification is shown in Fig. 6.

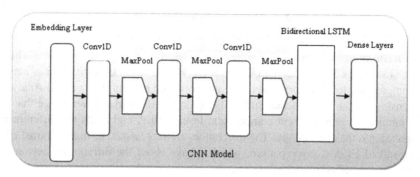

Fig. 6. CNN Model for Text Classification

The proposed model uses three datasets to experiment the model. Real and Fake news dataset from kaggle, MediaEval Tweets dataset and SMS Spam collection dataset from kaggle.

3.2 Audio Classification

Audio analysis is about understanding audio signals captured by digital devices. Audio processing requires Librosa package. Librosa is a python package with bundle of functions used for audio analysis. Librosa helps to visualize the audio signals. Audio signals cannot be used as input in its raw form due to noise. It is always better to extract features from audio signals and use that as input to neural networks for efficient classification. Mel Frequency Cepstral Coefficient (MFCC) is a technique for extracting features from the audio input. Librosa.feature.mfcc() is the method used to extract MFCC features. MFCC generates independent features that capture the dynamics of the fraudulent portions of the audio. Two datasets, Fake Audio from kaggle and a custom dataset with fake audio taken from ASVSpoof dataset and real audio take from VidTIMIT dataset are used. Experiments were performed on the datasets to obtain best accuracy. Figure 7 shows the layers of the optimum model identified for Audio classification in the proposed system.

3.3 Image Classification

Images have variable resolutions, sizes etc. For efficient functionality and performance, the images are first preprocessed to maintain constant dimensions and resolution, the

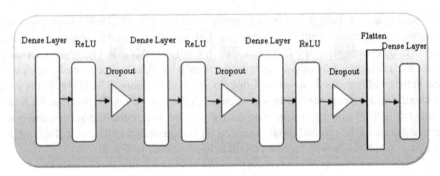

Fig. 7. Model for Audio Classification

mean RGB value is subtracted from each pixel of the image in the dataset. When an image is saved as JPEG after tampering, there will be significant differences between the compression levels of original image and modified portion. Error Level Analysis is a forensic method that attaches different coloring to the parts of the image that have been tampered (with different compression levels). ELA highlights the differences in compression rates of an image. The differences are represented as high-contrast edges. The result of ELA is error pattern, which speaks about the differences between the original and modified portions.

In Fig. 8, for real image ELA image looks dark whereas in the fraudulent image ELA has bright white colour in the section of the image which has been tampered. In proposed model, after experimentation, it is observed that ELA images given as input to CNN give higher accuracy when compared to normal images.

Real image and its ELA image from CASIA2 dataset

Fake image and its ELA image from CASIA2 dataset

Fig. 8. Error Level Analysis

Convolution Neural Network (CNN). An optimum CNN is required to get the best accuracy for the classification needed. The following layers are used in the proposed model.

Convolution Layer. Is the first layer of the CNN architecture, it is meant to extract features of the images using convolutional mathematical operations performed on the image and a filter of size (m × m). The dot product of the filter and a specific part of the image matrix is taken by sliding the filter over the image matrix. This operation gives feature map as output which learns the image corners and edges. The proposed model used small filter sizes of (2 × 2) or (3 × 3) which gave better accuracy, number of filters used were 128, 256 or 384 in each of the convolution layer. **The Pooling layer** is used to decrease the size of the feature map to decrease the computational costs required to process the feature map. Further, it also helps in extracting dominant features required to train the model effectively. Max Pooling 2D is chosen in the proposed model to extract the most dominant features with stride 2 and same padding.

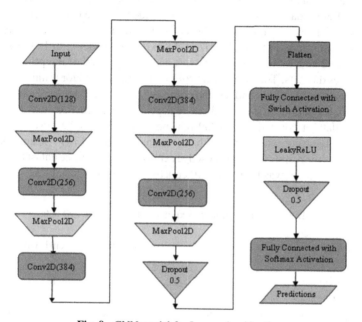

Fig. 9. CNN model for Image classification

Fully Connected Layer. It connects every neuron to connect to every other neuron in between the layers. The fully connected layer uses output from convolution layer and the Pooling layer to make best possible predictions as a vector of probabilities. This layer takes flattened input from previous layers and is used as last layers of proposed CNN architecture. The proposed model uses Dense class from the Keras library as the output layer. **Dropout:** Since CNN models sometimes result in overfitting problem, where the model works well with training data but does not give the same results on test datasets. Dropout layer addresses overfitting problem and also reduces the size of the model. The proposed model includes two Dropout layers with 0.5 i.e., 50% of the nodes are dropped out randomly. **Activation functions:** decide which feature should be considered and which can be ignored. Popularly used activation functions are: Sigmoid,

Softmax, ReLU and Swish. Each one of the activation functions is best for each type of classification. The proposed model uses Swish activation function for inner layers. Swish activation function is a smooth, non-monotonic function that gives consistent results, better than ReLU. Swish function is more suitable for deep networks used for Image classification [6]. The last dense layer uses Softmax activation function. Figure 9 presents the CNN model for Image classification.

4   Experimental Setup

The proposed work performed various experiments to choose the best performing techniques for fake content detection for each type of media. Many experiments were conducted on different datasets to choose the best sequence of layers for each of the three CNN models for text, image and audio content. The experiments are performed on 11th Gen Intel(R) Core(TM) i7-1165G7 @ 2.80 GHz processor with 16 GB RAM. The Table 1, Table 2 and Table 3 present the test accuracy of each of the proposed models against various datasets. The datasets are split in the ratio 80: 20 for training and testing.

The datasets used to train and test the proposed_text_model are Real and Fake News dataset from Kaggle consisting of 3159 real posts and 3116 fake text posts, MediaEval_2015 dataset consisting of 1209 real posts and 2546 fake posts, SMS SPAM dataset from kaggle consisting of 4825 ham(original) posts and 747 – spam(fake) posts. Table 1 presents the results of the Proposed_Text_Model on the three datasets. The model Proposed_Text_Model was trained for 10 epochs, with a batch size of 32.

Table 1. Comparison of proposed model against three text datasets

S.No	Dataset	Real & Fake	Accuracy %	Precision %	Sensitivity %	Specificity %
1	Real and Fake News-Kaggle	Real-3159, Fake-3116	89.8	88.9	89.8	89.7
2	MediaEval_Tweets	Real-1209, Fake-2546	94.9	93.3	99.8	84.3
3	SMS SPAM	ham-4825, Spam- 747	95.5	65.5	100	100

For Image posts, three datasets: Real and Fake faces, CASIA and CASIA2.0 were identified and experimented with the proposed model. CASIA 2.0 dataset originally consists of 7492 authentic images and 5125 Tampered images. CASIA originally consists of 812 authentic images and 921 forged images. CASIA and CASIA 2.0 are popular datasets on which many papers have published their experimental results. Both the datasets are downloaded from Kaggle. Real and Fake faces dataset is downloaded from kaggle consisting of 960 fake images and 1081 real images. The proposed work conducted experiments on 650 real and 650 fake images from each of the three datasets separately. The three datasets contain varying image sizes from 188 × 187 to 324 ×

256. Table 2 presents the results of our proposed model against the three datasets. The proposed image model was trained for 20 epochs with a batch size of 32.

Table 2. Comparison of proposed model against three image datasets

S.No	Dataset	Real & Fake	Accuracy %	Precision %	Sensitivity %	Specificity %
1	Real and Fake Faces	Real-650, Fake-650	96.6	100	93.9	100
2	CASIA	Real-650, Fake-649	73.4	68.8	84.3	62.8
3	CASIA2	Real-650, Fake-650	87.0	89.3	85.2	89

Real and Fake Faces is a simple dataset which gives very good accuracy, but CASIA and CASIA 2.0 are very challenging datasets with images of different sizes and even different types (TIF and JPG in CASIA 2.0) giving lesser accuracy. Figure 10 displays the accuracy graph and loss graph of the proposed_image_model on CASIA dataset.

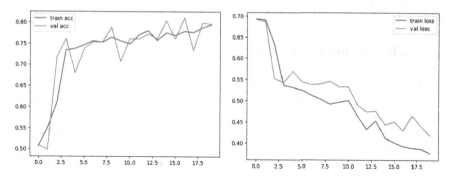

Fig. 10. Accuracy Graph and Loss Graph of the model on CASIA dataset

Audio Classification included techniques like Librosa and MFCC techniques for feature extraction which are fed into a CNN model. Two datasets, Fake Audio from kaggle with 2264 real audio and 2370 fake audio and a custom dataset is created with a combination of 4635 fake audio clips taken from ASVSpoof dataset and 1682 real audio clips taken from VidTIMIT dataset. Experiments were performed on the datasets to obtain best accuracy. The datasets consists of varying size audio in wav file format ranging from 1 to 5 s.

The CNN model gave best results for real and fake audio detection. The Fig. 11 presents the Accuracy graph and Loss graph of the proposed audio model with the custom dataset. Table 3 presents the test set results obtained by the proposed model with two datasets with 10 epochs.

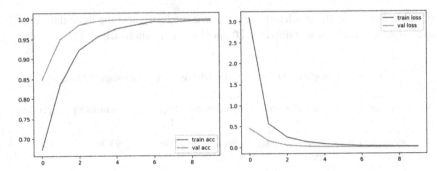

Fig. 11. Accuracy Graph and Loss Graph of audio model on VidTIMIT and ASVSpoof2015 dataset

Table 3. Comparison of proposed model against two audio datasets

S.No	Dataset	Real & Fake	Accuracy %	Precision %	Sensitivity %	Specificity %
1	Real and Fake audio from Kaggle	Real-2264, Fake-2370	99.7	100	98.6	100
2	VidTIMIT and ASVSpoof	Real-1682, Fake-4635	99.8	100	99.7	100

5 Conclusion and Future Scope

Existing research work mostly focused on fraudulent content detection on any one type of media files. The proposed system provides a framework that uses separate techniques and CNN models to identify the phony text, image and audio files. The comparison of proposed model against existing work in regard with few popular datasets is presented in Table 4 for text, Table 5 for images and Table 6 for Audio. Some of the existing research work did not specify details like number of epochs and are thus not displayed in Table 4 and Table 6.

Table 4 explains that the proposed_text_model performed reasonably well on a popular dataset and achieved 94.9% accuracy with just 10 epochs. The table compares the test accuracy of the proposed_text_model with existing state of art models.

Table 5 presents the comparison of the proposed_image_model with existing state of art models on a common CASIA 2.0 dataset. It is clearly seen that the proposed_image_model effectively achieves 87% accuracy with just 20 epochs.

Table 6 presents the comparison of the proposed_audio_model with the existing state of art models and achieves 99.8% accuracy with just 10 epochs.

Experiments were conducted on at least three datasets of each type of media to develop an optimum CNN which gives consistent results for all parameters and all datasets. Compared to the State of Art methods, the proposed work gave good accuracy with simplified models that take very less computational power and give efficient results in minimum number of epochs. To handle enormous number of posts on social media

Table 4. Comparison of proposed text framework against existing models

S.No	Paper	Dataset Size	Dataset	Methodology	Accuracy
1	Sawinder Kaur. et. al. [7]	Real-1865, Fake-2118	Kaggle	TF-IDF, CV, HV, Passive aggressive classifier	98.3%
2	Christina Boididou et. al. [2]	Real-6225, Fake-9404	Verification Corpus	Tweet, User based feature extraction and LR and RF classification	94.4%
3	Proposed Text_Model	Real-1209, Fake-2546	MediaEval	Gensim, CNN	94.9%

Table 5. Comparison of proposed image framework against existing models on CASIA2.0 dataset

S.No	Paper	Dataset Size	Methodology	Epochs	Accuracy
1	Villan et. al. [5]	Real-4000, Fake-4000	ELA, Metadata, CNN	1000	83%
2	Taksir et. al. [14]	Real-500, Fake-500	Shallow CNN	300	79%
3	Bhuvanesh et. al. [6]	Real-7492, Fake-5124	ELA, EfficientNetB0	300	87.1%
4	Proposed Image_Model	Real-650, Fake-650	ELA, CNN	20	87.0%

Table 6. Comparison of proposed audio framework against existing models

S.No	Paper	Dataset Size	Dataset	Methodology	Accuracy
1	Shilpa et. al. [12]	25000 audio clips	ASV Spoof	Spectrogram, CNN	99%
2	Tianyun et. al. [10]	29,284 audio clips on 1 s	FILM and MUSIC corpus	MFCC, SVM, CNN	99%
3	Proposed Audio_Model	Real-1682 Fake-4635	VidTimit & ASV Spoof	MFCC, CNN	99.8%

platforms every fraction of second, there is a vital requirement of a simplified model. This work presents simple models that can work on simple configuration to detect fraudulent text, image and audio posts and achieves 94.9% accuracy for textual posts, 87% accuracy for image posts and 99.8% accuracy for audio posts with minimum number of epochs.

There is a requirement to further come up with much simpler models that can run even on mobile devices, so that the detection of fraudulent content can be done on all devices. The fake content posted on social media can be of other different forms like videos, memes, and deepfakes etc. The work can be extended to detect the other types of media also and to increase the accuracy of image posts with minimum epochs. The work in future can also address the impact of contextual factors, such as cultural differences or regional variations in use of language as the proposed model may not effectively detect such features.

References

1. Study: On Twitter, false news travels faster than true stories. https://news.mit.edu/2018/study-twitter-false-news-travels-faster-true-stories-0308. Accessed 04 May 2023
2. Boididou, C., Papadopoulos, S., Zampoglou, M., Apostolidis, L.: Detection and visualization of misleading content on Twitter (2017). Springer London Ltd, Part of Springer Nature
3. Viral Images From 2021 That Were Totally Fake. https://gizmodo.com/9-viral-images-from-2021-that-were-totally-fake-1848250856/slides/8. Accessed 04 May 2023
4. de Rezende, E.R.S., Ruppert, G.C.S., Carvalho, T.: Detecting computer generated images with deep CNN. In: SIBGRAPI Conference (2017)
5. Villan, M.A., Kuruvilla, K., Paul, J., Elias, E.P.: Fake image detection using machine learning. IRACST – Int. J. Comput. Sci. Inf. Technol. Secur. (IJCSITS) 7(2) (2017)
6. Singh, B., Sharma, D.K.: Predicting image credibility in fake news over social media using multi-modal approach. Neural Comput. Appl. **34**, 21503–21517 (2021). Springer Nature
7. Kaur, S., Kumar, P., Kumaraguru, P., Automating fake news detection system using multi-level voting model. Soft Comput. **24**(12), 9049–9069 (2019)
8. Korshunov, P., Marcel, S.: Speaker inconsistency detection in tampered video. In: 26th European Signal Processing Conference (EUSIPCO) (2018)
9. Nasar, B.F., Sajini, T., Lason, E.R.: Deepfake detection in media files - audios, images and videos. In: IEEE Recent Advances in Intelligent Computational Systems (RAICS), 03–05 December 2020
10. Liu, T., Yan, D., Wang, R., Yan, N., Chen, G.: Identification of fake stereo audio using SVM and CNN. Information **12**(7), 263 (2021)
11. Li, Y., Chang, M.-C., Lyu, S., Oculi, I.I.: Exposing AI generated fake face videos by detecting eye blinking. In: IEEE International Workshop on Information Forensics and Security (WIFS). IEEE (2018)
12. Lunagaria, S., Parekh, C., Fake audio speech detection. IJIRT 7(1) (2020). ISSN 2349-6002
13. Sudiatmika, I.B.K., Rahman, F., Trisno, T., Suyoto, S.: Image forgery detection using error level analysis and deep learning. TELKOMNIKA (Telecommun. Comput. Electron. Control) **17**(2), 653–659 (2018)
14. Majumder, Md.T.H., Alim Al Islam, A.B.M.: A tale of a deep learning approach to image forgery detection. In: 5th International Conference on Networking, Systems and Security (NSysS), pp. 1–9. IEEE (2018)

Machine Translation Systems for Official Languages of North-Eastern India: A Review

Amit Kumar Roy$^{(\boxtimes)}$ ⓘ and Bipul Syam Purkayastha ⓘ

Department of Computer Science, Assam University, Silchar, India
amitroy.cs@gmail.com

Abstract. Language is the fundamental communication tool, and translation is a key instrument for understanding knowledge in an unknown language. Machine Translation (MT) is a Natural Language Processing tool where automated mechanisms are used to convert text from one natural language into another while retaining the sense of the text same. Though MT is a prime research field in India for many years, very limited work for the official languages of northeastern India has been done. The region is home to a diverse set of languages, many of which are classified as endangered or vulnerable. As such, there is a growing need for MT systems to facilitate communication and improve access to information in these languages. This paper shed light on the work carried out for these languages in the domain of MT and encourages researchers to advance exploration in the field. The review concludes by identifying areas for future research and development in the field of MT for the official languages of North-eastern India, including the need for more resources and tools to support the development of MT systems, as well as greater collaboration between researchers, language experts, and other stakeholders. It also provides a brief overview of how different MT methods operate.

Keywords: NLP · MT · SMT · RBMT · NMT · EBMT

1 Introduction

India is a diverse country and its diversity is shown in its languages too. Though English and Hindi are the most used language for communication and official purposes, we have 22 more languages of official status. The Indian parliament only transacts in Hindi or English. English is commonly used for administrative purposes such as parliamentary and judicial proceedings, as well as correspondence between the central and provincial governments. Thus, there is a need for translation of these English language documents into other official languages. There are 8 states in North-eastern India, with a population of 45,486,784 people according to the 2011 census. The official languages of these 8 states of North-Eastern India are listed below.

Arunachal Pradesh – English.
Assam – Assamese, Bengali, Bodo, English.
Manipur – Manipuri (Meitei), English.

K. Dasgupta et al. (Eds.): CICBA 2023, CCIS 1956, pp. 301–315, 2024.
https://doi.org/10.1007/978-3-031-48879-5_23

Meghalaya –Khasi, Garo, English.

Mizoram – English, Mizo.

Nagaland – English.

Sikkim – English, Nepali, Bhutia, Lepcha.

Tripura – Bengali, English, Kokborok.

Machine translation (MT) is one of the significant research domains in the field of AI and computational linguistics, as it allows individuals to grasp unknown linguistic knowledge without the assistance of a human interpreter. However, MT systems for languages with low-resource, especially for the official languages of North-eastern India, are still in their nascent stage due to the finite availability of digital resources and research focus. The aim of this review is to provide a comprehensive understanding of the current state-of-the-art MT systems for the official languages of North-eastern India and to identify the gaps and opportunities for future research in this area. The insights of this research study will prove beneficial to NLP and MT researchers and developers, particularly for low-resource languages. This paper will discuss the available MT system in Assamese, Bodo, Meitei (Manipuri), Khasi, Mizo, and Nepali languages. There is no available work in Garo and Kokborok languages as per our familiarity.

Following is a description of how the paper has been set up: Sect. 2 discusses the various MT methodologies. The development of MT for the various official languages of northeastern India is then demonstrated in Sect. 3. Section 4 discusses the numerous difficulties encountered when creating MT systems for these languages, the methodologies employed by various researchers, and the effectiveness assessments of the current systems. Section 5 covers the conclusion.

2   Machine Translation and Its Approaches

Machine Translation is an application of NLP, that pertains to translation between natural languages by using automated computing. It is a sub-domain of Computational Linguistics and Artificial Intelligence which is concerned with the development of computer systems to translate speech or text data among two natural languages. MT systems are very useful in fields such as travel, trade, health care, and other day-to-day activities. It helps people of different places to communicate and cooperate with each other. The MT system can be classified into two paradigms based on its core methodology - The Rule-based approach (RBMT) and the Corpus-based approach (CBMT). Combining the features of these two major paradigms Hybrid approach (HMT) of MT is born (Fig. 1).

2.1   Rule-Based Translation

The rule based method was the initial technique employed for MT. A software programme to process the rules, a bilingual or multilingual lexicon, and a set of rules constitute an RBMT system. The rules are written by linguistic experts, which plays a major role in syntactic processing, semantic interpretation, and contextual processing of language. Sentences in any natural language can take on a wide range of structures, which means translation takes a great deal of understanding of both the syntax and semantics of the source as well as target languages, which is the fundamental disadvantage of RBMT systems.

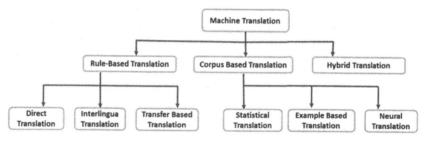

Fig. 1. Different Approaches of Machine Translation.

Direct Translation. A bilingual dictionary is employed in this MT approach, and the input text is translated directly word-by-word. To produce the results, some syntactical rearrangement is then performed. [1] (Fig. 2).

Fig. 2. Direct Machine Translation.

Interlingua Translation. In this MT approach, the input text is first converted into Interlingua, a middle form that is independent of languages, further, this interlingua is translated into the target output text [2] (Fig. 3).

Fig. 3. Interlingua Machine Translation.

Transfer Based Translation. It is similar to interlingua translation and creates a translation from an intermediate representation that mimics the meaning of the input text, but it depends partially on the source language as well as the target language [3]. At first, the Source Language (SL) parser produces the syntactic representation of SL text, then it is converted into equivalent Target Language (TL) oriented representations, and finally, with the help of a TL morphological analyzer output TL text is produced (Fig. 4).

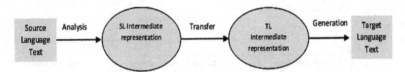

Fig. 4. Transfer Based Machine Translation Approach.

2.2 Corpus-Based Translation

The most popular translation methodology in use today is corpus-based machine translation(CBMT). A corpus is a collection of vast text, structured and authentic. By using it, the CBMT approach overcomes the knowledge acquisition problem of RBMT and is therefore also known as Data Driven MT.

Statistical Translation. The Statistical Machine Translation (SMT) approach assumes that every statement in one language has a plausible translation in another. There are numerous ways to translate a sentence from one language to another. SMT is a data-driven statistical approach that uses knowledge and statistical models gathered from bilingual parallel corpora to translate natural language texts [4]. Three different components constitute the system: the Language Model (LM), which calculates the probability of the target language; the Translation Model (TM), which aids in computing the conditional probability of target sentences given the source sentence; and the Decoder, which maximises the product of the probabilities generated by LM and TM (Fig. 5).

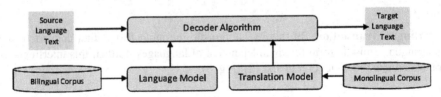

Fig. 5. Statistical Machine Translation Approach.

Example-Based Translation. In these systems, a set of sentences of the source language and their corresponding translation sentences of the target language are stored and these example sentences are used to translate input source text into output target text [5]. There are two modules in an EBMT system: the retrieval unit, which looks through the corpus for an equivalent text and its translation for a given source text, and the adaptation unit, which modifies the obtained translation to produce the final, accurate translation (Fig. 6).

Neural Translation. In this approach, Neural Networks are used to develop a statistical model for MT. Neural Machine Translation (NMT) system is an end-to-end direct learning approach to MT [7]. NMT framework has been developed with the help of two neural networks: an encoder that computes a representation for each source sentence and a decoder that takes the encoder output as input and produces translation one word at a time, thus decomposing the conditional probability (Fig. 7).

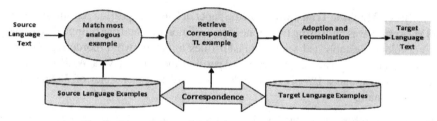

Fig. 6. Example Based Machine Translation Approach [6].

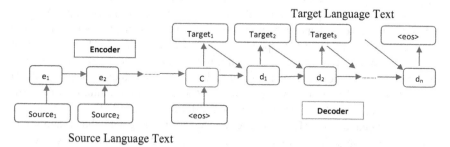

Fig. 7. Neural Machine Translation Approach.

2.3 Hybrid Translation

Such techniques are generated by taking advantage of both the RBMT and CBMT systems. The key idea of hybrid translation approaches is to use a linguistic approach based on rules to parse the source input text and then find the correct interpretation in the target language using a non-linguistic approach [8].

3 Machine Translation Systems in North-Eastern India

MT has been an active research subject in India since 1991. Some systems have been designed for Manipuri and Assamese, the two most widely spoken languages of the North-East India, which are classified in the Indian constitution's Eighth Schedule. Some more languages are still being researched, and relatively few of these works have been documented. The MT systems for the official languages of northeastern India are discussed in the following section.

3.1 Progresses in the Assamese

Assamese is one of the official languages of the North-Eastern state Assam. The language comes under the Indo-Aryan sub-part of the Indo-European language family. The Assamese language is spoken by 1,53,11,351 native people of Assam as per the census report of 2011. The writing system for the Assamese language uses Bengali scripts. The language uses Subject-Object-Verb (SOV) sentence formatting.

Rule-Based Machine Translation. In the paper of Das et al. [10], an Assamese-English RBMT system was built using two monolingual dictionaries and one bilingual dictionary. The developers established several transfer rules to handle word reordering and other grammatical issues. They employed the Apertium tool to achieve a WER (word error rate) of 53.80% and a PWER (Post-independent Word Error Rate) of 36.96% in the Tourism domain.

Statistical Machine Translation. Barman, et al., [9] developed a phrase based statistical translation technique from English to Assamese. They also built an embedded transliteration system to address the translation problem associated with extremely open word classes such as Proper, Noun, and Out Of Vocabulary words. Utilizing Assamese WordNet Synset, they enhanced the translation outcome by swapping out terms with the most pertinent synonym for that specific context. Baruah, et al., [11], then developed an SMT system that can translate between English and Assamese with the help of the Moses tool. They also entrenched a transliteration system to achieve a better result. The BLEU score for English to Assamese was 5.02 and that for Assamese to English is 9.72. The authors of [12] described a method for developing an SMT system that would provide translated text from English to Assamese. For training data, the system used an Assamese and English bilingual text corpus. It computed the Assamese text sequence with the highest likelihood of being translated from the matching English language using various statistical factors. The method was evaluated with a corpus of approximately 5000 sentences and yielded promising results. Das and Baruah [13], created an SMT system integrated with a transliteration system for the Assamese to English language. The LM was built with the help of IRSTLM and TM with GIZA++ in the Moses tool. The system was trained with a corpus of 8000 sentences and got a BLEU score of 11.32. Further, Kalita and Islam [14], developed an SMT system for Bengali to Assamese MT utilizing Moses. The system was trained with a bilingual corpus of 17100 sentence that obtained a 16.3 BLEU score. Hussain, et al. [15], built an N-gram-based SMT system for English and Assamese. A corpus of 15000 parallel sentences of English and Assamese was used to train the system. The system had been tested in the SRILM with four orders. They used phrase based MARIE decoder for preparing the translation and found that the decoder trained with Bilingual Language Model (BLM) along with Target Language Model (TLM) works better as compared to the system trained with BLM alone.

Neural Machine Translation. Laskar et al., [30], designed two systems using the Neural technique to machine translation: one with a sequence-to-sequence RNN with an attention mechanism and the second with the transformer model with self-attention mechanism. When using the transformer model in both forward and reverse translation modes, the systems achieved a higher average BLEU score. The acquired BLEU scores were 10.03 for the En-As translation and 13.10 for the As-En translation (Fig. 8).

3.2 Progresses in the Bodo

Bodo (also pronounce as Boro) is one of the official languages of the North-Eastern state Assam. The language is a member of the Sino-Tibetan language family's Bodo-Garo

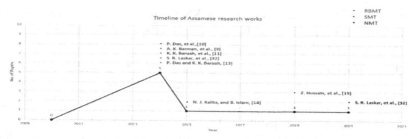

Fig. 8. The Timeline of papers for Assamese Language

sub-branch. Primary Bodo is spoken by 14,82,929 Bodo people of Assam, Bengal, and Nepal as per the census report of 2011. The Bodo language uses the Devanagari script officially, but formerly Latin and Bengali scripts are also used. The sentence format of this language is Subject-Object-Verb (SOV).

Statistical Machine Translation. Islam and Purkayastha [16], created a Phrase Based SMT system based on English to Bodo parallel corpus for the Tourism domain. The performance of the system was calculated by the BLEU score of 65.09. Islam, et al. [17], further continued their previous research and introduced more domains like News, Health, General, and Agriculture to the existing system and the combined performance was evaluated. With an increase in Multi-domain performance of the system was degraded, but it provided the best result in the general domain (38.12). Daimary et al., [31], developed a Bodo to English SMT system using parallel Bodo-English corpora for the travel and tourism industries. They have observed that the quality and result of the translation may be improved by increasing the amount of parallel sentences in each domain parallel corpus (Fig. 9).

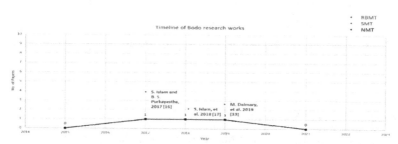

Fig. 9. The Timeline of papers for Bodo Language

3.3 Progresses in the Khasi

Khasi is the native language of the Khasi people of Khasi and Jaintia Hills, as well as one of Meghalaya's official languages. The language is spoken by 14,31,344 people of Meghalaya, Assam, and neighboring Bangladesh according to the 2011 census of India.

This language belongs to the Northern Mon–Khmer sub-branch of the language family Austro-Asiatic and uses Latin and Bengali scripts for writing. The sentence format in the Khasi language is the same as English, that is Subject-Verb-Object (SVO).

Rule-Based Machine Translation. Rapthap and Das [22], created a rule-based MT system that translates from English language to Khasi language.

Statistical and Neural Machine Translation. In the paper of Thabah and Purkayastha [23], they created and compared the SMT, supervised NMT, and unsupervised NMT systems with a parallel corpus of Khasi language. The accuracy of unsupervised NMT was very low (0.28%) as compared to supervised NMT (74.56%) and SMT (78.15%).

Singh and Hujon [32] focused on translating English into Khasi using two epitomes of translation: statistical and neural machine translation approaches. The translation quality of SMT and NMT systems for low-resource and domain-specific settings is thoroughly examined. The SMT Baseline model's performance was highest in comparison to the other models, as it achieved an 8.9 BLEU score. Further, Thabah and Purkayastha [33] extended their prior work by creating a Cross-lingual language model based NMT system using the self-attention based transformer model with a slight adjustment on the BERT model. With BLEU accuracy scores of 39.63 for English-Khasi translation and 32.69 for Khasi-English translation, respectively, this combination significantly improved language translation (Fig. 10).

Fig. 10. The Timeline of papers for Khasi Language

3.4 Progresses in the Manipuri

Meitei (Meiteilon) is also known as Manipuri, based on the name of the state Manipur where it is mainly spoken and has the status of the official language. Meitei is the native language of 17,61,079 people of Manipur and also for a good number of people in Assam, Tripura, Bangladesh, and Myanmar. Meitei is the third most widely spoken language of Northeastern India after Bengali and Assamese. It has its own writing script called Meitei-Mayek, but the Bengali script is the most widely used one. The language's sentence format is Subject-Object-Verb (SOV), and it is part of the Sino-Tibetan language family, the Kuki-Chin sub-branch.

Statistical Machine Translation. In the paper of Singh and Bandyopadhyay [18], a Manipuri language Example Based MT system was presented. The authors utilize news corpora for the MT system. For phrase level alignment, they used POS tagging, morphological analysis, NER, and chunking on a parallel corpus. The system scores 3.361 on the NIST and 0.137 on the BLEU. In their next paper Singh and Bandyopadhyay, [19] experimented with an English–Manipuri SMT system using factored model and the output is improved with morphological information and semantic relations. The NIST score and BLEU score of the system are 5.10 and 16.873 respectively. This paper also reflects that higher accuracy and fluency can be achieved with sentences of length 15 or below. Further, Singh and Bandyopadhyay [20], then extended their previous work and built the first ever bi-directional SMT systems using factored model for Manipuri-English language pair. This system achieved an improvement in fluency and adequacy of both outputs with a BLEU score of 16.873 for English to Manipuri translations and 17.573 for Manipuri to English translations. Singh, and Bandyopadhyay [21] combined Support Vector Machine based reduplicated multi-word named entities, and transliterated non-named entities into the phrase based Manipuri-English SMT. The accuracy of the developed system has also been compared with the baseline model and found better with BLEU and NIST scores of 15.023 and 5.21 respectively. Laitonjam and Singh [36], focused on determining the feasibility and outlining of difficulties in developing unsupervised SMT models for the English and Manipuri language pairs using comparable corpora and the Monoses toolkit. They found that using transliteration pairings with weakly supervised cross-lingual embedding generation on Monoses produced the best results, with BLEU scores of 3.50 for English-Manipuri and 6.64 for Manipuri-English when using Monoses with Re-score across both phrase translation probabilities and lexical weights.

Neural Machine Translation. Singh and Singh [34] worked on developing an unsupervised neural MT system for the English Manipuri languages, that uses backtranslation with an additional target (Manipuri) side multiple test reference, a denoising autoencoder, a shared encoder based on a transformer model, and language-specific decoders. Though the accuracy achieved by that system was a bit low as compared to other available systems, it still outperforms the baseline unsupervised machine translation model and attained a BLEU score of 3.1 for English to Manipuri and 2.7 for Manipuri to English respectively. Singh et al., [35], later on, analysed English-Manipuri MT using several supervised & unsupervised SMT & NMT approaches. They also generated a big parallel corpus of 74 thousand parallel sentences in the English-Manipuri language pair. Moses and Fairseq toolkits are used for supervised & unsupervised SMT & NMT systems. With a BLEU score of 13.3, the supervised PBSMT system outperforms all others in English-to-Manipuri translation, while the Manipuri-to-English translation supervised NMT with transformer architecture and Byte Pair Encoding achieved the maximum BLEU score of 17.1. A pre-trained word embedding model for Manipuri was developed by Huidrom and Lepage [37] using fastText (EM-FT), and subsequently, the neural machine translation system's skipgram model was trained on monolingual Manipuri text. The observations are taken several times with and without EM-FT, for different architectures (viz. RNN, GRU, Transformer, etc.) and discovered that the Transformer architecture performs better with the EM-FT fastText than all others with or without EM-FT. It has also been found that increasing the amount of data from various domains used for training and testing has a detrimental effect on translation accuracy (Fig. 11).

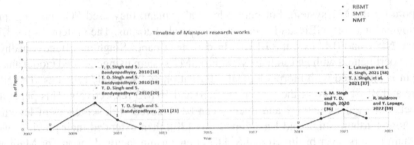

Fig. 11. The Timeline of papers for Manipuri Language

3.5 Progresses in the Mizo

Mizo (Duhlian, Mizo twang) is the second official language of Mizoram, India's 29th state. This language belongs to the Sino-Tibetan language family on the Kuki-Chin sub-branch. Mizo is written in Bengali-Assamese Script and Latin Script. According to the 2011 census, 8,30,846 native people of Mizoram and neighboring states speak this language along with a few tribes of Bangladesh and Burma (Myanmar). The Mizo word constituting 'mi' means 'people' and 'zo' means 'hills', which combinedly means the language of people of hills. The sentence format in the Mizo language is Object-Subject-Verb (OSV).

Statistical and Neural Machine Translation. The work of Pathak, et al., [24], contains both SMT and NMT systems for the Mizo language. A Phase Based SMT system was developed using Moses toolkit which got an accuracy of 2.2 whereas the NMT system was developed with OpenNMT toolkit which obtained an accuracy of 1.825 in that same test set. The highest BLEU scores obtained by the systems are 22.37 for SMT and 22.60 for NMT. Thihlum, et al., [29], developed a neural approach based machine translation system for the Mizo-English language pair in this research. The author concentrated on analysing the efficiency of the NMT approach in improving the system's translation based on the BLEU score. Despite the fact that the system was trained and tested on a tiny corpus, it achieved the highest BLEU score of 25.05 with Bible text after tuning the parameters. The paper of Lalrempuii, et al., [28], presented an NMT system with BiLSTM and Transformer model. The authors also compared the result of these systems with PBSMT. The system was trained with 66,648 parallel sentences of English – Mizo language and achieved the best BLEU score of 18 with the transformer model and sentence length between 1 to 15 words. The most recent work is done by Khenglawt, et al., [27], the authors implemented the NMT, both the RNN model and the transformer model, for the English Mizo language pair with the OpenNMT toolkit. They also compared their result with BERT fused NMT system with they had prepared and achieved higher accuracy. The BLEU scores are, English-to-Mizo (RNN model) 16.98, (Transformer model) 17.86, (BERT fused) 28.59 after some post-processing (Fig. 12).

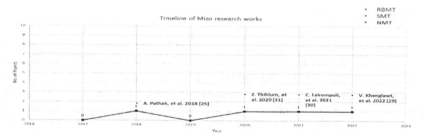

Fig. 12. The Timeline of papers for Mizo Language

3.6 Progresses in the Nepali

Nepali is one of the official languages of the North-Eastern state Sikkim. It is also called Khas Kura or Gorkhali in some contexts. The language belongs to the Eastern Pahari sub-branch of the Indo-Aryan language family. Nepali is spoken by 29,26,168 people of Sikkim, Assam, and West Bengal, and 12,300,000 speakers within Nepal as per the census report of 2011. It is also spoken in some parts of Bhutan too. The Nepali language uses the Devanagari script and the sentence formatof is Subject-Object-Verb (SOV).

Rule Based Machine Translation. In the paper of Shrestha [25], Nepali text (Unicode) was tokenized, the syllabic breakdown was conducted, and the root word and associated features of that word in the source language (Nepali) were found and mapped to the comparable sentential feature structure of the target language (English).

Statistical Machine Translation. Paul and Purkayastha [4] used the SMT approach to create an MT system for Nepali that can convert English sentences into their most likely Nepali equivalent. They utilised the Moses tool on a corpus of 5000 sentences and attained a 67.5% accuracy.

Neural Machine Translation. This NMT with attention mechanism was developed by Laskar et al., [26] for similar language translation of WMT19. The parallel Hindi-Nepali dataset was used to train the NMT systems, and they were then tested and assessed in both languages. Official results released at the WMT19 shared task show that the system performed well on the BLEU contrastive system type, scoring 53.7 (Hindi to Nepali) and 49.1 (Nepali to Hindi) (Fig. 13).

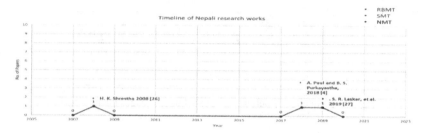

Fig. 13. The Timeline of papers for Nepali Language

4 Discussion

Research work on Machine translation is growing both in the world and in India. But more effort is needed for the official languages of North East India. Machine translation for the Garo, Bhutia, Lepcha and Kokborok languages still requires significant effort from the government and scientific community. To the best of our knowledge, no such systems or tools have been built for these languages till date. In this review, we tried to accumulate all the papers on Machine Translation systems for the official languages of North-Eastern India whose summarized distribution can be seen in Table 1 and Fig. 14.

Table 1. Language and approach based distribution of publications.

Languages	No. of Publications		
	RBMT	SMT	NMT
Assamese	1	6	1
Bodo	0	3	0
Khasi	1	2	3
Manipuri	0	5	3
Mizo	0	1	3
Nepali	1	1	1

It is observed that statistical method of machine translation is most widely used approach. This is due to the dearth of digital parallel corpora for these languages and SMT's superior performance with relatively low resource data compared to NMT. The improved reordering of sentences, inflection, fluency in output, and availability of some corpora has led to some research work in NMT over the past few years. It was also noted that several researchers used an unsupervised strategy for SMT and NMT, but that the results were subpar when compared to supervised methods in each paper.

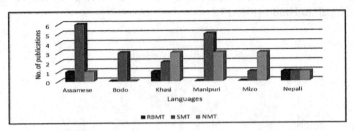

Fig. 14. Frequency of publications based on language and approaches.

The study also revealed that some preprocessing or postprocessing with the baseline system improves the precision and fluency of the translated outputs. For machine translation, the size of the corpus is a crucial aspect; as the training corpus grows, so does the translation's accuracy. In some papers, transliteration plays a major role in providing articulate translation from one natural language to another [38].

5   Conclusion

The paper discussed the different techniques of MT along with their basic architecture. We also highlighted a major breakthrough in MT for some of the official languages of North East India. From the study, we found that almost all MT systems for these languages are based on rule based, or statistical approaches, and very less work is done on the neural approach, which is a more popular and efficient way of MT. The prime objective of our paper is to summarize and analyze the available research on MT for the official languages of North-Eastern India which will encourage students, researchers, and private as well as government agencies towards advance exploration in the field. Additionally, efforts should be made to improve the quality of data used in training these systems, which can be achieved through the creation of more comprehensive and diverse language datasets. Overall, the paper highlights the need for continued research and development in this area to enable effective communication and information dissemination among the diverse linguistic communities of northeastern India.

References

1. Sanyal, S., Borgohain, R.: Machine translation systems in India (2013)
2. Dave, S., Parikh, J., Bhattacharyya, P.: Interlingua based English Hindi machine translation and language divergence. Mach. Transl. **16**, 251–304 (2002)
3. Okpor, M.D.: Machine translation approaches: issues and challenges. In: Proceedings of IJCSI, vol. 11, Issue 5, No. 2, September 2014
4. Paul, A., Purkayastha, B.S.: English to Nepali statistical machine translation system. In: Proceedings of the International Conference on Computing and Communication Systems, pp. 423–431 (2018)
5. Zhou, M., Huang, J.X., Huang, C.N., Wang, W.: Example based machine translation system. U.S. Patent: US 7,353,165 B2 (2008)
6. Sinhal, R.A., Gupta, K.O.: A pure EBMT approach for English to Hindi sentence translation system. In. J. Mod. Educ. Comput. Sci. **7**, 1–8 (2014)
7. Wu, Y., et al.: Google's neural machine translation system: bridging the gap between human and machine translation. arXiv abs/1609.08144 (2016)
8. Chatterji, S., Roy, D., Sarkar, S., Basu, A.: A hybrid approach for bengali to hindi machine translation. In: Proceedings of 7th ICON, pp. 83–91 (2009)
9. Barman, A.K., Sarmah, J., Sarma, S.K.: Assamese WordNet based quality enhancement of bilingual machine translation system. In: Proceedings of the Seventh Global Wordnet Conference, pp. 256–261. University of Tartu Press, January 2014
10. Das, P., Baruah, K.K., Hannan, A., Sarma, S.K.: Rule based machine translation for Assamese-English using Apertium. Int. J. Emerg. Technolog. Comput. Appl. Sci. **8**(5), 401–406 (2014)
11. Baruah, K.K., Das, P., Hannan, A., Sarma, S.K.: Assamese-English bilingual machine translation. Int. J. Nat. Lang. Comput. **3**(3), 73–82 (2014). https://doi.org/10.5121/ijnlc.2014.3307
12. Singh, M.T., Borgohain, R., Gohain, S.: An English-Assamese machine translation system. Int. J. Comput. Appl.Comput. Appl. **93**(4), 1–6 (2014)

13. Das, P., Baruah, K.K.: Assamese to English statistical machine translation integrated with a transliteration module. Int. J. Comput. Appl.Comput. Appl. **100**(5), 0975–8887 (2014)
14. Kalita, N.J., Islam, B.: Bengali to Assamese statistical machine translation using Moses (Corpus based). In: Proceedings of the International Conference on Cognitive Computing and Information Processing (2015)
15. Hussain, Z., Dutta Borah, M., Hannan, A.: N-gram based machine translation for English-Assamese: two languages with high syntactical dissimilarity. Proc. Int. J. Eng. Adv. Technol. (IJEAT) **9**(2) (2019). ISSN 2249-8958
16. Islam, S., Purkayastha, B.S.: English to Bodo phrase-based statistical machine translation. In: Proceedings of 10th International Conference on Advanced Computing and Communication Technologies, APIIT SD, pp. 207–217, Panipat. Haryana, India (2017)
17. Islam, S., Purkayastha, B.S.: English to Bodo statistical machine translation system using multi-domain parallel corpora. In: Proceedings of 15th International Conference on Natural Language Processing, pp. 80–86, Patiala, India (2018)
18. Singh, T.D., Bandyopadhyay, S.: Manipuri-English example based machine translation system. Int. J. Comput. Linguist. Appl. **1**(1–2), 201–216 (2010)
19. Singh, T.D., Bandyopadhyay, S.: Statistical machine translation of English–Manipuri using morpho-syntactic and semantic information. In: Proceedings of the Association for Machine Translation in the Americas (2010)
20. Singh, T.D., Bandyopadhyay, S.: Manipuri-English bidirectional statistical machine translation systems using morphology and dependency relations. In: Proceedings of SSST-4, Fourth Workshop on Syntax and Structure in Statistical Translation, pp. 83–91, COLING, Beijing (2010)
21. Singh, T.D., Bandyopadhyay, S.: Integration of reduplicated multiword expressions and named entities in a phrase based statistical machine translation system. In: Proceedings of the 5th International Joint Conference on Natural Language Processing, pp. 1304–1312, Chiang Mai, Thailand (2011)
22. Rapthap, B.J., Das, P.: Review: English to Khasi translation system. Int. J. Comput. Appl. (0975 – 8887) **179**(9) (2018)
23. Thabah, N.D.J., Purkayastha, B.S.: Khasi to English neural machine translation: an implementation perspective. Int. J. Eng. Adv. Technol. (IJEAT) **9**(2) (2019). ISSN 2249-8958
24. Pathak, A., Pakray, P., Bentham, J.: English-Mizo machine translation using neural and statistical approaches. Neural Comput. Appl.Comput. Appl. (2018). https://doi.org/10.1007/s00 521-018-3601-3
25. Shrestha, H.K.: Rule based machine translation system in the context of Nepali text to English text(2008)
26. Laskar, S.R., Pakray, P., Bandyopadhyay, S.: Neural machine translation: Hindi ↔ Nepali. In: Proceedings of the Fourth Conference on Machine Translation (WMT), Volume 3: Shared Task Papers (Day 2), pp. 202–207 (2019)
27. Khenglawt, V., Laskar, S.R., Pal, S., Pakray, P., Khan, A.K.: Language resource building and English-to-Mizo neural machine translation encountering tonal words. In: Proceedings of the WILDRE-6 Workshop @LREC2020, pp. 48–54 (2022)
28. Lalrempuii, C., Soni, B., Pakray, P.: An improved English-to-Mizo neural machine translation. Trans. Asian Low-Resourc. Lang. Inf. Process. **20**(4), 1–21 (2021)
29. Thihlum, Z., Khenglawt, V., Debnath, S.: Machine translation of english language to Mizo language. In: 2020 IEEE International Conference on Cloud Computing in Emerging Markets (CCEM), pp. 92–97 (2020)
30. Laskar, S.R., Pakray, P., Bandyopadhyay, S.: Neural machine translation for low resource Assamese–English. In: Maji, A.K., Saha, G., Das, S., Basu, S., Tavares, J.M.R.S. (eds.) Proceedings of the International Conference on Computing and Communication Systems.

LNNS, vol. 170, pp. 35–44. Springer, Singapore (2021). https://doi.org/10.1007/978-981-33-4084-8_4

31. Daimary, M., Sarma, S.K., Rahman, M.: Bodo to English statistical machine translation system. Int. J. Comput. Sci. Eng. **7**(5), 1731–1736 (2019)

32. Singh, T.D. Hujon, A.V.: Low resource and domain specific english to khasismt and nmt systems. In: 2020 International Conference on Computational Performance Evaluation (ComPE), pp. 733–737. IEEE (2020)

33. Thabah, N.D.J., Purkayastha, B.S.: Low resource neural machine translation from English to Khasi: a transformer based approach. In: Proceedings of the International Conference on Computing and Communication Systems: I3CS 2020, vol. 170, p. 3. NEHU, Shillong, India (2021)

34. Singh, S.M., Singh, T.D.: Unsupervised neural machine translation for english and Manipuri. In: Proceedings of the 3rd Workshop on Technologies for MT of Low Resource Languages, pp. 69–78 (2020)

35. Singh, T.J., Singh, S.R., Sarmah, P.: English-Manipuri machine translation: an empirical study of different supervised and unsupervised methods. In: 2021 International Conference on Asian Language Processing (IALP), pp. 142–147 (2021). https://doi.org/10.1109/IALP54817.2021.9675167

36. Laitonjam, L., Singh, S.R.: Manipuri-English machine translation using comparable corpus. In: Proceedings of the 4th Workshop on Technologies for MT of Low Resource Languages (LoResMT2021), pp. 78–88 (2021)

37. Huidrom, R., Lepage, Y.: Introducing EM-FT for Manipuri-English neural machine translation. In: Proceedings of the WILDRE-6 Workshop @LREC2020, pp. 1–6 (2022)

38. Roy, A.K., Paul, A., Purkayastha, B.S.: Statistical and syllabification based model for Nepali machine transliteration. In: Mukhopadhyay, S., Sarkar, S., Dutta, P., Mandal, J.K., Roy, S. (eds.) CICBA 2022. CCIS, vol. 1579, pp. 19–27. Springer, Cham (2022). https://doi.org/10.1007/978-3-031-10766-5_2

An Introduction to KDB: Knowledge Discovery in Biodiversity

Moumita Ghosh[1] , Sourav Mondal[1], Anirban Roy[2] ,
and Kartick Chandra Mondal[1(✉)]

[1] Department of Information Technology, Jadavpur University, Kolkata, India
kartickjgec@gmail.com
[2] West Bengal Biodiversity Board, Kolkata, India

Abstract. The most basic method of experimentation using data mining algorithms is the command prompt. A convenient approach of interactive graphical user interfaces can be supplied for data exploration to build up complex studies. A graphical user interface gives an upgraded status for experimental data mining. An innovative proposal for employing data mining methodology on biodiversity data is shown in this article through the KDB (Knowledge Discovery in Biodiversity). It provides a platform for domain researchers to apply their datasets to domain-specific data mining algorithms for further analysis. A convenient interactive graphical user interface is provided for data exploration for the biodiversity domain to build up complex studies. The proposed data mining methods are developed in Java, while the website is built in PHP.

Keywords: Knowledge discovery · Computational Biodiversity ·
Ecological Preservation · Data Mining · Computational Approach

1 Introduction

The term biodiversity refers to the complete range of living organisms. It is the single most important factor underlying the earth's symmetry. Biodiversity conservation is essential to preserve a sustainable environment integrated with a biological community of living species and their nonliving components in a balanced form. Nowadays, preserving biodiversity is a critical issue since it is difficult to conduct sufficient monitoring of individual components, their changing characteristics through time, and driving causes. Data mining can reach these obligations offering a collection of computational approaches.

Biodiversity and Ecosystem Informatics [21] is a new and interdisciplinary field. Its promising advances have already been recognised by biologists, natural resource managers, and computer scientists. Data mining includes algorithmic processes and computational paradigms that assist computers in recognising patterns in databases, performing prediction and estimate, and often improving their behaviour through data cooperation. Data mining is becoming increasingly important in engineering and information systems, and it has been effectively

K. Dasgupta et al. (Eds.): CICBA 2023, CCIS 1956, pp. 316–331, 2024.
https://doi.org/10.1007/978-3-031-48879-5_24

used to address a wide range of scientific and technical concerns. Because of their ability to extract knowledge, frequent itemset mining, frequent closed itemset mining, and other methods are widely used in data mining [9, 13, 16–18].

As of now, the significance of frequent itemset mining in the field of biodiversity knowledge extraction has not been clearly defined. However, after market basket analysis, it has clear uses in the field of bioinformatics [16] for discovering noteworthy patterns. In bioinformatics, GUI-based apps have been discovered to be common data mining tools [3]. This type of approach has yet to be discovered for the analysis of biodiversity data. We coined the term "computational biodiversity" [7], which refers to the application of computational methods to ecological conservation and biodiversity research. The objective is to identify underlying knowledge that may be beneficial to biodiversity scientists, foresters, stakeholder groups, and others. Originally, this concept relied on a variety of computational methodologies applied to main species biodiversity data pertaining to occurrence and presence/absence.

The proposed software system's purpose is to introduce researchers to the facility that may be accessible by using algorithmic techniques to analyse biodiversity data. At first, the system merely delivers a rich selection of sophisticated algorithms for data mining jobs. Furthermore, KDB serves as a digital data repository that domain researchers can use as a data repository. Statistics and visualisation tools, as well as data preprocessing operations, may be introduced in the near future to facilitate the use of graphical user interfaces.

The goal of this paper is to introduce a prototype for incorporating data mining tasks into primary biodiversity data analysis. Figure 1 depicts the general block diagram for showing KDB's working flow. To begin, three fundamental algorithmic operations have been provided in this section to highlight the power of data mining algorithms. These are three types of mining: frequent itemset mining, frequent closed itemset mining, and association rule mining. For binary datasets, frequent closed itemset mining is synonymous with biclustering. Several assembled datasets are also included. By selecting a dataset, potential users can apply a specific algorithm.

In summary the main contribution made to this paper is:

1. presenting an experimental platform for researchers in the biodiversity sector.
2. including techniques that are specifically designed for working with binary species occurrence datasets, although they are relevant to other datasets as well.
3. providing primary biodiversity data those have been digitised

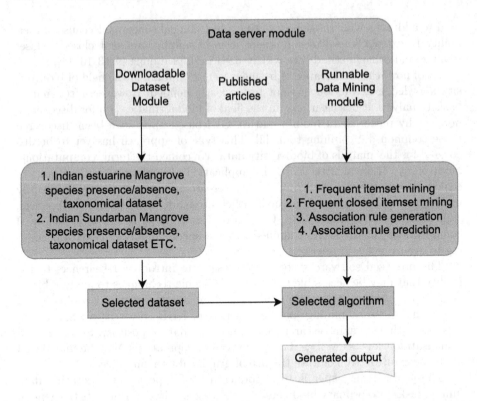

Fig. 1. WorkFlow of the proposed work

The following sections comprise the entire document. We have provided a short description of several panels in KDB in the Sect. 2. Section 3 discusses a few studies regarding the application of data mining. Another goal of KDB initiative is to provide an inventory of digitised primary biodiversity data and is presented in Sect. 4. This section provides an explanation for the currently listed biodiversity datasets. The Sect. 5 compares a few data mining tools. Finally, Sect. 7 brings the paper to a conclusion.

2   Exploring KDB

The model is available at: https://knowledgedb.ml. It has five unique panels that are brought in by tabs at the top and perform five different functions. Figure 2 depicts the web application screenshot for the Home page. The web page for the Technical Documentation is highlighted in Figs. 3, 4, and 5. Figures 6, and 7 depict web application screenshots for the Datasets, and Algorithms, respectively. The relevant journal and conference publications are listed, and shown in Figs. 8 and 9.

Figure 2 shows the Home screen, which presents the notion of Computational Biodiversity. The suggested field of work has been detailed in the About us section. This panel also includes the section Technologies, which lists the technologies that were used to create this website. The members of this project are listed in the next section, Our team. A brief theoretical overview of the data mining approach is provided in the Technical Documentation panel that is displayed in Figs. 3, 4 and 5. Introduction, Motivation and contribution, Data mining approach, Indian mangrove, and Sundarban mangrove are all aspects of this panel. Figure 6, Datasets panel, shows the options for uploading and downloading datasets. We began by compiling a few datasets. These datasets are intended for Indian mangrove and Sundarban mangrove primary biodiversity data. Figure 7 shows the Algorithms panel, which contains a list of data mining activities. It is structured in such a way that the user can select a specific data mining algorithm that corresponds to a specific operation. The user can then select the dataset to which the algorithm will be applied. The articles related to the data mining algorithms and application on biodiversity are listed under the Publications tab, which is seen in Figs. 8 and 9.

Fig. 2. Homepage tab

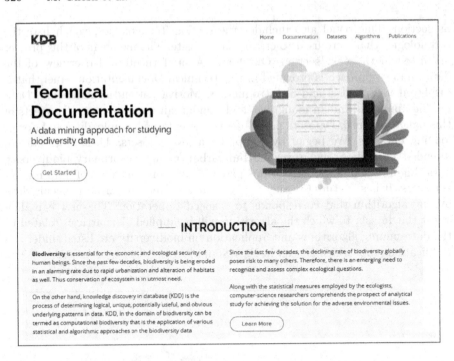

Fig. 3. Technical Documentation tab (Introduction)

— MOTIVATION AND CONTRIBUTION —

Forests are the natural security forces that have immense ecological service in controlling a number of climate catastrophy, preventing soil erosion, inhibiting inward ingression of sea in mangrove area and providing ecological niche for animals and livelihood for humans. Inspite of the great importance, loss of forest is prominent in India.
For example, a case study reveals that in between 1986 to 2012, 124.418 sq. km. mangrove forest cover has been lost. Different causes like over exploitation and illegal forest cutting, pollution, climate change etc. are identified as the most dominant factors for degradation of forest ecosystem.

Thus there is an urgent need of cause-effect analysis that would be helpful in safeguarding this precious ecosystem through proper management. Mainly statistical analysis techniques are used in a few research articles but those are only confirmatory analysis techniques with respect to researchers' understanding.

But data mining tools perform exploratory analysis where it is concerning with detecting and describing pattern within data, identifying predictor variables and discovering the forms of relationships between predictors and response.

The beneficial use of data mining is already proven where statistical analysis is unable to find out whether there is any relationship between abiotic and biotic factors on ichthyoplankton samples collected from a freshwater reservoir of Legal Amazon. Here, the use of data mining technique, the Apriori algorithm, helps in generating association rule regarding the understanding of the process of fish spawning in Tocantins River.
Thus knowledge discovery in data mining process is capable of identifying valid, potentially useful and understandable pattern which is not a new application in biodiversity domain. But very few research contribution can be found particularly in this domain.

Our main contribution can be summarized in two broad categories:

- Digitized downloadable datasets formations: Datasets on mangroves in Sundarban, as well as India, based on the gathered data from multiple online resources are formed. Multiple number of mangroves along with their associates are identified from different observational studies taken from both the published and unpublished literature.

- Application of domain specific algorithms: Novel algorithms along with information retrieval strategy is proposed.

— DATA MINING APPROACH —

Data Mining Tools and Packages in computer science yields interesting analytical results that could be applied on biodiversity data. Here our intension is to design a novel and efficient, domain specific data mining algorithm.

The proposed algorithm will become useful for the researchers and for the users working on the primary biodiversity data for the conservation and management of the fragile ecosystem.

- Frequent Itemsets
- Frequent Closed Itemsets
- Biclustering
- Association Rule Mining

Fig. 4. Technical Documentation tab (Motivation and contribution)

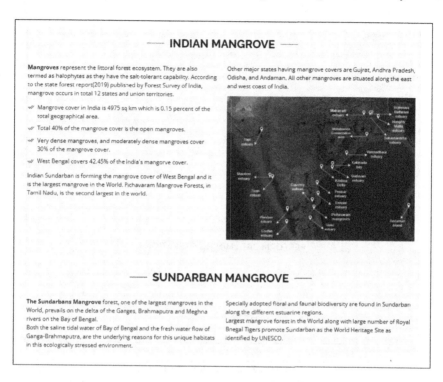

Fig. 5. Technical Documentation tab (Indian and Sundarban Mangrove)

Fig. 6. Datasets tab

Fig. 7. Algorithms tab

3   Application

The fundamental goal of KDB was to extract knowledge from primary biodiversity data. This section focuses on a few examples of successful applications of the proposed data mining methodologies on primary biodiversity datasets.

In [13], the application of frequent closed itemset mining on mangrove occurrence data was presented. To construct an off-the-shelf method to assess biodiversity presence/absence data, we used the FIST [16] approach, which employs association rule mining and biclustering approaches. The impacts of soil pH and water salinity on mangrove community and biodiversity indices are investigated in this study. The association rules can estimate potential sites for mangrove species expansion by estimating the likelihood of introducing a new species to a certain location. Our research generates lists of commonly co-occurring species and supportive regions. It could aid in the restoration of mangrove ecosystems by identifying the most likely species missing from a certain region, possibly owing to extinction.

We demonstrated the efficient implementation of the combined technique of bi-clustering and association rule mining in [10] on a manually curated real dataset of flora and fauna. We create a set of criteria that ecologists can use to get a summary of closely occuring member lists, a predicted list of sites for member expansion, and so on. As a result, our findings may help to preserve estuarine variety, paving the way for future regional investigations.

Fig. 8. Publications tab (List of journals)

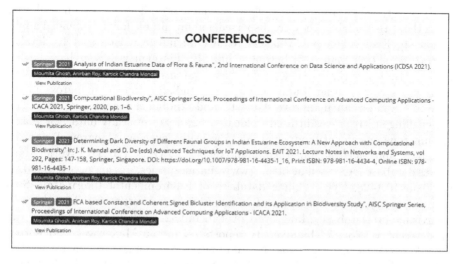

Fig. 9. Publications tab (List of Conferences)

The research in [9] combines data mining and statistics to lead us in the right direction for biodiversity restoration in a specific study region. This work recommended using the dark diversity function to the presence-absence dataset prior to the rule mining procedure. The purpose is to collect data on the missing part of the species occurrence data.

In [12], constant and coherent signed biclusters are identified utilising a novel strategy to mining a multiple-signed dataset. We concluded that identifying sensitive regions and unprotected or endangered species using a signed bicluster retrieval from a spatio-temporal dataset of species versus region would be advantageous for biodiversity conservation. It would also help environmentalists save or restore a declining species, a community, or even an ecosystem. Recently, [8] presented another key idea for an excessive salinity-affected mangrove community restoration technique in which hyper-salinity might be reduced by the establishment of suitable salt marshes. A case study of the Sundarban coastal area has been conducted, taking into account significant environmental/habitat characteristics such as salinity, pH, soil texture, and tidal amplitude, as well as data on the occurrence of mangroves, salt marshes, and mangrove associates. This study demonstrates a coexistence pattern among salt marshes, namely among mangroves and mangrove associates. Interspecies connections have also been hypothesised based on co-existence evidence.

4   Datasets

Another purpose of the KDB is to give primary biodiversity datasets of species. Exploration of unpublished data/statistics must be strengthened in order to identify the prevailing gap in knowledge in biodiversity. Primary data on biodiversity is a critical necessity for successfully completing ecosystem conservation [1]. However, these data are typically unavailable or difficult to obtain, and even when they are available, they are dispersed and unsuitable for the intended application [4]. Even when policymakers require an integrated dataset to develop a strategic action plan, [15] becomes difficult. Through web searches and literature studies, several datasets, database systems, and articles were located using key terms such as "Indian mangrove", "Indian estuarine mangrove biodiversity", "Sundarban mangrove dataset", and "Indian mangrove dataset". The snowballing strategy was utilised to locate extra relevant study data. We looked at numerous prominent biodiversity data websites, such as, Mangrove Reference Database and Herbar- ium (Dahdouh-Guebas F. (Ed.) (2021)), World Mangroves database (Accessed at http://www.marinespecies.org/ma ngroveson2021-04-30.doi:10.14284/460), Online database of Environmental Information System portraying mangrove cover of Indian states and territories (http://www.frienvis.nic.in/Database/Mangrove-Cover-in-India2444.aspx). In addition, the most recent versions of biodiversity reports on Indian Mangroves were sorted for references to mangrove-specific information, including a distinct statistics published by WWF on the State of the Art Report on Biodiversity in Indian Sundarbans [6], a report from Forest Survey of India (http://www.frienvis.nic.in/

Database/Mangrove-Cover-Assessment-20192489.aspx), and [2,5] are two significant book sources of our findings.

KDB now has assembled and preprocessed datasets mostly consisting of Indian mangroves. Below in Subsect. 4.1, a brief description for the included datasets is given.

4.1   Dataset Descriptions:

1. *Presence/ absence of Indian estuarine mangroves*: This dataset contains presence/absence data of 34 mangroves along 19 estuaries situated at east and west coasts of India. These estuaries are: Wandoor mangroves, Hooghly-Matla eatuary, Subarnarekha estuary, Brahmani-Baitarani estuary, Bhitarkanica estuary, Mahanadi mangroves, Vamsadhara estuary, Godabari estuary, Kakinada bay, Krishna delta, Pennar estuary, Ennore estuary, Cauvery estuary, Pichavaram Mangroves, Cochin estuary, Zuari estuary, Mandovi estuary, and Tapi estuary.

2. *Taxonomic details of Indian Estuarine Mangroves:* This dataset contains the taxonomic information (*Genus, Family, Order, Superorder, Class, Phylum*) for 34 Indian mangroves. The data was organized primarily from the World Register of Marine Species (http://www.marinespecies.org/aphia.php\ ?p=taxdetails&id=211508), the Integrated Taxonomic Information System (http://www.itis.gov/), the National Center for Biotechnology Information (https://www.ncbi.nlm.nih.gov/taxonomy), the Global Biodiversity Information Facility (https://www.cbif.gc.ca/eng/).

3. *Presence/ absence of Indian Sundarban mangroves:* Multiple forest blocks comprise the Sundarban delta region of India [6]. The southern region is comprised of Bagmara, Gona, Mayadwip, and Ajmalmari. The northern blocks consist of Jhilla, Pirkhali, and Panchmukhani. Harinbhanga, Khatuajhuri, and Arbesi constitute the eastern blocks. Chottohardi, Matla, and Netidhopani form up the western blocks. Chamta, Chandkhali, and Goasaba comprise up the core blocks. The blocks that constitute the 24 Parganas (South) Forest Division are Herobhanga, Ajmalmari, Dhulibhasani, Chulkati, Thakuran, Saptamukhi, and Muriganga. 82 mangroves have been identified for this dataset.

4. *Taxonomic details of Indian Sundarban Mangroves:* This dataset contains the taxonomic information (*Genus, Family, Order, Superorder, Class, Phylum*) for 82 number of Indian Sundarban mangroves. The taxonomic data was organized as mentioned before.

5. *Indian estuarine data of fish species:* We have curated a presence-absence binary dataset of fish from Indian coastal locations [5]. There are 20 major estuaries recognised throughout India's long coastal area, and 762 fish species occurrence data are displayed. 15 estuaries are taken from India's east coast. Among them are HooghlyMatla, Baitarani-Brahmani, Mahanadi, Rushikulya, Bahuda, Vamsadhara, Nagavali, Godavari, Krishna, Penner, Ennore, Adyar, Veller, and Cauveri. The west coast of India is defined by the rivers Cochin, Zuari, Mandovi, Tapi, and Narmada.

6. *Indian estuarine data of flora and fauna:* Along the long coastal area of India along the east and west coasts, 20 estuaries have been considered. Hooghly-Matla, Subarnarekha, Baitarani-Brahmani, Mahanadi, Rushikulya, Bahuda, Vamsadhara, Nagavali, Godavari, Krishna, Penner, Ennore, Adyar, Veller, and Cauveri: these 15 estuaries are from the east coast. Cochin, Zuari, Mandovi, Tapi, and Narmada are situated at the west coast of India. Along the estuaries, occurrence data of 23 faunal groups and 3 floral groups have been curated [10].

7. *Inner, middle and outer estuarine dataset of mangrove, saltmarsh, and environmental factors*
These datasets of outer estuarine blocks, middle estuarine blocks, and inner estuarine blocks contain the existence record of estuary-specific distinct salt marshes, mangroves, and mangrove associates data, as well as other environmental parameters (such as salinity, pH, soil texture, and tidal amplitude) across the columns. The rows represent the recognised blocks for the outer, middle, and inner estuarine zones.

Table 1. Dataset details

Sl No.	Dataset Name	Row data	No of Rows	Column data	No of Columns
1	Presence/ absence of Indian estuarine mangroves	Indian estuarine mangroves	34	Indian estuaries	19
2	Taxonomic details of Indian estuarine mangroves	Indian estuarine mangroves	34	Indian estuaries	19
3	Presence/absence of Indian Sundarban mangroves	Indian Sundarban mangroves	82	Indian Sundarban Blocks	22
4	Taxonomic details of Indian Sundarban mangroves	Indian Sundarban mangroves	82	Indian Sundarban Blocks	22
5	Indian estuarine data of fish species	Fish species	760	Estuaries	20
6	Indian estuarine data of flora and fauna	floral and faunal groups	3 floral groups and 23 faunal groups	Indian estuaries	20
7	Inner estuarine dataset of mangrove, saltmarsh, and environmental factors	Inner estuarine blocks	7	Salt marsh: 11, Mangrove: 16, Mangrove associates: 7, Other factors: 4	38
8	Middle estuarine dataset of mangrove, saltmarsh, and environmental factors	Middle estuarine blocks	7	Salt marsh: 11, Mangrove: 12, Mangrove associates: 4, Other factors: 4	31
9	Outer estuarine dataset of mangrove, saltmarsh, and environmental factors	Outer estuarine blocks	8	Salt marsh: 11, Mangrove: 5, Mangrove associates: 0, Other factors: 4	20

5   Comparison with Data Mining Tool

The modern world is heavily reliant on data, the majority of which is available in both structured and unstructured formats. Because much of the data is unstructured, a process and system are required to extract the information that is useful from the data. Material is also necessary to convert it into a comprehensible and useful format. There are several tools available for data mining activities that extract data efficiently. Some useful open source data mining tools are as follows:

Table 2. General characteristics of a few data mining tools

Tool name	Source	Prog. language	GUI/ Command line	Main purpose
WEKA	https://www.cs.waikato.ac.nz/ml/weka/	JAVA	Both	Mining of general data
RAPID MINER	http://rapidminer.com	JAVA	GUI	Mining of general data
Orange	http://orange.biolab.si	JAVA	Both	Mining of general data
FIST	https://sites.google.com/site/mrkartickchandramondal/direct-links/implementations-and-tools/trovefist?authuser=0	JAVA	Command Line	Mining of bioinformatics data
KDB	https://knowledgedb.ml	JAVA	GUI and Manual	Mining primarily biodiversity data

Weka has four different functionalities. These are the command-line interface (CLI), Explorer, Experimenter, and Knowledge flow. Weka is also primarily focused on classification and regression problems rather than descriptive statistics and clustering methods. Support for big data, text mining, and semi-supervised learning is also currently restricted [14].

RapidMiner has a visually appealing and user-friendly graphical user interface. It provides several statistical graphs as well as an application wizard that provides pre-built workflows for a variety of data mining activities [14].

Orange Canvas provides an organised view of supporting features divided into multiple categories, such as, classification, regression, evaluation, association, etc.

FIST [19] supports the data mining application of frequent closed itemset mining and association rule mining for both binary and textual datasets. Primarily, it was derived for the genetic dataset in the bioinformatics domain. But it can be applied to any other dataset provided in a specific format.

KDB is under development and primarily built for the biodiversity domain. The proposed data mining algorithms can be applied to any other dataset too. The user-guided R snippets are specifically related to the data mining tasks on species data.

6　Comparative Discussion on Multiple Previous Case Studies

This section briefly discusses the comparison among the reported results from multiple case studies. This part is listed in Table 3. The goal of the study, datasets under consideration, findings, and significance are all underlined here.

Table 3. Comparative discussion among the reported results from multiple studies

Reference	Aim	Dataset used	Findings	Significance
[8]	The goal of this research is to find a novel mangrove restoration approach by evaluating the frequent co-existence status of salt marshes, mangroves, and mangrove associates in various zones of deteriorated mangrove patches for species-rich propagation.	Datasets on mangrove, salt marsh and mangrove associates. Refer to dataset 7, 8, and 9 in Table 1	– Co-existence pattern of salt mash and salt marsh along the salinity gradient – Co-existence patterns of salt marshes, mangroves, and mangroves associates with various environmental conditions – Likely inter-species association based on current co-existence data	Understanding the distribution characteristics of salt marsh, mangrove, and mangrove associates, as well as environmental factors, can aid in decision-making. This paradigm is valuable for both academia and stakeholders, particularly environmentalists and protection authorities, in controlling salt marsh expansion and mangrove restoration.
[11]	By linking the concept of dark diversity, this work aims to reveal the standpoint of computational biodiversity as a counterweight to biodiversity loss.	Indian estuarine data of fauna is studied here. Refer to dataset 6 in Table 1.	Using dark diversity computation on the dataset before processing rule mining jobs allows us to examine the likelihood of faunal occurrence in totally absent part. These rules would create possible habitat for several faunal groups.	This research has presented the proposition of using the dark diversity function to the presence-absence dataset before the rule mining procedure. The reason for this is to obtain information about the missing portion of the occurrence data.
[13]	Interpreting biodiversity data, exploratory data analysis via box plot visualisation, z-score normalisation, histogram analysis, and data discretization, use of data mining on species data	Use of Indian Sundarban data on mangroves at 29 sites and the environmental factors. [Data source: [20]]	– The mangrove vegetation is more influenced by salinity than pH. – Finding information about the mangrove ecology in particular, – Identifying potential plantation locations based on salt content, – Conducting a species diversity analysis, and observing how salinity affects N2Div modulation	As interdisciplinary collaboration has already been adopted in research. The current study stresses and attempts to demonstrate the utility of data mining in biodiversity data analysis. A complete knowledge of raw data, exploratory data analysis, and therefore data conversion in system-relevant format is demonstrated.
[10]	Understanding the significance of the estuarine ecosystem, this paper focuses on Indian estuarine data analysis of flora and fauna and demonstrates the effective application of data mining in such analysis.	Indian estuarine data of fauna (occurrence data and presence/ absence data) is studied here. Refer to dataset 6 in Table 1.	In addition to the discretized categorical data, we created and evaluated the dataset displaying presence only data. This study reveals finer details for each class concerning their level of occurrences, co-occurrences, and for each estuary concerning their consistency in diversity.	This kind of information assists ecologists in maintaining estuarine biodiversity by formulating policies and appropriate procedures.

7   Conclusion and Future Work

To summarize the subject, computational methods adoption in the field of biodiversity is extremely substantial and in demand since it entails the ability to deal with heterogeneous and big scale data. These methods provide precise, accurate indicators as well as the ability to deal with large amounts of data efficiently. In a nutshell, KDB can be viewed as a building prototype for the application of data mining approaches to ecology. Despite the fact that Weka, Orange, and RapidMiner provide the majority of the desired qualities for a fully functional and adaptive platform, KDB can be considered of as a new addition to this set of data mining techniques when it comes to ecological datasets. Unlike other tools, KDB also acts as a data repository of primary biodiversity data. As of right now, there is no data pre-processing mechanism incorporated in the proposed work. Already pre-processed datasets are used that can directly be applied to the algorithms. In the future, procedures for pre-processing data and incorporating data from other web resources might be introduced. Furthermore, there is currently no association with data visualization in the proposed work. It could be addressed in the future. The data mining algorithms, and datasets will be updated continuously to keep the website updated. In the future, we would like to add more algorithms that could have good use in biodiversity information retrieval. Also, other datasets, not only limited to species biodiversity data, rather an ecosystem biodiversity and genetic biodiversity could be examined in the future.

Acknowledgements. The authors are grateful to the Department of Science & Technology, Government of India, New Delhi, for financial assistance under the scheme of WOS-A (Women Scientist Scheme A) to carry out this Ph.D. research project.

Supplementary Material

The required software requirement specification (SRS) document, data flow diagram (DFD), use case diagram and the software development life cycle are attached in the supplementary material.

References

1. Ball-Damerow, J.E., et al.: Research applications of primary biodiversity databases in the digital age. PloS one **14**(9), e0215794 (2019)
2. Banerjee, L.K.: Biodiversity of the Sundarbans: status and challenges. In: Sharma, A.K., Roy, D., Ghosh, S.N. (eds.) Biological Diversity-Origin. Evolotion and Conservation, pp. 327–375. Viva Books, New Delhi (2012)
3. Barkow, S., Bleuler, S., Prelić, A., Zimmermann, P., Zitzler, E.: Bicat: a biclustering analysis toolbox. Bioinformatics **22**(10), 1282–1283 (2006)
4. Barve, V.: Discovering and developing primary biodiversity data from social networking sites: a novel approach. Eco. Inform. **24**, 194–199 (2014)
5. Chandra, K., Raghunathan, C., Dash, S.: Current status of Estuarine Biodiversity in India, pp. 1–575. the Director, Zool. Surv. India, Kolkata (2018)

6. Danda, A.A., Joshi, A.K., Ghosh, A., Saha, R.: State of art report on biodiversity in Indian Sundarbans. World Wide Fund for Nature-India, New Delhi (2017)
7. Ghosh, M., Mondal, K.C.: Computational biodiversity. In: Mandal, J.K., Buyya, R., De, D. (eds.) Proceedings of International Conference on Advanced Computing Applications. AISC, vol. 1406, pp. 739–750. Springer, Singapore (2022). https://doi.org/10.1007/978-981-16-5207-3_60
8. Ghosh, M., Mondal, K.C., Roy, A.: Recognition of co-existence pattern of salt marshes and mangroves for littoral forest restoration. Ecol. Inform. **71**, 101769 (2022)
9. Ghosh, M., Roy, A., Mondal, K.C.: Determining dark diversity of different faunal groups in Indian estuarine ecosystem: a new approach with computational biodiversity. In: Proceedings of International Conference on Emerging Applications of Information Technology (EAIT-2020), pp. 1–10 (2020). https://doi.org/10.1007/978-981-16-4435-1_16
10. Ghosh, M., Roy, A., Mondal, K.C.: Analysis of Indian estuarine data of flora & fauna. In: Saraswat, M., Roy, S., Chowdhury, C., Gandomi, A.H. (eds.) Proceedings of International Conference on Data Science and Applications. LNNS, vol. 287, pp. 393–410. Springer, Singapore (2022). https://doi.org/10.1007/978-981-16-5348-3_31
11. Ghosh, M., Roy, A., Mondal, K.C.: Determining dark diversity of different faunal groups in Indian estuarine ecosystem: a new approach with computational biodiversity. In: Mandal, J.K., De, D. (eds.) EAIT 2021. LNNS, vol. 292, pp. 147–158. Springer, Singapore (2022). https://doi.org/10.1007/978-981-16-4435-1_16
12. Ghosh, M., Roy, A., Mondal, K.C.: FCA-based constant and coherent-signed Bicluster identification and its application in biodiversity study. In: Mandal, J.K., Buyya, R., De, D. (eds.) Proceedings of International Conference on Advanced Computing Applications. AISC, vol. 1406, pp. 679–691. Springer, Singapore (2022). https://doi.org/10.1007/978-981-16-5207-3_57
13. Ghosh, M., Roy, A., Mondal, K.C.: Knowledge discovery of Sundarban mangrove species: a way forward for managing species biodiversity. SN Comput. Sci. **3**(1), 1–14 (2022)
14. Jovic, A., Brkic, K., Bogunovic, N.: An overview of free software tools for general data mining. In: 2014 37th International Convention on Information and Communication Technology, Electronics and Microelectronics (MIPRO), pp. 1112–1117. IEEE (2014)
15. König, C., Weigelt, P., Schrader, J., Taylor, A., Kattge, J., Kreft, H.: Biodiversity data integration-the significance of data resolution and domain. PLoS Biol. **17**(3), e3000183 (2019)
16. Mondal, K.C.: Algorithms for data mining and bio-informatics, Ph. D. thesis, Université Nice Sophia Antipolis (2013)
17. Mondal, K.C., Pasquier, N.: Galois closure based association rule mining from biological data. Biological Knowledge Discovery Handbook, pp. 761–802 (2013). https://doi.org/10.1002/9781118617151.ch35
18. Mondal, K.C., Pasquier, N., Mukhopadhyay, A., da Costa Pereira, C., Maulik, U., Tettamanzi, A.G.B.: Prediction of protein interactions on HIV-1-human PPI data using a novel closure-based integrated approach. In: International Conference on Bioinformatics Models, Methods and Algorithms, pp. 164–173. SciTePress (2012)
19. Mondal, K.C., Pasquier, N., Mukhopadhyay, A., Maulik, U., Bandhopadyay, S.: A new approach for association rule mining and bi-clustering using formal concept analysis. In: Perner, P. (ed.) MLDM 2012. LNCS (LNAI), vol. 7376, pp. 86–101. Springer, Heidelberg (2012). https://doi.org/10.1007/978-3-642-31537-4_8

20. Rashid, S.H., Böcker, R., Hossain, A.B.M.E., Khan, S.A.: Undergrowth species diversity of Sundarban mangrove forest Bangladesh in relation to salinity. Ber. Inst. Landschafts-Pflanzenökologie Univ. Hohenheim **17**, 41–56 (2008)
21. Schnase, J.L., Cushing, J., Smith, J.A.: Biodiversity and ecosystem informatics. J. Intell. Inf. Syst. **29**(1), 1–6 (2007). https://doi.org/10.1007/s10844-006-0027-7

Segmented-Based and Segmented-Free Approach for COVID-19 Detection

Asifuzzaman Lasker[1], Mridul Ghosh[2], Sahana Das[3], Sk Md Obaidullah[1], Chandan Chakraborty[4], Teresa Goncalves[5], and Kaushik Roy[6(✉)]

[1] Department of Computer Science and Engineering, Aliah University, Kolkata 700160, India
[2] Department of Computer Science, Shyampur Siddheswari Mahavidyalaya, Howrah 711312, India
[3] School of Computer Science, Swami Vivekananda University, Kolkata 700121, India
[4] Department of Computer Science and Engineering, National Institute of Technical Teachers' Training and Research, Kolkata 700106, India
[5] Computer Science Department and ALGORITMI Center, University of Évora, Évora, Portugal
tcg@uevora.pt
[6] Department of Computer Science, West Bengal State University, Barasat 700126, India
kaushik.mrg@gmail.com

Abstract. According to WHO, lung infection is one of the most serious problems across the world, especially for children under five years old and older people over sixteen years old. In this study, we designed a deep learning-based model to aid medical practitioners in their diagnostic process. Here, U-Net based segmentation framework is considered to get the region of interest (ROI) of the lung area from the chest x-ray images. Two standard deep learning models and a developed CNN model comprise this framework. A deep ensemble framework method is presented to detect COVID-19 disease from a collection of chest X-ray images of disparate cases in both segment-free and segmented-based lung images. Different public datasets were used for segmentation and classification to test the system's robustness. The performance of segmentation and classification approaches returns promising outcomes compared to the state-of-the-art.

Keywords: Deep learning · Lung disease · Ensemble · Chest X-ray · Segmentation

1 Introduction

Chest radiography is the most popular and effective imaging modality for diagnosing lung diseases, such as tuberculosis, lung cancer, emphysema, atelectasis, pneumothorax, and others. Many diagnostic technologies are available, but X-ray is widely used, cheap, non-invasive, and easy to acquire. Several fields of

K. Dasgupta et al. (Eds.): CICBA 2023, CCIS 1956, pp. 332–342, 2024.
https://doi.org/10.1007/978-3-031-48879-5_25

research have been transformed by Deep Learning techniques over the last few years [1–4]. Deep learning techniques are particularly beneficial in the medical field because imaging data sets, such as retinal images, chest X-rays, and brain MRIs, show promising results with improved accuracy. X-ray machines provide inexpensive and quicker results for scanning various human organs in hospitals. In most cases, X-ray images are interpreted manually by radiologist experts. Data scientists can use deep learning to train those captured images for detecting lung diseases, which will substantially assist to medical experts. It will be helpful in developing countries where an X-ray facility exists, but an expert is still elusive. The convolutional neural network (CNN) [5,6] is effective, particularly effective among various deep learning classifiers [7,9] due to its ability to handle spatial data. According to CNN results, image data can be mapped to precise and expected output with high accuracy.

Segmentation of X-ray images is necessary for better lung disease classification. It is necessary to first separate the area of interest from the entire image. Segmentation divides the image into a series of regions based on characteristics of the image that are almost constant throughout the regions. Segmenting the lungs plays an important role in developing a computer-aided diagnosis system for lung infections [8]. Automated or semi-automated image segmentation is aimed at extracting the area or region of interest (ROI) in an image.

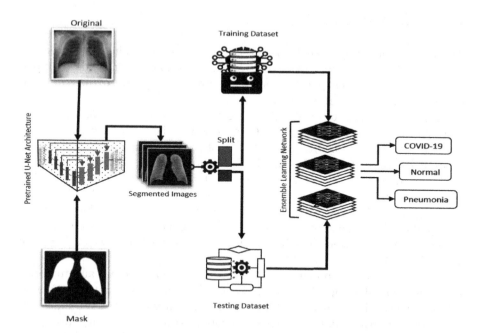

Fig. 1. Flowchart of our proposed work.

The objective of this technique is to elicit quantitative information about an organ of interest, including morphometric data. In segmentation problems, there are two related tasks to consider: object recognition and delineation [10]. The first task in this process is to determine where the object is located in the image in order to determine its position. During the object delineation task, the composition of an object is depicted to determine its character.

For cost-effective diagnosis of COVID-19, lung images play a significant role since this disease affects the lungs. Since pneumonia and COVID-19, the textures may not be differentiable to the naked eye by the inexperienced expert, which causes improper diagnosis. For this reason, a machine learning-based strategy is needed to get the enhanced performance of detection. Figure 1 represents the complete flowchart of our work. The following are the contribution of this work:

- A U-Net-based architecture is build for segmenting the ROI of lungs area for the whole chest image.
- We designed a CNN-based architecture to detect COVID-19.
- Standard deep learning framework are deployed to find out the performance.
- Deep ensemble framework was developed to get higher performance compared to the single models.
- A comparative study with state-of-the-art was performed.

2   Related Works

The state-of-the-art research described the different deep learning-based methods that used chest X-ray images for disease identification. Recently, deep ensemble methods have been popular among researchers [22] due to their inherent advantage in system performance.

Lasker et al. [11] proposed a lightweight stacked ensemble approaches with three pretrained deep learning and a CNN network. The accuracy values of three datasets are 97.28%, 96.50%, and 97.41% implemented using three different public datasets. In another work [19], they presented a stack ensemble framework for lung x-ray image segmentation based on U-Net architecture. In this U-Net architecture, three deep learning models were used as encoders: MobileNetV2, InceptionResNetV2, and EfficientNetB0. An experiment was conducted on the three public lung segmentation datasets in order to compare the proposed architecture to the conventional U-Net model. The dice coefficient was 3.02%, and the IoU was 3.43%.

Gour et al. [14] proposed a stacked-based CNN architecture and to detect COVID-19 on radiological images. They considered the discrimination attributes of the various submodels and their combination. They collected CT images to generate to prepare a dataset and accumulated X-ray images from three public datasets to create another X-ray image dataset. The sensitivity score for multiclass x-ray images was 97.62, and the sensitivity score for CT images was 98.31%. Chatterjee et al. [12] suggested a class imbalance-based classification method to detect COVID-19 disease using a variational autoencoder (VAE). Gayathri et al.

[13] presented a method that explored comprehensive computer-aided diagnosis using the CNN, autoencoder based strategy to classify diseases.

Authors in [18] developed deep features from DL models. The deep features were classified with the help of different traditional algorithms. The highest accuracy of the classification achieved by using MLP reached 96.81%. In [15,16] a pre-trained deep learning model for lungs disease detection was suggested. Chowdhury et al. [16] used the generalization feature from the deep learning model to address the issue of bottleneck convolution, which causes a lot of redundant information generation during the model-building process.

3 Methodology

3.1 Segmentation

We have used U-Net based architecture for segmenting lungs region. In deep learning models, large samples are often required for training to get higher performance, but in the case of U-Net architecture, the performance is still good for less sample size. The U-Net segmentation approach differs from other segmentation approaches like FCN, SegNet, and DeeplabV3+ because it uses skip connections of the semantic features rather than transmissions of high-level semantic features in the same stage. This way, the final recovered map will integrate more low-level features, and multiple-scale features will be fused, resulting in deep supervision and multi-scale prediction.

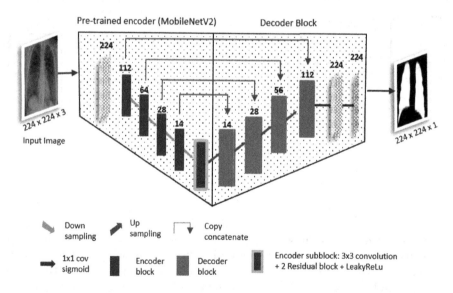

Fig. 2. Proposed U-Net architecture for segmenting lungs area.

The U-net architecture utilizes two parts, an encoder and a decoder. Pre-trained MobileNetV3 was used in the encoder part. This model has an input size of $224 \times 224 \times 3$ and an output size of $224 \times 224 \times 1$. We tested a variety of pre-training networks as the backbone, and MobileNeV2 had the most impressive results. In order to reduce pretrained architecture complexity, the value of alpha in MobileNetV2 is fixed to 0.35. The filter size of the decoder was the same as that of the encoder. A total of four filter sizes are used in the decoder block: 16, 32, 64, and 128. This pre-trained U-Net architecture is depicted in Fig. 2.

3.2 Classification

C3M2D Framework

CNN is a deep learning technique that is highly effective at segmenting, detecting, and identifying several imaging modalities in the medical field. In general, there are three types of layers in CNN: convolution, pooling, and dense. We designed a C3M2D (Three convolution layers, One maxpooling layer, and two dense layers) framework for segregating COVID-19 lung images from the above mention class of images. In the C3M2D framework, the input images with dimensions SxSxC (S and S is the row and column of the image, and C denotes channel) are fed to 5×5 convolutional layers having 32 filters, which are followed by two 3×3 convolutional layers with 16 mask which is fed to a 3×3 maxpool layer. Then 256, 128 dimensional fully connected layers are used, followed by 3-dimensional dense layers for classification. This C3M2D network is presented in Fig. 3.

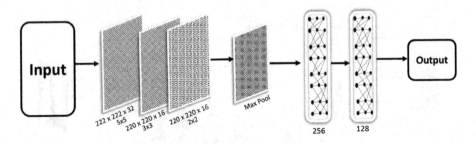

Fig. 3. The structure of C3M2D framework

Deep Ensemble Framework. In order to increase classification accuracy, ensemble learning incorporates several classification models into one coherent system. In general, ensemble models provide a better robustness level than deep learning models. This study used a horizontal voting strategy 12 to predict the final class tag by multiplying the predicted probabilities generated by the softmax functions of ResNet152, MobileNetV3, and C3M2D models. Due to the limited size of our training dataset, a horizontal voting scheme was chosen to avoid overfitting through an unstable classification error rate. The highest accuracy score is assigned to the image group that accurately identifies the disease. To represent the ensemble process, we can use the following formula.

$$F = \arg \max \prod_{k_j}^{k_i \epsilon P} k_j \tag{1}$$

The proposed deep ensemble framework is depicted in Fig. 4. In this framework, the predictions from three models are used in a majority voting ensemble process where the final prediction is obtained after multiplying the individual prediction. Since here, three models are considered, j is set to 3.

4 Experiment

4.1 Evaluation Protocols

Several performances measures are considered to assess the segmentation and classification outcomes: Dice Coefficient(DC), Intersection over Union(IoU), Accuracy, Loss, Precision, and Recall.

DC: The overlap area (A) is divided between the predicted segment(S) and the ground truth by their sum. This is expressed as follows:

$$\text{Dice Coeff} = \frac{2.A(S_{pred} \bigcap S_{g.true})}{A(S_{pred} + S_{g.true})} \tag{2}$$

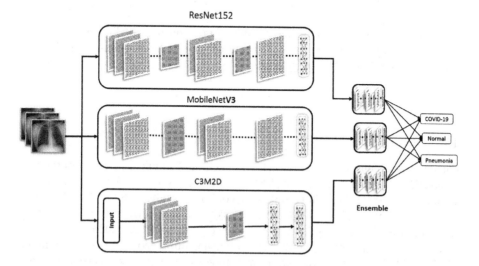

Fig. 4. Proposed deep ensemble framework for COVID-19 detection

IoU: The connection between ground truth and predictions is calculated using IoU metrics. It represents intersection and union ratios using labeling and predicted outcomes. Here is the formula for calculating the IoU score.

$$IoU = \frac{A(S_{pred} \cap S_{g.true})}{A(S_{pred} \cup S_{g.true})} \tag{3}$$

The True Positive rate (tp), the False Negative rate (fn), the True Negative rate (tn), and the False Positive rate (fp) are essential parameters here.

Accuracy (ACC): The accuracy of a prediction is evaluated using the following equation.

$$ACC(\varphi) = \frac{tp + tn}{tp + tn + fp + fn} \tag{4}$$

Precision: In terms of disease prediction, precision is a value that represents a positive prediction. Based on false positives and true positives, a predicted value is calculated.

$$Precision(\varphi) = \frac{tp}{tp + fp} \tag{5}$$

Recall: Using sensitivity, you can determine how many patients were detected as positive where the person was actually infected.

$$Recall(\epsilon) = \frac{tp}{tp + fn} \tag{6}$$

F1-score: Focusing on one single value as false positive or false negative may lead to overlooking another value. To combat this problem, we used the f1-score, which balances Precision and Recall.

$$f1 - score = 2(\frac{\varphi * \epsilon}{\varphi + \epsilon}) \tag{7}$$

4.2   Dataset

For image segmentation, we used three benchmark public datasets Montgomery County(MC), Shenzhen Hospital(SH), and Japanese Society of Radiological Technology (JSRT) in these datasets containing 662, 138, and 247 images, respectively and their corresponding mask. The MC, SH, and JSRT datasets each contain images of different resolutions, such as 4892×4020, 2048×2048, and 3000×3000 pixels. Training performance is improved by resizing all images to 224×224 dimensions to maintain homogeneity. For classification, we used RYDLS-20-v2 [21]. This dataset contains 2678 chest X-rays of three different classes.

4.3   Training Regime

To achieve better results, different hyperparameters were used in the proposed U-Net segmentation architecture. The batch size, learning rate, and number of epochs in these cases are 64, 0.0001, and 100, respectively. Figure 5 illustrates four different learning curves based on these parameters.

4.4   Results

In Table 1 performance of the proposed approach is shown using the single models and deep ensemble framework for both segmented-free and segmented-based approaches. It is observed that there is a gain in accuracy using the deep ensemble model compare to the single models by 4.9%, 3.6%, 2.97%for segmented based approach and 5.73%, 3.5%, 3.2% gain for segmented free approaches. It is observed that the segmented-based approach has a loss of 10.89% in accuracy even though there is a loss, the segmented approach can be justified when the dataset is large. We also considered 20 milliseconds (ms) less inference time and 50 megabytes(Mb) less memory usage.

The confusion matrix of segmented image using deep ensemble framework is shown in this Fig. 6.

In Table 2 the comparative study with the Teixeira et al. is presented. It is observed that for both segmented and segmented free approaches our methods gives 1.5%, high in accuracy and 1.3% improved f1-score.

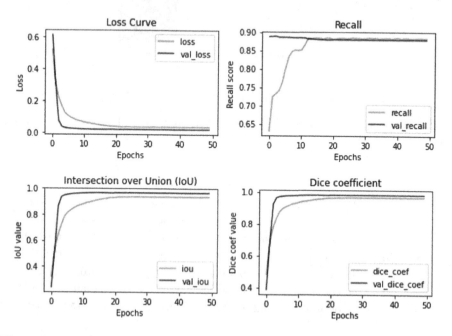

Fig. 5. Training Curve of horizontal voting, (a) Training for Segmented Image (b) Training Curve for Non-Segmented Image

Table 1. The perfomance of single and Deep ensemble model for both segmented and segmented free approach for COVID-19 detection.

Data Pattern	Framework	Precision	Recall	F1-score	Accuracy
Segmented	MobileNetV3	0.8652	0.8619	0.8623	0.8619
	ResNet152	0.8758	0.8742	0.8743	0.8742
	CNN	0.8782	0.8772	0.8770	0.8812
	Proposed method	0.9125	0.89159	0.8960	0.9109
Segmented-Free	MobileNetV3	0.9405	0.9437	0.9421	0.9473
	ResNet152	0.9019	0.9209	0.9110	0.9209
	CNN	0.9323	0.9341	0.9332	0.9393
	Proposed method	0.9485	0.9530	0.9507	0.9562

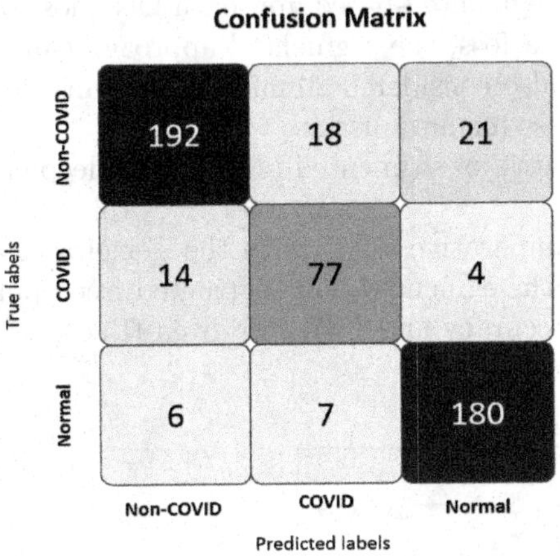

Fig. 6. Confusion matrix of segmented image

Table 2. Comparative study of F1-score of the proposed and state-of-the-art using RYDLS-20-v2 [21].

Data Pattern	Framework	COVID-19	Lung Opacity	Normal	Macro-Avg
Segmented	VGG16	0.8300	0.8800	0.9000	0.8700
	ResNet50V2	0.7800	0.8700	0.9100	0.8642
	InceptionV3	0.8300	0.8900	0.9200	0.8672
	Proposed method	**0.8919**	**0.9100**	**0.9310**	**0.9109**
Segmented-Free	MobileNetV3	0.9400	0.9100	0.9100	0.9200
	ResNet50V2	0.9100	0.9000	0.9200	0.9100
	InceptionV3	0.8600	0.9000	0.9100	0.9000
	Proposed method	**0.9520**	**0.9212**	**0.9315**	**0.9321**

5   Conclusion

The chest x-ray images are segmented to find out the ROI of the lungs using U-Net-based architecture is presented. A deep ensemble framework work is proposed to detect COVID-19 disease from the pool of chest X-ray images of normal, Pneumonia, and COVID-19 for both segment-free and segmented lung images. This framework is composed of two standard models and a developed CNN network. It has been observed that for the segmented-free approach, the accuracy of COVID-19 detection, then the segmented approach significantly improved. Though the performance of the segmented-based approach is less, this approach is essential for huge volumes of data where memory consumption is an issue for the low-resource platform. In the future, we will consider improving the segmentation-based approach's performance by considering new deep-learning models. We plan to develop a lightweight system to ease deploying in the resource-constrained platform to consider the low-cost and efficient diagnosis of lung diseases.

References

1. Lasker, A., Obaidullah, S.M., Chakraborty, C., Roy, K.: Application of machine learning and deep learning techniques for Covid-19 screening using radiological imaging: a comprehensive review. SN Comput. Sci. **4**(1), 65 (2022)
2. Ghosh, M., Roy, S.S., Mukherjee, H., Obaidullah, S.M., Santosh, K.C., Roy, K.: Understanding movie poster: transfer-deep learning approach for graphic-rich text recognition. Visual Comput. **38**(5), 1645–1664 (2022)
3. Wang, G., et al.: A deep-learning pipeline for the diagnosis and discrimination of viral, non-viral and COVID-19 pneumonia from chest X-ray images. Nat. Biomed. Eng. **5**(6), 509–521 (2021)
4. Ghosh, M., Mukherjee, H., Obaidullah, S.M., Santosh, K.C., Das, N., Roy, K.: LWSINet: a deep learning-based approach towards video script identification. Multimedia Tools Appl. **80**(19), 29095–29128 (2021)
5. Ghosh, M., Mukherjee, H., Obaidullah, S.M., Roy, K.: STDNet: a CNN-based approach to single-/mixed-script detection. Innov. Syst. Softw. Eng. **17**(3), 277–288 (2021)
6. Ambati, A., Dubey, S.R.: AC-CovidNet: attention guided contrastive CNN for recognition of covid-19 in chest x-ray images. In: Raman, B., Murala, S., Chowdhury, A., Dhall, A., Goyal, P. (eds.) CVIP 2021, vol. 1567, pp. 71–82. Springer, Cham (2022). https://doi.org/10.1007/978-3-031-11346-8_7
7. Tripathi, A., Jain, A., Mishra, K.K., Pandey, A.B., Vashist, P.C.: MCNN: a deep learning based rapid diagnosis method for COVID-19 from the X-ray images. Revue d'Intelligence Artificielle **34**(6), 673–682 (2020)
8. Stifanic, D., et al.: Semantic segmentation of chest X-ray images based on the severity of COVID-19 infected patients. EAI Endorsed Trans. Bioeng. Bioinf. **1**(3) (2021)
9. Ghosh, M., Obaidullah, S.M., Gherardini, F., Zdimalova, M.: Classification of geometric forms in mosaics using deep neural network. J. Imaging **7**(8), 149 (2021)

10. Ghosh, M., Obaidullah, S.M., Santosh, K.C., Das, N., Roy, K.: Artistic multi-character script identification using iterative isotropic dilation algorithm. In: Santosh, K.C., Hegadi, R.S. (eds.) RTIP2R 2018. CCIS, vol. 1037, pp. 49–62. Springer, Singapore (2019). https://doi.org/10.1007/978-981-13-9187-3_5

11. Lasker, A., Ghosh, M., Obaidullah, S.M., Chakraborty, C., Roy, K.: LWSNet-a novel deep-learning architecture to segregate Covid-19 and pneumonia from x-ray imagery. Multimedia Tools Appl. 82(14), 21801–21823 (2023)

12. Chatterjee, S., Maity, S., Bhattacharjee, M., Banerjee, S., Das, A.K., Ding, W.: Variational autoencoder based imbalanced COVID-19 detection using chest X-ray images. New Gener. Comput. 41(1), 25–60 (2023)

13. Gayathri, J.L., Abraham, B., Sujarani, M.S., Nair, M.S.: A computer-aided diagnosis system for the classification of COVID-19 and non-COVID-19 pneumonia on chest X-ray images by integrating CNN with sparse autoencoder and feed forward neural network. Comput. Biol. Med. 141, 105134 (2022)

14. Gour, M., Jain, S.: Automated COVID-19 detection from X-ray and CT images with stacked ensemble convolutional neural network. Biocybern. Biomed. Eng. 42(1), 27–41 (2022)

15. Hira, S., Bai, A., Hira, S.: An automatic approach based on CNN architecture to detect Covid-19 disease from chest X-ray images. Appl. Intell. 51(5), 2864–2889 (2021)

16. Chowdhury, M.E., et al.: Can AI help in screening viral and COVID-19 pneumonia? IEEE Access 8, 132665–132676 (2020)

17. Ravi, V., Narasimhan, H., Chakraborty, C., Pham, T.D.: Deep learning-based meta-classifier approach for COVID-19 classification using CT scan and chest X-ray images. Multimedia Syst. 28(4), 1401–1415 (2022)

18. Lasker, A., Ghosh, M., Obaidullah, S.M., Chakraborty, C., Roy, K.: Deep features for COVID-19 detection: performance evaluation on multiple classifiers. In: Das, A.K., Nayak, J., Naik, B., Vimal, S., Pelusi, D. (eds.) CIPR 2022, vol. 480, pp. 313–325. Springer, Singapore (2022). https://doi.org/10.1007/978-981-19-3089-8_30

19. Lasker, A., Ghosh, M., Obaidullah, S.M., Chakraborty, C., Goncalves, T., Roy, K.: Ensemble stack architecture for lungs segmentation from X-ray images. In: Yin, H., Camacho, D., Tino, P. (eds.) IDEAL 202, vol. 13756, pp. 3–11. Springer, Cham (2022). https://doi.org/10.1007/978-3-031-21753-1_1

20. Oktay, O., et al.: Attention u-net: learning where to look for the pancreas. arXiv preprint arXiv:1804.03999 (2018)

21. Teixeira, L.O., et al.: Impact of lung segmentation on the diagnosis and explanation of COVID-19 in chest X-ray images. Sensors 21(21), 7116 (2021)

22. Ghosh, M., Chatterjee, S., Mukherjee, H., Sen, S., Obaidullah, S.M.: Text/Non-text scene image classification using deep ensemble network. In: Mandal, J.K., Buyya, R., De, D. (eds.) Proceedings of International Conference on Advanced Computing Applications. AISC, vol. 1406, pp. 561–570. Springer, Singapore (2022). https://doi.org/10.1007/978-981-16-5207-3_47

23. Ghosh, M., Baidya, G., Mukherjee, H., Obaidullah, S.M., Roy, K.: A deep learning-based approach to single/mixed script-type identification. In: Chaki, R., Chaki, N., Cortesi, A., Saeed, K. (eds.) Advanced Computing and Systems for Security: Volume 13. LNNS, vol. 241, pp. 121–132. Springer, Singapore (2022). https://doi.org/10.1007/978-981-16-4287-6_9

24. Ghosh, M., Roy, S.S., Mukherjee, H., Obaidullah, S.M., Gao, X.Z., Roy, K.: Movie title extraction and script separation using shallow convolution neural network. IEEE Access 9, 125184–125201 (2021)

A Study of Word Embedding Models for Machine Translation of North Eastern Languages

Basab Nath[1], Sunita Sarkar[1(✉)], and Narayan C. Debnath[2]

[1] Department of Computer Science and Engineering, Assam University, Silchar, India
sarkarsunita2601@gmail.com, som.cse@live.com
[2] School of Computing and Information Technology, Eastern International
University, Thu Dau Mot, Binh Duong, Vietnam
Narayan.debnath@eiu.edu.vn

Abstract. Neural Machine Translation (NMT) has experienced significant growth in recent years and is now a well-established field. Despite
being the most popular machine translation solution, NMT's performance on low-resource language pairs is inferior to that of high-resource
language pairs because of the lack of large parallel corpora for these
languages.This paper explores how pre-trained word embedding models,
specifically FastText and Word2Vec, can enhance the translation performance of NMT (neural machine translation) systems for low resource
English-Assamese, English-Manipuri, and English-Nepali language pairs.
We have compared the performance of NMT systems trained with the use
of these pre-trained word embedding models and evaluated the results
on test sets of English-Assamese, English-Manipuri, and English-Nepali
translations. The resukts indicate that the use of FastText significantly
improves the translation performance of NMT systems for both language pairs, with an average increase in BLEU score of 5.6, 7.3, and
4.4 points for English-Assamese, English-Manipuri, and English-Nepali,
respectively. We have also discussed the potential challenges and limitations of using pre-trained word embedding models for NMT in low-
resource languages and suggested directions for future work in this area.

Keywords: Low resource languages · Neural machine translation ·
Transformers · Word Embeddings · FasText · Word2Vec

1 Introduction

India is a linguistically diverse country, with over 1500 languages spoken in
addition to its 121 major languages [20]. Three of these languages, Assamese,
Manipuri, and Nepali, are of great cultural and historical significance and are
widely spoken in India's northeastern region. Assamese [16,20] is the primary
language of the Indian state of Assam, as well as certain regions of Arunachal
Pradesh and Nagaland. Manipuri [9] is the main language of Manipur as well as

K. Dasgupta et al. (Eds.): CICBA 2023, CCIS 1956, pp. 343–359, 2024.
https://doi.org/10.1007/978-3-031-48879-5_26

certain parts of Assam and Tripura. Nepali, which is spoken in parts of Sikkim and serves as the official language of Nepal, West Bengal, and other northeastern states of India, Despite their importance, there has been limited research on the use of Neural Machine Translation (NMT) for translating these low-resource languages. NMT systems [1] require large, high-quality parallel corpora to achieve superior translation performance, which is often challenging for languages with limited resources. However, there is a growing demand for NMT systems for these languages to improve cross-cultural communication, especially in the fields of education, tourism, and business. In order to construct a translation system of superior grade, an NMT system requires a large corpus of text that is of high quality. As a result, NMT systems are frequently only effective in languages with a large number of parallel sentences [2,3].

The present research work aims to address the limited research on the use of Neural Machine Translation (NMT) for low-resource languages, specifically Assamese, Manipuri, and Nepali, which are of great cultural and historical significance in India's northeastern region. The primary motivation behind this study is to enhance cross-cultural communication, especially in the fields of education, tourism, and business, by developing NMT systems for these languages. To achieve this goal, we examine how pre-trained word embedding models can improve the translation performance of NMT systems for these low-resource languages. We compare the performance of pre-trained models with traditional NMT systems using BLEU metrics. Our research findings can offer valuable insights into the application of pre-trained models in enhancing NMT for low-resource languages. Therefore, this research work can make a significant contribution to the field of NMT.

The entirety of the paper is broken up into these parts: In Sect. 2, a short list of related works is given. Section 3 discusses about the background study, and Sect. 4 demonstrates the data preprocessing, Model building, and system description. In Sect. 5, the evaluation and results are given, and in Sect. 6, the conclusion and future work are described.

2   Literature Review

Despite numerous efforts dedicated to the machine translation of various low-resource Indian languages, Assamese, Manipuri, and Nepali have received considerably less attention. In 2014, Loung et al. [5] highlighted the issue of infrequent words in NMT systems when translating sentences. In 2016, Sennrich et al. [6] the issue of limited vocabulary in NMT networks. They noted that NMT models can only produce accurate results when the model size is kept constant. In 2020, Barman et al. [16] investigated the use of NMT to translate Assamese to and from other Indo-Aryan languages. They trained an NMT system on a parallel corpus and evaluated its translation performance on test sets for both directions. They found that the NMT system was able to achieve good translation performance, with an average BLEU score of 30.12 on the test sets. One study that examined the use of NMT for English-Manipuri translation is "Introducing EM-FT for Manipuri-English Neural Machine Translation" by Rudali H and Yves L

[15] (2020). In this study, the authors introduced a new approach called "EM-FT" (Expert-Moderated Fine-Tuning), which involves fine-tuning a pre-trained NMT model on a small parallel corpus of Manipuri and English sentences with the guidance of a human expert. On a sample of English-Manipuri translations, they investigated EM-FT's efficiency and found that it was able to achieve good translation performance, with a BLEU score of 27.14. Singh et al. [14] (2020) investigated the use of unsupervised neural machine translation (NMT) for the translation of Manipuri, a low-resource language, to English. Unsupervised NMT refers to the use of NMT without the need for parallel data, which is typically required to train an NMT system.

In the WMT19 shared task, author [7] used a combination of a monolingual corpus and parallel dataset to train a neural machine translation system, resulting in a BLEU score of 12.8 on the test set. Another author [8] also used a small parallel training dataset, but with the addition of multiple input modalities, leading to a BLEU score of 28.45. Salam Michael et al. [9] proposed a method that draws from aligned and unaligned linguistic resources in order to improve translation performance. The author conducted experiments on a small dataset of parallel English-Manipuri sentences and reported that the semi-supervised method improved the translation performance compared to a supervised approach that only uses parallel data. Additionally, the author found that the use of monolingual data was particularly beneficial for languages with low resources. Based on the findings, it seems that the proposed semi-supervised method may be a valuable solution for machine translation in other low-resource languages as well. Artetxe and Schwenk (2021) [23] proposes a method for unsupervised cross-lingual representation learning that improves neural machine translation without parallel data. The paper discusses the limitations of traditional methods and reviews related works on unsupervised learning of cross-lingual representations using monolingual data or bilingual dictionaries. Das et al.(2022) [24] presents a literature survey on the challenges of neural machine translation for Indic languages and reviews previous solutions proposed to overcome them. The paper introduces its own approach that combines various techniques and achieves improved translation quality on multiple Indic language pairs. According to [12], Samanantar has amassed 49.7 million sentence pairs for eleven Indic languages and English, in addition to IndicTrans, a transformer-based approach for producing high-quality translations. The machine translation of English-Assamese, English-Manipuri, and vice-versa is very much in its infancy at the present time.

The literature survey presented in the section highlights the lack of attention given to low-resource Indian languages, specifically Assamese, Manipuri, and Nepali, in machine translation research. While previous studies have proposed various approaches for machine translation of these languages, we aim to contribute to this field by proposing a new model structure for the English-Manipuri language pair, which incorporates various word embedding algorithms and attention mechanisms to improve translation performance.

3 Background

3.1 Word Embeddings

Word embedding is a technique in natural language processing that allows for the conversion of words into numerical values, creating a compact representation of words that mean the same thing. The numerical values are determined automatically through training rather than being hard-coded. This method aids in capturing the semantic connections among words and may used in various NLP problems [18] (Fig. 1).

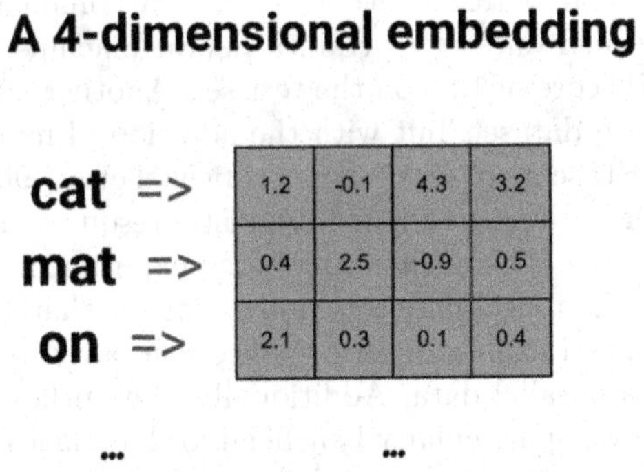

A 4-dimensional embedding

cat =>	1.2	-0.1	4.3	3.2
mat =>	0.4	2.5	-0.9	0.5
on =>	2.1	0.3	0.1	0.4

•••   •••

Fig. 1. Word Embeddings architecture

The preceding illustration shows a typical word embedding. In this system, each word is represented by a 4-by-4 vector of floating-point numbers. The 4-by-4 format refers to a 4-dimensional vector where each dimension is represented by a floating-point number. When discussing word embedding, each word is assigned a unique 4-by-4 vector that represents its meaning in a high-dimensional space. These vectors are learned during the training process of the neural network, and the embedding for a word can be looked up in the database by simply searching for the corresponding vector. The vector representation captures the semantic relationships between words, allowing for more effective language processing in machine learning models. An embedding can also be viewed as a "lookup table." Once these weights are learned, encoding a word is as simple as searching up the dense vector that best describes it in the database. We have used two types of word Embedding Algorithms for this research:

1. Word2Vec (W2V): Word2Vec [5] is a technique for achieving word embeddings of a given sentence; Skip Gram and Common Bag of Words (CBOW) are the two techniques for achieving this. CBOW predicts the word by using the context of each word as input. Skip-gram is used to predict the context word for a given target word. Both algorithms have their benefits and drawbacks. Skip-gram works well with tiny data sets and more accurately captures rare words. CBOW is significantly faster and provides a better representation of frequent terms.

2. FasText: FastText [9,21] is an open-source and free library that was developed by Facebook's AI Research team for NLP applications, including text categorization. The library can handle large datasets with millions of text examples and work with multiple languages. FastText is based on the word embedding technique, which representing words as vectors in a continuous space. The algorithm used in FastText is a variant of word2vec, which is a popular word embedding algorithm.

3.2 Byte Pair Encoding

Byte Pair Encoding (BPE) [6] is a subword tokenization method used in NMT, which originated from information theory, is lossless data compression method in which the most frequent pair of consecutive bytes is swapped out for a byte that is not present in the data. When tokenizing word sequences, NLP systems such as Transformer based NMT models and Large language Models (LLM) such as GPT-2 use a variation of this technique. When textual data is cleaned and prepared to be fed to the model, Byte Pair Encoding [4] is used. A word in BPE is divided into separate characters. For each unique word in the vocabulary, a count is kept. The special stop token "</w>" is added at the end of each word.

Consider the vocabulary terms "clever," "smart," "oldest," and "wildest," which occur three times, four times, six times, and three times, respectively. In BPE, these words will be split into characters , and the vocabulary will be formed along with their occurrence count as,

'smart </w>': 3, 's marter </w>': 4, 'o l d e s t </w>': 6, 'w i l d e s t </w>': 3

3.3 Transformers

The Transformer is an attention-based neural network architecture [13]. For applications requiring the ability to translate one sequence into another Word sequences from one language to another are translated using the Transformer architecture. The transformer is a model that differs from traditional sequence-to-sequence models, which typically rely on recurrent neural networks (RNNs) or convolutional neural networks (CNNs). Instead, the Transformer exclusively uses self-attention mechanisms to connect various positions within a single sequence and generate a representation of that sequence. By utilizing self attention method, the transformer is capable of attending to every position within the input sequence and generating a corresponding representation for each position. These representations can then be utilized to produce the output sequence. The Transformer uses an encoder and decoder to process input sentences in a specific language and translate them to a target language. The encoder uses attention layers to process each phrase in the input sentence, while the decoder works in a linear manner and pays attention only to the elements it has already translated. The decoder's initial attention layer focuses on previous decoder input, while the second layer uses the encoder output to ensure accurate translation despite differences in language morphology or sentence context (Fig. 2).

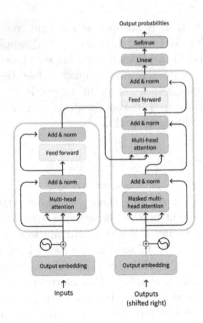

Fig. 2. The Transformer architecture

Attention Mechanism. Transformer [22] models are constructed using unique layers that are referred to as attention layers, which is a significant characteristic of these models. When it comes to the manner in which each word is represented, the attention layer instructs the model to concentrate on particular terms in the sentence that we provide it.

Scaled Dot Product Attention. Transformers use a "Scaled Dot-Product Attention" [13]to obtain the context vector:

$$\text{Attention}(Q, K, V) = \text{softmax}\left(\frac{QK^T}{\sqrt{d_k}}\right) V$$

3.4 BLEU

BLEU (Bilingual Evaluation Understudy) [11] is a widely used metric for evaluating machine translation quality. The method evaluates the resemblance between a proposed translation and one or multiple reference translations by comparing their respective n-gram sequences, which are sequences of words. Based on the number of matching n-grams, a score is calculated. The formula for the BLEU score is as follows:

$$\text{BLEU} = \text{BP} \cdot \exp\left(\sum_{n=1}^{N} w_n \log p_n\right) \tag{1}$$

where,

- p_n is the geometric mean of the modified n-gram precision.
- W_n is the positive weights.

4 Methodology

This paper describes the construction of three NMT systems, each utilizing a transformer-based model and W2V/FastText embeddings for a different language pair:

1. English-Assamese and vice-versa.
2. English-Manipuri and vice-versa.
3. English-Nepali and vice-versa.

In our primary test we trained our model using Word2Vec. Word2Vec word embeddings for Assamese, Manipuri, and Nepali are trained. However, as of yet, no research has been published that compares Word2Vec and FasText for Assamese, Manipuri, or Nepali. On our parallel corpus, we train multidimensional word embeddings. We selected Word2Vec as our preferred embedding method due to its ability to train embeddings with a shallow neural network and its reported success in comparison to other embedding techniques for morphologically complex languages. Using 22 iterations of training data consisting of sentences written in Assamese, Manipuri, and Nepali, we trained a skip-gram model. In the second set of tests that we conducted, we focused solely on developing a pretrained word embedding model for the Assamese, Manipuri, and Nepali languages. Specifically, we decided to go with fastText since it is able to incorporate subword information throughout the training process by making use of character n-gram embeddings. For morphologically rich languages, Certain prior findings on pre-trained word embeddings suggest that fastText outperforms word-level approaches such as GloVe and word2vec. In order to train skip-gram models, we used a parallel corpus. As part of the NMT models' training procedure, we integrated pre-existing word embedding.

The step-by-step working of **Word2Vec (W2V)** and **FastText** word embeddings are as follows :

1. preprocessing of Data: Raw text data must first be preprocessed. This includes removing punctuation, converting all letters to lowercase, and splitting the text into individual words. The resulting text is a list of tokenized sentences.

Building n-grams: Next, FastText builds n-grams from the tokenized sentences. An n-gram is a set of n contiguous words in a sequence of text. For example, in the sentence "I like to play soccer", the 2-grams (or bigrams) would be "I like", "like to", "to play", and "play soccer". FastText is a natural language processing library that can generate n-grams from text data, and by default, it uses 5-grams to represent text.

2. Building a vocabulary: FastText builds a vocabulary of all unique n-grams in the tokenized sentences. Each n-gram is assigned a unique integer index. Initializing word embeddings: FastText initializes word embeddings for each word in the vocabulary. The word embeddings are initialized randomly or with pre-trained embeddings if available. Word2Vec assigns random weights for each feature in input layer.

3. Model Training: The subsequent stage involves training the FastText model. This involves iterating over the tokenized sentences, computing the gradient of the loss function, and updating the word embeddings using stochastic gradient descent. FastText employs the negative log probability of the predicted class as its loss function. Word2Vec computes dot product between input and output layers.

4. Predicting the class: Once the model is trained, it is used to predict the class of new text data. The text is first tokenized and n-grams are built. The model then utilises a vector computed by weighting the total of the word embeddings for each n-gram in the text to make a prediction about the class. Word2Vec applies softmax activation function on output layer values.

5. Fine-tuning the model: Finally, the FastText model is fine-tuned by retraining it on new data or adjusting the hyperparameters like learning rate, epochs, and hidden layer size.

Each system is trained with the help of the Fairseq Sequence Modeling Toolkit. The Modeling kit is free and open-source. We have trained multilingual models for this research, meaning English-Assamese, English-Manipuri and English-Nepali in one go as well as Assamese-English, Manipuri-English and Nepali-English. The process of building a system typically involves several key steps, including data cleaning, system learning, and testing of system. Each of these steps is crucial to the overall success of the system.

4.1   Data for Training

We have used the NLLB dataset and modified it to meet our requirements. The dataset includes 5161159 English-Assamese and 448538 English-Manipuri sentences. For training, we chose 50000 sentences at random from the entire dataset. These sentences have been further segmented into training, testing, and validation sets for the purposes of processing. We grouped the datasets into three categories, namely test, tune/validate, and train, using the proportions 10: 10: 80. The data presented in Table 1 can provide additional insight into the corpus.

Table 1. Corpus Statistics

Content	English	Assamese	Manipuri	Nepali
Sentences	50000	50000	50000	50000
Mean	17.62	13.23	14.01	14.23
Median	11.0	9.0	10.0	10.2
Max Length	158	142	162	154
Vocabulary Count	63,457	77,588	74,387	73000
Test Set Count	5000	5000	5000	5000
Validation Set Count	5000	5000	5000	5000
Train Set Count	40000	40000	40000	40000

4.2 Fairseq

Fairseq, a toolkit for sequence modelling, enables researchers and programmers to design custom models for various tasks such as translation, summarization, language modelling, and text production. We utilized Fairseq in our work to achieve essential outcomes. The PyTorch foundation of the toolkit facilitates distributed training across numerous GPUs and machines.

4.3 Model Construction

Transformer Based NMT Model. Long-sentence translation can be improved using a GRU-based model or even an LSTM-based model, but this comes at the expense of accuracy and parallelization is severely constrained. The transformer [13] model is presented as a solution to these problems. The attentional mechanism that employs the transformer model is known as "self-attention." It's the best NMT model available at the moment. The encoder and decoder layers in the transformer's encoder-decoder model are self-attentional and fully coupled. There are two distinct components involved in both the encoding and decoding procedures: a feed-forward network and a multi-head self-attention mechanism. A multi-head attention sub-layer was included in the decoder to facilitate parallelization.

By utilizing the transformer architecture and the fairseq toolbox, it is possible to train the NMT model by following a series of steps. -

1. Preparing the training data: Preprocessing the data to prepare it for training. This includes tasks such as tokenization, lowercasing, and filtering out sentences that are too long or contain rare words.
2. Training the word embeddings: Using the FastText toolkit to train word embeddings on the parallel corpus. This will create a set of word vectors that can be used to represent the words in the training data. We used skip-gram training algorithm to train our word embeddings. We have also used fairseq to train Word2Vec word embeddings.

3. Training the transformer model: Using the fairseq toolkit to train a transformer model on the parallel corpus and the FastText word embeddings. We have defined custom hyper-parameters for out training which are listed in Tables 2 and 3.
4. Evaluate the model: The translation performance of a test set of sentences from the source language to the target language can be evaluated by utilizing a metric like BLEU (Bilingual Evaluation Understudy) after applying the trained transformer model for translation, By doing so, we can effectively evaluate the caliber of the translations produced by the model and identify any areas for improvement.

The loss that our model witnessed in both the training and validation sets has been included in Fig. 3. Also, we have included our model structure for further understanding of the process.

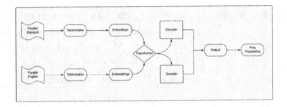

Fig. 3. Proposed Model Structure for Emglish ⟺Manipuri Language Pair

5 Evaluation and Result

In this study, we investigated the use of pre-trained word embedding models, specifically FastText and Word2Vec, to improve the translation performance of NMT systems for English-Assamese, English-Manipuri, and Emglish-Nepali language pairs. We used the BLEU score as the evaluation metric, and used the mteval-v13a tokenizer to convert Assamese to English and Manipuri to English. Due to the inability of BLEU-Tokenizer to function with Indic languages, we implemented the indicNLP tokenizer prior to running BLEU in order to tokenize the text.Tables 2 and 3 provide information on the model parameters for different word embedding algorithms. The findings of our study illustrate that employing pre-trained word embedding models can notably enhance the translation performance of NMT systems for low-resource languages such as Assamese and Manipuri. Specifically, our results showed an average increase in BLEU score of 5.6, 7.3 and 4.4 points for English-Assamese, English-Manipuri and English-Nepali, respectively, when using FastText. Tables 4, 5, and 6 display the experimental outcomes of the system in terms of the BLEU score.Figure 5 is a bar chart showing the BLEU score performance of several models.

These results suggest that pre-trained word embeddings is a useful resource for NMT of low-resource languages, particularly when parallel data is limited. It is worthwhile to note, however, that there is still a chance of improvement in the performance of NMT systems for low-resource languages. Potential challenges and limitations of using pre-trained word embedding models for NMT of low-resource languages include the need for domain-specific data and resources and the potential for mismatch between the training data and test data (Figs. 4 and 6).

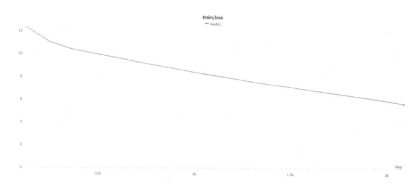

Fig. 4. Training set loss

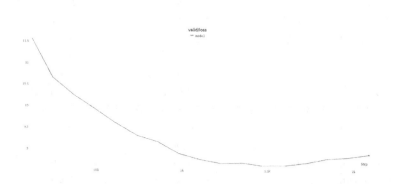

Fig. 5. Validation set loss

In this study, we evaluated the performance of our proposed Transformer models for English-Assamese, English-Manipuri and English-Nepali language pairs using various input data. In order to showcase the efficiency of our models, we have provided Tables 7 through 16, which exhibit the input, desired output, and actual output produced by the models.

The results indicate that for both Indic-English and English-Indic translations, our Transformer model with Probabilistic FastText performed well. This

Table 2. Model Parameters using Word2Vec

Parameters	English ⟺ Assamese	English ⟺ Manipuri	English ⟺ Nepali
Model	Transformer	Transformer	Transformer
Number of Epochs	22	22	22
Input Embeddings	512	512	512
FFD	1024	1024	1024
Attention Heads	8	8	8
Encoder-Decoder	6	6	6
Cost Function	Log Loss	Log Loss	Log Loss
Optimizer	Adam	Adam	Adam
Learning Rate	annealing scheduler	annealing scheduler	annealing scheduler
Label Smoothing	0.2	0.2	0.2
Warmup steps	3000	3000	3000
Batch Size	4096	4096	4096
Word Embeddings	Word2Vec	Word2Vec	Word2Vec

Table 3. Model Parameters using FasText

Parameters	English ⟺ Assamese	English ⟺ Manipuri	English ⟺ Nepali
Model	Transformer	Transformer	Transformer
Number of Epochs	22	22	22
Input Embeddings	512	512	512
FFD	1024	1024	1024
Attention Heads	8	8	8
EDL	6	6	6
Cost Function	Log Loss	Log Loss	Log Loss
Optimizer	Adam	Adam	Adam
Learning Rate	annealing scheduler	annealing scheduler	annealing scheduler
Label Smoothing	0.2	0.2	0.2
Warmup steps	3000	3000	3000
Batch Size	4096	4096	4096
Word Embeddings	FasText	FasText	FasText

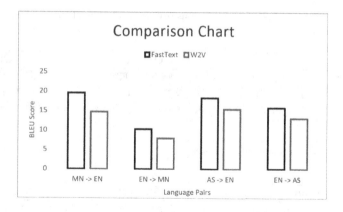

Fig. 6. Bar chart for performance comparison in terms of BLEU score.

Table 4. BLEU Scores for various Word Embeddings in Manipuri-English pair

Word Embedding	English to Manipuri	Manipuri to English
Word2Vec	7.9	14.7
FastText	10.3	19.6

Table 5. BLEU Scores for various Word Embeddings on Assamese-English pair

Word Embedding	English to Assamese	Assamese to English
Word2Vec	13.1	15.4
FastText	15.8	18.3

Table 6. BLEU Scores for various Word Embeddings on Nepali-English pair

Word Embedding	English to Nepali	Nepali to English
Word2Vec	4.3	11.7
FastText	8.7	16.2

was observed in both forward and backward translation directions. However, a detailed analysis of the generated translations using the provided test set revealed that the current NMT method still requires further improvement to produce accurate translations (Tables 8, 9, 10, 11, 12, 13, 14, 15 and 16).

Table 7. Sample Translation by Transformer model English to Assamese using Word2Vec (W2V)

Input	Target Output	Predicted Output
Why am I seeing this	মই এয়া কিয় দেখি আছোঁ	কিয় এইটো দেখিছেঁা
But thats not possible	কিন্তু ই সম্ভৱ নহয়।	কিন্তু সেয়া সম্ভৱ নহয়।
I had so much going on	মই বহু সংঘৰ্ষ কৰিবলগীয়া হৈছিল।	মোৰ ইমানবোৰ চলি আছিল।

Table 8. Sample Translation by Transformer model English to Assamese using Fast-Text

Input	Target Output	Predicted Output
Why am I seeing this	মই এয়া কিয় দেখি আছোঁ	মই এইটো কিয় দেখিআছো
But thats not possible	কিন্তু ই সম্ভৱ নহয়।	কিন্তু সেয়া সম্ভৱ নহয়
I had so much going on	মই বহু সংঘৰ্ষ কৰিবলগীয়া হৈছিল।	মোৰ বহুত চলি আছিল

Table 9. Sample Translation by Transformer model English to Manipuri using Fast-Text

Input	Target Output	Predicted Output
bright sun is shining in the sky	মখা তানসূ তমলোঙা খিজাঙনী	মমা মপানা পমদুনা পুৰকখিবদু
i will drink the pomegranate juice	মমা মপানা পমদুনা পুৰখাবাদো	অমতা ভায়বা অচুম্বা ঈশ্বৰ অদু কনানো
i have never seen such a thing before	অঙাং অমনা মসি তৌবা ঙম্বা তাই।	অঙাং অমনা মসি তৌবা ঙম্বা তাই

Table 10. Sample Translation by Transformer model English to Manipuri using Word2Vec (W2V)

Input	Target Output	Predicted Output
bright sun is shining in the sky	মখা তানসূ তমজখিগনি।	মখা তানসূ তমজখিগনি
i will drink the pomegranate juice	মমা মপানা পমদুনা পুৰকখিবদু	মমা মপানা পমদুনা পুৰকখিবদু।
i have never seen such a thing before	অঙাং অমনা মসি তৌবা ঙম্বা তাই।	অঙাং অমনা মসি তৌবা ঙম্বা তাই

Table 11. Sample Translation by Transformer model Assamese to English using Word2Vec (W2V)

Input	Target Output	Predicted Output
ধেই কি জীৱন ৰে এইটো?	What is this life?	What the hell is this life?
তাতে তেওঁৰ পৰিয়াল থাকে।	He has a family there.	He has a family there.
পুতুও বৰকৈ সহজ হ🔲ব নোৱাৰিলে।	It could not have been easy.	It couldn't have been easier.

Table 12. Sample Translation by Transformer model Assamese to English using Fast-Text

Input	Target Output	Predicted Output
ধেই কি জীৱন ৰে এইটো?	What is this life?	Hey what life is this?
তাতে তেওঁৰ পৰিয়াল থাকে।	He has a family there.	His family lives there.
পূতুও বৰকৈ সহজ হ'ব নোৱাৰিলে॥	It could not have been easy.	It too couldn't be very easy.

Table 13. Sample Translation by Transformer model Manipuri to English using Fast-Text

Input	Target Output	Predicted Output
মদুগি মওংসিনা ঙখি ঐবু নাহ্না	i cannot eat meat and fish	i cannot eat meat and fish
ওফিসনা শিৱবা থৱক খুদিংমক তৌখি।	I will go to the market after office hours.	I will go to the market after office hours.
অচুম্ৱ ধৰ্ম অমখঙা লৈবৰা	Let us spread the message of non-violence and peace	Let us spread the message of non violence and peace

Table 14. Sample Translation by Transformer model Manipuri to English using Word2Vec (W2V)

Input	Target Output	Predicted Output
মদুগি মওংসিনা ঙখি ঐবু নাহ্না	i cannot eat meat and fish	i can't eat meat and fish
ওফিসনা শিৱবা থৱক খুদিংমক তৌখি।	I will go to the market after office hours.	I may go to the market after office hours
অচুম্ৱ ধৰ্ম অমখঙা লৈবৰা	Let us spread the message of non-violence and peace	Let's spread the message of non violence and peace

Table 15. Sample Translation by Transformer model English to Nepali using fastText.

Input	Target Output	Predicted Output
It happened after the death of Saul when David was returned from the slaughter of the Amalekites	यो घटना शाऊलको मृत्युपछि भएको थियो। जब दाऊद अमालेकीहरूको मारेर फर्कका थिए	यो शाऊलको मृत्यु पछि भयो जब दाऊद अमालेकीहरूलाई मारेर फर्किए

Table 16. Sample Translation by Transformer model English to Nepali using Word2Vec(W2V).

Input	Target Output	Predicted Output
It happened after the death of Saul when David was returned from the slaughter of the Amalekites	यो घटना शाऊलको मृत्युपछि भएको थियो। जब दाऊद अमालेकीहरूको मारेर फर्कका थिए	यो शाऊलको मृत्यु भएको केही दिन पछिको कुरा हो दाऊदले अमालेकीहरूलाई हराएर पछि सिकलग गए

6   Conclusion

In this study, we examined the effectiveness of three different word embedding algorithms in the context of low-resource language pairs: English-Assamese and English-Manipuri and English-Nepali. Specifically, we compared the performance of the FasText algorithm to that of the widely-used Word2Vec algorithm. Our results indicate that the FasText algorithm performed better when applied to the Transformer model using the same parameters. To further improve translation quality, we plan to conduct additional research by training Transformer-based models using a larger amount of data and fine-tuning the parameters in the future. Additionally, our objective is to assess the performance of these models on a more extensive selection of low-resource languages and contrast the outcomes with those of other state-of-the-art techniques.

References

1. Koehn, P., Knowles, R.: Six challenges for neural machine translation. In: Proceedings of the First Workshop on Neural Machine Translation (2017). https://doi.org/10.18653/v1/w17-3204
2. Sutskever, I., Vinyals, O., Le, Q.V.: Sequence to sequence learning with neural networks. In Advances in Neural Information Processing Systems, vol. 27, pp. 3104–3112 (2019). http://papers.nips.cc/paper/5346-sequence-to-sequence-learning-with-neural-networks.pdf
3. Cho, K., Merrienboer, B. V., Bahdanau, D., Bengio, Y.: On the properties of neural machine translation: encoder-decoder approaches. In: Proceedings of SSST-8, Eighth Workshop on Syntax, Semantics and Structure in Statistical Translation (2014). https://doi.org/10.3115/v1/w14-4012
4. Shibata, Y., et al.: Byte pair encoding: a text compression scheme that accelerates pattern matching (1999)
5. Luong, M.T., Sutskever, I., Le, Q.V., Vinyals, O., Zaremba, W.: Addressing the rare word problem in neural machine translation. arXivpreprint arXiv:1410.8206 (2016)
6. Sennrich, R., Haddow, B., Birch, A.: Neural Machine translation of rare words with subword units. In: Proceedings of the 54th Annual Meeting of the Association for Computational Linguistics, vol. 1: Long Papers) (2016). https://doi.org/10.18653/v1/p16-1162
7. Mondal, R., Nayek, S.R., Chowdhury, A., Pal, S., Naskar, S.K., van Genabith, J.:JU-Saarland submission to the WMT2019 English-Gujarati translation shared task. In: Proceedings of the Fourth Conference on Machine Translation, Shared Task Papers, Day 1, vol. 2, pp. 308–313 (2019)
8. Meetei, L.S., Singh, T.D., Bandyopadhyay, S.: WAT2019: English-Hindi translation on Hindi visual genome dataset. In: Proceedings of the 6th Workshop on Asian Translation, pp. 181–188 (2019)
9. Singh, S.M., Singh, T.D.: Low resource machine translation of English-Manipuri: a semi-super-vised approach. Expert Syst. Appl. **209**(2022), 118–187 (2022)
10. Laskar, S.R., Pakray, P., Bandyopadhyay, S.: Neural machine translation: Hindi-Nepali. In: Proceedings of the Fourth Conference on Machine Translation, vol. 3: Shared Task Papers, Day 2 (2019). https://doi.org/10.18653/v1/w19-5427
11. Papneni, K., Roukos, S., Ward, T., Zhu, W.: BLEU: a method for automatic evaluation for machine translation. In: Proceedings of the 40th Annual Meeting of the Association for Computational Linguistics (ACL) (2002)
12. Ramesh, G., et al.: Samanantar: the largest publicly available parallel corpora collection for 11 Indic languages. arXiv arXiv:cs.CL/2104.05596 (2021)
13. Vaswani, A., et al.: Attention is all you need. In: Proceedings of the 31st International Conference on Neural Information Processing Systems, NIPS 2017, Long Beach, CA, USA, 4–9 December 2017, pp. 6000–6010. Curran Associates Inc., Red Hook (2017)

14. Michael, S., Singh, D.: Unsupervised neural machine translation for English and Manipuri. In: Proceedings of the 3rd Workshop on Technologies for MT of Low Resource Languages, Suzhou, China, pp. 69–78. Association for Computational Linguistics (2020)

15. Huidrom, R., Lepage, Y.: Introducing EM-FT for Manipuri-English neural machine translation. In: Proceedings of the WILDRE-6 Workshop within the 13th Language Resources and Evaluation Conference, Marseille, France, pp. 1–6. European Language Resources Association (2022)

16. Baruah, R., Mundotiya, R.K., Singh, A.K.: Low resource neural machine translation: assamese to/from other Indo-Aryan (Indic) languages. ACM Trans. Asian Low-Resour. Lang. Inf. Process. **22**(1), Article 19, p. 32 (2023).https://doi.org/10.1145/3469721

17. Madhani, Y., et al.: Aksharantar: towards building open transliteration tools for the next billion users. arXiv preprint arXiv:2205.03018 (2022)

18. Hassan, A., Alom, F., Chowdhury A.S., Khan, N.: Neural machine translation for Bengala-English language pair. In: 22nd International Conference of Computer and Information Technology (ICCIT) (2019)

19. Le, N.T., Sadat, F., Menard, L., Dinh, D.: Low-resource machine transliteration using recurrent neural networks. ACM Trans. Asian Low-Res. Lang. Inf. Process. **18**(2), Article 13, p. 14 (2019) (2019).https://doi.org/10.1145/3265752

20. Nath, B., Sarkar, S., Das, S., et al.: Neural machine translation for Indian language pair using hybrid attention mechanism. Innov. Syst. Softw. Eng. (2022). https://doi.org/10.1007/s11334-021-00429-z

21. Joulin, A., Grave, E., Bojanowski, P., Mikolov, T.: Bag of tricks for efficient text classification. In: Proceedings of the 15th Conference of the European Chapter of the Association for Computational Linguistics, vol. 2, Short Papers, pp. 427–431(2017)

22. Radford, A., Wu, J., Child, R., Luan, D., Amodei, D., Sutskever, I.: Language models are unsupervised multitask learners. OpenAI Blog **1**(8), 9 (2019)

23. Artetxe, M., Schwenk, H.: Unsupervised cross-lingual representation learning for neural machine transation. Trans. Assoc. Comput. Linguist. (TACL) **9**, 177–192 (2021)

24. Das, S.B., Biradar, A., Mishra, T.K., Patra, B.K.: Improving multilingual neural machine translation system for Indic languages. ACM Trans. Asian Low-Res. Lang. Inf. Process. (TALLIP) **21**(1), 1–17 (2022)

Author Index

Printed in the United States
by Baker & Taylor Publisher Services